	DATE DUE		

DAVID COPPERFIELD

Major Literary Characters

CHELSEA HOUSE PUBLISHERS

Major Literary Characters

DAVID COPPERFIELD
Charles Dickens, *David Copperfield*

ROBINSON CRUSOE
Daniel Defoe, *Robinson Crusoe*

DON JUAN
Molière, *Don Juan*
Lord Byron, *Don Juan*

HUCK FINN
Mark Twain, *The Adventures of Tom Sawyer, Adventures of Huckleberry Finn*

CLARISSA HARLOWE
Samuel Richardson, *Clarissa*

HEATHCLIFF
Emily Brontë, *Wuthering Heights*

ANNA KARENINA
Leo Tolstoy, *Anna Karenina*

MR. PICKWICK
Charles Dickens, *The Pickwick Papers*

HESTER PRYNNE
Nathaniel Hawthorne, *The Scarlet Letter*

BECKY SHARP
William Makepeace Thackeray, *Vanity Fair*

LAMBERT STRETHER
Henry James, *The Ambassadors*

EUSTACIA VYE
Thomas Hardy, *The Return of the Native*

TWENTIETH CENTURY

ÁNTONIA
Willa Cather, *My Ántonia*

BRETT ASHLEY
Ernest Hemingway, *The Sun Also Rises*

HANS CASTORP
Thomas Mann, *The Magic Mountain*

HOLDEN CAULFIELD
J. D. Salinger, *The Catcher in the Rye*

CADDY COMPSON
William Faulkner, *The Sound and the Fury*

JANIE CRAWFORD
Zora Neale Hurston, *Their Eyes Were Watching God*

CLARISSA DALLOWAY
Virginia Woolf, *Mrs. Dalloway*

DILSEY
William Faulkner, *The Sound and the Fury*

GATSBY
F. Scott Fitzgerald, *The Great Gatsby*

HERZOG
Saul Bellow, *Herzog*

JOAN OF ARC
William Shakespeare, *Henry VI*
George Bernard Shaw, *Saint Joan*

LOLITA
Vladimir Nabokov, *Lolita*

WILLY LOMAN
Arthur Miller, *Death of a Salesman*

MARLOW
Joseph Conrad, *Lord Jim, Heart of Darkness, Youth, Chance*

PORTNOY
Philip Roth, *Portnoy's Complaint*

BIGGER THOMAS
Richard Wright, *Native Son*

CHELSEA HOUSE PUBLISHERS

Major Literary Characters

DAVID
COPPERFIELD

Edited and with an introduction by
HAROLD BLOOM

17351 ·
CHELSEA HOUSE PUBLISHERS
New York ◊ Philadelphia

Jacket illustration: Illustration by "Phiz" (H. K. Browne) from the
first publication of *David Copperfield* (20 parts, May 1849–November 1850)
(Courtesy of Oxford University Press). *Inset:* Cover design for
the wrapper of the monthly parts of *David Copperfield* (Berg Collection,
New York Public Library).

Chelsea House Publishers

Editor-in-Chief   Remmel T. Nunn
Managing Editor   Karyn Gullen Browne
Picture Editor   Adrian G. Allen
Art Director   Maria Epes
Manufacturing Director   Gerald Levine

Major Literary Characters

Senior Editor   S. T. Joshi
Associate Editor   Richard Fumosa
Designer   Maria Epes

Staff for DAVID COPPERFIELD

Researcher   Jerome J. Aliotta
Picture Researcher   Wendy Wills
Assistant Art Director   Noreen Romano
Production Manager   Joseph Romano
Production Coordinator   Marie Claire Cebrián

Printed and bound in the United States of America

First Printing

1   3   5   7   9   8   6   4   2

Library of Congress Cataloging-in-Publication Data

David Copperfield / edited and with an introduction by Harold Bloom.
p.   cm.—(Major literary characters)
Includes bibliographical references and index.
ISBN 0-7910-0937-8.—ISBN 0-7910-0992-0 (pbk.)
1. Dickens, Charles, 1812–1870. David Copperfield.   I. Bloom, Harold.
II. Series.
PR4558.D38   1992
823'.8—dc20
91-14978
CIP

CONTENTS

THE ANALYSIS OF CHARACTER

Harold Bloom

"Character," according to our dictionaries, still has as a primary meaning a graphic symbol, such as a letter of the alphabet. This meaning reflects the word's apparent origin in the ancient Greek *charactēr,* a sharp stylus. *Charactēr* also meant the mark of the stylus' incisions. Recent fashions in literary criticism have reduced "character" in literature to a matter of marks upon a page. But our word "character" also has a very different meaning, matching that of the ancient Greek *ēthos,* "habitual way of life." Shall we say then that literary character is an imitation of human character, or is it just a grouping of marks? The issue is between a critic like Dr. Samuel Johnson, for whom words were as much like people as like things, and a critic like the late Roland Barthes, who told us that "the fact can only exist linguistically, as a term of discourse." Who is closer to our experience of reading literature, Johnson or Barthes? What difference does it make, if we side with one critic rather than the other?

Barthes is famous, like Foucault and other recent French theorists, for having added to Nietzsche's proclamation of the death of God a subsidiary demise, that of the literary author. If there are no authors, then there are no fictional personages, presumably because literature does not refer to a world outside language. Words indeed necessarily refer to other words in the first place, but the impact of words ultimately is drawn from a universe of fact. Stories, poems, and plays are recognizable as such because they are human utterances within traditions of utterances, and traditions, by achieving authority, become a kind of fact, or at least the sense of a fact. Our sense that literary characters, within the context of a fictive cosmos, indeed are fictional personages is also a kind of fact. The meaning and value of every character in a successful work of literary representation depend upon our ideas of persons in the factual reality of our lives.

Literary character is always an invention, and inventions generally are indebted to prior inventions. Shakespeare is the inventor of literary character as we know it; he reformed the universal human expectations for the verbal imitation of personality, and the reformation appears now to be permanent and uncannily inevitable. Remarkable as the Bible and Homer are at representing personages, their characters are relatively unchanging. They age within their stories, but their habitual modes of being do not develop. Jacob and Achilles unfold before us, but without metamorphoses. Lear and Macbeth, Hamlet and Othello severely modify themselves not only by their actions, but by their utterances, and most of all through *overhearing themselves,* whether they speak to themselves or to others. Pondering what they themselves have said, they will to change, and actually do change, sometimes extravagantly yet always persuasively. Or else they suffer change, without willing it, but in reaction not so much to their language as to their relation to that language.

I do not think it useful to say that Shakespeare successfully imitated elements in our characters. Rather, it could be argued that he compelled aspects of character to appear that previously were concealed, or not available to representation. This is not to say that Shakespeare is God, but to remind us that language is not God either. The mimesis of character in Shakespeare's dramas now seems to us normative, and indeed became the accepted mode almost immediately, as Ben Jonson shrewdly and somewhat grudgingly implied. And yet, Shakespearean representation has surprisingly little in common with the imitation of reality in Jonson or in Christopher Marlowe. The origins of Shakespeare's originality in the portrayal of men and women are to be found in the *Canterbury Tales* of Geoffrey Chaucer, insofar as they can be located anywhere before Shakespeare himself. Chaucer's savage and superb Pardoner overhears his own tale-telling, as well as his mocking rehearsal of his own spiel, and through this overhearing he is emboldened to forget himself, and enthusiastically urges all his fellow-pilgrims to come forward to be fleeced by him. His self-awareness, and apocalyptically rancid sense of spiritual fall, are preludes to the even grander abysses of the perverted will in Iago and in Edmund. What might be called the character trait of a negative charisma may be Chaucer's invention, but came to its perfection in Shakespearean mimesis.

The analysis of character is as much Shakespeare's invention as the representation of character is, since Iago and Edmund are adepts at analyzing both themselves and their victims. Hamlet, whose overwhelming charisma has many negative components, is certainly the most comprehensive of all literary characters, and so necessarily prophesies the labyrinthine complexities of the will in Iago and Edmund. Charisma, according to Max Weber, its first codifier, is primarily a natural endowment, and implies a primordial and idiosyncratic power over nature, and so finally over death. Hamlet's uncanniness is at its most suggestive in the scene of his long dying, where the audience, through the mediation of Horatio, itself is compelled to meditate upon suicide, if only because outliving the prince of Denmark scarcely seems an option.

Shakespearean representation has usurped not only our sense of literary character, but our sense of ourselves as characters, with Hamlet playing the part of the largest of these usurpations. Insofar as we have an idea of human disinterestedness, we tend to derive it from the Hamlet of Act V, whose quietism has about it a ghostly authority. Oscar Wilde, in his profound and profoundly witty dialogue, "The Decay of Lying," expressed a permanent insight when he insisted that art shaped every era, far more than any age formed art. Life imitates art, we imitate Shakespeare, because without Shakespeare we would perish for lack of images. Wilde's grandest audacity demystifies Shakespearean mimesis with a Shakespearean vivaciousness: "This unfortunate aphorism about art holding the mirror up to Nature is deliberately said by Hamlet in order to convince the bystanders of his absolute insanity in all art-matters." Of *Hamlet*'s influence upon the ages Wilde remarked that: "The world has grown sad because a puppet was once melancholy." "Puppet" is Wilde's own deconstruction, a brilliant reminder that Shakespeare's artistry of illusion has so mastered reality as to have changed reality, evidently forever.

The analysis of character, as a critical pursuit, seems to me as much a Shakespearean invention as literary character was, since much of what we know about how to analyze character necessarily follows Shakespearean procedures. His hero-villains, from Richard III through Iago, Edmund, and Macbeth, are shrewd and endless questers into their own self-motivations. If we could bear to see Hamlet, in his unwearied negations, as another hero-villain, then we would judge him the supreme analyst of the darker recalcitrances in the selfhood. Freud followed the pre-Socratic Empedocles, in arguing that character is fate, a frightening doctrine that maintains the fear that there are no accidents, that overdetermination rules us all of our lives. Hamlet assumes the same, yet adds to this argument the terrible passivity he manifests in Act V. Throughout Shakespeare's tragedies, the most interesting personages seem doom-eager, reminding us again that a Shakespearean reading of Freud would be more illuminating than a Freudian exegesis of Shakespeare. We learn more when we discover Hamlet in the Freudian Death Drive, than when we read *Beyond the Pleasure Principle* into *Hamlet.*

In Shakespearean comedy, character achieves its true literary apotheosis, which is the representation of the inner freedom that can be created by great wit alone. Rosalind and Falstaff, perhaps alone among Shakespeare's personages, match Hamlet in wit, though hardly in the metaphysics of consciousness. Whether in the comic or the modern mode, Shakespeare has set the standard of measurement in the balance between character and passion.

In Shakespeare the self is more dramatized than theatricalized, which is why a Shakespearean reading of Freud works out so well. Character-formation after the passing of the Oedipal stage takes the place of fetishistic fragmentings of the self. Critics who now call literary character into question, and who proclaim also the death of the author, invariably also regard all notions, literary and human, of a stable character as being mere reductions of deeper pre-Oedipal desires. It

becomes clear that the fortunes of literary character rise and fall with the pres-
tige of normative conceptions of the ego. Shakespeare's Iago, who wars against
being, may be the first deconstructionist of the self, with his proclamation of "I
am not what I am." This constitutes the necessary prologue to any view that
would regard a fixed ego as a virtual abnormality. But deconstructions of the self
are no more modern than Modernism is. Like literary modernism, the
decentered ego came out of the Hellenistic culture of ancient Alexandria. The
Gnostic heretics believed that the psyche, like the body, was a fallen entity,
mechanically fashioned by the Demiurge or false creator. They held however
that each of us possessed also a spark or pneuma, which was a fragment of
the original Abyss or true, alien God. The soul or psyche within every one of
us was thus at war with the self or pneuma, and only that sparklike self could be
saved.

Shakespeare, following after Chaucer in this respect, was the first and remains
still the greatest master of representing character both as a stable soul and a
wavering self. There is a substance that endures in Shakespeare's figures, and there
is also a quicksilver rendition of the unsettling sparks. Racine and Tolstoy, Balzac and
Dickens, follow in Shakespeare's wake by giving us some sense of pre-Oedipal
sparks or drives, and considerably more sense of post-Oedipal character and
personality, stabilizations or sublimations of the fetish-seeking drives. Critics like Leo
Bersani and René Girard argue eloquently against our taking this mimesis as the only
proper work of literature. I would suggest that strong fictions of the self, from the
Bible through Samuel Beckett, necessarily participate in both modes, the sublima-
tion of desire, and the persistence of a primordial desire. The mystery of Hamlet
or of Lear is intimately invested in the tangled mixture of the two modes of
representation.

Psychic mobility is proposed by Bersani as the ideal to which deconstructions
of the literary self may yet guide us. The ideal has its pathos, but the realities of
literary representation seem to me very different, perhaps destructively so. When
a novelist like D. H. Lawrence sought to reduce his characters to Eros and the
Death Drive, he still had to persuade us of his authority at mimesis by lavishing upon
the figures of *The Rainbow* and *Women in Love* all of the vivid stigmata of
normative personality. Birkin and Ursula may represent antithetical and uncanny
drives, but they develop and change as characters pondering their own pronounce-
ments and reactions to self and others. The cost of a non-Shakespearean representation is enormous. Pynchon, in *The Crying of Lot 49* and *Gravity's Rainbow*,
evades the burden of the normative by resorting to something like Christopher
Marlowe's art of caricature in *The Jew of Malta*. Marlowe's Barabas is a marvelous
rhetorician, yet he is a cartoon alongside the troublingly equivocal Shylock. Pynchon's personages are deliberate cartoons also, as flat as comic strips. Marlowe's
achievement, and Pynchon's, are beyond dispute, yet they are like the prelude and
the postlude to Shakespearean reality. They do not wish to engage with our hunger
for the empirical world and so they enter the problematic cosmos of literary
fantasy.

No writer, not even Shakespeare or Proust, alters the available stock that we agree to call reality, but Shakespeare, more than any other, does show us how much of reality we could encounter if only we retained adequate desire. The strong literary representation of character is already an analysis of character, and is part of the healing work of a literary culture, which implicitly seeks to cure violence through a normative mimesis of ego, *as if it were stable,* whether in actuality it is or is not. I do not believe that this is a social quest taken on by literary culture, but rather that we confront here the aesthetic essence of what makes a culture *literary,* rather than metaphysical or ethical or religious. A culture becomes literary when its conceptual modes have failed it, which means when religion, philosophy, and science have begun to lose their authority. If they cannot heal violence, then literature attempts to do so, which may be only a turning inside out of the critical arguments of Girard and Bersani.

I conclude by offering a particular instance or special case as a paradigm for the healing enterprise that is at once the representation and the analysis of literary character. Let us call it the aesthetics of being outraged, or rather of successfully representing the state of being outraged. W. C. Fields was one modern master of such representation, and Nathanael West was another, as was Faulkner before him. Here also the greatest master remains Shakespeare, whose Macbeth, himself a bloody outrage, yet retains our imaginative sympathy precisely because he grows increasingly outraged as he experiences the equivocation of the fiend that lies like truth. The double-natured promises and the prophecies of the weird sisters finally induce in Macbeth an apocalyptic version of the stage actor's anxiety at missing cues, the horror of a phantasmagoric stage fright of missing one's time, of always reacting too late. Macbeth, a veritable monster of solipsistic inwardness but no intellectual, counters his dilemma by fresh murders, that prolong him in time yet provoke him only to a perpetually freshened sense of being outraged, as all his expectations become still worse confounded. We are moved by Macbeth, however estrangedly, because his terrible inwardness is a paradigm for our own solipsism, but also because none of us can resist a strong and successful representation of the human in a state of being outraged.

The ultimate outrage is the necessity of dying, an outrage concealed in a multitude of masks, including the tyrannical ambitions of Macbeth. I suspect that our outrage at being outraged is the most difficult of all our affects for us to represent to ourselves, which is why we are so inclined to imaginative sympathy for a character who strongly conveys that affect to us. The Shrike of West's *Miss Lonelyhearts* or Faulkner's Joe Christmas of *Light in August* are crucial modern instances, but such figures can be located in many other works, since the ability to represent this extreme emotion is one of the tests that strong writers are driven to set for themselves.

However a reader seeks to reduce literary character to a question of marks on a page, she will come at last to the impasse constituted by the thought of death, her death, and before that to all the stations of being outraged that memorialize her own drive towards death. In reading, she quests for evidences that are strong representations, whether of her desire or her despair. Such questings constitute the necessary basis for the analysis of literary character, an enterprise that always will survive every vagary of critical fashion.

EDITOR'S NOTE

This volume brings together a representative selection of the best criticism that has been devoted to David Copperfield, considered as a major literary character. I am grateful to Jerry Aliotta for his devoted aid in editing this book.

My introduction centers upon the apparent colorlessness of David Copperfield, in comparison to his vivid account of nearly everyone else in the story. A selection of extracts from the criticism of Copperfield follows, tracing the history of his reception, from Dickens himself through Matthew Arnold, G. K. Chesterton, Virginia Woolf, and George Orwell, on to the criticism of J. Hillis Miller and Angus Wilson.

Full-scale critical essays begin with Gwendolyn G. Needham's study of what Dickens rather curiously called David Copperfield's "undisciplined heart." A remarkable essay by James R. Kincaid analyzes the rhetoric of humor of Dickens's treatment of David, while Bert G. Hornback concentrates upon mythological aspects.

Memory, both open and repressed in Dickens's autobiographic portrait of Copperfield, is the theme of Robin Gilmour, after which Norman Talbot shrewdly analyzes David's name and namings. Mark M. Hennelly, Jr., traces change and its evasions in the portrait of David, after which John P. McGowan examines the limits of realism in that portrait.

David as a sexual being is considered by Iain Crawford, while Chris R. Vanden Bossche emphasizes elements of social class and familial background in the hero. A darker tone is invoked by Edwin M. Eigner, who centers on Copperfield's elegiac strain, his sense of mortality.

Virginia Carmichael invokes the contemporary psycholinguistics of Lacan in order to set David in the context of the Freudian family romance. In this book's final essay, Alexander Welsh searchingly analyzes Copperfield's belated response to his early hardships.

INTRODUCTION

David Copperfield is the great original of all the portraits of the artist as a young man, including Joyce's representation of Stephen Dedalus. There are vast perplexities attendant upon Copperfield, many of them doubtless connected to the labyrinthine need of Charles Dickens both to portray and to refuse to confront his own past. Yet the central truth about Dickens burns through Copperfield's personality and character: we are observing the genesis and the early development of a great novelist. What matters about Copperfield is what matters most about Dickens: story is born. If the novel ever has achieved Shakespearean exuberance and profusion, it is in Dickens. David Copperfield at first seems eclipsed by the marvelous figures around him: Edward Murdstone, Steerforth, Rosa Dartle, Uriah Heep, Micawber, Peggotty, Aunt Betsey Trotwood. Grand grotesques, or the self-obsessed, doom-eager Steerforth, alike have a vitality that the ruminating and ever-belated David appears to lack. But they already are *his* creatures, and he is at work creating them more truly and more strange before he can begin to realize his relation to them. Our odd sense that David keeps catching up to himself is one of the beautiful peculiarities that mark him as a strikingly original literary character. He is the novelist as a child and as a young man, at first nearly helpless and then somewhat hapless, but with the ear, the eye, the veritable touch of the novelist fully matured.

Of Copperfield we remember, after we have closed his book, mostly individual qualities that we tend to find in ourselves: guilty aspirations disowned yet still ongoing; an energetic fantasy life that blends into dreadful realities; an extraordinary preoccupation with the self. What is different in David are the pragmatic consequences of his repressed intensities: they ensue in the disasters of those whom he loves. Steerforth, Ham, Dora all die that Copperfield the novelist may live as a novelist; they are vicarious atonements for David's vocation. If he seems colorless to us, that is because we see the violent colors of Heep, Micawber, Murdstone, and Steerforth only as he sees them. They live and die in him; they are his frontier concepts, his way of both projecting what he cannot bear in his self, and introjecting what he cannot reject in his own fantasies. No one reads *Ulysses* for Joyce's

1

Stephen, who can be as much a sensible emptiness as David Copperfield frequently is. But the sublime Poldy, the potent Molly, even the outrageous Buck Mulligan more than fill Stephen's empty heart. David Copperfield knows more than he incarnates, because he learns the secret of the novelist's patient labor of the negative. Like Dickens, Copperfield becomes a more-than-Carlyle, by working prodigiously before the coming of the night.

And yet, as a personality, how could Copperfield ever become Dickens? Any good biography of Dickens gives us a personage who overgoes his own characters. Indeed, when I read about Dickens, I sometimes cannot believe that he was an actual Victorian novelist. He seems instead to be a character in a great drama, unwritten only because no Victorian Shakespeare was there to compose it. No man, woman, child anywhere in a Dickens novel is nearly as theatrical, vitalistic, and darkly Rabelaisian a being as Dickens himself. Copperfield, though evidently his favorite literary creation, excludes nearly every overt quality that made Dickens so singular and overwhelming a performer, on stage and off. We cannot imagine Dickens sketching his outward self as Copperfield; a protagonist so rammed with life would not need a Steerforth as the true object of his drive towards storytelling. It is David's curiously endearing (if exasperating) trait to get things wrong until getting them right mends little or nothing. We trust David to tell the truth long before he begins to understand the truth. That is why we can accept the "stage fire" (as Ruskin called it) that seems excessive in David's account of his early sorrows and sufferings. The childhood of Copperfield is a tormented story but a magnificent one, and what it reveals is not only David's endurance but his fighting qualities, the storyteller's unique combat with death. Even as a child, the novelist knows that telling his story not only mitigates disaster but postpones death, postpones it because even death wants to hear Copperfield's story, the story of how stories need to go on being told.

Did Dickens, in order to evade a full identification of his hero with himself, fall into the error of making David so foolish as to exasperate us too consistently? If one gave only a plot summary of the novel, one might think so. David is so consistently wrong in judging both characters and events that bald summary might disengage him from our sympathies. Yet that is precisely what does not happen as we read along in David's narrative. Our fellow-feeling for him abides in later years, even as it does if one first reads his book at the age of ten (as I did). He portrays himself as endlessly naive, but we receive his perpetual innocence as being our own. The child never dies in David, and the childlike (not childish) apprehension of other selves is David Copperfield's unique gift to us. It is because David's spirit imbues us that we can apprehend the proto-Falstaffian gusto of Micawber and the authentic bogeyman quality of Uriah Heep. Our perspective upon them is curiously Pickwickian, because a strong touch of the unabashed innocence of Pickwick endures in Copperfield. It is almost as though his childhood descents into Hell have strengthened David into an ascension to the state of what William Blake called "Organized Innocence." Hence we receive both the restraint and the open vision that makes David's mode of comedy possible. Take as representative this, after David is delegated by Mrs. Micawber to raise some cash in order to stock the much depleted Micawber family larder:

> At last Mr Micawber's difficulties came to a crisis, and he was arrested early one morning, and carried over to the King's Bench Prison in the Borough. He told me, as he went out of the house, that the God of day had now gone down upon him—and I really thought his heart was broken and mine too. But I heard, afterwards, that he was seen to play a lively game at skittles, before noon.
>
> On the first Sunday after he was taken there, I was to go and see him, and have dinner with him. I was to ask my way to such a place, and just short of that place I should see such another place, and just short of that I should see a yard, which I was to cross, and keep straight on until I saw a turnkey. All this I did; and when at last I did see a turnkey (poor little fellow that I was!), and thought how, when Roderick Random was in a debtors' prison, there was a man there with nothing on him but an old rug, the turnkey swam before my dimmed eyes and my beating heart.
>
> Mr Micawber was waiting for me within the gate, and we went up to his room (top story but one), and cried very much. He solemnly conjured me, I remember, to take warning by his fate; and to observe that if a man had twenty pounds a-year for his income, and spent nineteen pounds nineteen shillings and sixpence, he would be happy, but that if he spent twenty pounds one he would be miserable. After which he borrowed a shilling of me for porter, gave me a written order on Mrs. Micawber for the amount, and put away his pocket-handkerchief, and cheered up.

David overreacts to the pathos of Micawber, but the Falstaffian Micawber is too insouciant to stay down. It is young Copperfield who is overwhelmed, blending together sight and Smollett's fiction into one visionary entity, until Micawber rouses him again. What matters here, as elsewhere, is David's voice: gentle, emotional, in excess of the object, benign, and always trembling with a repressed intensity, with the barely concealed half-memories of his own childhood distress. Yet that intensity is compounded of love as much as of sorrow, and David's love for the Micawbers, which we share, is clearly based upon his love for his own parents. Micawber just about *is* John Dickens: amiable, delightful, feckless, overrhetorical, financially hopeless, but also always loving. David makes mistake after mistake, misjudges and misinterprets, but also never ceases to love every benevolent figure in the book, even when like Steerforth they do not behave benignly. And though this may seem sentimental, that is the secret of David's strength as a literary character: he is a profoundly loving person, and the love persuades us. When David loves, we love (except for the impossibly idealized Agnes!), and we learn to trust in the authenticity of that love.

Identification with David Copperfield (and through him with Charles Dickens) becomes the joyous franchise of the reader of this autobiographical novel. Unlike Micawber, Steerforth, Uriah Heep, David lacks the extraordinary actuality with which Dickens, at his best, could imbue literary character. Such actuality rivals Shakespeare in his comic mode, but then David is not a comic character, although he is a humorous one, portrayed by Dickens with affectionate irony and shrewd self-knowledge. Instead of vividness, Dickens subtly conferred upon David a kind of blankness, a void before creation, the sense of the novelist-in-waiting. The single trait besides loving-kindness that most marks David is anxiety or anxious expectations. This is not the anxiety of the compulsive neurotic but of the storyteller, who seems to know, in the depths, that telling the tale will be therapeutic for him, even as it tends to heal us. Violence and fraud shadow David's world, as they shadow ours, but his gift is somehow to know, almost from the start, that being able to tell the story is being made capable of healing violence and eradicating fraud.

Lacking all color himself, David Copperfield develops the power to render others with immense color. Yet as we look back upon his novel, we realize that we have accepted a kind of illusion, because David is as much loved as he loves others. We see him at last, not as he sees himself, but as the object of the sustaining love of nearly all whom he loves. Though David matures in self-control, in the disciplining of his own heart, what is most valuable in him never has to mature at all.

—H. B.

CRITICAL EXTRACTS

CHARLES DICKENS

I am within three pages of the shore; and am strangely divided, as usual in such cases, between sorrow and joy. Oh, my dear Forster, if I were to say half of what *Copperfield* makes me feel to-night, how strangely, even to you, I should be turned inside-out! I seem to be sending some part of myself into the Shadowy World.

—CHARLES DICKENS, Letter to John Forster (October 21, 1850), *The Letters of Charles Dickens*, ed. Graham Storey, Kathleen Tillotson, and Nina Burgis (Oxford: Clarendon Press, 1988), Vol. 6, p. 195

HENRY F. CHORLEY

That this is in many respects the most beautiful and highly finished work which the world has had from the pen of Mr. Dickens, we are strongly of opinion. It has all the merits to which the author already owes a world-wide popularity; with some graces which are peculiar to itself—or have been but feebly indicated in his former creations. In no previous fiction has he shown so much gentleness of touch and delicacy of tone,—such abstinence from trick in what may be called the level part of the narrative,—so large an amount of refined and poetical yet simple knowledge of humanity. The Chronicler himself is one of the best heroes ever sketched or wrought out by Mr. Dickens. Gentle, affectionate and trusting,—his fine observation and his love of reverie raise David Copperfield far above the level of sentimental lovers or hectoring youths whose fortunes and characters are too often in works of this sort made the axles on which the action and passion of the story turn. The loving, imaginative child—with his childish fancies perpetually reaching away towards heights too high for childhood to climb—his rapid and sympathetic instincts for enjoyment—his quick sense of injustice,—his tremulous foresight of coming griefs,—the boy seduced by the fascinating qualities of a dangerous friend,— the youth's boy-love for his child-wife,—that love itself never faltering even to the end, yet by a fine instinctive information leading his mind to dim glimpses of a higher domestic happiness at which he might have aimed,—all these are outlined, filled in and coloured without one stroke awry or one exaggerated tint to mar the por-traiture. Few authors would have so finely comprehended the step-child's mixture of awe and curiosity under the tyranny of that she-turnkey Miss Murdstone,—few could have touched the strange, inexplicable shrinking of the orphan when he makes one of the pleasure party of the merry and beneficent undertakers, Omer and Joram,—few could have so nicely indicated the relish which, in spite of their sorrows, their shabbiness, their difficulties, their fustian and their prosing, David could not help finding in the society of Mr. and Mrs. Micawber. In coarser hands this must have become a taste for bad company.—Then, over all there hangs that mournful sentiment which, being the natural accompaniment of all personal reviews of the past, never in its saddest expressions takes the tone of sentimentalism; but follows the narrative like a low, sweet—and true—music:—beginning with the narrator's first look out on his father's cold grave in the churchyard against which every night his mother's door is barred, and only ending with the last line that chronicles the gains, the trials and the losses of a life.

—HENRY F. CHORLEY, Review of *David Copperfield, Athenaeum,*
November 23, 1850, pp. 1209–10

CHARLES DICKENS

I remarked in the original Preface to this Book, that I did not find it easy to get sufficiently far away from it, in the first sensations of having finished it, to refer to it with the composure which this formal heading would seem to require. My interest in it was so recent and strong, and my mind was so divided between pleasure and regret—pleasure in the achievement of a long design, regret in the separation from many companions—that I was in danger of wearying the reader with personal confidences and private emotions.

Beside which, all that I could have said of the Story to any purpose, I had endeavored to say in it.

It would concern the reader little, perhaps, to know how sorrowfully the pen is laid down at the close of a two-years' imaginative task; or how an Author feels as if he were dismissing some portion of himself into the shadowy world, when a crowd of the creatures of his brain are going from him for ever. Yet, I had nothing else to tell; unless, indeed, I were to confess (which might be of less moment still) that no one can ever believe this Narrative, in the reading, more than I believed it in the writing.

So true are these avowals at the present day, that I can now only take the reader into one confidence more. Of all my books, I like this the best. It will be easily believed that I am a fond parent to every child of my fancy, and that no one can ever love that family as dearly as I love them. But, like many fond parents, I have in my heart of hearts a favourite child. And his name is DAVID COPPERFIELD.

—CHARLES DICKENS, "Preface" to *David Copperfield*
(London: Chapman & Hall, 1867)

JOHN FORSTER

The *Copperfield* disclosures formerly made will for ever connect the book with the author's individual story; but too much has been assumed, from those revelations, of a full identity of Dickens with his hero, and of a supposed intention that his own character as well as parts of his career should be expressed in the narrative. It is right to warn the reader as to this. He can judge for himself how far the childish experiences are likely to have given the turn to Dickens's genius; whether their bitterness had so burnt into his nature, as, in the hatred of oppression, the revolt against abuse of power, and the war with injustice under every form displayed in his earliest books, to have reproduced itself only; and to what extent mere compassion for his own childhood may account for the strange fascination always exerted over him by child-suffering and sorrow. But, many as are the resemblances in Copperfield's adventures to portions of those of Dickens, and often as reflections occur to David which no one intimate with Dickens could fail to recognize as but the reproduction of his, it would be the greatest mistake to imagine anything like a complete identity of the fictitious novelist with the real one, beyond the Hungerford scenes; or to suppose that the youth, who then received his first harsh schooling in life, came out of it as little harmed or hardened as David did. The language of the fiction reflects only faintly the narrative of the actual fact; and the man whose character it helped to form was expressed not less faintly in the impulsive impressionable youth, incapable of resisting the leading of others, and only disciplined into self-control by the later griefs of his entrance into manhood. Here was but another proof how thoroughly Dickens understood his calling, and that to weave fact with fiction unskillfully would be only to make truth less true.

The character of the hero of the novel finds indeed his right place in the story he is supposed to tell, rather by unlikeness than by likeness to Dickens, even where intentional resemblance might seem to be prominent. Take autobiography as a design to show that any man's life may be as a mirror of existence to all men, and the individual career becomes altogether secondary to the variety of experiences received and rendered back in it. This particular form in imaginative literature has too often led to the indulgence of mental analysis, metaphysics, and sentiment, all in excess: but Dickens was carried safely over these allurements by a healthy judgment and sleepless creative fancy; and even the method of his narrative is more simple here than it generally is in his books. His imaginative growths have less luxuriance of underwood, and the crowds of external images always rising so vividly before him are more within control.

Consider Copperfield thus in his proper place in the story, and sequence as well as connection will be given to the varieties of its childish adventure. The first warm nest of love in which his vain fond mother, and her quaint kind servant, cherish him; the quick-following contrast of hard dependence and servile treatment; the escape from that premature and dwarfed maturity by natural relapse into a more perfect childhood; the then leisurely growth of emotions and faculties into manhood; these are component parts of a character consistently drawn. The sum of its achievement is to be a successful cultivation of letters; and often as such imaginary discipline has been the theme of fiction, there are not many happier conceptions of it. The ideal and real parts of the boy's nature receive development in the proportions which contribute best to the end desired; the readiness for impulsive attachments that had put him into the leading of others, has underneath it a base of truthfulness on which at last he rests in safety; the practical man is the outcome of the fanciful youth; and a more than equivalent for the graces of his visionary days, is found in the active sympathies that life has opened to him. Many experiences have come within its range, and his heart has had room for all. Our interest in him cannot but be increased by knowing how much he expresses of what the author had himself gone through; but David includes far less than this, and infinitely more.

That the incidents arise easily, and to the very end connect themselves naturally and unobtrusively with the characters of which they are a part, is to be said perhaps more truly of this than of any other of Dickens's novels. There is a profusion of distinct and distinguishable people, and a prodigal wealth of detail; but unity of drift or purpose is apparent always, and the tone is uniformly right. By the course of the events we learn the value of self-denial and patience, quiet endurance of unavoidable ills, strenuous effort against ills remediable; and everything in the fortunes of the actors warns us, to strengthen our generous emotions and to guard the purities of home. It is easy thus to account for the supreme popularity of *Copperfield*, without the addition that it can hardly have had a reader, man or lad, who did not discover that he was something of a Copperfield himself. Childhood and youth live again for all of us in its marvellous boy-experiences. Mr. Micawber's presence must not prevent my saying that it does not take the lead of the other novels in humorous creation; but in the use of humour to bring out prominently the ludicrous in any object or incident without excluding or weakening its most enchanting sentiment, it stands decidedly first. It is the perfection of English mirth. We are apt to resent the exhibition of too much goodness, but it is here so qualified by oddity as to become not merely palatable but attractive; and even pathos is heightened by what in other hands would only make it comical. That there are also faults in the book is certain, but none that are incompatible with the most masterly qualities; and a book becomes everlasting by the fact, not that faults are not in it, but that genius nevertheless is there.

—JOHN FORSTER, *The Life of Charles Dickens* [1872–74] (London:
J. M. Dent & Sons, 1966), Vol. 2, pp. 105–7

MATTHEW ARNOLD

Much as I have published, I do not think it has ever yet happened to me to comment in print upon any production of Charles Dickens. What a pleasure to have the opportunity of praising a work so sound, a work so rich in merit, as *David Copperfield!* 'Man lese nicht die mitstrebende, mitwirkende!' says Goethe: 'Do not read your fellow-strivers, your fellow-workers!' Of the contemporary rubbish which is shot so plentifully all round us, we can, indeed, hardly read too little. But to contemporary work so good as *David Copperfield* we are in danger of perhaps not paying respect enough, of reading it (for who could help reading it?) too hastily, and then putting it aside for something else and forgetting it. What treasure of gaiety, invention, life, are in that book! what alertness and resource! what a soul of good nature and kindness governing the whole!

—MATTHEW ARNOLD, "The Incompatibles" [1881], *Irish Essays*
(London: Smith, Elder & Co., 1882), pp. 43–44

WILLIAM SAMUEL LILLY

Dickens's young men are, as a rule, impossible. They are well-nigh all of the same inane type. He seems to have got them out of an Adelphi melodrama. But David Copperfield, who is a transcript from his own troublous and distressed childhood and youth, is, at all events, human.

—WILLIAM SAMUEL LILLY, "Dickens," *Four English Humorists
of the Nineteenth Century* (London: John Murray, 1895), p. 14

G. K. CHESTERTON

I do not like the notion of David Copperfield sitting down comfortably to his tea-table with Agnes, having got rid of all the inconvenient or distressing characters of the story by sending them to the other side of the world. The whole thing has too much about it of the selfishness of a family which sends a scapegrace to the Colonies to starve with its blessing. There is too much in the whole thing of that element which was satirised by an ironic interpretation of the epitaph "Peace, perfect peace, with loved ones far away." We should have thought more of David Copperfield (and also of Charles Dickens) if he had endeavoured for the rest of his life, by conversation and comfort, to bind up the wounds of his old friends from the seaside. We should have thought more of David Copperfield (and also of Charles Dickens) if he had faced the possibility of going on till his dying day lending money to Mr. Wilkins Micawber. We should have thought more of David Copperfield (and also of Charles Dickens) if he had not looked upon the marriage with Dora merely as a flirtation, an episode which he survived and ought to survive. And yet the truth is that there is nowhere in fiction where we feel so keenly the primary human instinct and principle that a marriage is a marriage and irrevocable, that such things do leave a wound and also a bond as in this case of David's short connection with his silly little wife. When all is said and done, when Dickens has done his best and his worst, when he has sentimentalised for pages and tried to tie up everything in the pink tape of optimism, the fact, in the psychology of the reader, still remains. The reader does still feel that David's marriage to Dora was a real marriage; and that his marriage to Agnes was nothing, a middle-aged compromise, a taking of the second best, a sort of spiritualised and sublimated marriage of convenience. For all the readers of Dickens Dora is thoroughly avenged. The modern world (intent on anarchy in everything, even in Government) refuses to perceive the permanent element of tragic constancy which inheres in all passion, and which is the origin of marriage. Marriage rests upon the fact that you cannot have your cake and eat it; that you cannot lose your heart and have it. But, as I have said, there is perhaps no place in literature where we feel more vividly the sense of this monogamous instinct in man than in David Copperfield. A man is monogamous even if he is only monogamous for a month; love is eternal even if it is only eternal for a month. It always leaves behind it the sense of something broken and betrayed.

But I have mentioned Dora in this connection only because she illustrates the same fact which Micawber illustrates; the fact that there is at the end of this book too much tendency to bless people and get rid of them. Micawber is a nuisance. Dickens the despot condemns him to exile. Dora is a nuisance. Dickens the despot condemns her to death. But it is the whole business of Dickens in the world to express the fact that such people are the spice and interest of life. It is the whole point of Dickéns that there is nobody more worth living with than a strong, splendid, entertaining, immortal nuisance. Micawber interrupts practical life; but what is practical life that it should venture to interrupt Micawber? Dora confuses the housekeeping; but we are not angry with Dora because she confuses the housekeeping. We are angry with the housekeeping because it confuses Dora. I repeat, and it cannot be too much repeated that the whole lesson of Dickens is here. It is better to know Micawber than not to know the minor worries that arise out of knowing Micawber. It is better to have a bad debt and a good friend. In the same way it is better to marry a human and healthy personality which happens to attract you than to marry a mere housewife; for a mere housewife is a mere housekeeper. All this was what Dickens stood for; that the very people who are most irritating in small business circumstances are often the people who are most delightful in long stretches of experience of life. It is just the man who is maddening when he is ordering a cutlet or arranging an appointment who is probably the man in whose company it is worth while to journey steadily towards the grave. Distribute the dignified people and the capable people and the highly business-like people among all the situations which their ambition or their innate corruption may demand; but keep close to your heart, keep deep in your inner councils the absurd people. Let the clever people pretend to govern you, let the unimpeachable people pretend to advise you, but let the fools alone influence you; let the laughable people whose faults you see and understand be the only people who are really inside your life, who really come near you or accompany you on your lonely march towards the last impossibility. That is the whole meaning of Dickens; that we should keep the absurd people for our friends. And here at the end of *David Copperfield* he seems in some dim way to deny it. He seems to want to get rid of the preposterous people simply because they will always continue to be preposterous. I have a horrible feeling that David Copperfield will send even his aunt to Australia if she worries him too much about donkeys.

I repeat, then, that this wrong ending of *David Copperfield* is one of the very few examples in Dickens of a real symptom of fatigue. Having created splendid beings for whom alone life might be worth living, he cannot endure the thought of his hero living with them. Having given his hero superb and terrible friends, he is afraid of the awful and tempestuous vista of their friendship. He slips back into a more superficial kind of story and ends it in a more superficial way. He is afraid of the things he has made; of that terrible figure Micawber; of that yet more terrible figure Dora. He cannot make up his mind to see his hero perpetually entangled in the splendid tortures and sacred surprises that come from living with really individual and unmanageable people. He cannot endure the idea that his fairy prince will not have henceforward a perfectly peaceful time. But the wise old fairy tales (which are the wisest things in the world, at any rate the wisest things of worldly origin), the wise old fairy tales never were so silly as to say that the prince and the princess lived peacefully ever afterwards. The fairy tales said that the prince and princess lived happily ever afterwards: and so they did. They lived happily, although it is very likely that from time to time they threw the furniture at each other. Most marriages, I think, are happy marriages; but there is no such thing as a contented marriage. The whole pleasure of marriage is that it is a perpetual crisis. David Copperfield and Dora quarrelled over the cold mutton; and if they had gone on quarrelling to the end of their lives, they would have gone on loving each other to the end of their lives; it would have been a human marriage. But David Copperfield and Agnes would agree about the cold mutton. And that cold mutton would be very cold.

—G. K. CHESTERTON, *"David Copperfield"* [1907], *Appreciations and Criticisms of the Work of Charles Dickens* (London: J. M. Dent & Sons, 1911), pp. 132–36

VIRGINIA WOOLF

Like the ripening of strawberries, the swelling of apples, and all other natural processes, new editions of Dickens—cheap, pleasant-looking, well printed—are born into the world and call for no more notice than the season's plums and strawberries, save when by some chance the emergence of one of these masterpieces in its fresh green binding suggests an odd and overwhelming enterprise—that one should read *David Copperfield* for the second time. There is perhaps no person living who can remember reading *David Copperfield* for the first time. Like *Robinson Crusoe* and *Grimm's Fairy Tales* and the Waverly Novels, *Pickwick* and *David Copperfield* are not books, but stories communicated by word of mouth in those tender years when fact and fiction merge, and thus belong to the memories and myths of life, and not to its esthetic experience.

—VIRGINIA WOOLF, *"David Copperfield"* [1925], *The Moment and Other Essays* (New York: Harcourt, Brace, 1948), p. 75

S T E P H E N   L E A C O C K

One of the strangest things in the book *David Copperfield* is David Copperfield himself. Few people perhaps have noted the fact, but many will admit it when said, that there is, so to speak, no such person. David is merely the looking glass in which we see the other characters, the voice through which they speak. He himself has no more character than a spiritualist medium. He tells us, for example, that he wrote stories for the press, but we don't believe him. He tells us all about his career, his attempts to enter law, his struggle with shorthand reporting, but we take no stock in it. None of it seems real. And none of it is. Our interest is purely in the people who circulate in David's life, Betsy Trotwood, and the Micawbers, Uriah Heep and his mother, and Mr. Spenlow, and, above all, Dora. But in David himself not at all: he is ruined, and we don't feel a pang; goes up in fortune or down or sideways—it doesn't seem to matter. All we want is to hear what happened to the others, not to him.

This instinctive attitude of the reader is entirely justified. It arises out of the origin of the book. Dickens, as everybody knows, planned to write an autobiography, to set down in writing especially all the early recollections of the sufferings of his own life. He began the task. He wrote out various early chapters of his life: then found the revelation too intimate, too poignant, and abandoned it. Later on he changed it into the story of David Copperfield, and in the changing the whole nature of the thing is altered. In the autobiography such as he meant to write the interest is in himself. We can see that in the burning passages which describe the humiliation of little Copperfield degraded to ignoble work, an outcast, on the edge of want and on the fringe of destitution: this is not David Copperfield; this is little Dickens. There are touches of this all through the book, though the intensity washes out of them as it goes on. In the written novel, the autobiography, the revelation of the author's soul, is overwhelmed and absorbed by the characters in the book. If David Copperfield has a soul, we don't care about it. The effect is as if the other characters spoke through the medium of David and sometimes Charles Dickens himself used the medium to do a little talk of his own. The book is therefore neither a real autobiography nor a real novel in first person impersonal. If this is bad art, it doesn't matter. For Dickens there were no more rules of art than there were rules of battle for Napoleon.

It is a supreme excellence of the book that the interest rises continually. For many readers, David's meeting with Dora and his falling in love seem to bring the story to a culmination of interest, when all the points run together, like lights focussed on a single spot. Yet Dora does not come in until the twenty-sixth chapter—halfway through the book. It is a wonderful evidence of the genius of Dickens that could introduce a new character and a new interest at such a stage of the narration. Few writers would even attempt such a thing, and fewer still succeed in it.

Dora herself is one of the great triumphs of the book. The falling in love of David Copperfield, sudden, catastrophic, and idyllic, is one of the masterpieces of

English literature. It is so marvellously written that to readers young enough in mind it comes with all the freshness and glory of love itself. The magic words transpose the scene, and the reader shares the exaltation felt by David, carried away on the wings of the morning.

—STEPHEN LEACOCK, "Flood Tide 1845–1850," *Charles Dickens: His Life and Work* (Garden City, NY: Doubleday, Doran, 1934), pp. 144–46

GEORGE BERNARD SHAW

⟨. . .⟩ David was, for a time at least, Dickens's favorite child, perhaps because he had used him to express the bitterness of that episode in his own experience which had wounded his boyish self-respect most deeply. For Dickens, in spite of his exuberance, was a deeply reserved man: the exuberance was imagination and acting (his imagination was ceaseless, and his outward life a feat of acting from beginning to end); and we shall never know whether in that immensely broadened outlook and knowledge of the world which began with *Hard Times* and *Little Dorrit,* and left all his earlier works behind, he may not have come to see that making his living by sticking labels on blacking bottles and rubbing shoulders with boys who were not gentlemen, was as little shameful as being the genteel apprentice in the office of Mr. Spenlow, or the shorthand writer recording the unending twaddle of the House of Commons and its overflow of electioneering bunk on the hustings of all the Eatans-wills in the country.

⟨. . .⟩ Comparing David Copperfield with Pip, believe, if you can, that there was no revision of his estimate of the favorite child David as a work of art and even as a vehicle of experience. The adult David fades into what stage managers call a walking gentleman. The reappearance of Mr. Dickens in the character of a black-smith's boy may be regarded as an apology to Mealy Potatoes.

—GEORGE BERNARD SHAW, "Preface" to *Great Expectations* (Edinburgh: R. & R. Clark, 1937), pp. v–vi

GEORGE ORWELL

One crying evil of his time that Dickens says very little about is child labour. There are plenty of pictures of suffering children in his books, but usually they are suffering in schools rather than in factories. The one detailed account of child labour that he gives is the description in *David Copperfield* of little David washing bottles in Murdstone & Grinby's warehouse. This, of course, is autobiography. Dickens himself, at the age of ten, had worked in Warren's blacking factory in the Strand, very much as he describes it here. It was a terribly bitter memory to him, partly because he felt the whole incident to be discreditable to his parents, and he even concealed it from his wife till long after they were married. Looking back on this period, he says in *David Copperfield:*

It is a matter of some surprise to me, even now, that I can have been so easily thrown away at such an age. A child of excellent abilities and with strong powers of observation, quick, eager, delicate, and soon hurt bodily or mentally, it seems wonderful to me that nobody should have made any sign in my behalf. But none was made; and I became, at ten years old, a little labouring hind in the service of Murdstone & Grinby.

And again, having described the rough boys among whom he worked:

No words can express the secret agony of my soul as I sunk into this companionship . . . and felt my hopes of growing up to be a learned and distinguished man crushed in my bosom.

Obviously it is not David Copperfield who is speaking, it is Dickens himself. He uses almost the same words on the autobiography that he began and abandoned a few months earlier. Of course Dickens is right in saying that a gifted child ought not to work ten hours a day pasting labels on bottles, but what he does not say is that *no* child ought to be condemned to such a fate, and there is no reason for inferring that he thinks it. David escapes from the warehouse, but Mick Walker and Mealy Potatoes and the others are still there, and there is no sign that this troubles Dickens particularly. As usual, he displays no consciousness that the *structure* of society can be changed. He despises politics, does not believe that any good can come out of Parliament—he had been a Parliamentary shorthand writer, which was no doubt a disillusioning experience—and he is slightly hostile to the most hopeful movement of his day, trade unionism.

—GEORGE ORWELL, "Charles Dickens" [1939], *Dickens, Dali and Others*
(New York: Reynal & Hitchcock, 1946), pp. 8–10

W . S O M E R S E T   M A U G H A M

Dickens wrote *David Copperfield* in the first person. This straightforward method served him well, since his plots were often complicated, and the reader's interest was sometimes diverted to characters and incidents that have no bearing on the story's course. In *David Copperfield* there is only one major digression of this kind, and that is the account of Dr. Strong's relations with his wife, his mother and his wife's cousin; it does not concern David and is in itself tedious. I surmise that he used this episode to cover on two occasions a lapse of time which otherwise he didn't know what to do with: the first was the years that David spent at school at Canterbury, and the second was the period between David's disappointment with Dora and her death.

Dickens did not escape the danger that confronts the author of a semi-biographical novel in which himself is the principal character. David Copperfield at the age of ten was put to work by his stern stepfather, as Charles Dickens was by *his* father, and suffered from the "degradation" of having to mix with boys of his own age, whom he did not consider his social equals, in the same way as Dickens, in the fragment of autobiography which he gave to Forster, persuaded himself that he had suffered. Dickens did all he could to excite the reader's sympathy for his hero, and indeed, on the celebrated journey to Dover, when David ran away in order to seek the protection of his aunt Betsey Trotwood, a delightful, amusing character, he loads his dice without scruple. Innumerable readers have found the narration of this escapade wonderfully pathetic. I am made of sterner stuff. I am surprised that the little boy should have been such a ninny as to let everyone he came across rob and cheat him. After all, he had been in the factory for some months and had wandered about London early and late; one would have thought that the other boys at the factory, even though they were not up to his social standard, would have taught him a thing or two; he had lived with the Micawbers and pawned their bits and pieces for them, and had visited them at the Marshalsea: if he had really been the bright boy he is described to be, even at that tender age he would surely have acquired some knowledge of the world and enough sharpness to fend for himself. But it is not only in his childhood that David Copperfield shows himself sadly incompetent. He is incapable of coping with a difficulty. His weakness with Dora, his lack of common sense in dealing with the ordinary problems of domestic life, are almost more than one can bear; and he is so obtuse that he does not guess that Agnes is in love with him. I cannot persuade myself that in the end he became the successful novelist we are told he did. If he wrote novels, I suspect that they were more like those of Mrs. Henry Wood than those of Charles Dickens. It is strange that his creator should have given him none of his own drive, vitality and exuberance. David was slim and good-looking; and he had charm, or he would not have attracted the affection of almost everyone he encountered; he was honest, kindly and conscientious; but he was surely a bit of a fool. He remains the least interesting person in the book. Nowhere does he show himself in so poor a light, so feckless, so incapable of dealing with an awkward situation, as in the monstrous scene between Little Em'ly and Rosa Dartle in the attic in Soho which David witnesses but, for the very flimsiest reason, makes no attempt to stop. This scene affords a good example of how the method of writing a novel in the first person may result in the narrator being forced into a position so shockingly false, so unworthy of a hero of fiction, that the reader is justly indignant with him. If described in the third person, from the standpoint of omniscience, the scene would still have been melodramatic and repellent, but, even though with difficulty, credible. But of course the pleasure one gets from reading *David Copperfield* does not arise from any persuasion one may have that life is, or ever was, anything like what Dickens describes. That is not to depreciate him. Fiction, like the kingdom of heaven, has many mansions, and the author may invite you to visit whichever he chooses. One has just as much right to exist as another, but you must suit yourselves to the surroundings into which you are led. You must put on different spectacles to read *The Golden Bowl* and to read *Bubu de Montparnasse. David Copperfield* is a fantastication, sometimes gay, sometimes pathetic, on life, composed out of recollections and wish-fulfillments by a man of lively imagination and warm feelings. You must read it in the same spirit as you read *As You Like It*. It provides an entertainment almost as delightful.

—W. SOMERSET MAUGHAM, "Charles Dickens and *David Copperfield*" [1948],
The Art of Fiction: An Introduction to Ten Novels and Their Authors
(London: William Heinemann, 1954), pp. 159–61

ROBERT HAMILTON

The most remarkable thing about Dickens as a man, his many-sidedness, was also the most remarkable thing about him as a creative artist; and the two were closely related. The many aspects of his personality and character were reflected in the rich variety of his characters. He had in him elements of Pickwick, Swiveller, Bailey Junior, and even Quilp and Pecksniff, to name only a few. We should therefore expect to find a particularly intimate side of him in a novel such as *Copperfield* based directly on autobiographical fragments of his own life. Yet David remains one of his quietest and least personal creations, increasingly so with his growth from youth to manhood. The young David is not so much a person as a narrator and a symbol—a symbol of normal childhood everywhere. He embodies a universal experience of childhood; and it is this universal quality pervading the particular, the characters, places, and events observed by the narrator, that makes the writing so intimate. There are, it is true, directly autobiographical elements in *Copperfield,* but these relate more to events than to the personality of David. Dickens idealised his childhood. From the little we know, he must have been much more temperamental than David. David is sweet-tempered (apart from the Murdstone episode, which was exceptional) but nobody could have called Dickens that at any time, and certainly nobody would ever have called him "Daisy." By contrast, Pip is much more alive, and much more like his creator—touchy, vain, but fundamentally good-hearted. Of course, the adult David is completely unlike the adult Dickens, as unlike as a lamb to a fiery steed. But here we are concerned with the child.

It is very difficult, almost impossible, to create a convincing child character. Children in general lack the individuality of adults. Personality has not yet developed, and such personality as exists tends to be inhibited by imitativeness, which itself partly proceeds from lack of personality. But there is another reason for the impersonality of David which is bound up with the autobiographical form in fiction. Paradoxically, in the first person character is objectivised: in the third person, subjectivised. To make this clear. When a novelist employs the first person, the narrator tends to become artificial, due partly to the self-consciousness of the effort. He is not writing straightforward autobiography which concerns himself and his doings, but projecting an aspect of himself into the narration, creating a fictional self. At the same time, this self has to stand back from the narrative with sufficient detachment from other characters and events not to get in their way, and thus becomes rather disembodied. Conversely, fiction written in the usual third person often reveals far more of the author's character. Just because he is not consciously describing some aspect of himself, the unconscious elements of his character come into play. For example, Dickens would be inclined to idealise the ego that was expressed in David, and in doing so (particularly in the case of childhood, when he is describing himself at one remove) would guard against the self-revelation of undesirable traits; but when he was creating Swiveller or Quilp, he would be so engrossed in these objective characters that the Swiveller and Quilp-like elements in himself would be incorporated unconsciously. For all these reasons, the young David, though delightful, is not a very real or convincing figure.

—ROBERT HAMILTON, "Dickens's Favourite Child," *Dickensian* No. 291
(June 1, 1949), pp. 141–42

J. HILLIS MILLER

If *Dombey and Son* is Dickens' most mature treatment of the child-parent relationship, *David Copperfield* is the first of his novels to organize itself around the complexities of romantic love. For the first time marriage, in a more than conventional way, is seen as offering a solution to the problem of solitude and dispossession. And if earlier novels contained many varied examples of good or bad parents or children, *David Copperfield* repeats in several minor stories the theme of marriage (Annie and Dr. Strong; Traddles and Sophy; the bad marriage of Betsey Trotwood—which has made her, like Miss Havisham, already overshadowed when we meet her by a definitive event in her past).

But one must mention here, even if only digressively, one of the great triumphs of Dickens' genius: Mr. Micawber. Most of Dickens' comic eccentrics achieve only a hollow or superficial identity, and are either destroyed by their situations, move from them into the nothingness of pure façade, or, like Captain Cuttle, really cease to be comic grotesques, and become more or less serious characters. But Micawber escapes either alternative by carrying to its very limit the strategy of the assumed role. For once the comedian is supremely successful, or at least a magnificent failure. Such is "the latent power of Mr. Micawber" that he can always completely spiritualize his situation and thus escape it. Even when he is literally caught and imprisoned, he can spring out in a moment by a mere redefinition of what has happened: "You find me, fallen back, *for* a spring." This perpetual transcendence of spirit over concrete reality takes a special form: it is transcendence through language. If the manipulation of words is a fundamental expression of human freedom, Micawber must be said to tax this resource to the utmost. He throws forth a perpetual stream of metaphors, clichés, and hyperboles. He writes letters on every possible occasion, letters which, even if they assert his acceptance of his doom ("The fair land of promise lately looming on the horizon is again enveloped in impenetrable mists, and for ever withdrawn from the eyes of a drifting wretch whose Doom is sealed!"), effectually escape from reality by transcending it linguistically. "Mr. Micawber's enjoyment of his epistolary powers," as

David says, ". . . really seemed to outweigh any pain or anxiety that the reality could have caused him."

Perhaps, indeed, there is a secret identity between the linguistic enterprise of Micawber and that of Dickens himself, as it is transposed into the attempt by David Copperfield to tell all that he remembers about himself and about his experience. For *David Copperfield*, as everyone knows, is Dickens' most personal book. Its point of genesis is the autobiographical fragment (published in Forster's *Life*) which describes Dickens' early life and his painful experiences as a blacking factory drudge. But, more than this, the narrative of *David Copperfield* is the clearest account we have anywhere of the secret springs of Dickens' imagination, of the mixture in his creative impulse of "childish recollections and later fancies, the ghosts of half-formed hopes, the broken shadows of disappointments dimly seen and understood, the blending of experience and imagination." Here we can find directly asserted the link between the gift of creative imagination and the point of view of the alienated child: "When my thoughts go back now, to that slow agony of my youth, I wonder how much of the histories I invented for such people hangs like a mist of fancy over well-remembered facts! When I tread the old ground, I do not wonder that I seem to see and pity, going on before me, an innocent romantic boy, making his imaginative world out of such strange experiences and sordid things."

The "mists of fancy," then, are inseparable from "well-remembered facts," and we must define Dickens' creative genius as not so much a brilliantly distorted view of reality in the present as the continuing memory of the way he once saw things long ago—as a child. Here is a way to account for the omnipresence of the locution "as if" in Dickens' most brilliant metaphorical transformations. The "as if" admits the fictitious nature of a surrealist view of persons or things. It testifies to the copresence of Dickens' childish view and his mature, disillusioned view, and points to the persistence of the former as the source of what we think of as the distinctively Dickensian imagination. Like many another Victorian, Dickens continued to possess his creative power only by keeping what William Empson, speaking of nineteenth-century poetry generally, has called a "tap-root" to childhood. But here, strangely enough, it is a childhood of separation and distance from all people and things, rather than of a Wordsworthian unity with nature.

David Copperfield, at any rate, is before everything a novel of memory, a *Bildungsroman* recollecting from the point of view of a later time the slow formation of an identity through many experiences and sufferings. As David says: "this narrative is my written memory."

The novel is full of references to memory and to its operations, reminding us again and again that these are reminiscences drawn up from what David calls "the sea of my remembrance," and haloed with "a softened glory of the Past, which nothing could have thrown upon the present time."

There are first of all passages which assert the pictorial vividness of memory, the way certain remembered scenes start up bidden or unbidden from the past and are relived in imagination in all their concrete and sensuous immediacy:

Can I say of her face—altered as I have reason to remember it, perished as I know it is—that it is gone, when here it comes before me at this instant, as distinct as any face that I may choose to look on in the crowded street?

All this, I say, is yesterday's event. Events of later date have floated from me to the shore where all forgotten things will reappear, but this stands like a high rock in the ocean.

I do not recall it, but see it done; for it happens again before me.

But we also find the experience of a superimposition of past and present via the associative link of some specific sensation in the present. For David, as for Marcel in À la recherche du temps perdu, a smell or a sound in the present can be a *signe mémoratif* producing the miracle of affective memory:

There were two great aloes, in tubs, on the turf outside the windows; the broad hard leaves of which plant . . . have ever since, by association, been symbolical to me of silence and retirement.

The feeling with which I used to watch the tramps, as they came into the town on those wet evenings, at dusk, . . . came freshly back to me; fraught, as then, with the smell of damp earth, and wet leaves and briar, and the sensation of the very airs that blew upon me in my own toilsome journey.

The scent of a geranium leaf, at this day, strikes me with a half comical, half serious wonder as to what change has come over me in a moment; and then I see a straw hat and blue ribbons, and a quantity of curls, and a little black dog being held up, in two slender arms, against a bank of blossoms and bright leaves.

But this mode of memory is not, for David, a difficult or rare occurrence, as it is for Marcel. Memories come easily, touched off by the slightest voluntary or involuntary associative stimulus, and crowd into the mind of the autobiographer:

I don't know why one slight set of impressions should be more particularly associated with a place than another, though I believe this obtains with most people, in reference especially to the associations of their childhood. I never hear the name, or read the name, of Yarmouth, but I am reminded of a certain Sunday morning on the beach, the bells ringing for church, little Em'ly leaning on my shoulder, Ham lazily dropping stones into the water, and the sun, away at sea, just breaking through the heavy mist, and showing us the ships, like their own shadows.

I now approach a period of my life, which I can never lose the remembrance of, while I remember anything; and the recollection of which has often, without my invocation, come before me like a ghost, and haunted happier times.

The present for the grown-up David is no desiccated emptiness watered occasionally and fortuitiously by the sudden rains of memory. The multitudinous past, as in the case of Henry James, is in danger of swamping, engulfing, the present, and overrunning all its attempts to put the past or the present in coherent order: "There was that jumble in my thoughts and recollections, that I had lost the clear arrangement of time and distance. Thus, if I had gone out into the town, I should not have been surprised, I think, to encounter some one who I knew must be then in London. So to speak, there was in these respects a curious inattention in my mind. Yet it was busy, too, with all the remembrances the place naturally awakened; and they were particularly distinct and vivid. . . . Something within me, faintly answering to the storm without, tossed up the depths of my memory, and made a tumult in them." But this tendency to be, in certain states of excitement, thrown into tumultuous confusion by memory is countered by a distance one usually feels between David and even the most intensely relived of his memories. He separates himself from them, and holds them at arm's length, even while reliving them. There is no Proustian doctrine of the transcendence of time through a merger of past and present: "I have stood aside," says David, "to see the phantoms of those days go by me." The past is, for Dickens, definitively past, and lost in the ocean of things that once were, and are no longer: "Yet the bells . . . told me of the many, never old, who had lived and loved and died, while the reverberations of the bells . . . , motes upon the deep of Time, had lost themselves in air, as circles do in water."

But, though the past can never be fully recaptured, nevertheless all David's memories hang together to form a whole, the integrated continuum of his past life as it has led by stages up to his present condition. All David's memories are linked to one another. Any one point radiates backward and forward in a multitudinous web connecting it to past and future:

> I was so filled with the play, and with the past—for it was, in a manner, like a shining transparency, through which I saw my earlier life moving along. . . .

> . . . I had reason to remember it thereafter, when all the irremediable past was rendered plain.

> I now approach an event in my life, so indelible, so awful, so bound by an infinite variety of ties to all that has preceded it, in these pages, that, from the beginning of my narrative, I have seen it growing larger and larger as I advanced, like a great tower in a plain, and throwing its forecast shadow even on the incidents of my childish days.

We recognize eventually that this novel has a duration and a coherence denied to all the third-person narratives among Dickens' novels. The spiritual presence of the hero organizes all these recollected events, through the powerful operation of association, into a single unified pattern which forms his destiny. At first David, as a child, can only experience isolated fragments of sensation, without possessing any power to put these together to form a coherent whole: "I could observe, in little pieces, as it were; but as to making a net of a number of these pieces, and catching anybody in it, that was, as yet, beyond me." But in the end the protagonist can boast that he has fabricated his own destiny by living through these experiences, and holding them together with the magnetic field of his mind. Without his organizing presence the world might fall back into disconnected fragments.

However, there are also throughout the novel repeated references to a very different kind of unifying presence, a presence external to the hero, guiding his life, and casting into any moment of time foreshadowings, presentiments, of the future, and echoes of the past. This providential spirit has determined the cohesion of events and their inalterable necessity. The hero has not made his own life and given himself a developing identity through the psychological power of memory; his destiny and identity and those of other people have been made by a metaphysical power, the power of divine Providence:

> Is it possible, among the possibilities of hidden things, that in the sudden rashness of the child and her wild look so far off, there was any merciful attraction of her into danger, any tempting her towards him permitted on the part of her dead father, that her life might have a chance of ending that day.

> . . . from the greater part of the broad valley interposed, a mist was rising like a sea, which, mingling with the darkness, made it seem as if the gathering waters would encompass them. I have reason to remember this, and think of it with awe; for before I looked upon those two again, a stormy sea had risen to their feet.

> "Ay, Mas'r Davy. I doen't rightly know how 'tis, but from over yon there semed to me to come—the end of it like;". . . . The remembrance of this . . . haunted me at intervals, even until the inexorable end came at its appointed time.

Which of these interpretations is the correct one? Or is there some way they can be reconciled? To do so would be to allow David to have his cake and eat it, to be both self-determining and justified and determined from the outside. To see how the novel escapes from its dilemma will be to reach the very heart of its central dramatic action: the developing relationship between David and Agnes.

David has, during his childhood of neglect and misuse, been acutely aware of himself as a gap in being. He has seemed to himself to be "a blank space . . . , which everybody overlooked, and yet was in everybody's way," cast away among crea-tures with whom I had no community of nature," "a somebody too many." Even after his marriage to Dora he has felt, in a phrase which is repeated again and again in the novel, an "old unhappy loss or want of something never to be realised." After he is married to Dora, he wishes that his child-wife "had had more character and purpose, to sustain me, and improve me by; had been endowed with power to fill up the void which somewhere seemed to be about me." The center of David's life, then, is the search for some relationship to another person which will support his life, fill up the emptiness within him, and give him a substantial identity. And the turning point of his destiny is his recognition that it is Agnes who stands in that relation to him: ". . . without her I was not, and I never had been, what she thought me"; "What I am, you have made me, Agnes." After this recognition, he must "discipline" his "undisciplined heart" by renouncing any claim on Agnes, and, through that renunciation, become worthy of possessing her at last as his wife. David in the end has altogether escaped from his initial condition of emptiness and nonbeing, when his life was "a ruined blank and waste." He stands in an unmediated relation to that which is the source of his being and the guarantee of the solidity of his selfhood: "Clasped in my embrace, I held the source of every worthy aspiration I had ever had; the centre of myself, the circle of my life, my own, my wife; my love of whom was founded on a rock!" David's relation to Agnes is a late example of that transposition of religious language into the realm of romantic love which began with the poets of courtly love, and which finds its most elaborate Victorian expression in *Wuthering Heights*. David has that relation to Agnes which a devout Christian has to God, the creator of his selfhood, without whom he would be nothing.

But has David chosen these roles for Agnes and himself, or has he simply assented to them passively? If the former is the case, then David's existence is returned in a way to the same emptiness, since he has no power in himself to validate Agnes as his human goddess. And if the latter possibility is the case, then David is a mere puppet, manipulated by his destiny. Dickens contrives to have it both ways for David, and in having it both ways he achieves the only satisfactory solution to his problem. On the one hand, since David has been for so long ignorant of the place Agnes has in his life, and has finally discovered it for himself, he can say truthfully: "I . . . had worked out my own destiny." And, on the other hand, two striking passages assert covertly that Agnes has been all along secretly destined for him by a benign Providence:

> He seemed to swell and grow before my eyes; the room seemed full of the echoes of his voice; and the strange feeling (to which, perhaps, no one is quite a stranger) that all this had occurred before, at some indefinite time, and that I knew what he was going to say next, took possession of me.

> "If you had not assured us, my dear Copperfield, on the occasion of that agreeable afternoon we had the happiness of passing with you, that D. was your favourite letter," said Mr. Micawber, "I should unquestionably have supposed that A. had been so."

> We have all some experience of a feeling, that comes over us occasionally, of what we are saying and doing having been said and done before, in a remote time—of our having been surrounded, dim ages ago, by the same faces, objects, and circumstances—of our knowing perfectly what will be said next, as if we suddenly remembered it! I never had this mysterious impression more strongly in my life, than before he uttered those words.

Both of these passages describe experiences of *déjà vu*, the strange sensation of autohypnosis in which one feels oneself to be reënacting a scene which has occurred before, long ago in the past, or in another life. Both are connected with

Agnes. And both have a peculiar characteristic: in each case David not only feels that it has all happened before, but also that he knows what is about to happen. In other words, both experiences are oriented toward the future, and seem to indicate that the future is already mapped out and fated to happen in a certain way. Both experiences are covert premonitions of the place Agnes is to have in David's life. But at the time David cannot understand the divine hints, and is left to work out his own destiny. It is only long afterward, in the perspective of his total recollection of his life, that David can understand these moments and give them their true value. Only then can he see that it is not so much his own mind as the central presence of Agnes which organizes his memories and makes them a whole: "With the unerring instinct of her noble heart, she touched the chords of my memory so softly and harmoniously, that not one jarred within me; I could listen to the sorrowful, distant music, and desire to shrink from nothing it awoke. How could I, when, blended with it all, was her dear self, the better angel of my life?" David, then, has both made himself and escaped the guilt which always hovers, for Dickens, over the man who takes matters into his own hands.

Years later, *Great Expectations* was to be a radical revaluation of this solution of Dickens' central problem, but the next novel, *Bleak House*, reopens the issue in a different way by questioning the compatibility of the psychological and metaphysical ways of putting a fragmented world together and organizing it into a coherent whole. *Bleak House* represents in a way the watershed peak of Dickens' career. Here, in a novel in which, as Dickens said, he "purposely dwelt upon the romantic side of familiar things" (Preface to the first edition), he makes the first of his large-scale attempts to synthesize in a single complex whole the familiar and the romantic, the objective facts of all the life of his age, and his own dreamlike apprehension of those facts as they appeared when transposed within the interior regions of his imagination.

—J. HILLIS MILLER, *"David Copperfield," Charles Dickens: The World of His Novels* (Cambridge, MA: Harvard University Press, 1958), pp. 150–59

J. B. PRIESTLEY

David Copperfield belongs to no group of works, has no companions in his fiction, cannot be compared with any other of his novels: whether it is his masterpiece or not even one of his most important works, it stands by itself.

Before he had thought of *David Copperfield*, while he was wondering what to do next, after *Dombey and Son* was off his hands, his friend and adviser, Forster, suggested that the new novel might be a story told in the first person. It happened that Dickens had already written in secret some chapters of autobiography. It also happened that various events round about this time brought painful reminders of his early life. So *David Copperfield* was born. But it is far from being—as many novels have been—so much autobiography dressed up as fiction. There is in it an elaborate and often subtle transmutation. For instance, Dickens's father and mother are not present in the novel as whole characters; various aspects of them are divided among various characters. Again, David Copperfield's adventures in child-hood and youth are not Dickens's, but on the other hand both have the same psychological and emotional basis. David's first marriage, to the childish Dora, represents old daydreams, first remembered and then critically considered: it is what *might* have happened if young Dickens had had his way and had married Maria Beadnell. Throughout this novel there is a very complicated delicate relation between autobiography and fiction, what has been remembered and what has been invented.

It was the first favourite for so long probably because it has more charm than any other of Dickens's novels. As pieces of writing the early chapters are unques-tionably the best. This is the world of childhood as few novelists anywhere have been able to capture it. Dickens is a poet here. He is also an innovator in highly subjective narrative, and for this, even now, he has not been given sufficient credit. As far as the first third of the book is concerned, we are ready to join in the praise and applause of his contemporaries. This account of David's childhood is indeed a masterpiece. But the last third of the book, with David an adult, does not make us laugh (in spite of the glorious Micawbers) and cry and marvel, as it did earlier readers. We feel that the magic has gone, that there is a falling off even by the usual standards of good fiction. The action is forced and incredible. Once out of the nightmares and enchantments of childhood, David is rather a dull young man. It is not that these chapters are really bad Dickens, but they seem to us now a descent and a disappointment after those wonderful early passages. We cannot enjoy it all as much as his contemporary readers and he himself did.

—J. B. PRIESTLEY, *Charles Dickens: A Pictorial Biography* (New York: Viking Press, 1962), pp. 76–79

MAURICE BEEBE

If David seems to lack at least one quality of the typical artist-hero—egotism—it is perhaps because he has an excess of another—passivity. A more aggressive boy would hardly have taken as much abuse from Murdstone as David did before he finally struck back. Later, when David leaves the factory and makes his bid for freedom, it is again only because he has been driven to desperation. For a boy as passive as David, adversity so extreme that it forces him to act is a positive stimulus to his personal development.

The abilities that nature gives—to observe, imagine, and concentrate—are common to many children, David himself assures us, and are not sufficient to make an artist. The young David is almost inseparable from his surroundings, unaware of his individuality, until he becomes estranged by the alteration in his domestic situa-tion. When his mother remarries and has Murdstone's child, David becomes in-creasingly aware of his alienation. His desperate need for a "kind word at that season," a word not given, reminds us of Proust's Marcel overwhelmingly conscious of his aloneness on the night when his mother refused to give him the usual goodnight kiss. David, formerly a bright, responsive child, becomes increasingly "sullen, dull, and dogged. I was not made the less so by my sense of being daily more and more shut out and alienated from my mother. I believe I should have been stupefied but for one circumstance." The circumstance is the usual one in portraits of the artist—the retreat to the dream-world of books. David, like other artists from Anton Reiser to Proust's Marcel, discovers *The Arabian Nights* and other stories of romantic adventure. Through reading and imaginative reverie David is able to move from the real world of pain and loneliness into a private "great good place."

Once we recognize the temperament which nature gives to David, the estrangement which makes him aware of his individuality, and the retreat into imagination, his later development as an artist seems inevitable. From reading stories in the attic at home to telling stories to Steerforth and the other boys at school— "What ravages I committed on my favourite authors in the course of my interpretation of them"—is a likely progression, and it stems partly from David's need to establish himself as a person, to communicate—if not with others, then with himself. "I was alone in the world," he says of his first days in London, "and much given to record that circumstance in fragments of English versification." This verse writing precedes the loss of his aunt's money and helps us realize that his turning to reporting and writing is not entirely accidental. Without the adversity, though, David would presumably have remained an amateur poet. The loss of the money forces David to overcome his passivity and to find his own way in the world, armed with the temperament and the talent of the artist.

That we find in David the usual components of the artistic temperament and in his life a typical progression to an artistic vocation may help to persuade us that David is capable of becoming a successful author. It does not, however, assure us that *David Copperfield* is a superior portrait of the artist nor explain what makes Dickens' novel a more distinguished work of art than the other artist-novels of its time. We recognize the temperament and the development of David as typical of the contemporaneous view of the artist, because the same concepts of the artist are stated explicitly in books like *Contarini Fleming* and *Ernest Maltravers*. Dickens' distinction is that, unlike the other writers of the period, he does not impose a theory of the artist upon his hero, but lets the vocation emerge as the result of David's unique experience—does not, in fact, consciously write a portrait-of-the-artist novel until, writing his own life story in symbolic form, he discovers that his hero, like himself, has become an artist almost unawares.

—MAURICE BEEBE, "Art as Experience," *Ivory Towers and Sacred Founts:
The Artist as Hero in Fiction from Goethe to Joyce* (New York:
New York University Press, 1964), pp. 92–93

ANGUS WILSON

If critics were asked to name an English novel worthy to stand among the great fiction of all time—*War and Peace* and so on—*David Copperfield* was very likely to be their choice. This great reputation had been handed down from Victorian times. It still remains a highly esteemed and very popular novel, but I doubt if most critics now would rank it quite so highly either among world fiction or among Dickens's own works. Told in the first person, it is Dickens's great internal—what used to be called 'psychological'—novel, a Proustian novel of the shaping of life through the echoes and prophesies of memory. As such, it is beautifully told. We are always conscious of David looking back and asking himself when this happened or that happened, did I have any intuition of where it was leading me? And when he decides now and again that, yes, there were intimations, overtones that had led him to feel apprehensive, or restless, or sad, so beautifully is the book constructed that we forget altogether that it is an artefact, made up by Dickens, and we consider only the reliability of David Copperfield as a guide to the meaning of his own past life; and usually we are convinced, so balanced and careful and real is the sense of remembered things, that David is a valuable guide, that this is how it happened. In this sense *David Copperfield*, the least socially integrated of Dickens's novels, the most internal, is paradoxically the most 'real'. In part as with Proust's Marcel, this is because with D. C. (David Copperfield) we are so close to the reality of C. D. (Charles Dickens). But it is so even more because of Dickens's superb artistry in the management of the narratives, of the echoes and the overtones of memory. In this one respect *David Copperfield* seems to me quite the artistic equal of *A la recherche du temps perdu*.

The book is admirably constructed in another way, for this recall of the past is also David's lesson of life. From the shape of his past he learns that we cannot live in dreams, that, in the popular Victorian quotation from Longfellow, 'life is real, life is earnest'; he learns to strengthen his will; he finds achievement through discipline and duty; he learns, in short, 'true happiness'.

Above all, he learns that romantic love (the sort of love that had so cruelly hurt Dickens in the collapse of his hopes for Maria Beadnell), a love that distorts and falsifies our view of the loved one, can bring only unhappiness and regret. This is splendidly shown in David's own life, where we see that the little, spoilt child-wife, who was his mother, is absolutely repeated in his choice of a little, spoilt child-wife, Dora (modelled upon Maria Beadnell). But Dickens was not content with that; and one of the glories of the novel is the way in which the theme is repeated again and again in a series of different relationships: David's worship of his friend, Steerforth, already made trivial and false by the worship given him by *his* mother; old Dan Peggotty's worship and spoiling of his niece, Emily; Doctor Strong's blind worship of *his* child-wife, Annie; Aunt Betsy's romantic, ruined marriage; Mr. Wickfield's blind concern for his daughter, Agnes, which ruins not her but himself. So subtly are these told that they seem (often to modern critics disconcertingly) like a series of unconnected stories; yet after one has closed the book, the repetition of theme is what leaves a strong impact. All this, and the complete mastery of scene and character (the Micawbers, Heep, Steerforth, Rosa Dartle, the Murdstones, all for the price of one book!) and narrative certainly make *David Copperfield* a sort of masterpiece. And yet at the end of it, I think, there is a disagreeable sense that this most inner of Dickens's novels is the most shallow, the most smoothly running, the most complacent—indeed, in the pejorative use of that word, the most Victorian.

The reasons for this are in part social and in part something deeper. David learns the lessons of life, and through hard work and the acquirement of a steady will, he becomes a famous novelist: 'I had advanced in fame and fortune, my domestic joy was perfect,' is what he tells us of himself. 'Having some foundation for believing, by this time, that nature and accident had made me an author, I pursued my vocation with confidence. Without such assurance I should certainly have left it alone, and bestowed my energy on some other endeavour. I should have tried to find out what nature and accident had really made me, and to be that, and nothing else.' And again, 'the more praise I got, the more I tried to deserve.' There is nothing wrong with all this; Dickens did work hard at his craft to improve the great powers that nature had given him. There are many letters to aspiring writers over his whole career, stressing this point. For those who liked to dwell on the sober, hardworking, competent, efficient, commonsensical side of Dickens, which, as I said in an earlier chapter, is certainly a great part of him, *David Copperfield* will be a very sympathetic book. But although the demonic, driven side of Dickens may have been exaggerated, it *is* there and it constitutes a great deal of the unique side of his genius. There is nothing of it in David.

But, it may well be objected, David Copperfield is not Charles Dickens; to demand this is to impose our knowledge of biographical background on a work of fiction. Very well, but I think one still asks in a book which tells us of an author's genesis some indication greater than an assertion of natural capacity improved by hard work, and this without demanding of Dickens any aesthetic view of the purpose of life such as we get from Proust. David Copperfield as a writer (and it is to this that his story brings us) is too much like Trollope as he tells us he was in his autobiography. In the long run, by making art so much a matter of moral duty, Dickens diminishes it as he criticized Thackeray for doing, although in a different way.

But this sort of philistine, bourgeois, complacent view of his powers as a writer only reflects the social and ethical whole of the book. No novel of Dickens is so bounded by middle-class horizons. Once or twice in the novel—at the Water-brooks's dinner party, and when considering Mr. Spenlow's complacent view of the machinery of law—Dickens the social critic peeps out through David. But for the rest it seems as though David's battle to emerge from the pains and the illusions of his childhood and youth have left him exhausted, fit only for the comfortable domestic fireside with his good angel, Agnes, and the round of good works that she suggests his fame demands of him.

When David returns from his healing travels after the deaths of Dora and Steerforth, Agnes asks, 'Have you any intention of going away again?' 'What does my sister say to that?' 'I hope now . . . I think you ought not, since you ask me. Your growing reputation and success enlarge your power of doing good; and if *I* could spare my brother, perhaps the time could not.' Dickens in this philanthropic and Unitarian phase of his life may have thought that his literary genius was intended solely to make him powerful in 'doing good', but we cannot. And we know that an author who could see society and its evil so wholly as he had done in *Dombey and Son* will not find 'good work' enough as a solution. Indeed in the next chapter we shall see that he did not. *David Copperfield* on the social level is the epitome of Victorian bourgeois morality. But its insufficiency is deeper than purely social. David's life of good works must be seen in a Christian context, but it is exactly here that the novel, and with it Dickens's very sincere Christian beliefs, seem inadequate to give meaning to life. He has mocked at romantic love, at the distorting power of passion, and he makes his case; yet the complacent domestic fireside of Agnes seems an empty thing to put in its place. He has inveighed against the cruel Calvinist creed of the Murdstones and he more than makes his case; yet a Christianity of 'doing good' seems somehow as empty without grace as his wonderful social observation does when denied the total view of society which he had glimpsed in *Dombey and Son* and was to see whole in his next novel, *Bleak House*. This is perhaps why Dickens, in compensation, gives one of the finest portrayals in fiction of that secular semblance of grace, called charm, in the marvellously living character of Steerforth.

—ANGUS WILSON, *"David Copperfield," The World of Charles Dickens*
(London: Martin Secker & Warburg, 1970), pp. 213–16

A. H. GOMME

David Copperfield is in one respect a more centrally organised book than *Great Expectations*, in that it is written in the first person and tells (directly) only the narrator's experiences. At the same time, being told by the hero, it purports to register (directly) only the hero's opinions and attitudes. Yet we hardly need Dickens's self-confessed partiality for this novel, or his introduction of autobiographical elements within it, to confirm our sense that David is in league with his author. As a child, until he reaches Dover and finds sympathy and affluence at one go, he is always an object of pity simply because he is so ill-used, and so we are pretty well bound to be on his side. When he is grown up we know that he behaves foolishly, and his admission of this is amusingly told:

> I lived primarily on Dora and coffee. In my love-lorn condition, my appetite languished; and I was glad of it, for I felt as though it would have been an act of perfidy towards Dora to have a natural relish for my dinner.

But David remains essentially the morally reliable centre who feels and expresses the right opinions about Uriah Heep and Annie and Mr. Peggotty and the rest: even his too ready acceptance of Steerforth is insisted on as a good fault, the result of too much love. So in the event David inevitably becomes a prig; and his lack of moral growth means that he himself can be little more than a recorder of things that happen to him (or to others) without deeply affecting him.

The story is presented as if it were the subject of a memoir—David in narrating 'cannot always remember' details: the device is transparent, for we all know that the book is a novel, and the author can 'remember' anything he chooses to. But a genuine memoir almost always consists of a fairly loose string of experiences tied together by the accident of their happening to or coming within the ken of one person. Most human lives have no more than this accidental coherence. Likewise there is no guiding theme to *David Copperfield*, only a bundle of stories in which the narrator is haphazardly involved. Moreover David himself is not interesting enough to keep the reader keenly alert to the effects of his adventures on him: he happens to take a leading part in some of the stories, but his main function is to be the universal moral recorder. This is in any case a tricky part for a first-person narrator to keep up; but the identification of author and narrator leads to further strains. David is not by nature satirically or even ironically given; yet the book contains large-scale satirical portraits which have to be conveyed through him. This does not present any special difficulties in Mr. Micawber's case, for he largely describes himself through his speeches and letters; but with Uriah Heep we are up against something different. He is one of Dickens's most venomous creatures, and the author's dislike is patent. The portrait may well be, even as satire, overdrawn—that is not here at issue. What is to the point is that much of the reader's impression of him is gained not through what he does or says, but through David's description of his appearance and the impression he makes. His writhings are real enough, but it is impossible at times to avoid a feeling of special pleading against him, of Dickens with his knife in Uriah using the sensitive, fair-minded David to force the reader's attitude. It is made a point against him that not only does he pretend to a humility which in truth he does not own, but that he has a coarse accent and drops his aitches—which would be relevant if he also pretended to gentility, but he does not. That suggests snobbery in Dickens as well as in David, which becomes really vicious in the scene in which David is obsessed by Heep's physical repulsiveness.

—A. H. GOMME, *Dickens* (London: Evans Brothers, 1971), pp. 174–76

NORREN FERRIS

At first glance, it is difficult for the reader of *David Copperfield* to understand why Charles Dickens selects Wilkins Micawber as David's steadfast companion. As master of circumlocution, Micawber is a perverter of words. This characteristic makes him an unlikely comrade for the adult David, an author who uses words in order that he might "reflect [his] mind" on paper—that he might discover whether he really is "the hero of [his] own life."

For the person who attaches the importance to words that David does, it is vital that he be able to comprehend the power words have to both reflect *and* distort an image. If David's words are to reflect his mind accurately, he must fully comprehend this power. It is precisely for this reason that Dickens introduces the character of Wilkins Micawber to the young boy David. Micawber's circumlocutions can be compared to his house, which "was shabby like himself, but also, like himself, made all the show it could." If David can be trained to see this shabbiness, he will be better able to discern his own mind's reflections.

From Micawber's first appearance in the novel, his speech is characterized by a steady fusillade of nouns, verbs, adjectives, and adverbs strung together by a series of dashes and conjunctions. Reading these, the reader soon comes to expect the terse, direct statement preceeded by "in short" that follows Micawber's circumlocutions. It is the difference between what is said before and after the "in short" that David must be brought to understand.

Micawber's circumlocutory phrasing followed by the "in short" statement recurs again and again in the novel whenever Micawber is experiencing frustration. For example, the first encounter between David and Micawber occurs during one of the many instances of deep financial stress in the Micawber household. "In short" appears four times. Each time the characteristic phrase follows a torrent of descriptives referring to Micawber's house—a painful reminder of his present pecuniary state of affairs:

> "I am," said the stranger, "thank Heaven, quite well. I have received a letter from Mr Murdstone, in which he mentions that he would desire me to receive into an apartment in the rear of my house, which is at present unoccupied—and is, in short, to be let as a—in short," said the stranger, with a smile and in a burst of confidence, "as a bedroom—the young beginner whom I have now the pleasure to—" and the stranger waved his hand, and settled his chin in his shirt-collar.

> "My address," said Mr Micawber, "is Windsor Terrace, City Road. I—in short," said Mr Micawber, with the same genteel air, and in another burst of confidence—"I live there."

> "Under the impression," said Mr Micawber, "that your peregrinations in this metropolis have not as yet been extensive, and that you might have some difficulty in penetrating the arcana of the Modern Babylon in the direction of the City Road,—in short," said Mr Micawber, in another burst of confidence, "that you might lose yourself—I shall be happy to call this evening, and install you in the knowledge of the nearest way."

In each of these examples, the circumlocutions preceeding "in short" are used by Micawber to try to hide the fact that his financial affairs are not what he would have them to be. It is only in the more direct phrase following the "in short" that Micawber admits the actual financial conditions.

In *Bleak House*, Dickens reserves the "in short" exposure of meaningless verbalization for dramatizing the extent of legal circumlocutions. The *Bleak House* narrator's description of Mr. Snagsby's law stationer's office is one example: "In the shade of Cook's Court, at most times a shady place, Mr. Snagsby has dealt in all sorts of blank forms of legal process; in skins and rolls of parchment; in paper—foolscap, brief, draft, brown, white, whitey-brown, and blotting; in stamps; in office-quills, pens, ink, India-rubber, pounce, pins, pencils, sealing-wax, and wafers; in red tape and green ferret; in pocket books, almanacks, diaries, and law lists; in string boxes, rulers, inkstands—glass and leaden, penknives, scissors, bodkins, and other small office-cutlery; in short, in articles too numerous to mention; ever since he was out of his time, and went into partnership with Peffer."

For many years David is deceived by Micawber's circumlocutions. As a young boy he is well aware of Micawber's financial state, yet his most vivid recollection is that Micawber spoke "with a certain condescending roll in his voice, and a certain indescribable air of doing something genteel, which impressed me very much." Part of young David's failure to see past the wordy passages could be due to his young age. On the other hand, it could be a result of the father-figure the debtor represented for him. Recalling one scene with Micawber, David quotes the man's parting words to him: "If, in the progress of revolving years, I could persuade myself that my blighted destiny had been a warning to you, I should feel that I had not occupied another man's place in existence altogether in vain." Understandably, for David, "another man's place" is the place of David's deceased father.

As the son seeks to emulate the father, so David seeks to model himself after Micawber. He does so however, by implementing the Micawber speech pattern when dealing with frustration. On four occasions, three directly and one indirectly, David reverts to the use of "in short," Micawber's identifying verbal trait, and each of these instances is important in that it represents a time of frustration in the narrator's life.

In contrast to the financially unfortunate Micawber, David's frustrations are centered in his human loves, Agnes and Dora. His first attempt at the circumlocutional method of problem-solving occurs the morning after Agnes has beheld a drunk Trot at the theater. Humiliated, David recalls his feeling when he later goes to visit Agnes: "She looked so quiet and good and reminded me so strongly of my airy fresh school days at Canterbury, and the sodden, smoky, stupid wretch I had been the other night, that, nobody being by, I yielded to my self-reproach and shame, and—in short, made a fool of myself." The attempt to rationalize his actions (or diminish their humiliating backlash) through the lengthy scourging he administers to himself, does not erase the "in short" of the matter. It still stands that David had made a fool of himself the night before.

During his struggle to master the hieroglyphics of shorthand, David again tries to hide the failures he repeatedly encountered through the process, in some Micawber-like circumlocutions:

> When I had groped my way, blindly, through these difficulties, and had mastered the alphabet, which was an Egyptian Temple in itself, there then appeared a procession of new horrors, called arbitrary characters; the most despotic characters I have ever known; who insisted, for instance, that a thing like the beginning of a cobweb, meant expectation, and that a pen-and-ink skyrocket stood for disadvantageous. When I had fixed these wretches in my mind, I found that they had driven everything else out of it; then, beginning

again, I forgot them; while I was picking them up, I dropped the other fragments of the system; in short, it was almost heart-breaking.

This passage might also be interpreted as a miniature picture of David's large-scale
attempt to put the pieces of his entire life together. Early in the novel, the narrator
reflects that, as a child, "I could observe, in little pieces, as it were; but as to making
a net of a number of these pieces, and catching anybody in it, that was, as yet,
beyond me." Assuming that David is still working on the net, the "in short" in this
passage deals with an even greater frustration than the surface battle against shorthand. On neither level, however, does the long-winded reiteration of the problem
reduce, in any way, the problem's existence. The fact remains for David that the
experience is an agonizing one—almost heartbreaking.

David resorts to circumlocution a third time while composing a bulky letter to
Julia Mills. In reflecting on the letter, he recalls that "I signed myself, hers distractedly;
and I couldn't help feeling, while I read this composition over, before sending it by
a porter, that it was something in the style of Mr Micawber." While we do not have
the exact content of the letter available for our perusal, David's realization that the
epistle reflects something of Micawber suggests that perhaps the familiar "in short"
(and preceeding verbiage) were included in the body of the letter. That David
makes such a note to himself at this point in his narrative further indicates his
awareness of whose footsteps he has followed.

Finally, a beaten David resorts to "in short" after he has reduced Dora to tears
when arguing with her about the way they manage their affairs:

> Dora would not allow me, for a long time, to remove the handkerchief.
> She sat sobbing and murmuring behind it, that, if I was uneasy, why had I ever
> been married? Why hadn't I said, even the day before we went to church, that
> I knew I should be uneasy, and I would rather not? . . . in short, Dora was so
> afflicted, and so afflicted me by being in that condition, that I felt it was of no
> use repeating this kind of effort, though never so mildly, and I must take some
> other course.

The questions, Dora raises in the preceeding circumlocutions are of no real importance here, as David has begun to realize. Instead, the reality—the "in short"—
of the situation is that, regardless of what the answers to those questions are, David
is still being forced to abandon his present course, that of disciplining his wife in the
techniques of bookkeeping.

The lesson *David Copperfield* teaches about coping with life's frustrations by
means of words does not end with the folly of large volumes of symbols and
syllables disguising the reality of the "in short." The climax occurs when Micawber
strips away the circumlocution and, before an astonished David, vehemently attacks
Uriah Heep. Whether or not Micawber actually learns from past experience that
his liberal sprinkling (or, perhaps flooding) of words does not expunge reality is left
open to debate. When Micawber denounces Heep in this dramatic scene, he does
so—and does so effectively—without the need of an "in short" to expose the

circumlocution for what it is. The only time the phrase is found in the discourse, occurs at the onset of the verbal lashing but is quickly cut off—almost swallowed, in a gulp—by Micawber, as if he recognizes that without the circumlocution, there is no need for an "in short":

"What are you waiting for?" said Uriah. "Micawber! did you hear me tell you not to wait?"

"Yes!" replied the immovable Mr Micawber.

"Then why *do* you wait?" said Uriah.

"Because I—in short, choose," replied Mr Micawber, with a burst.

But Micawber's exuberant flow of words does not appear curtailed in the remaining pages of the novel. David records his aunt's perplexity with Micawber's extreme wordiness as she exclaims, "Letters!...I believe he dreams in letters!"

An older, more knowledgeable David, however, is no longer deceived by the circumlocutional pattern of speech. It is the "in short" that is the true reflection of a situation—not the excessive verbiage that serves, instead, to distort. After all, admits David, "the meaning or necessity of our words is a secondary consideration, if there be but a great parade of them."

—NORREN FERRIS, "Circumlocution in *David Copperfield*," *Dickens Studies Newsletter* 9, No. 2 (June 1978): 43–46

DONALD HAWES

'Generally, Mr. Dickens, as if in revenge for his own queer name, does bestow still queerer ones upon his fictitious creations.' That comment, made in January 1849 by an anonymous reviewer of *The Haunted Man* in *Macphail's Edinburgh Ecclesiastical Journal*, is typical of many made at that time and afterwards. There was nothing new, of course, in grotesque or grotesquely meaningful naming, a practice perhaps as old as fiction itself. In the eighteen-thirties and eighteen-forties, nomenclature used by Carlyle, for one, included Teufelsdröckh, Plugson of Undershot, Sir Jabesh Windbag, and Pandarus Dogdraught. After Dickens's death, Hardy widely used freakish names, sometimes—but not invariably—for suggestions of characterisation or symbolism: Aeneas Manston, Bathsheba Everdene, Eustacia Vye, Damon Wildeve. But for sheer quantity and exuberance of invention, Dickens's fictional names stand apart, although, as G. L. Brook has reminded us, 'the names of major Dickensian characters are now so familiar that we tend to forget how unusual some of the best-known names are.' The fascination names held for him is revealed in personal and literary ways; three well-known pieces of evidence for this are his fondness for nicknames in real life as well as in fiction, the Christian names he gave his sons, and the Privy Council Education lists of names in his Memoranda for possible future use.

Turning from the general to the particular, I want to examine the name, and names, of David Copperfield. It is a commonplace in Dickensian criticism that David Copperfield, while he may not be a completely neutral personage, is nevertheless not a complete and colourful character who immediately springs to life. As J. Hillis Miller has observed, 'the center of David's life, then, is the search for some relationship to another person who will support his life, fill up the emptiness within him, and give him a substantial identity.' Another commentator, Trevor Blount, goes somewhat further in remarking that 'as the novel proceeds David's character is pieced together from the fragments of him realized in the people he meets.' Assuming that Dickens had some such conception in mind when he embarked on the novel, we can infer that his problem was to find for his hero a name which was not indicative of one particular 'humour' (as 'Murdstone' is), which was not noticeably eccentric or comic (as 'Micawber' or 'Peggotty' is), but which satisfied the novelist's own predilection for something striking. Dickens would not have been content with using a name like 'Tom Jones', however ordinary or neutral his hero was intended to be.

As often, he worked hard at getting the name he thought most appropriate. Forster tells us:

> In this particular instance he had been undergoing doubts and misgivings to more than the usual degree. It was not until the 23rd of February [1849] he got to anything like the shape of a feasible title. 'I should like to know how the enclosed (one of those I have been thinking of) strikes you, on a first acquaintance with it. It is odd, I think, and new; but it may have A's difficulty of being "too comic, my boy." I suppose I should have to add, though, by way of motto, "And in short it led to the very Mag's Diversions. *Old Saying.*" Or would it be better, there being equal authority for either, "And in short they all played Mag's Diversions. *Old Saying?*"
>
> "Mag's Diversions.
Being the personal history of
Mr. Thomas Mag the Younger,
Of Blunderstone House."
>
> This was hardly satisfactory, I thought; and it soon became apparent that he thought so too, although within the next three days I had it in three other forms. "*Mag's Diversions,* being the Personal History, Adventures, Experience, and Observation of Mr. David Mag the Younger, of Blunderstone House." The second omitted Adventures, and called his hero Mr. David Mag the Younger, of Copperfield House. The third made nearer approach to what the destinies were leading him to, and transformed Mr. David Mag into Mr. David Copperfield the Younger and his great-aunt Margaret; retaining still as his leading title, *Mag's Diversions.*

Dickens refers in his letter to an 'old saying'. The *Oxford English Dictionary* informs us that 'Mag', a 'playful shortening of 'Margaret', was used as a personal name in various proverbial phrases, such as 'Mag's (or Meg's) delight or diversions', which signified 'the deuce and all' or 'the very mischief.' 'Mag's tales' meant 'nonsense or trifling.' Dickens seems to have liked the sound of 'mag', as he uses it, or a variant of it, as a component in other names. Apart from Magwitch, there are Magg (in 'Our Vestry'), Maggy (in *Little Dorrit*), Peter Magnus (in *Pickwick Papers*), Magsman (the narrator of 'Going into Society'), Mrs Miggot (*Uncommercial Traveller*, 14), Miss Miggs (in *Barnaby Rudge*), Mogley (in *Nicholas Nickleby*), Mugby Junction (in the Christmas story of that name), Muggleton (in *Pickwick Papers*), and Sir Alfred Muggs (in 'Sentiment'). But Forster was right in thinking 'Mag' unsatisfactory, because it suggests jocularity or mischief, just as 'Nickleby' and 'Chuzzlewit' may be considered unsuitable surnames for Nicholas and Martin, who are plain and neutral figures.

In addition to the evidence supplied by Forster, there are the lists made by Dickens on a manuscript sheet of possible beginnings, endings, and complete names: Stone, bury, Flower, Brook, Well, Boy, Field; Wellbury, Flowerbury, Magbury, Copperfield, Copperfield; Trotfield, Trotbury, Spankle, David, Copperboy, Topflower, Copperstone; Charles Copperfield. The first list consists of words that could be complete names or components of names; it will be observed that they denote natural features, creatures, objects, or places. Perhaps there is in these a conscious or unconscious Wordsworthian element; perhaps they are meant to suggest a typical, traditional Englishness, vaguely associated with the countryside; or perhaps Dickens chose them simply because they exist, singly or in combination, in many common English surnames. The second list makes use of many of these words, and the final repetition of 'Copperfield' shows Dickens's satisfaction with his coinage. The third list is more facetious, and except for 'David' seems obviously unsuited for Dickens's purpose, although he made use of 'trot', 'field', 'Copper', and 'stone' for characters' names in the novel.

'Coinage' may be the correct term for 'Copperfield', since the manuscript lists suggest that Dickens developed the name himself. It is, in fact, an actual surname, although a fairly rare one; there are only four examples in the 1975 London telephone directory, and it is not listed in the dictionaries of surnames I have consulted. Perhaps 'copper' suggested itself to Dickens because he had previously considered 'mag', a word used in the nineteenth century for a halfpenny, a copper coin; Dickens was familiar with the word, which occurs in *Bleak House*, Ch. 23. It is noteworthy that 'copper' is a metal which is 'malleable, ductile, and very tenacious' (*OED*) and which is used for ordinary, inexpensive coins and medals. Although it is not so precious and valuable as gold and silver, it is worthy and practical. If Dickens had called his hero 'Goldfield' or 'Silverfield', he would have conjured up images of wealth, ostentation, and flashiness; by using 'copper' instead of 'gold' or 'silver', he suggests a fitting plainness and honesty. 'Field', the second component of the name, is frequently found as the last syllable of an English surname—Duffield, Greenfield, Hurstfield—and so gives an air of normality to his hero. Besides the literal meaning of 'field', there is its signifying 'an area or sphere of action, operation, or investigation; a wider (or narrower) range of opportunities, or of objects, for labour, study, or contemplation; a department of study or speculation' (*OED*). The complete name, 'Copperfield', can therefore suggest not only the hero's essential but not extraordinary worthiness, durability, and malleability, but also the area and scope relating to the exercise and development of those personal qualities; there are, in addition, suggestions of familiar Englishness and perhaps (as previously suggested) of characteristics that can loosely be called natural and Wordsworthian. We should note, too, that David Copper*field* is finally united to Agnes Wick*field*, as Sylvère Monod points out. Each name symbolically echoes the other, and the long-expected marriage between David and Agnes is perfected as a complete harmony.

The significance of Dickens's temporarily considering 'Charles' as a Christian name for his hero needs no comment. As it was, he chose 'David', which was a rather more unusual choice than may appear today. For 'David' was not a popular name in England in 1850. In 1863, Charlotte Yonge observed that it 'has continued a distinctively Scottish name,' and it was also, of course, widely used in Wales. Eminent nineteenth-century men named David were usually Scottish: Livingstone, Wilkie, Masson. The name rarely appears in fiction of the time, although Sarah Fielding's hero, David Simple, had appeared in 1744. Scott, not surprisingly, occasionally used 'David' or 'Davie' (for example, for Jeanie and Effie Deans' father), but no major character in the works of Thackeray, Trollope, George Eliot, George Meredith, the Brontës, or Mrs Gaskell bears the name. Dickens had used it in novels before *David Copperfield*, but exclusively for minor or lower-class characters: the Cheerybles' butler, a grave-digger in the *Old Curiosity Shop*, Ch. 54, and David Crimple, Montague Tigg's associate in his bogus Assurance Company. Dickens's source for 'David' is likely to have been the Bible rather than Scotland: R. F. Pechey, a contributor to the *Dickensian*, goes so far as to say indeed that 'for all, or nearly all of his principal characters, in most of his books, he extracted his "Christian names" from the Bible.' 'David' is Hebrew in origin, from a lullaby word meaning 'darling' first, and then 'friend' generally. Its Biblical associations make it notably appropriate for the hero of Dickens's novel. The Old Testament David was 'a man after [God's] own heart just as *David Copperfield*, the novel (and its hero above all, one assumes), was its author's 'favourite child.' For both heroes, courage and skill, amongst other praiseworthy qualities, outweigh defects of character. Two further parallels suggest themselves, but these may be over-fanciful. First, each David has a Uriah as a rival for the woman he desires, although this comparison cannot be extended into particulars: the Biblical Uriah's grim fate is far distant from David Copperfield's slapping Heep's face and from Micawber's exposure of his fraudulent activities—and Uriah's final appearance in prison is a comic episode. Secondly, each David in his youth is devoted to a male friend, although here again the details of the relationship are not comparable. Apart from these specific suggestions, which admittedly can be thought to be far-fetched, the name 'David' was likely to convey impressions of fallibility as well as strength—impressions, that is, of a hero with certain flaws—to nineteenth-century readers with their ready and knowledgeable acquaintance with the Bible.

'David Copperfield', then, clearly illustrates Harry Stone's statement that 'Dickens thought long about his characters' names, and frequently modified a name until it carried just the connotations he desired. And the principal connotations were neatly summed up by Frank A. Gibson: 'there is pure metal, if not pure gold, as well as nature and history in the name.' In addition to having fairly numerous and enlightening connotations, it fulfilled Dickens's requirements, and doubtless his readers' expectations as well, by having a distinctive but not wildly idiosyncratic form. Forster must have been the first to observe the fact that the initials of the hero's name reversed those of the author. 'He was much startled when I pointed this out,' Forster writes, 'and protested it was just in keeping with the fates and chances which were always befalling him. "Why else," he said, "should I so obstinately have kept to that name when once it turned up?" '

Sylvère Monod has pointed out the 'interesting innovation' that 'is introduced into the designation of the characters in *David Copperfield*. It is the frequent use of different names or different forms of one name, applied to the same character by various members of his or her own circle, a device which emphasises the differences in the nature of the relationships involved.' Betsey Trotwood's comments and renamings are striking instances of this practice; in her usage, Trotwood, 'Murderer', 'Barkis', 'our military friend' (suggested by the schoolboys' nickname, the Old Soldier), and 'Little Blossom' replace respectively David, Murdstone, Peggotty, Mrs Markleham, and Dora. Monod further observes that almost every character in the novel has his or her own way of addressing David. This point is made again by A. E. Dyson, who discusses its implications more fully than Monod. I think that it is worth yet another examination, since such an analysis takes us into the heart of the novel.

First of all, it is necessary to discriminate between what is significant and what is not, between modes of address that are conventional and those that have a meaning peculiar to David's character and circumstances. For instance, the use of the surname by itself in addressing a male was common in schools and also amongst adult men (and some women) of all classes; indeed, this usage still exists in England, particularly in some public schools, although outside school life it has been dying out rapidly since the end of the last war. Traddles and Mr Micawber are simply following convention when they call their friend 'Copperfield', although admittedly the trisyllabic name suits Mr Micawber's grandiloquence and perhaps also helps him to feel that he is David's social equal. Similarly, Mrs Micawber's 'Master Copperfield', which she changes in later years to 'Mr Copperfield,' is the way one would expect her to address him. Dyson thinks that she calls David 'Master Copperfield' 'affectionately, though vaguely, since she has only a misty idea who he is.' She may be affectionate but vague, but this is surely not shown by her use of these names. It is difficult to see what else she could call him. In 1850, any woman in her social position who was an acquaintance and not a relative or close friend would naturally call him 'Master Copperfield' or 'Mr Copperfield', as 'David' would have been considered too informal. I would also say that Mr Murdstone's 'David' has little significance. He is almost alone in calling the hero by this name, and Dyson thinks that this is 'a sinister use, measured and cruel, and intended to degrade him like a dog.' Of course, Murdstone thinks it necessary to humiliate David, as he warns him, but I cannot agree that the use of his full Christian name shows this. It is not a name associated with a dog or any other animal. It simply shows, I think, that Mr Murd-stone wants to emphasise to David and his mother that David is a boy and not a baby, and that he is not to be treated any longer as a mother's darling. In any case, what other name could Mr Murdstone employ? A man of his 'firmness', even if he were kindly disposed to the boy, would normally use the unabbreviated Christian name instead of 'Davy.' But 'Master Davy' or 'Mas'r Davy', frequently used by members of the Peggotty family, nicely combines affection with a proper respect— a respect that has no suggestion of servility or snobbishness but that again is conventional, in that it is a recognition by the coarser and less well-educated members of society of a superiority in culture and refinement. So far, then, we observe that Dickens is mostly following accepted practice in making his personages address David in a certain way, although suggestions of characterisation and attitude may also be present, such as Mr Micawber's orotundity of speech and the Peg-gottys' fondness for David.

A more obviously telling use of normal modes of address is Uriah's frequent apologetic correction of 'Master' to 'Mister'. This cunning belittling is one clear indication, out of many, of David's own uncertainty about his maturity and social status. Several of the ways in which he is addressed show various kinds and degrees of this lack of assurance. When Miss Murdstone first meets him, she greets him as 'boy' (ch.4); at the Yarmouth inn, where he breaks his journey to Salem House, his dinner is paid for, disconcertingly, in the name of 'Master Murdstone' (ch. 5); even to Mr Mell, he is at first just 'the new boy' (ch. 5); the pasteboard placard he is forced to wear at the school implies that he is a dog (ch. 5); Creakle seems not to know his name, but calls him 'boy' or 'sir' (ch. 6); Quinion, remembering Murd-stone's joking allusion, insists that David is 'Brooks of Sheffield' (ch. 10); to the boys and men in Murdstone and Grinby's warehouse, he is 'the little gent' or 'the young Suffolker', although two of them sometimes call him 'David' (ch. 11); the 'long-legged man' with the donkey-cart addresses him as 'Sixpenn'orth of bad ha'pence (ch. 12); David's name, so Mrs Steerforth informs him, 'has not lived in [her] memory' (ch. 20); Mrs Crupp always calls him 'Mr Copperfull' (ch. 26); Littimer, who deferentially uses 'sir' to his face, called him 'Young Innocence' behind his back, according to Miss Mowcher (ch. 32).

Steerforth's nicknaming him 'Daisy' is meant, as Rosa Dartle realises, to show that he thinks David is 'young and innocent' (ch. 20), but these are qualities that he envies as well as mocks. Betsey Trotwood's renaming him 'Trotwood Copperfield' is partly to signify her identifying him with the girl who should have been born, partly to demonstrate her desire that he should be unlike his father (whose Chris-tian name was also David), and partly to emphasise the fact that he is to 'make another beginning' (as the heading to ch. 15 makes clear)—she renames him only after her defeat of the Murdstones and the consequent rejection of most of his previous existence. The new name is marked in his new clothes with 'indelible marking-ink' (ch. 14). Agnes' use of the new name is one of the factors that sharply differentiate her from Dora, who nicknames him 'Doady.' 'Trotwood', originally meant by Dickens to denote Aunt Betsey's briskness of mind and body, is closely applicable to David in that phase of his life when he feels impelled to make as much effort and progress as possible, urged on by his aunt and Agnes, both of whom habitually address him as 'Trot' or 'Trotwood.' 'What I had to do,' says David, 'was, to take my woodman's axe in my hand, and clear my own way through the forest of difficulty, by cutting down the trees until I came to Dora. And I went on at a mighty rate, as if it could be done by walking' (ch. 36). Dare one say that he would trot through the wood? Dora's 'Doady', which was 'a corruption of David' (ch. 41), seems also to be a pun on 'dote' (or 'doat', to use another spelling possible in the nineteenth century): 'What could I do,' exclaims David after a difference of opinion with Dora, 'but kiss away her tears, and tell her how I doted on her, after that!' (ch. 41). It also reflects, in a way, her own foolishness, with its suggestion of 'Dodo' (Celia's pet name for her sister, Dorothea, in *Middlemarch*).

Leaving aside those modes of address that were relatively or completely commonplace, we can observe and appreciate, therefore, how closely Dickens brings us by means of his hero's various names to the vital purpose of the novel, as formulated in the comments I have quoted from J. Hillis Miller and Trevor Blount. They immediately clarify David's 'search for some relationship' and consequently 'a substantial identity', and they illuminate the process of piecing together his character 'from the fragments of him realised in the people he meets.' Interpretation of the different names and styles can be an interpretation of the stages in the development of his character, his social status, his emotions (particularly anxiety and love), and his personal relationships.

—DONALD HAWES, "David Copperfield's Names," *Dickensian* No. 385 (May 1978): 81–87

ROSEMARIE BODENHEIMER

David Copperfield, a story describing the growth out of innocence through loss, might seem to be the Dickens novel most nearly pastoral in tone and subject; and its stress on the recollection of childhood invites comparisons with Wordsworth's *Prelude*, published in the same year. As Dickens' first first-person narrative, it also raises the possibility that description might resonate as self-description: that landscape might work as an image of character. The occasional descriptions of natural scenes do indeed figure David's state of mind, rather than blot it into generality, and their images are gracefully and imaginatively generated from the condition of feeling itself. Yet these descriptions are surprisingly rare, and interestingly dependent on conventional literary images of landscape.

The myth of pastoral innocence is briefly invoked in the chapter entitled "I Observe," where the first-person retrospective narrative transforms Eden into a psychological condition:

> And now I see the outside of our house, with the latticed bedroom windows standing open to let in the sweet-smelling air, and the ragged old rooks'-nests still dangling in the elm-trees at the bottom of the front garden. Now I am in the garden at the back, beyond the yard where the empty

pigeon-house and dog-kennel are—a very preserve of butterflies, as I re-member it, with a high fence, and a gate and padlock; where the fruit clusters on the trees, riper and richer than fruit has even been since, in any other garden, and where my mother gathers some in a basket, while I stand by, bolting furtive gooseberries, and trying to look unmoved. A great wind rises, and the summer is gone in a moment.

This lost paradise, where the fruit is "riper and richer than fruit has ever been since, in any other garden," draws its charm from the way Dickens gives light mythological pressure to domestic detail. Psychologically placed as an image of nostalgia for childhood and possession of the mother, the Eden myth rings with a mixture of loss and gentle comedy. Eve-like, Clara Copperfield gathers fruit, while David's furtive "bolting" plays on the guilt and pretense of the fallen world. David knows that this Eden is only "a preserve of butterflies"; all the more substantial animals have left already. And the "great wind" prefigures the upheaval and loss which are to shape the storm and the crisis of the novel.

In the double consciousness created by the narrator, "Eden" is linked with the remembering mind; it is the metaphor which shapes the feeling of nostalgia. The writing moves in the direction of giving a simultaneous description of mind and place, as it does again, in another way, during the storm scene it anticipates. In the chapter entitled "Tempest," David tells the story of the shipwreck and the death of Steerforth, but pauses for a paragraph to describe the sea: it "confounded me . . . it seemed to scoop out deep caves in the beach, as if its purpose were to under-mine the earth." He goes on to talk about the waves as though they were earth landscapes gone mad: "Undulating hills were changed to valleys, undulating valleys . . . were lifted up to hills . . . the ideal shore on the horizon, with its towers and buildings rose and fell . . . "; finally, "I seemed to see a rending and upheaving of all nature." The disturbance takes the metaphorical form of reliable land structures rearranged and rendered dizzily unstable, creating a correlative for the inner dis-ordering of David's structures of feeling about Dora and Steerforth—a state that is not expressed in any other way than in the frantic actions necessary at this crisis of plot. The act of description is thus partly a self-description, though less a creation of "character" than of a generalized psychic upheaval, an apocalyptic change.

Near the end of the novel, a mountain landscape serves to record David's response to Dora's death. Wandering in the frozen heights of the Alps, David encounters "awful solitudes," which directly echo Wordsworth's account of his Alpine crossing in the (then recently published) *Prelude*. This reference is followed up by a sequence of description which may be an attempt to imitate the form of Wordsworth's experience: an emotion is missed at the heights, but another is unexpectedly granted further down the path: "If those awful solitudes had spoken to my heart, I did not know it," David says; apparently he is so distraught that he is immune to the sublime. Once down in the valley, however, he describes a picture-postcard landscape, with an enclosed and protected valley, shepherd voices, a tumbling stream, lonely cottages, and a "bright evening cloud." With some success, the movement of the narrative eye down the valley makes the description suggest an inner movement of reintegration and release: the frozen heights give way to a picturesque thaw. David's psychic geography, overturned and jumbled by the losses of the storm, seems to rebuild itself in the vision of a stable landscape.

Yet this sort of reading gives way before the tone; the real pressure of the passage falls on the sentimental connection with Dora's death. Having received hardly a narrative comment, that event has quickly faded into its stereotype, the untimely death of a young girl. As this paragraph proceeds, the organ music for the dead returns: nature is supernaturalized, the clouds are heavenly, and the shepherd voices seem "not earthly music." Then, "All at once, in this serenity, great Nature spoke to me; and soothed me to lay down my weary head upon the grass, and weep as I had not wept yet, since Dora died!"

Few readers could be much convinced by Nature's voice; the voice of Agnes in the letter which David carries in his pocket, for use at this juncture, carries a good deal more force in his regeneration. The point is that Wordsworth and nature are called upon to do the work of memorializing Dora's death before the narrative proceeds on to Agnes; that they stand in for the complexity of feeling, the mixture of grief and relief, which the all-too-convenient death should actually elicit. Here emotional truth rather than truth to class is at stake; but the conjuring of nature-poetry, while sophisticated in one way, also provides a decoy, shifting attention from a particular history of emotional experience to a generalized pattern of intense feeling.

Despite their inward references, the descriptions in *David Copperfield* do not endow their narrator-hero with a very particular character. The lost garden, the tempest, and the Alpine landscape are well-established literary emblems, and un-clearly related to one another; they provide images for nostalgia, tumult, and reintegrated feeling which allow us to sympathize with the generalized experience of loss. These descriptions, increasingly subtle in detail, do stand for psychological conditions. Yet David's history remains a conventional account of growth, a senti-mental pilgrim's progress which does not depend in any essential way on the distortions and corrections of his personal vision. It was not until he wrote *Great Expectations* that Dickens created a fully resonant conjunction of landscape and point of view.

—ROSEMARIE BODENHEIMER, "Dickens and the Art of Pastoral,"
Centennial Review 23, No. 4 (Fall 1979): 485–61

NEIL GRILL

To the outcast and to the orphan there is but one search along many roads and that is for a shelter, a refuge, in a word, for a home. In the world of Charles Dickens's *David Copperfield*, it is enough that the wind abates, the stomach is not empty and the light glows in the window. It is enough in a world with too few parents and that number diminishing as the night comes on—it is enough simply not to be homeless.

In one sense *David Copperfield* may be seen as a book of coverings (and uncoverings), coverings of well-beloved graves, the caul or covering on his body at birth, coverings of motives as with Steerforth or of David himself in his first marriage, coverings of David's skin on his dream flight to freedom and Aunt Betsey, and most importantly, the coverings or roofs of the many houses in the book.

If autobiography differs from history in the former's insistence on repeating emotionally charged symbols or images, David's writing is, indeed, autobiographical in its repetition of "house" imagery. All autobiography and all writing is selective, and what David cannot stop himself from selecting out of a world of infinite choice are houses and the traces of family living in them, crippled, overpowered, widowed, orphaned, sacrificed, and deserted. It is part of the fabric of David's mind and memory, pervading his descriptions and even the dialogues that he reports to the reader. Thus, early in the book's first chapter, Miss Betsey Trotwood asks David's mother what has become of the rooks near the house, and she replies, "It was quite a large rookery; but the nests were very old ones, and the birds have deserted them a long while." The theme of the deserted house is repeated again in the next chapter when David sees "our house" out of the past containing a backyard with a "pigeon-house on a pole ... without any pigeons in it; a great dog-kennel in a corner, without any dog." The dog kennel is memorably filled at the end of chapter 3 with the frightening creature who resembles the newly married Mr. Murdstone, and the pigeon-house on a pole appears, virtually unchanged, in *Great Expectations* when Pip first enters Satis House, a deserted place down to the pigeon-house in the brewery yard where there were "no pigeons in the dove-cot, no horses in the stable, no pigs in the sty." David also alludes to creatures who are not in their proper homes when, while walking on the beach with Emily, he sees, as reflections of them both, "stranded star-fish," which he places "carefully back into the water."

In *David Copperfield,* houses and rooms take on an almost human vividness as they mirror David's perception of the differing emotional textures each house reveals. Thus, his description of Murdstone and Grinby's warehouse as a rat's dwelling prepares us for his evocation of a child's life as a "little labouring hind." David describes it as the last house at the bottom of a narrow street, a crazy old house "literally overrun with rats." He concludes by saying that the dirt and rottenness, the squeaking and scuffling of the rats are things, "not of many years ago, in my mind, but of the present instant."

This terrifying house near water (another central symbol in the novel) is clearly contrasted with another house on the sea, that of Mr. Peggotty and his adopted family, who all appear at one familial remove from David's perception of them. He tells us that if Mr. Peggotty's house were Aladdin's palace he couldn't be more charmed by it and he is taken with the "delightful door cut in the side" and the fact that it was a real boat intended to be lived in on dry land. The importance for David of the warmth of this "delicious retreat" and its protection against the world outside are clearly seen when he exclaims: "To hear the wind getting up out at sea, to know that the fog was creeping over the desolate flat outside, and to look at the fire, and think that there was no house near but this one ... was like enchantment."

A house with a fire which can withstand the wind and the invading sea is, surely, one of the most basic, visible and elemental images of human civilization. It takes on, also, in *David Copperfield*, added reality when we consider the fates of Ham and Emily's fathers—both "drowndead"—and, more importantly, the climactic tempest that takes the lives of Ham and Steerforth near the end of the novel.

David's preoccupation with houses and the influence he feels they have over his own life, both for good or ill, are apparent throughout the novel. For him, hallways, rooms and staircases are haunted with a kind of elemental power. When he states after his mother remarries, "If the room to which my bed was removed were a sentient thing that could give evidence, I might appeal to it at this day," he is suggesting this power. Thus, immediately upon reaching Aunt Betsey's property (after a six-day journey through streets and highways with no roof), he finds a sense of peace and order in his aunt's house facing the sea. He is led to a neat cottage with a cheerful bow-window in front of which is a garden full of flowers, "carefully tended and smelling deliciously."

The home of Mr. Wickfield and Agnes, too, is seen as a force for solidity and good, at first, although it will soon fall beneath Heep's weak shadow. He describes the house, in fact, in terms that he will use again in speaking of Agnes's good influence over him. With his new school books under his arm he feels his uneasiness melting away because of the "influence in Mr. Wickfield's old house." Agnes, herself, is immediately connected in David's mind with another type of shelter, that of a church and its stained glass windows. In this often repeated link between Agnes and the stained window, David is also connecting her with the religious images he uses in describing his own mother. He cannot recall where or when he has seen a stained glass church window in his childhood, but he immediately feels as Agnes turns toward him that something of its "tranquil brightness" will be associated with her forever. Indeed, perhaps, the single most direct connection in the book between human beings and houses occurs when David tells us he cherishes a "general fancy as if Agnes were one of the elements of my natural home."

If a place can have a softening or positive influence, it can also cut off light and life. When David returns to Mrs. Steerforth's house late in the novel, we should not be very surprised to find Mrs. Clennam or Miss Havisham waiting behind its dismal, life-denying and lifeless closed shutters. He tells us, startlingly, that if he were a casual passer-by, he would have thought that some childless person lay dead inside.

The link between houses and people becomes even more apparent when we observe how and in what contexts Dickens sees houses as reflections of specific characters in the novel. These characters, like Agnes, above, are defined by, or themselves define, the dwellings they inhabit. In searching for the residence of Traddles, David senses that Mr. Micawber is not only on the premises but, in a sense, has become a part of them. In the general air of the place he finds, "an indescribable character of faded gentility" which made it unlike all the other houses in the street and which "reminded [him] still more of Mr. and Mrs. Micawber."

Indeed, Mr. Micawber's search for a permanent residence and his fortuitous appearances and disappearances add another set of echoes to the sense of transience and homelessness in the novel. In his fantasy world, Mr. Micawber describes a home that would be acceptable to him as one in the upper part of a house over some "respectable place of business" where they might "live, comfortably and reputably, for a few years." In one of Micawber's last outbursts before emigrating, he opens his arms to the major evils besetting him and "houselessness" is high on the list.

Other characters in the novel are also described or seen as parts of buildings. David sees Uriah Heep, for example, as a gargoyle when, leaning out of a window, he sees "one of the faces on the beam-ends" looking at him sideways and "fancied it was Uriah Heep got up there somehow." Mr. Dick, too, we are told, at one point, "seemed neither to advance, nor to recede. He appeared to have settled into his original foundation, like a building."

If one can be identified with a building, one can also personify one. In the case of Rosa Dartle, David's imagination portrays her as being "a little dilapidated—like a house—with having been so long to let." David also connects the emotional life of his characters with the theme of home and homelessness when he (perhaps oversentimentally) has Emily state in her blotted farewell letter to Ham, "When I leave my dear home—my dear home—oh, my dear home!—in the morning . . ." It is striking, too, that human beings and houses are verbally joined when Mr. Peggotty defines the word "beein" for David: "A 'beein' signifies, in that dialect, a home."

The far-reaching obsession in the novel to equate people with specific places or spaces they move in may finally be seen in Dickens's treatment of even such a relatively minor figure as Martha. The force of Dickens's description captures the world of dust, mud, and garbage that was to reappear in *Our Mutual Friend*. The landscape of unfinished buildings wasting away is mirrored in the incompleted, fragmented dreams of the neighborhood's occupants. On what Dickens calls a melancholy waste of road, "carcases of houses, inauspiciously begun and never finished, rotted away." Here, too, last year's handbills offering rewards for drowned men float upon "the ooze and slush to the ebb-tide." Dickens makes clear the bridge between the exterior world of buildings and streets and the interior world of his characters when he describes Martha, on the verge of suicide, looking at the water, as if she "were a part of the refuse it had cast out, . . . left to corruption and decay."

The image of the house does not appear in *David Copperfield* merely in descriptions or in David's propensity for finding correspondences between people and houses. It becomes the central concept and, indeed, the central *word* in the crucial episode that will determine—once and for all—the authority in the new Murdstone household, and thus determine David's future. Clara, in her one visible protest against Mr. Murdstone's vaunted "firmness," seeks to be consulted about certain household plans being made by Mr. and Miss Murdstone, the real couple in the home. David tells us that his mother "did not suffer her authority to pass from her without a shadow of a protest." Then the dialogue itself beautifully illustrates how power can be wielded in a family merely by words and the proper tonalities. Authority (or at least the shadow of its last rays) moves through carefully but potentially violent stages and David, ever observant by necessity, catches the nuances:

> "It's very hard," said my mother, "that in my own house—"
> "*My* own house?" repeated Mr Murdstone. "Clara!"
> "*Our* own house, I mean," faltered my mother, evidently frightened—"I hope you must know what I mean, Edward—it's very hard that in *your* own house I may not have a word to say about domestic matters."

The passage of authority here and the continuing attempt to keep Clara a child is also symbolized by the transferring of keys from Clara to Miss Murdstone. David suggests also the close and almost automatic connection between keys and prisons in Dickens when he informs us that from that time on Miss Murdstone kept the keys in "her own little jail all day, and under her pillow all night."

The dramatic power for Dickens in the word "home" may be observed also in the scene of verbal misunderstanding between Rosa Dartle and Emily. Rosa, in an earlier scene, had already stated concerning Mr. Peggotty's house and family that "I would trample on them all . . . I would have his house pulled down." In the scene with Emily, Rosa, in speaking of Steerforth's house, asks Emily, "Do you know what you have done? Do you ever think of the home you have laid waste?" Emily answers her in a long, emotional speech in which she repeatedly refers to Mr. Peggotty's home. Rosa's response indicates clearly the force of the word "home" in the novel: "*Your* home! Do you imagine that I bestow a thought on it . . . Your home! . . . I speak of *his* home—where I live."

This emphasis upon the home, appearing as it does around every corner, wherever David turns, in whatever he overhears, is given perhaps its clearest expression by him after he is literally and emotionally re-covered after his flight to Aunt Betsey and her home facing the sea: "I prayed that I might never be houseless any more, and never might forget the houseless."

Dickens's vision of a warm house on the water is quite similar to that revealed in Virginia Woolf's portrait of Mrs. Ramsay's windowed, but protective house, in *To the Lighthouse*. Beyond obvious surface correspondences such as Mr. Peggotty's light in the window, what is especially noteworthy is the manner in which both authors describe houses that time and change have worn away. Mrs. Woolf, like Dickens, sees the world in terms of houses, in terms of rooms, windows, doors. In the marvelous "Time Passes" section, she describes the decaying house Lily Briscoe returns to after ten years and the forces of nature pressing upon, flooding the house:

> Nothing, it seemed, could survive the flood, the profusion of darkness which, creeping in at keyholes and crevices, stole round window blinds, came into bedrooms . . . The nights now are filled with wind and destruction; the trees plunge and bend and their leaves fly helter skelter until the lawn is plastered

with them and they lie packed in gutters and choke rain pipes and scatter damp paths.

Dickens, too, in describing David returning to his birthplace at Blunderstone, writes of darkness, rain, leaves, shadows on the wall, the toppling of trees and the closing of blinds. In both authors, then, there is a clear sense of an attack upon a living thing. Dickens writes:

> . . . it pained me to think of the dear old place as altogether abandoned; of the weeds growing tall in the garden, and the fallen leaves lying thick and wet upon the paths. I imagined how the winter would howl round it, how the cold rain would beat upon the window-glass, how the moon would make ghosts on the walls of the empty rooms, watching their solitude all night.

Later in the novel he describes, as Mrs. Woolf does, the "great changes in my old home," the ragged nests, the trees "lopped and topped out of their remembered shapes," and the garden run wild with half the house's windows shut.

For both Dickens and ourselves, then, the eternal image of the house may refer to our individual selves, our total identities, and its windows to our eyes, our vision, the pathways to our minds. However, the house in *David Copperfield*, as we have seen, recurs most significantly as a symbol of the basic human need for warmth and protection in a world of impermanence and flux. For Dickens himself, haunted by early separations from his own family, the themes of home and home-lessness take on almost immeasurable emotional poignancy. As John Forster has written of Dickens's reunion with his family during the blacking factory period: "What was to him the greatest pleasure of his paradise of a lodging, was its bringing him again, though after a fashion sorry enough, within the circle of home."

—NEIL GRILL, "Home and Homeless in *David Copperfield*," *Dickens Studies Newsletter* 11, No. 4 (December 1980): 108–11

CRITICAL ESSAYS

Gwendolyn B. Needham

THE UNDISCIPLINED HEART
OF DAVID COPPERFIELD

Author, critic, and public have distinguished *The Personal History and Experience of David Copperfield the Younger* by proclaiming it their favorite of all Dickens's works. Much has been written to explain this unusual triple accord, much on the novel's merits and defects. Among many valuable discussions it is surprising that the contribution of the theme of the undisciplined heart to the novel's power has not been more thoroughly appreciated. Study of the part played by theme reveals its importance: it emphasizes and illumines the character of David, showing that his function is far greater than that of narrator; it works within the novel's frame of retrospection to shape the structure; it gives deeper significance to and closer integration of minor episodes with the novel's larger unity; thus it contributes largely to the novel's total effect and pervading tone.

The theme of the undisciplined heart, implicit from the beginning, Dickens does not state explicitly until about three-fourths through the story. In the emotion-charged climax of the Strong episode, the young wife summarizes her history in three memorable phrases which ring forever in David's mind and heart: "The first mistaken impulse of an undisciplined heart." "There can be no disparity in marriage like unsuitability of mind and purpose." "My love was founded on a rock."[1] The highly dramatic presentation is characteristic, but few have noted the significance of Dickens's long and careful preparation for it. Study of the Strong episode in relation to the whole novel demonstrates that from its inception the episode's *raison d'être* is statement and illustration of the theme, and that for maximum effect Dickens planned the episode's development to coincide at the right moment with the emotional development of his hero. The extended dramatized statement of theme, involving five separately placed chapters, thus helps shape the order and treatment of material in the middle half of the novel.[2] How thereafter the theme's further development affects the arrangement of material is easily perceptible. Only with the entire story in mind, however, can one clearly perceive its implicit presence in the first part and then appreciate the full contribution the theme makes to the novel.

From *Nineteenth-Century Fiction* 9, No. 2 (September 1954): 81–107.

Although David declares his concern is with his personal life, not his writings, since "They express themselves, and I leave them to themselves" (p. 727; p. 889), his own story, ironically enough, has not always been left to express itself. Because Dickens included some authentic autobiographical data, many studies of the novel focus attention on Dickens's character rather than on David's, whose importance to the novel is accordingly minimized and the theme of his undisciplined heart neglected. George Gissing declares David is "decidedly not the hero of his own story";[3] Stephen Leacock dismisses him as "merely the looking glass in which we see the other characters, the voice through which they speak. He himself has no more character than a spiritualist medium."[4] Ernest Baker believes David "emerges a real man" but leaves only "a pleasant but not very memorable impression." He comes near the truth when he says the story relates "how the boy's character was tried, his mind shaped, and his imagination fed, by all the different things that befell him,"[5] but with Dickens in mind rather than David, Baker unfortunately misses the significant last step—and *his heart disciplined*. Percy Lubbock rightly points out that "the far stretch of the past" makes the shape of the book; that the lesser dramas instead of controlling the novel "sink into the level of retrospect"; that the story is a "clear case for narration in person"; but mistakenly concludes, "Nothing was lost, because the sole need is for the reader to see what David sees; it matters little how his mind works, or what the effect of it all may be upon himself. . . . [He] offers a pair of eyes and a memory, nothing further is demanded of him."[6] Lubbock accounts for the over-all form, but not for the novel's power. He fails to consider the importance of David's character and overlooks the fact that within the frame of retrospection, the theme helps shape the selection and arrangement of material.

Those who regard David as only a pair of eyes and ears forget that what they see and hear is colored and heightened by David's feeling. As G. K. Chesterton observes, the novel's characters are romantically felt; "they are not exaggerated as personalities are exaggerated by an artist; they are exaggerated as personalities are exaggerated by their own friends and enemies. The strong souls are seen through the glorious haze of the emotions that strong souls really create."[7] It is David who provides this "glorious haze." We do not see his person so distinctly because we are so often within him and both feel his vibrant personality and feel through it. David's capacity for feeling, his sensitivity to the emotional tone of personal relationships, as well as his remarkable powers of observation, make his story live. Just as David's feeling pervades, colors, and gives significance to the story, so the story in turn reveals David's character and traces his emotional growth. Dickens has David as older narrator continually comment on his feeling *then* and *now*, thus skillfully indicating the varying intensity, importance, and permanence of the experiences in his emotional development while at the same time rendering their account more vivid, poignant, or humorous. The reader may recall numerous examples besides the following:

> As I recall our being opposed thus, face to face, I seem again to hear my heart
> beat fast and high. . . . God help me, I might have been improved for my whole

ıht have been made another creature perhaps, for life, by a kind word
ason (pp. 48–49). I admired and loved him, and his approval was
ough. It was so precious to me, that I look back on these trifles now
ing heart (p. 98). I now approach a period of my life which I can
he remembrance of while I remember anything, and the recol-
ich has often, without my invocation, come before me like a
ted happier times (p. 159). There is no doubt whatever that
ical young spooney; but there was a purity of heart in all this
events my having quite a contemptuous recollection of it, let me
laugh as I may (p. 414). I now approach an event in my life, so indelible, so
awful, so bound by an infinite variety of ties to all that has preceded it, in these
pages, that, from the beginning of my narrative, I have seen it growing larger
and larger as I advanced, like a great tower in a plain, and throwing its forecast
shadow even on the incidents of my childish days. For years after it occurred
I dreamed of it often (p. 826).

Study in their context shows how fully and variously Dickens used such comments.
They complete the characterization of the hero by revealing the kind of man the
boy David has become. They clarify the characterization of other personages by
enabling us to feel their personalities as David does and also perceive those qualities
which his later judgment discerns. They serve to guide, summarize, or forecast the
action and to connect various narrative links. But above all, these comments help
to prepare and arouse the reader emotionally.

All the events and people in David's written memory are bathed in his
emotions—saturated, steeped in feeling as David was steeped in Dora. This fact
impresses us forcibly when we hold this novel of retrospection in our own retrospect. We can see that just as "the knots and networks of action" sink into the level
of retrospect, the feeling proportionately rises and pervades the whole with its
radiating light and warmth. And it is the feeling evoked by the "wonderful show"
that goes straight to our heart and remains. Dickens's basic belief that "real love and
truth are stronger in the end than any evil and misfortune in the world" is the
foundation for the novel's prevailing tone—a melodic blend of bright humor, tender sorrow, and firm hope. A paraphrase of Dickens's words can best describe the
novel's lasting effect: "Of all [the novels] that Time has in his grip, there is none that
in one retrospection I can smile at half so much, and think of half so tenderly" (p.
514). Perhaps the chief artistic virtue, shining above other merits and overshad-
owing the defects, of that long retrospection, David Copperfield, is that it evokes
so perfectly the emotion natural to retrospection—the mingled tears and laughter
which most men feel as they review their past.

When we realize the preëminence of feeling, the importance in the novel of
hero and theme becomes manifest; David is feeling's main source, the theme its
guiding channel. David appropriately has traits typical of the man of sensibility—
innocence, simplicity, gullibility, benevolence, tenderness. If tears be an index of
sensibility, David supplies an overflow; they accompany almost every emotion—

joy, grief, shame, rapture, indignation, pity—and serve to relieve and refresh, soothe and exalt. Spiritually akin to Goldsmith and Sterne in his tender humanity,[8] Dickens, had he written in the eighteenth century, might well have called David's story, "The History of a Man of Feeling." He does not represent his hero as perfect, for the model of his history is Fielding's *Tom Jones*. A domestic occurrence records the literary fact. At the time when Dickens's mind was "running like a high sea" on plans for *Copperfield,* his sixth son was born (January 16, 1849), and Dickens wrote John Forster that he had changed the child's name from the intended "Oliver Goldsmith" to "Henry Fielding," as "a kind of homage to the style of work he was now bent on beginning."[9]

The example of Fielding probably influenced also Dickens's choice of theme. Fielding, concerned with his hero's way in the world, directly warns that Tom's innate goodness is not enough; he must learn prudence:

> Let this, my young readers, be your constant maxim, that no man can be good enough to enable him to neglect the rules of prudence; nor will Virtue herself look beautiful unless she be bedecked with the outward ornaments of decency and decorum. And this precept, my worthy disciples, if you read with due attention, you will, I hope, find sufficiently enforced by examples in the following pages (p. 96).

Dickens's theme of the undisciplined heart encompasses this truth and goes further; natural goodness plus prudence may win affectionate respect, but one must learn a higher wisdom of the heart if he would achieve inner strength and peace. The good heart must have no "alloy of self," must love humanity as well as persons. It must be self-reliant and possess constancy and fortitude in order to be strengthened, not conquered or merely softened, by adversity and sorrow. The good heart must learn the nature of "real truth and love" in order to overcome "evil and misfortune in this world." This is the discipline which David and every good man must achieve.

By use of David as narrator Dickens cannot make, as Fielding does, an early specific statement of his theme. He must present his details and enforcing examples implicitly until David's emotional development reaches the point where David himself can perceive his mistaken impulses and can realize his heart's need for discipline. To use this method effectively, Dickens must sufficiently characterize and soundly motivate his narrator-hero so that David's revelation to the reader of his character and of the developing theme and the fact of his own continued blindness are both rendered convincing. A brief survey of the story up to the explicit statement will show how well Dickens accomplished this task.

When we analyze David's character (and do not unconsciously deprive him, as is too often done, of those traits in which he most resembles his author-father), we find that although easily classifiable as a man of feeling, he emerges a real individual, lovable as boy, youth, and man. He is sensitively alive to the world about him and throws himself with romantic fervor into whatever he does or feels. He possesses honesty, loyalty, generosity, and modesty but lacks active courage. Delicate as a child, he was soon hurt bodily or mentally. Naturally timid, he has a passive fortitude, suffers without complaint (exemplified by his childhood London experience), but exhibits courage only when driven by desperation. He uses his native talents with earnest, persevering industry to win economic success and literary fame. The pervading sensibility of his loving heart wins affection but proves his own greatest weakness. His disposition is too pliant, too easily influenced. At times his loyalty is misplaced, his feeling misdirected or mistaken; his modesty often sinks into lack of self-confidence, his judgment into self-distrust. We must remember, above all, that he is very young. He does not reach twenty-one until the story is two-thirds over, is between twenty-six and twenty-seven at its close, and is thirty-seven when he narrates his history.

Both heredity and environment play their part in forming David's character. Through Aunt Betsey we learn how much he resembles his father and mother, from both of whom he derives his sensibility, earnest heart, and too pliant disposition. Copperfield, Sr., had "a delicate constitution," a dreamy romantic nature without judgment, and a predilection for "wax dolls"; his mother is "a simple affectionate Baby," who becomes an "unhappy, misdirected Baby," a "poor little fool" for trusting Murdstone. Although sure of David's principles (he follows her advice: "Never be mean in anything; never be false; never be cruel") and confident of his powers (he achieves an excellent scholastic record), Aunt Betsey fears his lack of firmness. She urges him to be "A fine firm fellow, with a will of your own. . . . with strength of character that is not to be influenced, except on good reason, by anybody, or by anything. . . . That's what your father and mother might both have been, Heaven knows, and been the better for it" (p. 289).

Aunt Betsey herself is the first example we meet of an undisciplined heart, but we do not recognize her as such until Dickens gives his purposely postponed explanation. In the opening chapter we learn enough of her oddities to prepare us for her abrupt departure, never to return, when "niece Betsey" arrives a little David. Knowledge of this formidable eccentric adds to the boy's suspense (also the reader's) in his desperate journey to Dover. Later we find her harsh rigidity hides a good heart that has been closed to the world since her younger husband's deceitful villainy. Embittered by the "first mistaken impulse of her undisciplined heart," Aunt Betsey renounced mankind (save simple Mr. Dick), developed a fixation against marriage, and became an eccentric recluse. Care and responsibility for the orphaned child opens her heart first to love for David, then for mankind; thus she achieves the disciplined heart and proves it by extending the charitable love to Dora that she had denied to Mrs. Copperfield (pp. 366, 672).

Easily recognizable is the example of the undisciplined heart presented by Mrs. Copperfield, who cannot "live under coldness or unkindness" and cannot bear either responsibility or discomfort. The disastrous results of his mother's weakness are clearly revealed in David's account of his childhood sufferings, although even as older narrator he expresses love and pity for her, never criticism. Incapable of understanding the child's unhappy bewilderment when he finds her remarried, she upbraids him and Peggotty for making her unhappy, "when one has the most right to expect [the world] to be as agreeable as possible." The little boy soon perceives Mr. Murdstone's overpowering influence: "I knew as well that he could mould her pliant nature into any form he chose, as I know, now, that he did it" (p. 47). Instead of expecting comfort from his mother, the child tries to help by staying out of the Murdstones' way: "I had perception enough to know that my mother was the victim always; that she was afraid to speak to me, or be kind to me, . . . that she was not only ceaselessly afraid of her own offending, but of my offending, and uneasily watched their looks if I only moved" (p. 125). Such conditions undoubtedly increased David's timidity and deepened that distrust of himself which he later observes, "has often beset me in life on small occasions, when it would be better away." Recall how often his lack of self-assertion makes him an easy victim to the tyranny of waiters, coachmen, and landladies.

What he unconsciously misses in his mother and sorely needs, the child finds in Peggotty—a love "founded on a rock," a trust and constancy on which he can rely. When she refuses to believe he has "bad passions," David observes, "there grew up in my breast a feeling for Peggotty which I cannot very well define. She did not replace by mother—no one could do that; but she came into a vacancy in my heart, which closed upon her, and I felt towards her something I have never felt for any other human being" (p. 64). What the child sensed, the reader can fully perceive—Peggotty has the disciplined heart; his mother's childish nature prevents her loving heart from ever achieving discipline. Fortunately for David's memory of her, his mother with death "winged her way back to her calm, untroubled youth, and cancelled all the rest." Dickens clearly makes the example of Mrs. Copperfield prophetic of David's experience with Dora, another "simple, affectionate Baby."

His school experiences first reveal weaknesses in David's own character. Although the boy cannot perceive Steerforth's faults nor Traddles' merits, his detailed account exposes them, and his comments as narrator plainly intimate the course of future events. David's erroneous valuation of his two friends, so long held, is the first example of his heart's "mistaken impulses." This error, understandable in the boy, not easily excusable in the young man, is destined to bring grief to David and grave trouble to others—sorrow for which David feels partly responsible. Critics who designate the whole Steerforth episode as extraneous, an "artistic blot" on the story, have not realized fully its purpose and use.[10] Both Steerforth and Traddles, absolute foils to each other, serve as foils to David. The stories of each friend's fate are intertwined and integrated with David's own story and with his emotional growth; their parts in the novel both illustrate and develop the theme. The child's self-distrust and need for loving approval—increased by his unhappiness at home—help explain his blind hero-worship of the older Steerforth. His champion's magnetic personality long represents what he himself would like to be but is not. The comic Traddles arouses David's affection but also his laughter—"I never think of that boy but with a strange disposition to laugh, and with tears in my eyes"—and he inevitably feels superior.

Misled by appearances, David long fails to appreciate Traddles' worth, honor, and honest friendship. Years afterwards, when Traddles frees the Wickfields from Heep's net, David confesses that "this was the first occasion on which I really did justice to the clear head, and plain, patient, practical good sense of my old school-fellow" (p. 798). Further illustrating the theme, Dickens contrasts the love of Traddles and Sophy ("the dearest girl—one in ten, you know") to that of David and Dora. Traddles and Sophy have unselfish hearts, "suitability of mind and purpose," and love "founded on a rock." David finds comparison impossible between their patient love and his and Dora's ecstasy. He cannot comprehend their unselfish consideration for Sophy's preposterous family; his impatient ardor rejects their motto, "Wait and hope." Only when the finally disciplined David returns from Europe does he appreciate how rich in happiness such a marriage as theirs will prove.

When David and Steerforth meet later, the overtures of the jaded young man, attracted by "Daisy's" fresh innocence, indicate true friendship to David's trusting heart: "As he had treated me at school differently from all the rest, I joyfully believed that he treated me in life unlike any other friend he had. I believed that I was nearer to his heart than any other friend, and my own heart warmed with attachment to him" (p. 316). Nourished by sensibility, this warmth inevitably blazes into a bright glorification of *friendship* in Steerforth that blinds David to realities. When Agnes warns of his "bad angel," Steerforth's image is so cemented in David's heart by all his "romantic feelings of fidelity and friendship" that he feels ashamed of entertaining even a momentary doubt. When Steerforth proclaims his philosophy of riding roughshod or smooth-shod over all obstacles to win a race, David merely wishes his friend had a race worthy of his great powers. Equally blinded by innocent love for Emily, David has no suspicion of the impending Yarmouth catastrophe. His shock and grief, therefore, are great when he learns of their elopement and witnesses the widespread disaster resulting from his friend's "roughshod" victory.

From this experience David could have learned much about the real nature of love, truth, and the disciplined heart, for the entire episode teaches this important lesson. In varying ways and degrees, all the principal characters, including himself, provide enforcing examples of the theme. Steerforth, Mrs. Steerforth, and Rosa Dartle, each marred by the "alloy of self," exemplify the misery to which the undisciplined heart can doom itself and bring innocent victims. David does perceive that mother and son are "alike in their moral constitution" and that her misguided mother-love has helped ruin the son. Her proud refusal to be reconciled except on her own terms perpetuates the tragedy which her son's passion has begun. Selfish in their love, she and Rosa Dartle are embittered, not softened, by grief and feel no compassion for others; they are doomed to wear out their desolate years in conflict and misery. Dickens sympathetically depicts some inner conflict in Steerforth, who passionately cries to David, "I wish to God I had had a judicious father these last twenty years!... I wish with all my soul I had been better guided! I wish with all my soul I could guide myself better!" (p. 338). He demonstrably lacks the discipline to deny his desires.

The Yarmouth folk all have honest hearts, but only Peggotty and Ham have completely disciplined love. Little Emily, desiring to be a lady and to shower fortune on her family, misjudges the nature of true love and follows her heart's "mistaken impulse." Through suffering and remorse she learns her lesson and thereafter devotes her life in unselfish goodness to others. Her generous uncle, rugged embodiment of simple virtue, yet has to learn pity for society's outcasts. He admits, "The time was when I thowt this girl Martha a'most like the dirt underneath my Em'ly's feet. God forgive me, there's a difference now!" and humbly cries to Martha, "God forbid as I should judge you!" (pp. 713; 720). He expresses compassion and gratitude by taking Martha with them to Australia. The calamity befalling the Yarmouth household also disciplines Mrs. Gummidge, hitherto selfishly engrossed in her own misfortunes. Aroused by others' sorrow, that "lone lorn creetur" ceases moaning about "everthink going contrairy," feels herself needed, and becomes a cheerful prop to Mr. Peggotty in his affliction.

Although David observes, "I could not meditate enough upon the lesson that I read in Mrs. Gummidge, and the new experience she unfolded to me," he is in no condition to apply the truths presented by the Yarmouth happenings. His friend's unworthiness elicits more tenderness than wisdom. He regrets the waste of qualities "that might have made him a man of a noble nature and a great name," and declares

> I am not afraid to write that I never had loved Steerforth better than when the ties that bound me to him were broken. . . . Deeply as I felt my own unconscious part in his pollution of an honest home, I believed that if I had been brought face to face with him, I could not have uttered one reproach. . . . I should have held in so much tenderness the memory of my affection for him (p. 478).

This last sentiment, so unmistakably that of a "man of feeling," reveals David's present inability to see and correct the weaknesses of his undisciplined heart. Dickens makes his hero's failure to learn from life's harsh lesson more plausible and also more excusable by showing him already entrapped in an intoxicating new emotion. How can David, "as enraptured a young noodle as ever was carried out of his five wits by love," profit by one mistake when his whole being is absorbed in a second? So dazzling is idealized love that even the shattered dream of friendship cannot darken it or cast a doubt on its reality. David confides,

> All this time, I had gone on loving Dora, harder than ever. Her idea was my refuge in disappointment and distress, and made some amends to me, even for the loss of my friend. The more I pitied myself, or pitied others, the more I sought for consolation in the image of Dora. The greater the accumulation of deceit and trouble in the world, the brighter and the purer shone the star of Dora high above the world. . . . I should have scouted the notion of her being simply human, like any other young lady, with indignation and contempt.

If I may so express it, I was steeped in Dora. I was not merely over head and ears in love with her, but I was saturated through and through (pp. 497–498).

This "very ecstasy of love" also prevents the young man (as age and inexperience had formerly prevented the boy) from reading correctly the lessons that life presents in the characters and fates of his Canterbury-London acquaintances: the Wickfields, the Heeps, the Strongs. Dickens links the stories of these people with each other (also "turns up" the Micawbers and brings in Traddles) and integrates them all with the story of David's developing character and life. Again we find Dickens using the principal characters to develop or illustrate some aspect of the theme. Heep, as villain, provides the contrast of the bad heart, the evil hypocrisy of which is only intensified by discipline. His fate proves that greed and cunning overreach themselves to fall before real truth and good. Agnes obviously demonstrates "the influence for all good" that can come from the disciplined heart; her father as clearly demonstrates the ruin to itself and the suffering to others that the undisciplined heart may bring. Through care for her father, Agnes learned as a child the responsibility of love and early arrived at emotional maturity. She realizes the causes of her father's warped love and its sad consequences, hides her own suffering, and strives for his restoration. Enslaved by alcohol, entrapped by Heep, Mr. Wickfield is shocked into the realization that he, rather than Uriah, is ultimately responsible for the ruin which has culminated in the villain's ignominious scheme to marry Agnes. He analyzes for David and the reader the lesson his life presents:

"Weak indulgence has ruined me. Indulgence in remembrance, and indulgence in forgetfulness. My natural grief for my child's mother turned to disease; my natural love for my child turned to disease. . . . I have brought misery on what I dearly love, I know—*you* know! I thought it possible that I could truly love one creature in the world, and not love the rest; . . . that I could truly mourn for one creature gone out of the world, and not have some part in the grief of all who mourned. Thus the lessons of my life have been perverted! I have preyed on my own morbid coward heart, and it has preyed on me. Sordid in my grief, sordid in my love, sordid in my miserable escape from the darker side of both, oh see the ruin I am, and hate me, shun me!" (p. 608).

One might deduce from Dickens's wholesale use of orphans (David, Emily, Ham, Traddles, Rosa Dartle; Steerforth, Uriah, Agnes, Annie, Dora are half-orphans) that he sought by this fact partially to extenuate their weaknesses. But in his characterization of parents, Dickens stresses how often parental love itself urgently requires discipline. Not one of them—Mrs. Copperfield, Mrs. Steerforth, Mr. Wickfield, Mr. Spenlow, Mrs. Markleham, or Mrs. Heep—is wise in love's expression; each unintentionally contributes to the child's troubles or unhappiness. These examples of misguided parents imply, of course, that wise training would help; but Dickens makes clear by David's own story that every individual has to learn for himself his need and to accept responsibility for disciplining his heart. Life's teachings prove instructive to David only when he can recognize his need and can apply them correctly to himself. Dickens uses the Strong episode to present this truth. Analysis in their context of its five chapters—Numbers 16, 19, 36, 42, and 45—shows how carefully Dickens integrated its development with David's emotional growth while dramatizing the theme's explicit statement.

In Chapter Sixteen the schoolboy David meets the Strongs, first supposes Annie to be the Doctor's daughter, then observes the household of benevolent sage, pretty wife, her "Old Soldier" mother, and her virile young cousin. Although the innocent child records with equal emphasis trivial and significant details, the knowing reader detects a probable "triangle" situation. At the scene's close, the sensitive boy is puzzled by the feeling look which Annie gives her husband; the older narrator signifies its importance:

> I cannot even say of what it is expressive to me now, rising again before my older judgment. Penitence, humiliation, shame, pride, love, and trustfulness, I see them all; and in them all, I see that horror of I don't know what. . . . It made a great impression on me, and I remembered it a long time afterwards, as I shall have occasion to narrate when the time comes (p. 260).

By Chapter Nineteen, David has finished school, is seventeen and ready to brave the world. Experienced in adolescent loves, he can now deduce why Mr. Wickfield distrusts Annie and disapproves of her intimacy with Agnes: "And now, I must confess, the recollection of what I had seen on that night when Mr. Maldon went away, first began to return upon me with a meaning it had never had, and to trouble me." He is haunted by the "impending shadow of a great affliction" that has "no distinct form in it yet" and feels "as if the tranquil sanctuary of my boyhood had been sacked before my face, and its peace and honour given to the winds" (pp. 296–297).

Two years pass before David again meets the Strongs. He has suffered from the Yarmouth happenings and has fallen in love with Dora. His aunt's loss of fortune has made work imperative. David is mature enough to profit by the economic experience but not by the emotional ones. With unusual care, Dickens provides a sound psychological basis for David's emotional state, which he pictures in detail. Neither Aunt Betsey's leading questions about Dora—"Not silly?" "Not light-headed?"—nor her intimated doubts can penetrate David's infatuation. Fearing that like his father, David has run after a "wax doll," and that like his mother, he has poured his soul into ill-judged love, his aunt urges him to seek deep earnestness. The nineteen-year-old lover can neither apply the warning of his mother's mistake nor conceive his love of "unfathomable profundity" as a boy-girl attachment. At Aunt Betsey's sad reiteration of "Blind, blind, blind!" David does observe, "And without knowing why, I felt a vague, unhappy loss or want of something overshadow me like a cloud." He has no suspicion that the "want" may lie within himself or Dora. Although love's proverbial blindness is excuse enough, Dickens makes David's infatuation still more probable by having the bewitching doll an almost exact replica of the lad's mother—prettily pettish, innocently vain, truly fond, charmingly childish.

As Peggotty once filled the "vacancy" left by his mother, so does Agnes now supply the "want" David vaguely feels; as the child on his nurse, the unthinking youth depends on Agnes' love, trust, and guidance. Dickens satisfactorily accounts for David's unawareness of the real nature of his love. When the two first meet as children, the boy immediately senses Agnes' greater maturity and feels her "quiet, good, calm spirit." He associates her "tranquil brightness" then and ever after with soft light shining through a church's stained-glass window. His imagination thus colors their relationship with a religious aura that causes him to venerate her goodness and to elevate her effectually beyond his reach. Their years in the same household with Agnes as listener, helper, and adviser lead him to regard her as a sister. Poor Agnes! Revered as an angel, beloved as a sister, she is the victim of David's romantic sensibility; he has etherealized her into a superior being, a removed spirit whose rays warm his heart and guide his path.

While the youth remains blind to the real nature of his love for both Dora and Agnes, his comments as older narrator reveal the actual state and intimate the eventual course of his two loves. For example, when writing Agnes of his secret engagement to Dora, the image of his "good angel" so calms his turbulent spirit that he is "soothed into tears" and fancies that in her "sacred" presence, "Dora and I must be happier than anywhere; as if, in love, joy, sorrow, hope, or disappointment—in all emotions—my heart turned naturally there, and found its refuge and best friend" (p. 515). Another time, he declares that she so directed "the wandering ardour and unsettled purpose within me, that all the little good I have done, and all the harm I have forborne, I solemnly believe I may refer to her. . . . Oh, Agnes, sister of my boyhood, if I had known then, what I knew long afterwards!—" (p. 546). To highlight this significant hint, Dickens contrives a typical theatrical coincidence. As David gazes at Agnes' window, thinking of her "calm, seraphic eyes," a street beggar wanders by muttering, "Blind! blind! blind!"

His "good angel" advises David of Dr. Strong's need for a secretary; the "star" of his universe inspires him to a frenzy of work; "Great is the labour; priceless the reward. . . . Dora must be won." Thus, in Chapter Thirty-six an eager worker and ardent lover enters the Strong menage and surveys the developing domestic situation. The omnipresent cousin, Jack Maldon, appears no longer a glamorous figure but a lazy dependent on the Doctor's bounty. The young worker's "ferocious virtue" condemns any man not "cutting down trees in the forest of difficulty"; the lover feels the emotional tension of a triangle. Aided by "Old Soldier's" mistaken insistence that Annie have entertainment, Maldon seems an increasing threat to the Doctor's peace and honor. With comic irony Dickens has the youth, so blind yet so sure in his knowledge of love, now wonder how the innocent old Doctor "could be so blind to what was so obvious." But David remains puzzled by Annie: "She did not look very happy, I thought; but it was a good face, or a very false one." David is filled with fears for the Strongs' future; the reader remains in suspense as to the true situation.

In the months intervening between Chapters Thirty-six and Forty-two, David's economic progress is steady but love's progress is not so smooth. Mr. Spenlow's disapproval, then his death, separate David from Dora. David's confession of a "lurking jealousy of Death" which pushes him out of Dora's thoughts shows the instinctive selfishness of undisciplined love. His very loyalty, fidelity, and earnestness help keep David an unconscious victim of his romantic imagination and mistaken impulses. His failure to make Dora understand that one cannot hew his way through a forest of difficulty with a guitar does not open his eyes to any "disparity of mind and purpose" or to the unsuitability of their union. If he occasionally wonders at Agnes' effect on him, his two fixed concepts of angel and sister satisfactorily explain it; his fascination with Dora prevents any suspicion of possible romantic love. The same reasons preclude his sensing Agnes' love for him. David's appeal to Agnes for advice in effecting his betrothal to Dora thus has a dramatic irony which Dickens makes both comic and pathetic. The youth's unconscious conflict of feelings lies beneath his conscious perplexity about himself. He thinks he is earnest, patient, and persevering, but "I get so miserable and worried, and am so unsteady and irresolute in my power of assuring myself, that I know I must want— shall I call it—reliance, of some kind? . . . When I have come to you, at last (as I have always done), I have come to peace and happiness" (pp. 596–597). Overpowered by feeling, he bursts into tears but knows not what they mean. When Agnes tactfully suggests that he rely on Dora, his dismayed excuses also fail to enlighten. He begs that Agnes will never marry Heep out of a sacrificial sense of duty: "Say you have no such thought, dear Agnes!—much more than sister! Think of the priceless gift of such a heart as yours, of such a love as yours!" The devastating irony pierces her calmness, as well it might, and David never forgets the momentary dimming of her "bright tranquillity." Relieved by her promise, David follows her advice "to do what is right," becomes officially betrothed to Dora, and believes he is supremely happy.

Thus in Chapter Forty-two Dickens presents a decided contrast between David's bright future and that of the Strongs. It grows steadily blacker. The despicable Heep, fearful that Mrs. Strong may injure his suit by putting "my Agnes up to higher sort of game," decides to interfere. To the unsuspicious Doctor, Uriah takes "the liberty of umbly mentioning . . . the goings-on" of Annie and her cousin, who are "too sweet on one another," and contrives to strengthen his case by cunningly forcing Mr. Wickfield and David to admit their fear that the young wife had married for "worldly considerations only." The aged husband's simple trust in his wife's integrity and fidelity remains unshaken, but he is crushed by the conviction of her marital unhappiness. Although he tries to hide his sorrow, Annie feels a change, and unaware of its cause, becomes silent and sad. As the weeks pass, their daily lives grow farther and farther separate. Their friends can only stand helpless and hopeless before the dark picture of increasing domestic unhappiness.

In the months that pass before the climax in Chapter Forty-five, several significant changes occur both in David and to him. Now twenty-one, he has come "legally to man's estate" and has enough physical and mental maturity to deserve the rank. He has successfully cut down "economic" trees and launched his writing career. Young David has achieved discipline of the body and mind; his heart remains undisciplined, unself-reliant. Marriage soon teaches the boyish husband that there are trees other than economic, ones far more difficult to fell, in life's forest of difficulty. His glorification of love makes adjustment to the actualities of marriage more perplexing and makes more acute his sense of loss on the discovery that love is not all of life. He finds "all the romance of our engagement put away upon a shelf, to rust—no one to please but one another—one another to please for life," a sobering thought indeed. The poignant emotion of David's secret unhappy bewilderment lies underneath the exquisitely humorous record of love's joys and vexations in Chapter Forty-four, "Our Housekeeping." Dismayed by their scrambled household and by futile efforts to reason with his pretty wife, David asks Aunt Betsey to advise Dora. Her refusal and sane counsel make him realize what marriage means, that he and Dora alone must work out their future. Their many abortive attempts end with Dora remaining a child-wife and him bearing all the burdens. David sums up his secret feelings:

> I am far from sure, now, that it was right to do this, but I did it for my child-wife's sake.... The old unhappy loss or want of something had, I am conscious, some place in my heart; but not to the embitterment of my life. When I walked alone in the fine weather, and thought of the summer days when all the air had been filled with my boyish enchantment, I did miss something of the realization of my dreams; but I thought it was a softened glory of the Past, which nothing could have thrown upon the present time. I did feel, sometimes, for a little while, that I could have wished my wife had been my counsellor; had had more character and purpose, to sustain me, and improve me by; had been endowed with power to fill up the void which somewhere seemed to be about me, but I felt as if this were an unearthly consummation of my happiness, that never had meant to be, and never could have been (p. 681).

David here reveals both his secret unhappiness and his present inability to analyze its true causes. This inability is suggestive of an unconscious refusal to face facts too painful to bear, an unconscious desire to preserve at all costs some golden remnants of his dream while acknowledging its imperfect round. He has not yet realized that every individual ultimately must supply himself the inner strength and purpose he needs. Dickens makes clear that David is rationalizing his loss as an ideal unattainable in this life, is trying to keep the feeling submerged and indefinable.

At this appropriate point in David's emotional development, Dickens presents the climactic resolution of the Strongs' domestic unhappiness. His integration of minor incident, major interest, character, theme, humor, and emotional tone gives the scene a powerful two-fold dramatic effect. Until now David could not have felt the full impact of the emotions he witnesses and the truths he hears. Knowing David's secret unhappiness, the reader feels both the drama of the Strongs and David's own inner drama, realizes even more clearly than the dazed youth the poignant applicability of the phrases uttered by Annie's anguished heart. Dickens solves the emotional impasse of the Strong estrangement by pure feeling, uncomplicated by intellect. Simple Mr. Dick with "the mind of the heart" can do what no one else dares—he effects an éclaircissement. Disclaiming any part in her mother's exploitation of the Doctor, Annie courageously lays bare the history of her heart. She publicly avows her gratitude to the Doctor for saving her from a girlish attraction to Maldon, a "'first mistaken impulse"; her deep appreciation of the marriage; her unwavering love and fidelity. Taken alone, this scene might well be termed melodramatic; placed in the context of the novel its high dramatic tone is justified by its direct statement of theme, by its resolution of the tense Strong episode, by its marking the climax of the hero's emotional development. Annie's words have defied David's vague unhappiness; he will have to face the knowledge that his heart is undisciplined, many of its impulses mistaken. At the scene's close, Dickens signifies with a nice poetic touch its effect on David, who walks home surrounded by happy chatter:

> I was thinking of all that had been said. My mind was still running on some of the expressions used. "There can be no disparity in marriage like unsuita-bility of mind and purpose." "The first mistaken impulse of an undisciplined heart." "My love was founded on a rock." But we were at home; and the trodden leaves were lying under-foot, and the autumn wind was blowing (pp. 700–701).

The symbols of "trodden leaves" and "autumn wind" mark the end of exu-berant youth and the beginning of man's graver responsibilities, suggest the suc-cessive shocks Death is to bring to David, and foreshadow the long gloomy night of despair David undergoes before he emerges with spirit strengthened and cleansed. The novel's dominant tone of bright cheer softens for a time to harmo-nize with the autumn wind blowing in David's heart and with the sad events he has to relate. Unable to rationalize away his "old unhappy feeling," David very humanly first acknowledges a lack in Dora rather than in himself: "But that it would have been better for me if my wife could have helped me more, and shared the many thoughts in which I had no partner—and that this might have been—I knew" (p. 734). He knows that they must accept responsibility for their appalling household and for encouraging the delinquency of their servants but fails to make Dora understand. To effect "a perfect sympathy," he vainly tries to form Dora's mind; all he effects is a separating shadow. Forced to analyze the shadow, he finally ac-knowledges his own undisciplined heart, accepts responsibility for it and for making their marriage as happy as possible:

> "The first mistaken impulse of an undisciplined heart." Those words of Mrs. Strong's were constantly recurring to me, at this time, were almost always present to my mind. I awoke with them, often, in the night; I remember to have even read them, in dreams, inscribed upon the walls of houses. For I knew, now, that my own heart was undisciplined when it first loved Dora; and that if it had been disciplined, it never could have felt, when we were married, what it had felt in its secret experience.

"There can be no disparity in marriage, like unsuitability of mind and purpose." Those words I remembered too. I had endeavoured to adapt Dora to myself, and found it impracticable. It remained for me to adapt myself to Dora; to share with her what I could, and be happy; to bear on my own shoulders what I must, and be happy still. This was the discipline to which I tried to bring my heart, when I began to think. It made my second year much happier than my first; and, what was better still, made Dora's life all sunshine (p. 735).

In dying Dora achieves an understanding denied her in life. She tells David that she was not fit to be a wife, would not have improved, that as the years passed, he would have wearied of his child-wife and could not have loved her so well, that "it is better as it is." The only plausible explanation for her perception is Dickens's phrase "mind of the heart"; Dora's love has sensed Agnes' love for David, his for Agnes, and probably also those changes in his feeling for herself that he thought safely hidden. David's "undisciplined heart is chastened heavily"; weeping, he thinks "with a blind remorse of all those secret feelings I have nourished since my marriage. I think of every little trifle between me and Dora, and feel the truth, that trifles make the sum of life. . . . Would it, indeed, have been better if we had loved each other as a boy and girl, and forgotten it? Undisciplined heart, reply!" (p. 810).

Culminating events prevent David's experiencing the full effect of grief, and the deaths of Ham and Steerforth augment his load of sorrow before he goes abroad. Chapter Fifty-eight, "Absence," is one long introspection in which Dickens has his hero undergo a period of despair and searching somewhat comparable to Carlyle's "Everlasting Nay" and "Everlasting Yea" in *Sartor Resartus*. Sorrow exposes the weakness of David's undisciplined heart as love has exhibited its mistaken ardor:

The desolate feeling with which I went abroad, deepened and widened hourly. At first it was a heavy sense of loss and sorrow . . . By imperceptible degrees, it became a hopeless consciousness of all that I had lost—love, friendship, interest; of all that had been shattered—my first trust, my first affection, the whole airy castle of my life; of all that remained—a ruined blank and waste, lying wide around me, unbroken, to the dark horizon.

If my grief were selfish, I did not know it to be so. . . . From the accumulated sadness into which I fell, I had at length no hope of ever issuing again. . . . When this despondency was at its worst, I believed that I should die. . . . Listlessness to everything, but brooding sorrow, was the night that fell on my undisciplined heart (pp. 857–858).

David wanders for months with "no purpose, no sustaining soul within me anywhere" and without the fortitude to write his friends. At last he awakens to some faint sense of beauty in nature and feels its softening influence (typical of the "man of sensibility"). A letter from Agnes stating the lesson of the disciplined heart lightens his night of despair. Agnes trusts that David would "turn affliction to good," would be exalted by trial, that in him "sorrow could not be weakness, but must be strength," that his purpose would gain from grief a "firmer and higher tendency," that he would labor on, and that as he had been taught by calamities and grief, so would he teach others. David understands the lesson, feels the night "passing from my mind," realizes his true love for Agnes, and knows, "I was not, and never had been, what she thought me; but that she inspired me to be that, and I would try" (p. 860). Through Nature's influence, restored interest in his fellow man, and his writing, David gradually wins his way back to health—to joy in working and pleasure in living.

The discipline his heart has gained enables him to analyze more objectively his past and present emotions:

> I cannot so completely penetrate the mystery of my own heart, as to know when I began to think that I might have set its earliest and brightest hopes on Agnes. I cannot say at what stage of my grief it first became associated with the reflection, that, in my wayward boyhood, I had thrown away the treasure of her love. I believe I may have heard some whisper of that distant thought, in the old unhappy loss or want of something never to be realized, of which I had been sensible. But the thought came into my mind as a new reproach and a new regret, when I was left so sad and lonely in the world.
>
> If, at that time, I had been much with her, I should, in the weakness of my desolation, have betrayed this. . . . I could not have borne to lose the smallest portion of her sisterly affection; yet, in that betrayal, I should have set a constraint between us hitherto unknown.
>
> I could not forget that the feeling with which she now regarded me had grown up in my own free choice and course. That if she had ever loved me with another love—and I sometimes thought the time was when she might have done so—I had cast it away. It was nothing, now, that I had accustomed myself to think of her, when we were both mere children, as one who was far removed from my wild fancies. I had bestowed my passionate tenderness upon another object, and what I might have done I had not done; and what Agnes was to me, I and her own noble heart had made her (pp. 861–862).

David first hopes that he might "cancel the mistaken past" and after "some indefinite probation" marry Agnes, but sufferingly decides that "in right and honour" he must not turn "to the dear girl in the withering of my hopes, from whom I had frivolously turned when they were bright and fresh. . . . I made no effort to conceal from myself now that I loved her—that I was devoted to her; but I brought the assurance home to myself that it was now too late, and that our long-subsisting relation must be undisturbed" (p. 862).

David recalls what Dora had said might happen to their marriage, mentally lives through those future years, and admits the truth of her prediction. He resolves to be corrected by that visioned future as if it had been a reality and determines to convert what might have been between him and Agnes into a means "of making me more self-denying, more resolved, more conscious of myself, and my defects and errors." After three years' absence, David is ready to return home, confident that he "could think of the past now, gravely, but not bitterly, and could contemplate the future in a brave spirit" (p. 874). He has learned that real love has no "alloy of self," that sorrow should strengthen, and—his final step toward emotional maturity—that one must himself develop the firmness, fortitude, and courage to guide his life in the right path. Knowledge, however, is not enough; the discipline his heart has learned must be tested and proved by action.

Dickens skillfully contrives a test which, plausibly motivated by his hero's character, dramatizes the novel's last bit of action. David's romantic nature has led him from the perception that unselfish love is capable of renunciation to the mistaken conclusion that for him renunciation is inevitable; his sensibility deepens the belief that he deserves thus to expiate his past mistakes; his conviction of her superiority and his modest deprecation of his own powers of attraction quench any hope of winning Agnes. A confident man of action would have unhesitatingly tried his fortune. But Aunt Betsey's well-meaning ambiguous hints only confirm David's conviction that Agnes loves another; he feels intensely his duty to act the part of brother and friend, to make her feel free to confide as he had confided his past loves to her. His awkward efforts only torture them both. When his suffering finally senses hers, his feverish sensibility promptly concludes that she has discovered his love and hesitates to confide her secret for fear of paining him! Crushed by failure in his "brother" role, he nerves himself to the sacrificial test:

> "For Heaven's sake, Agnes, let us not mistake each other after all these years, and all that has come and gone with them! I must speak plainly. If you have any lingering thought that I could envy the happiness you will confer; . . . that I could not, from my removed place, be a contented witness of your joy;—dismiss it, for I don't deserve it! I have not suffered quite in vain. You have not taught me quite in vain. There is no alloy of self in what I feel for you" (p. 906).

Having thus proved his hero's disciplined heart, Dickens rewards him with Agnes' hand and life-long love.

The theme's illumination of his "Personal History" shows David to be, while not a "heroic" figure, a very human hero who struggles with "many opportunities wasted, many erratic and perverted feelings constantly at war within his breast" (p. 638), and shows the story of his development to be paramount. In this conclusion Dickens demonstrates in the fates accorded the characters that "real love and truth are in the end stronger than evil and misfortune in this world." This affirmation cannot be dismissed as mere shallow optimism; his theme qualifies that only the disciplined heart can discern the nature of real love and truth, thus gaining power to conquer, and that such discipline is difficult and painful to achieve. Discipline alone is not enough; natural goodness, while essential, alone is not enough. Dickens shows by his villains that discipline intensifies the evil in their hearts, and shows by many examples that the undisciplined heart also can cause misery and trouble. Although delineated tenderly, Dora and Mrs. Copperfield exemplify that no matter how loving the heart, if mind and character are weak, discipline cannot be learned. Incapable of responsibility in the world, such people must be treated, loved, and protected as children. Dickens sympathetically allows them to die young—perhaps the kindest fate Life can provide for them and theirs. The theme helps control Dickens's use of poetic justice, making it more discriminating than is usual with him. The noble Ham and erring Steerforth meet the same fate. The good, including David, must earn their reward, the highest of which is not material gain but inner peace and strength; the bad are not all punished "to fit the crime." Creakle becomes a magistrate; Heep and Littimer are incarcerated, not "pulverized." Dickens's humor also salts the saccharinity and lightens the solemnity of poetic justice. The two arch-villains make captivity comfortable by duping Creakle with their expert rendition of his own hypocritical pose of Christian virtue. Rewarded by a judgeship and prosperity, Traddles and Sophy remain squeezed by their preposterously overcrowded household. That inimitable comic pair, the elastic Micawbers, whose falls, springs, and leaps have given such delight, are rewarded for their great "Spring of no common magnitude" to Australia. The land of the kangaroo appropriately proves their natural habitat; Micawber's final spring into public prominence as a magistrate is superbly extolled by his own magniloquent pen.

Dickens's study of emotional maturity deals with simple fundamentals; a more complex and profound study could hardly be expected from a man who apparently never learned to discipline his heart. Whether he realized the fact or to what extent his hero's achievement expresses a conscious or unconscious wish-fulfillment of his own are questions for his biographers to decide and a subject for another essay. Considering the novel in and by itself, we see that Dickens's use of theme helps shape the novel's inner structure, shows David the hero, and gives closer integration and deeper significance to his colorful and moving history. Understanding of the theme deepens our appreciation of *David Copperfield*.

NOTES

[1] A survey of Dickens criticism reveals that many enthusiastic admirers have loved him well, but not always wisely. I wish to give credit to a wise lover, my colleague, Mrs. Elizabeth R. Homann, for first suggesting the significance of these phrases to me.

[2] The edition of the novel used in this discussion is the Modern Library edition (New York, n.d.). Of the novel's 64 chapters and 923 pages, the five chapters spaced between Chapters 15 and 46 (Numbers 16, 19, 36, 42, and 45) begin on page 237 and end on page 701. Of the book's initial 20 installments, the episode's development extends from the 6th to the 16th installment.

[3] *Charles Dickens* (London, 1898), p. 101.

[4] *Charles Dickens* (New York, 1936), p. 144; see also Bruce McCullough, *Representative English Novelists: Defoe to Conrad* (New York, 1946), pp. 142–143.

[5] *History of the English Novel* (New York, 1936), VII, 288; 308; 239.

[6] *The Craft of Fiction* (New York, 1929), p. 130.

[7] *Charles Dickens* (London, 1910), pp. 194–195.

[8] Gissing, p. 29; p. 182.

[9] *The Life of Dickens*, edited by J. W. T. Ley (New York, 1928), p. 524.

[10] Baker, p. 283; Leacock, p. 147.

James R. Kincaid

DAVID COPPERFIELD: LAUGHTER AND POINT OF VIEW

'Again, I wonder with a sudden fear whether it is likely that our good old clergyman can be wrong, and Mr. and Miss Murdstone right, and that all the angels in Heaven can be destroying angels.' (IV)

'The world would not take another Pickwick from me now',[1] Dickens wrote as he began work on *David Copperfield*. The truth was that the world as he saw it would no longer maintain the beautiful vision of *Pickwick*, and *David Copperfield* was to be an exploration of the external pressures which severely limit the possibilities of creating the internal Eden Pickwick had proposed. The comic society, though rather tenuous in several other of Dickens's novels, is here pushed to the distant outskirts of the world and is embodied only in a collection of the most distinctly misfit: the imprisoned, the alienated, the mad, and the dying. The comedy of accommodation hinted at in *Martin Chuzzlewit* is emphatically denied here. Jonas Chuzzlewit has taken over much of the world, and the presumably invincible Bailey is now shown, in David, to be terribly vulnerable. There are no resurrections; only the very, very sad recording of defeats, limitations, compromises. *David Copperfield* is no comedy, but a farewell to comedy. It is, in fact, the most reluctant farewell to comedy on record.

For David is extremely sensitive to the comic vision; he is born in the midst of gentleness and joy, and he never forgets that atmosphere. It is certainly his misfortune that the Murdstones enter his life, but it might also be said that it is equally unfortunate that he had enjoyed such an idyllic childhood before the murderers arrived. He is thrown directly from a rich and imaginative Eden into a mean and restricted cashbox version of reality. He leaves for Yarmouth from a home which has nothing but joy and returns to a home which has none. No transition and no connection are ever established between these worlds, and as a result it is not possible for him to find in life either complete commercial rigidity or full imaginative joy.[2] Although he later enters pretty fully into the Murdstonean ethic, he never absolutely abandons the perspective of his fragile and pathetic mother: 'What a troublesome world this is, when one has the most right to expect it to be as agreeable as possible!' (IV). David is always haunted by the sense of something missing, 'the old unhappy loss or want of something', and, like his mother, has the

From *Dickens and the Rhetoric of Laughter* (Oxford: Oxford University Press, 1971), pp. 162–91.

comic sense that things ought to be better, that one has a right to Eden. But the comic and commercial, the lovely and the firm, are never brought together, and David becomes something of a representative nineteenth-century man, for whom the realm of the imaginative, the spiritual, and the ideal is divorced from the realm of the pragmatic, the commercial, and the real. And, in place of a resolution, he adopts a very representative operating principle: a self-congratulatory firmness, modified by a compensating sentimentality. One can say, of course, that he comes to terms with his world, but the price he is asked to pay is enormous.

He must, as he says so often, 'discipline' his heart.[3] It has struck many readers that this is a terribly reductive formula for a humane and responsive existence, that it is priggish, escapist, ugly, and narrow, that it denies the values that count—those of Dora, the Micawbers, and Mr. Dick—and that this 'disciplining' is partly a euphemism for desensitizing, falsifying, sentimentalizing. All these charges are true; they are fully supported by the novel. But it is equally true that the novel is never ironic in the sense of attacking its hero; it is never critical of David's decisions. But it is very sad about them. *David Copperfield*'s famous tone of melancholy[4] is created by more than its bittersweet reminiscences; it is perhaps more to the point that these are reminiscences of defeat, of a world now lost. David's course, from joy to a pain so intense that it admits of no escape but only of more or less inadequate evasion, is one which is at the centre of the experience of the last two centuries. Indeed, it helps explain the novel's immense and continuing popularity. The primary means of the attempted escape are also common ones: the important comic values are denied, and trivial antithetical values are loudly proclaimed. David tries very hard to turn his novel into a celebration of prudence, distrust, discipline, rigid and unimaginative conduct, and the commonest sense. It is a cause both of his pain and of the novel's greatness that he has terrible difficulty ever accepting these values; their inadequacy and irrelevance are signalled over and over again.

There are really two major kinds of signals: the commercial values do not help David, and, in addition, they are disproved by the beauty and power of the improvident and the undisciplined in the novel. First of all, David's own proclamations of prudent sanity are outgrowths of a rather complete fantasy life, an unhealthy substitute forced on him first by the Murdstones, later by Steerforth, and even by his aunt, rescue by whom ironically pushes him into the delusory world of the Strongs and the Wickfields and finally into the aura (not the arms) of Agnes, who is a vaporous and shadowy attitude rather than a woman. The firm pragmatism David mouths, in other words, is never solidly realized in his existence and is, therefore, largely a compensation for the fact that he can accept fully neither the comic reality of the Micawbers nor the black reality of the Murdstones. He is thus forced, subtly but insistently, into the position of impotence and delusion where, with Agnes, he believes that 'real love and truth are stronger in the end than any evil or misfortune in the world' (XXXV). On the next page, David says that Agnes is indeed strong in 'simple love and truth', and it is these *simple* qualities which he thinks will somehow deal with the complexity of Uriah Heep or Murdstone or Steerforth. This blind trust in a vague Providence can, in the end, lead to the awful suspicion that 'all the angels in heaven' really are 'destroying angels' (IV). The same reliance also often renders David passive and impotent. When Rosa Dartle viciously attacks Mr. Peggotty, for example, David can only sputter, 'Oh, shame, Miss Dartle! shame!', and he later listens next door while Rosa verbally flays the newly found Em'ly. It is lucky that there are active comic agents, such as Micawber, Traddles, Mr. Dick, and Mr. Peggotty, around to participate actively and creatively in arranging their lives. These people and others like them also establish a strong value system directly opposed to David's (and Murdstone's) firmness. It is a subversive structure which is constantly in evidence. Micawber, for instance, the architect and most enthusiastic builder of this system, does not simply wander in and out of the plot; he appears strategically and on schedule as apologist and propagandist of his sense of comic community.

Thus, as in many of Dickens's earlier novels, there is a basic dualism, a split between the comic world of the imagination, and the threatening and hostile world of practical or commercial 'reality'. In *David Copperfield* this split receives its most subtle and mature treatment. The novel also makes the most complex use of the rhetorical humour Dickens had mastered. Laughter is used to establish values, themes, and, paradoxically, the atmosphere of melancholy. *David Copperfield* is one of the funniest of Dickens's novels but also one of the saddest; for all of the fun is enlisted on the side of forces which are finally extinguished.

The crucial issue, then, is related to the technical one of point of view: the relation of the novel's established values to those gradually accepted by David and the control of our attitude toward both sets of value. It seems to me essential that we recognize that David is, in many key ways, neither the voice of the author nor the voice of the novel. In any case, there are three clearly distinguished stages in the novel, in which the conditions of David's life, the values suggested, and the rhetorical techniques all shift radically and significantly:

i. *Childhood joy.* Chapters I–III. This section, though quite short, is extremely important in that it establishes an image of Eden which is never absent from David's mind but which is realized later only in tantalizing brief snatches. The laughter in this section not only supports the comic values associated with David's happy childhood but, interestingly, encourages us to reject as harmless many of the threats which will later become more precisely defined and much more dangerous.

ii. *Isolation and fear.* Chapters IV–XIII. This black period, the period of Murdstone, Creakle, and the warehouse, functions as a direct contrast to the first and makes impossible for David the openness, spontaneity, and trust necessary for comedy. The humour in this section is similar to that in *Oliver Twist,* acting as rhetoric of attack in order to demand our sympathy for and identification with David. It also begins to build, through Micawber, an alternate system.

These first thirteen chapters are the novel's most crucial ones in determining the character of the hero; they are also among the finest in English literature in forming a complete fusion with their subject and creating a total imaginative iden-tification with the child: George Orwell said that when he first read the early chapters, 'the mental atmosphere . . . was so immediately intelligible to me that I vaguely imagined they had been written *by a child*'.[5] They suggest the absolute necessity of comic joy; they also suggest its impossibility. These chapters urge us to identify with David, to sympathize with a value structure, and then to recognize that the two will likely never come together. The rest of the novel can be seen as the development of these dichotomies and of this rhetoric of frustration and melancholy.

iii. *Fantasy and firmness.* Chapters XIV–LXIV. The remaining chapters explore David's attempts to deal with the hostile world about him, his dependence upon fantasy, and his pathetically ironic drift towards Murdstonean firmness and sentimentality. Laughter here is asked continually to reinforce the comic value system, identify the split between this system and the hero, and try to heal it. It trails off altogether as David moves to Agnes and Micawber moves to Australia. The impossibility of a comic society must finally, and sadly, be admitted.

I

In Chapter III, Em'ly relates her vision of a future filled with wealth, generosity, and gentility, to which David responds, 'This seemed to me to be a very satisfactory, and therefore not at all improbable, picture.' The equation of the satisfactory with the probable only holds in Paradise, but this is where David seems to be for the first years of his life: a 'garden at the back . . . a very preserve of butterflies, as I remember it, with a high fence, and a gate and padlock; where the fruit clusters on the trees, riper and richer than fruit has ever been since, in any other garden' (II). The padlocked gate and high fence are subtle and ominous hints, of course, but they are quiet ones, and we are encouraged to imagine, with the boy, that his Eden is complete. Even crocodiles are imaginatively transformed to vegetables, and all predation and terror are banished from this happy, non-competitive world, supported throughout this section by a basically protective humour. Like other issues in this first section, however, the crocodiles become harder and harder to dismiss as the novel goes on, and this first deceptive allusion begins a chain of more and more significant references to animals, reflecting more and more closely the darker themes of the novel, and causing the initial laughter at the crocodiles to backfire. The transposition of animals and human beings suggests a basic and threatening inhumanity.

As David's position at home changes from that of a petted and much-loved only child to that of a victimized and lonely outcast, he gradually appears, both to himself and to the Murdstones, as less than human. Finally, the Murdstones complete this dehumanization by forcing on him a placard, '*Take care of him. He bites.*' The irony packed into the word 'care' emphasizes the brutality of this treatment as does David's complete acceptance of his animality. After looking for the dog that is to wear the sign and finding it is for him, he rejects utterly his own humanity and suffers a 'dread' of himself (V). The transfer from Murdstone to Creakle does not at all change his feelings. The other boys pretend that he is a dog, and he soon looks at Creakle's school as a veritable kennel, twice referring to the boys as 'miserable little dogs' (VII), who bait the poor 'bull or bear', Mr. Mell, and who are harassed by a keeper who whips them, asking at the same time, 'Did it bite, hey?' (VII).

David begins to adopt this dehumanizing vocabulary himself, not, however, to attack but only to achieve comfort in a fantasy life. No doubt unconsciously but still consistently, he speaks of good people as harmless domestic animals and evil people as dangerous predatory beasts. For example, Mr. Chillip is 'an amiable bird' (I); Barkis is 'like a horse' (III); David's brother is 'a poor lamb' (IX); Dr. Strong is like 'a blind old horse' (XVI); Traddles says he is a 'fretful porcupine' (XLI); Dora's aunts are 'little birds' (XLI); Dora is 'a Mouse' (XLIV); and Mr. Dick and Aunt Betsey are like 'a sheperd's dog' and 'a sheep' (LII). On the other hand, Mr. Murdstone is like a vicious dog (III); Miss Murdstone is a 'Dragon' (XXXVIII); and together they are 'two snakes' (IV); the Goroo man lives in a 'den' and has the 'claws of a great bird' (XIII); Steerforth (after his seduction of Em'ly) is 'a spotted snake' (LI); Mrs. Markleham is 'a crocodile' (XLV); Rosa Dartle is 'lynx-like' and shows the 'fury of a wild cat' (XXIX); and Uriah Heep is called at various times a 'serpent' (XLIX), a 'red-headed animal' (XXV), an 'Ape' (XXXV), an 'eel' (XXXV), a 'red fox' (XXXV), and he and his mother are likened to 'two great bats' (XXXIX).

David is tempted to make his life over into a kind of fairy-tale, but even then a dark fantasy emerges: what chance, for instance, do the lambs and mice have against the serpents, the apes, and the wild cats? Our first laughter at the crocodiles thus supports a comic and non-predatory world, which is ultimately seen as impossible.

The deceptive humour of the crocodiles is only one example of a technique often repeated in the first section; in many ways the very first chapter functions as a kind of reverse paradigm of the entire novel, bringing up nearly all of what will be the major threats, only to dismiss them in humour. Thus the initial Eden is a complete one, established in delight and fully protected by our laughter. The dark life which comes later reverses the opening of the novel virtually point-by-point, insisting that we recognize explicitly the loss of the beauty and joy of the garden. Even the mild jokes on the heroic birth which open the novel are preludes to the anti-heroism of the inactive protagonist. The first extended joke, however, involves the sale, as a safeguard against drowning, of the caul with which David was born. It is bought by an old lady who never goes near the water and is nevertheless (or therefore) cited as proof of the efficacy of cauls. The joke not only brings up the key symbol of the sea,[6] later to be identified explicitly with death, but also introduces the central thematic issues of prudence, delusion, and egoism, only to ask us to dismiss them in laughter. In much the same way, Miss Betsey flounces on the scene to suggest the comic possibilities of what are later to be seen as very dark tendencies: rigidity and iron composure. Her composure, further, is clearly compensatory, and the jeweller's cotton she stuffs in her ears suggests the forcible exclusion of unpleasant threats. Her vision of young Betsey Trotwood Copperfield, who 'must be well brought up, and well guarded from reposing any foolish confidences where they are not deserved' (I), foreshadows David's later disciplining of his heart; and her blunt, mad attack on Dr. Chillip prefigures all the mad and hostile clashes with which the novel is filled. Of course, all these issues are prefigured in a negative way: they are banished from serious consideration. Their later appearance, therefore, comes with greater force and poignancy.

Even at this early stage there are hints of the fall to come, primarily those connected with 'The Gentleman in the Black Whiskers' who takes David off on a trip and exposes him to the first dehumanizing laughter of exclusion: the boy is 'Bewitching Mrs. Copperfield's incumbrance', and he is forced to propose a toast, 'Confusion to Brooks of Sheffield!' (II). The characters' laughter here does not reflect the expansive, protective humour found elsewhere in this section, but hostile and aggressive impulses. More ominous still is Mr. Murdstone's failure to join in the day's general merriment. David's future stepfather even goes so far as to reject hostility itself if it has a communal quality. He is a man who resists all notions of community and is therefore the most dangerous to a comic society.

Significantly, David is shipped off to Yarmouth while Murdstone steps in to take his place at home, thus creating the pattern of escape and retreat the boy will be tempted to follow throughout. Peggotty's boat-house is indeed the centre of a potentially comic world, where all darkness is drained off in laughter at Mrs. Gummidge, a wonderful parody of misery. David is an alien in this world, however, and instinctively sees it as a 'retreat', not as a creative and burgeoning garden but as an evasion of a threat he cannot possibly fight. The magnitude of those threats and the impossibility of David's combating them have already been hinted at, then, as early as the third chapter. More important, our laughter has identified the qualities which the novel never ceases to regard as paramount and which are never seen as any less real than the values of Murdstone, just more difficult to establish. Perhaps the key joke in the whole section is a very quiet one: Murdstone, David says, asked for and received a flower from Mrs. Copperfield: 'He said he would never, never, part with it any more; and I thought he must be quite a fool not to know that it would fall to pieces in a day or two' (II). David's natural realism is thrown against Murdstone's hypocritical sentimentality, forecasting not only the later union of firmness and evasion but establishing the child's perspective as clearly superior. David is completely unsentimental; his early comic world has been to him totally real and has never needed falsification to produce happiness. Our laughter is enlisted in support of the child and his values, and in opposition to the hideous Murdstone. Even after we recognize that Murdstone is not dismissable and that David's comic perspective is lost, the humour continually forces us to remember that for a brief time there was this lovely world.

II

But not for long; the Murdstones move in and establish a reign not only of physical cruelty but also of the gloomiest kind of self-mastery based on self-distrust:

'Control yourself, always control yourself!" (III). The 'firmness' on which they take their doctrinal stand is rooted in a vicious Calvinism, which distrusts spontaneity, natural affection, the basic goodness of undisciplined and unrestrained man, in short, the very bases of comedy; and the real conflict in the novel is between their 'control' and Micawber's wild self-indulgence, between cash-boxes and steaming punch. At this point, however, Murdstone's values are in complete control, and our laughter is often used much as it was in *Oliver Twist*, to identify the cruelty in these values, to expose the shadow of cruelty in ourselves, and to push us closer to the alienated child. The rhetoric in this section, then, is a rhetoric of attack, tempting us to be momentarily amused at what turn out to be dangerous threats, at Miss Murdstone's being a 'metallic lady altogether' who snaps, 'Generally speaking . . . I don't like boys. How d'ye do, boy?' (IV), or at her brother's elaborate puzzles involving double-Gloucester cheeses. We soon notice, though, that Miss Murdstone's dehumanizing, somewhat mad, treatment of David is really an accurate sampling of later confrontations, and Mr. Murdstone's puzzle, at which 'Miss Murdstone [is] secretly overjoyed', is only a type of the malicious wit common to all the many sadists in the novel. The hostility latent in this wit—and in any laughter it may have aroused—is unmistakably exposed in the horrible beating David receives for failing with the puzzle. Even worse than the beating, however, is the alienation of the boy from love and comfort, the door Murdstone symbolically throws up between David and his mother and nurse. The humour connected with the Murdstones, then, is meant finally to draw us closer to David and to his pain, confusion, and isolation.

It also enables us to understand better why he turns to romantic tales and eighteenth-century novels for 'my only and my constant comfort'. But instead of building an expansive and healthy imaginative life as it might this single comfort tends to become a narcotic, sustaining but dangerous. David still sees himself 'sitting on my bed, reading as if for life' (IV). It is, literally, for *life*. He begins here the fantasy role which never leaves him, although it does change form: from Steerforth and the story-telling in the dark, to the vague second childhood at Dover, to the tragically disrupted comic life with Dora, and finally to the less-than-substantial Agnes. Murdstone really gives David two choices: firmness or escape. He finally chooses to try for a combination, but now he only wants to escape. The awful fact is that these terrifying and impossible choices are being forced on a boy far too young to make them by himself. But he is completely alone; the good people are all on the other side of the locked door.

It is an interesting secondary function of the humour in this section to trivialize many of these good people or eliminate them from consideration. Mr. Barkis the carrier, for instance, is introduced as one of the most freakishly inhuman of Dickens's comic grotesques: 'I offered him a cake as a mark of attention, which he ate at one gulp, exactly like an elephant, and which made no more impression on his big face than it would have done on an elephant's' (V). This impassive man is a kind of joke on the absence of response and the non-humanity of the supposedly human. His affections are somehow connected to his gastric juices, and he decides then and there to make a play for the matter of those cakes, even though he has some considerable trouble getting her name straight. His magnificent phrase, 'Barkis is willin' ', seems a joke on the failure of commitment, a perfect image of a kind of absorbent stomach-creature that gulps everything into itself and renders human notions of intelligence and emotion ludicrous. He appears, in other words, as an apparent 'relief' figure to drain our apprehensions and to release some of the intensity created by David's plight. Barkis seems to be a comic Murdstone, no more human but not in the least threatening.

As it happens, though, Barkis truly is willin', and this curiously touching phrase begins really to separate him from Murdstone's values and to associate itself with openness and friendliness, with a limited but genuine comic expansiveness: 'I'm a friend of your'n. You made it all right, first. It's all right' (X). In the midst of hostility, meanness, and cruelty, this declaration is terribly important. It belies altogether the basis of any laughter at this 'great stuffed figure' (X). What happens here is that we are forced to recognize how unlikely and how rare are the manifestations of friendship in this black world, and how very precious are those who are willin'. We are also asked to take a much closer look at Barkis, and when we do, we see that this supposed comic grotesque is a very functional character indeed. After marrying Peggotty, he becomes obsessed not so much with money as with the prudent resolve to protect that money. His crazy box stands as a parody indictment not only of Murdstone's value system, but, ironically, of David's as well. He pokes at his box and announces:

> 'Old clothes.'
> 'Oh!' said I.
> 'I wish it was Money, sir,' said Mr. Barkis.
> 'I wish it was, indeed,' said I.
> 'But it AIN'T,' said Mr. Barkis, opening both his eyes as wide as he possibly could. (XXI)

Significantly, however, he continues, 'more gently': 'She's the usefullest and best of women, C. P. Barkis. All the praise that any one can give to C. P. Barkis she deserves, and more! My dear, you'll get a dinner to-day, for company; something good to eat and drink, will you?' (XXI). He is an insanely disjointed man, a daffy mixture of the generous and the 'near', and we see him, finally, as a heightened and dramatic symbol of the open and willing heart corrupted by the ossifying pressures of prudence, as a signal of the potential beauty of man but also of the great dangers of the world. His death encapsulates his functional humour. Flopped over on his box, literally protecting it with his life, he manages, just at the end, to show the inner strength of his comic and generous impulses:

> 'C. P. Barkis,' he cried faintly. 'No better woman anywhere!'
> 'Look! Here's Master Davy!' said Peggotty. For he now opened his eyes.
> I was on the point of asking him if he knew me, when he tried to stretch out his arm, and said to me, distinctly, with a pleasant smile:
> 'Barkis is willin'!'
> And, it being low water, he went out with the tide. (XXX)

This death is one of the most costly in the novel; it removes one of David's willing friends. The comic carrier, initially too weak and too far away really to help the boy, has become, by the time of his death, a comic indictment of the firmness David is moving towards. Our laughter at Barkis has helped to increase our sense of the importance of joy to David and to determine later how far he is moving away from the values of the carrier. Mr. Barkis has, in his way, presented a form of hope to David, but the form has been too distorted for the boy to recognize it, and the alternate pressures have been far too strong.

The more common function of our laughter in this section, in fact, is to insist on the strength of the camp of the firm and the hostile, and the more usual jokes are of the deceptive kind exemplified by the waiter whom David meets on his way to Creakle's school. The waiter seems at first to be very much like Sam Weller, hearty, open, and witty. He 'very affably' calls to David, using Sam's own terms, 'Now, six-foot! come on!' Even the stories he devises to cheat David of his food are so resourceful and wild with such apparently undirected hostility that we are very likely to laugh: A gentleman 'in breeches and gaiters, broad-brimmed hat, grey coat, speckled choker', he says, 'came in here . . . ordered a glass of this ale—*would* order it—I told him not—drank it, and fell dead. It was too old for him. It oughtn't to be drawn; that's the fact' (V). He does, indeed, seem not only witty but, as David says, 'so very friendly and companionable' that it comes as a shock that he is *only* a cheat, malicious and cruel. When David tells him he is going to school 'near London', the waiter invents a story of a boy at the same school, just David's age, whose ribs were broken 'with whopping'. He then insists on taking one of David's shillings as a tip and joins with the crowd in laughing at the boy's huge appetite. The apparent friendliness has been a guise, and the wit has been hostile and self-serving, isolating and hurting the helpless child. Dickens then rubs our noses in the consequences of this reversal, insisting over and over in the next few pages on David's loneliness ('more solitary than Robinson Crusoe'), his feeling of abandonement (no one calls for him at the booking-office, and he thinks for a time that 'Murdstone had devised this plan to get rid of me'), and his dehumanization (the clerk 'presently slanted me off the scale, and pushed me over to him, as if I were weighed, bought, delivered, and paid for').

He then moves to Creakle's school, where the deceptive humour is continued. We are invited to share in a kind of Hobbesian laughter at the man with no voice at all, but it is soon apparent that Creakle is no weakling to be dismissed. He is, rather, a continuation of Mr. Murdstone: 'I am a determined character. . . . That's what I am. I do my duty. That's what I do' (VI). 'Duty', we begin to understand, is a convenient euphemism which many characters—Murdstone, Creakle, Aunt Betsey, Mrs. Steerforth, Mr. Wickfield, Agnes, and later even David—use to cover sadism, sexual perversion, weakness, or incapacity. The world at Creakle's, then, is just as dark as the one at home, and David again turns to the only escape at hand, this time made more sinister in the figure of Steerforth, who begins by simply continuing the role of the waiter, cheating the boy of his money. He then forces David to retell his old stories in the dark, which even the young boy admits 'may not have been very profitable to me' since it encouraged all 'that was romantic and dreamy' (VII) in him. Steerforth does nothing to protect David from Creakle's mistreatment and, as a fantasy figure for the younger boy, is dangerous both to him and to others. The older boy symbolically joins hands with Creakle in expelling the one kindly figure, Mr. Mell, suggesting, in relation to David, the deadly union of determination with fantasy. More important, Steerforth does not really deflect the training in firmness away from David; he only encourages the dangerous tendencies to fantasy escape.

So David really has no choice. The forces of blackness close in around him and eventually make all happiness alien to him, isolating him from other men and implying that, in the face of his situation and the ugly world it suggests, all laughter is really self-centred and reprehensible. This attack on laughter is most pointedly illustrated by the undertaker, Mr. Omer, and his family. Mr. Omer is a character out of *Martin Chuzzlewit*, a relative of Mr. Mould's, who tries to build joy out of darkness, operating his business rather as if it were a confectioner's shop. In the environment of *David Copperfield*, however, such efforts seem callous, perhaps hideous. The ability to whistle to the happy rat-tat-tat of the hammer on the coffin is no longer applauded. David is met by Omer on his way home from school at the time of his mother's death. The undertaker takes David to his shop to measure him for mourning clothes and to check up on the progress of Mrs. Copperfield's coffin and the love-making of his daughter and his partner Joram. For a considerable space, the narrative focus is removed from David, and we are allowed to bask in the comic glow:

'Father!' said Minnie, playfully. 'What a porpoise you do grow!'

'Well, I don't know how it is, my dear,' he replied, considering about it. 'I *am* rather so.'

'You are such a comfortable man, you see,' said Minnie. 'You take things so easy.'

'No use taking 'em otherwise, my dear,' said Mr. Omer.

'No, indeed,' returned his daughter. 'We are all pretty gay here, thank Heaven! Ain't we, father?' (IX)

It sounds for a moment very much like a voice from Mrs. Todgers's. Soon, however, ugly hints intrude. 'I knew your father before you', Mr. Omer says in his continually amiable way, but then he continues, 'He lays in five and twen–ty foot of ground, if he lays in a fraction. . . . It was either his request or her direction, I forget which.' The fact that this is said 'pleasantly' makes it all the more ghastly. The joy begins to be as excluding and alienating to David as Murdstone's cruelty, and Dickens begins to insist more openly on the cruelty of any laughter. The three bustle David into a chaise and boisterously roll off, with Mr. Omer chuckling while Joram steals kisses from Minnie. Joram 'didn't appear to mind me at all', David says, and the humour has tempted us to be equally neglectful of the outcast and or-phaned boy. He admits finally that he is 'afraid of them'. 'I do not think I have ever experienced so strange a feeling in my life', he says, adding that he felt 'as if I were cast among creatures with whom I had no community of nature'. Anyone who can laugh, then, is a 'creature', unfeeling and awful. The image is one of an inverted Mrs. Jarley's or Mrs. Todgers's: the joy creates discomfort and excludes those who need it most. Ultimately it reinforces the pessimistic vision at the heart of the novel that sees a world in which the comic life is open only to a very few—and not at all to the hero.

It has been closed for him by the Murdstones, who have so mangled his youth that a part of his psychic life is now frozen. He sees all joy as past, as contained in the brief time before firmness entered his life: 'From the moment of my knowing of the death of my mother, the idea of her as she had been of late had vanished from me. I remembered her, from that instant, only as the young mother of my earliest impressions, who had been used to wind her bright curls round and round her finger, and to dance with me at twilight in the parlour. . . . The mother who lay in the grave, was the mother of my infancy; the little creature in her arms [David's dead brother], was myself, as I had once been, hushed for ever on her bosom' (IX). By the time the Murdstones send him out for his 'fight with the world' in the warehouse, he has already lost the chance for what he most wants and needs: the sort of life presented so brilliantly and so completely by the enemies of Murdstone and Grinby, cash-boxes, and firmness—Mr. and Mrs. Micawber. This great pair function to express periodically throughout the novel the beauty and importance of comic existence; because they do this so very well, they are the major cause of the book's final sadness. They remind us of nothing so much as of the life that has been stolen from David.

A. O. J. Cockshut has made the perceptive comment that it is never possible to give proportionate space to the Micawbers, that one, very literally, cannot say nearly enough.[7] The tendency (as is evident here) is to talk about analysing them rather than doing it. This is partly because Mr. Micawber is perhaps the most organically complete of comic characters; even his clothes (particularly the ornamental eye-glass and the 'imposing shirt-collar') are a part of his perfectly harmonizing style, suggesting the wonderful comic notion that man has the power to create himself. The difficulty, however, comes also from the enormously rich and various functional role Mr. and Mrs. Micawber play. They climax a great line of Dickens's comic characters and carry on the role of Sam Weller as tutor and seer, Dick Swiveller as parodist, Sairey Gamp as imaginative creator. They not only combine these parts but are truly greater than their sum. And in the novel they fail. All their kindness, their creative genius, their courage, and their infinite resiliency cannot keep David from the trap of the sentimental and the firm. But they do create a system of values which, with the help of characters like Mr. Dick, Peggotty, Barkis, and Miss Mowcher, and with the great support of our laughter, maintains one-half of the conflict in the novel: the approved but impossible life of the imagination.

It is often and truly said that Micawber builds worlds of delight out of words, but he finds joy not only in words but in arranging his unnecessary quizzing-glasses, not only in writing letters but in creating a 'library' out of a few books and a dressing table. Even more significant, his presence even distinguishes his house, making it 'unlike all the other houses in the street—though they were all built on one monotonous pattern' (XXVII). He is, above all, ornamental, which is to say, a walking attack on prudence and practicality. He and his wife live deeply in the commercial world only to make fun of it and turn potential sources of anxiety into rituals of cheer, motives for exquisite melodrama, and, most important, into exaggerated depths from which to rebound into joyous celebrations: 'I saw her lying (of course with a twin) under the grate in a swoon, with her hair all torn about her face; but I never knew her more cheerful than she was, that very same night, over a veal-cutlet before the kitchen fire, telling me stories about her papa and mama, and the company they used to keep' (XI). The principle seems totally to be one of resilience: the more the Micawbers are pushed downward the higher they spring back. In fact, much of the deepest-rooted humour of the Micawbers is based on this paradoxically mechanical elasticity, the sense that they do rebound automatically, rather like a rubber ball.

But beyond this there is the deep power of their conscious and courageous fight against an almost overwhelmingly dark and threatening social system. They act out a burlesque of their troubles, distancing their pain, of course, but also humanizing the almost inhuman. All disasters are welcomed as proof of their own exceptional humanity, giving rise to scenes of potential grand suicide, tragic sacrifice, and magnificent decisions of alliance: ' "Mr. Micawber has his faults. I do not deny that he is improvident. I do not deny that he has kept me in the dark as to his resources and his liabilities, both," she went on, looking at the wall; "but I will never desert Mr. Micawber!" ' (XII). A tradesman's bill is a small price to pay for the chance to play Cleopatra every day or two. And behind the ring of the phrases and the echo of a million melodramas is the continual thrill of the assertive, unrestrained, and glamorized ego of comedy: 'All I have to say on that score is, that the cloud has passed from the dreary scene, and the God of Day is once more high upon the mountain tops. On Monday next, on the arrival of the four o'clock afternoon coach at Canterbury, my foot will be on my native heath—my name, Micawber!' (XXXVI). By welcoming these small disasters from the commercial society and creatively transforming them, the Micawbers avoid the really greatest threats of that society: dehumanization and despair. They have found the great and complex secret of joy in a commercial world.

This secret is very difficult to decipher fully, but at least a few parts of it are clear. First, the Micawbers have absolutely renounced the system and (except for the brief lapse with Uriah Heep) make no concessions in their war against it. Dickens here separates completely the notion of the good heart from the notion of commercial success and thereby creates a greater Pickwick, incidentally solving the problem of what Mr. Pickwick did 'in the city' all those years. Micawber is a coalescence of the notions embodied in Mr. Pickwick and Sam and a clear renunciation of the Brownlow-Cheeryble concept. Second, they carry on the great subversive tradition of attacking the system by parody. Mr. Micawber is active here, particularly in his recurrent burlesque of the alert and ruthless businessman waiting to spring on the first opportunity, but the major burden is carried by his wife, whose 'business habits' and 'prudent suggestions' (XXXVI) he has learned to depend on. 'My disposition', she says, 'is eminently practical' (LVII), and she proves it over and over again with rigorous analyses which ought to make all corporate flunkies, government commissions, and faculty advisory groups blush: ' "We came," repeated Mrs. Micawber, "and saw the Medway. My opinion of the coal trade on that river is, that it may require talent, but that it certainly requires capital. Talent, Mr. Micawber has; capital, Mr. Micawber has not. We saw, I think, the greater part of the Medway, and that is my individual conclusion" ' (XVII).

But the Micawbers really spend comparatively little time on such negative parody functions. They are probably the most open and expansive of Dickens's comic characters, accepting with resounding confidence in themselves and their powers the whole range of the shabbiest existence and refusing any sort of escape or falsification. They suggest not only that life is bearable but that it can be wonderful. 'Experientia does it—as papa used to say' (XI). *Experientia* certainly does it for the Micawbers at any rate; it provides them with a chance to dedicate their lives to joy. There is no image so firmly associated with them as that of Mr. Micawber working happily in the midst of lemon-peel and sugar, rum, and steaming water, making a punch instead of a fortune and, as David says, enjoying himself more than any man he ever saw. ' "But punch, my dear Copperfield," said Mr. Micawber, tasting it, "like time and tide, waits for no man" ' (XXVIII). The subversive substitution is clear; Micawber transforms the clichés of the Murdstone economy into justifications for parties. The Micawbers are grandly anti-Malthusian, blissfully arguing that 'in our children we [live] again, and that, under the pressure of pecuniary difficulties, any accession to their number [is] doubly welcome' (XXVIII). Whatever doubts Mrs. Micawber's prudent family have on this point simply provide Mr. Micawber with an opportunity for splendid Byronic denunciations of that socially prominent group. The mean, niggardly, frightened spirit of order and balance was never more blatantly flouted than by Mrs. Micawber's always-busy 'Founts' or, for that matter, by Mr. Micawber's epistolary style, which takes arms specifically against the previous century's leading proponent of the organized and the clear-headed: 'I am about to establish myself in one of the provincial towns of our favoured island (where the society may be described as a happy admixture of the agricultural and the clerical) . . . Our ashes, at a future period, will probably be found commingled in the cemetery attached to a venerable pile, for which the spot to which I refer has acquired a reputation, shall I say from China to Peru?' (XXXVI).

Finally, the Micawbers are powerful because they love.[8] They are not only unembarrassed in their show of warmth to one another, but also to others, particularly David. This warmth is manifested most openly in the touching scene where, in leaving London, Mrs. Micawber looked down from the coach, saw how small David really was (she had been in the friendly habit of thinking of him as an equal), called him up on the coach, 'and put her arm round my neck, and gave me just such a kiss as she might have given to her own boy' (XII). Every speech of Mr. Micawber's asserts, though more indirectly, the same warm response. He comes into the blacking warehouse and begins his magnificent oratory to David, inter-

rupting it with an inevitable 'in short'. As inevitable as the self-parodying 'in short',
however, is its accompanying manner: 'with a smile and in a burst of confidence',
with an offer, in other words, of intimacy and connection. In the midst of the mad
hostility of cheating waiters, vicious tinkers, and raving Goroo men, Micawber's
undefensive warmth is strangely highlighted. Even his endless stream of letters
suggests his fight against the silence and systematic alienation of Murdstone's system.
The Micawbers are great, finally, because they offer, even in the face of this threat,
not mutual protection but mutual fun. Their comic society is undefensive and open.
'Friend of my youth, the companion of my earlier days' Micawber loves later to call
David, associating himself not only with the friendly Mr. Barkis but also, and more
specifically, with Falstaff's great and equally anti-prudent battle-cry, 'They hate us
youth'. Indeed they do, and there are few like Micawber who cannot only live with
hatred but transform it for his family and for others, even briefly for David, into
happiness.

But it is too late for David fully to accept the secret of existence offered him
by the Micawbers. All trust, openness, and hope for joy have been either extinguished or perverted in him. In addition, the Micawbers are forced to leave London, taking with them the answer both necessary and unavailable to David. Left
alone and without consolation of any sort, David runs away to Dover and to his
Aunt Betsey. His flight through the countryside, significantly, is like a tour through
the Chamber of Horrors: the donkey-driver, the tinker, the Goroo man, all fly out
and terrify him with their mad, uncaused hostility. Even in Dover, no one will tell
him where his aunt lives, simply because he is asking. The shopkeepers there, with
their immovable coldness, are paradigmatic of the nightmare world, alternately
chasing and rejecting the boy: 'not liking my appearance, [they] generally replied,
without hearing what I had to say, that they had got nothing for me' (XIII). They
surely do not, but David has nowhere else to go.

Aunt Betsey is a gentle and kindly person, but she does not have Mr. Micawber's secret. Instead of highly developed elasticity, she has a compensatory firmness; she lacks optimism, creative power, and imaginative hope. She and Mr. Dick
are themselves partly on the run, she from her husband, Mr. Dick from the relatives
who threaten to lock him up. In the artificial firmness which resolutely attacks not
real enemies but donkeys, and in the mad, gentle man who holds his head like 'one
of Mr. Creakle's boys after a beating' (XIII), he might be seen a combined image of
what David finally becomes. This retreat at Dover allows David to view his life 'like
one in a dream' (XV), and the repeated references to new beginnings carry an
ironic sense. He moves into an artificial and very fragile haven, where Aunt Betsey
counsels him to be firm, where Agnes takes Steerforth's place as reading partner,
and where, in 'the soft light of the coloured windows in the church' (XVI), Uriah
Heep and Jack Maldon can be dismissed in fantasy.

Aunt Betsey and Mr. Dick do try very hard, but in the end this collection of
outcasts is too defensive to help the boy much, and the humour connected with
them is deceptive. Nowhere is this deception more crucial than in Aunt Betsey's
encounter with the Murdstones. The refinement and reserve of much of this scene

seem to induce the kind of 'laughter of the mind' advocated by George Meredith.[9] Meredith sees the true Comic Spirit as 'a most subtle delicacy' (p. 3) employed in a truly cultivated way. Its function is calmly to expose Folly, to pour the light of common sense on the overblown, the disproportionate, and the self-important (p. 48). Miss Betsey's comments to the pompous Jane Murdstone provide just this kind of deflation:

> 'I so far agree with what Miss Trotwood has remarked,' observed Miss Murdstone, bridling, 'that I consider our lamented Clara to have been, in all essential respects, a mere child.'
> 'It is a comfort to you and me, ma'am,' said my aunt, 'who are getting on in life, and are not likely to be made unhappy by our personal attractions, that nobody can say the same of us.' (XIV)

Jane Murdstone is, at the end of the interview, left sputtering and angry, and her exposure seems complete. But what of the silent Mr. Murdstone? Meredith says the Comic Spirit pursues Folly to the end, 'never fretting, never tiring, sure of having her' (p. 33). But here there are strong indications that the enemy is not really overcome.

Far from being defeated, in fact, Jane Murdstone does reappear as Dora Spenlow's companion to harass David, and Mr. Murdstone is left to pursue his wicked ways, unencumbered by a child. Aunt Betsey's 'victory' has thus produced a disturbingly ironic result: Murdstone is relieved of a boy whom he had already thwarted to his satisfaction and who could now be nothing but a hindrance. He is left free to extend his malevolence to other weak mothers and helpless boys (see LIX). The originally benign scene thus becomes, by the end of the novel, a very dark one. The Comic Spirit which had seemed so effective is rendered powerless, and the civilized laughter is shown to be incomplete and inadequate. The final sugges-tion is that this kind of Murdstonean power is not available to the good, and in this light Agnes Wickfield's simple trust is misplaced and her position very dangerous. There are, it seems, two honourable positions open: the imaginative and happy subversive warfare of the Micawbers or a retreat from the battle. One either renounces the terms of the fight or is beaten.

III

The basic pattern of the novel, then, has been established. Only the outcasts are loyal and open to David; those in power are rigid and hostile. The boy then moves, in the rest of the novel, to look for an opening that is never there for long. Except for the comic joy of the outcasts, not available to him anyhow, he finds only the happy but dangerously flabby second childhood of the Wickfields or the hard, successful commercialism of Murdstone. The rest of his life can be seen as an attempt to combine the last two. Much of our laughter functions in this last section to remind us of the Eden David has lost, to show that the black world makes it impossible for him, and to suggest how limited his responses are.

He moves through a tragic marriage to the acceptance of simple notions of a disciplined heart, to a final union which seems to resolve none of the basic problems. He joins the firmly successful and the blurring escapists, the Agnes who is not only unable to stop Uriah Heep's subtle attacks on the Wickfield firm but who actually urges her father to enter into a partnership with Heep because she felt 'it was necessary for Papa's peace' (XXV). Peace indeed! It is significant that those who are opposed to Murdstone are equally opposed to this sort of peace, and, when they are shipped off to Australia at the end, it is suggested, perhaps, that they are irrelevant to the mature David but more likely that they are incompatible with nineteenth-century England. The letters from Micawber keep coming, though, to remind us of what is missing, and the humour is used more and more to define a lost world and to point towards the ironic position David moves close to: a gentler version of Murdstone, who likewise doesn't know that the flowers will wither in a day or so. Two instances of this sad and deceptive humour are especially prominent: the marriage to Dora and Micawber's exposure of Heep.

The Micawbers have all along been conducting a kind of triumphal Progress, parodying commerce and business in all the provinces of England and promoting their own brand of comic society. They function rhetorically to redefine all the important values and to measure David's increasing distance from them as he stuffily warns Traddles against his friends (XXVIII) and finally calls Micawber 'slippery' (XXXVI). These judgements, echoed, incidentally, in George Orwell's perverse conclusion that Micawber is nothing but a 'cadging scoundrel',[10] simply indicate two increasingly incompatible systems. Micawber's borrowing, as W. H. Auden points out in reference to another great borrower, Falstaff, is an important sign of community,[11] establishing a necessary interdependence. In return for money, Micawber gives language, punch, and happiness; these seem insufficient returns only to a perspective which takes money seriously, as David certainly does and as Micawber certainly does not. But Micawber does take joy seriously, and his positive function becomes more emphatic, moving to a climax in the wonderful denunciation and exposure of Uriah Heep (LII).

That Micawber ever gets into the clutches of Uriah suggests, I suppose, the extreme power of commercial forces which can enmesh, even briefly, such a clear-sighted enemy. There is even the darker suggestion that Micawber must engage himself for a time in their camp in order to acquire weapons, that only those who are in some way corrupted can fight at all. But there is, concurrently, the sense that Mr. Micawber is arranging for himself a new part to play, with new lines, new poses, new outfits, and new opportunities for exercising his wild imagination in mock forecasts of doom: 'For anything that I can perceive to the contrary, it is still probable that my children may be reduced to seek a livelihood by personal contortion, while Mrs. Micawber abets their unnatural feats, by playing the barrel-organ' (XLIX). Notice no factories or warehouses appear here; even his misery is fun. Finally, the general situation simply allows an extremely apt and aesthetically satisfying movement from the mysterious, secretive, and reserved back to the open, confident, and trusting. Mr. Micawber's organic unity is disrupted—'his very

eye-glass seemed to hang less easily, and his shirt-collar...rather drooped'
(XLIX)—and must be put right.

Equally significant is the nature of the villain. Uriah Heep is really a kind of
Alfred Jingle, resilient, courageous, witty, and very bitter. He is the product of a
hypocritical benevolence which produced charity schools that taught both humility
and firm assertiveness, and his response to David's simple reflections is both cutting
and valid:

> 'It may be [David said] profitable to you to reflect, in future, that there
> never were greed and cunning in the world yet, that did not do too much, and
> over-reach themselves. It is as certain as death.'
>
> 'Or as certain as they used to teach at school (the same school where I
> picked up so much umbleness), from nine o'clock to eleven, that labour was
> a curse; and from eleven o'clock to one, that it was a blessing and a cheer-
> fulness, and a dignity, and I don't know what all, eh?' said he with a sneer. 'You
> preach, about as consistent as they did.'

He is right in attacking the soft-headed, the sentimental, and the insensitive realism
that measures things against death and smugly assumes that anyone will choose the
most *profitable* course. To this rightness he adds a surprising wit, suggesting both
intelligence and, since he is so clearly cornered, real courage:

> 'You know what I want?' said my aunt.
> 'A strait-waistcoat,' said he.

But Uriah is vindictive. He is the apotheosis of the hurt and vengeful figure, part
victim and part villain, who had appeared earlier as Jingle, Fagin, Sim, and Quilp.
Micawber's victory is not over evil—only David views the fight in such narrow
terms—but over the sensitivity that pushed into violence and bitterness. Micawber affirms not goodness but comic optimism.

And he does so with the richness and rounded, complete perfection that
characterizes all his actions. The exposure is, first of all, wonderfully arranged by
Micawber, who uses his considerable talents as a stage-director to get every effect
right. He uses, of course, a letter as the means of the exposure, not because it is
in any sense necessary (Micawber is always an enemy of the necessary) but because
it is a fitting medium of the dramatic and the openly and articulately communicative.
He provides himself with a simple but brilliantly appropriate prop, a ruler. He
transforms this instrument of precision and order first to a kind of wand used to
point the grandest phrases and provide the most emphatic flourishes and then to
a mock duelling weapon to keep Uriah at bay. It is all very much like an extremely
imaginative child playing in an office, and it carries, on a much higher level, the same
implicit criticism of the office. Micawber also masquerades as a firm and aggressively
insistent champion of the right—he is called 'immovable'—and functions thereby as
an indirect lesson to all the truly firm that it is comic flexibility that really is
profitable.

The unique greatness of his triumph lies in its absolute lack of real personal vengeance. All his energy is directed toward gaiety, toward the relish that he has and that he gives to others in the endless fun available in words: 'In an accumulation of Ignominy, Want, Despair, and Madness, I entered the office—or, as our lively neighbour the Gaul would term it, the bureau—of the Firm, nominally conducted under the appellation of Wickfield and—HEEP, but, in reality, wielded by—HEEP alone.' He is obviously spurred on not so much by the desire to set things right as by the exquisite possibilities in the name HEEP. His letter is really a collection of 'triumphant flourishes', and the real victory is one of language. As he reaches the end of his charges, he is unable to hold on to the logical and orderly listing he had been straining to follow and he breaks out, just at the end, in a final phrase that destroys the logic but gives a mad and wonderful hint of the joy beyond logic: 'All this I undertake to show. Probably much more!' He completes the act decorously by folding up his letter and handing it 'with a bow to my aunt, as something she might like to keep'. The letter, we see, is what counts—not Heep. The scene ends with Micawber back in the arms of his wife, re-forming the comic unit and, like the Phoenix he is always invoking, starting off again on a life of improvidence, refreshed and confident: ' "Now, welcome poverty!" cried Mr. Micawber, shedding tears. "Welcome misery, welcome houselessness, welcome hunger, rags, tempest, and beggary! Mutual confidence will sustain us to the end!" '

Ultimately, though, the full context of the novel does not absorb the comic triumph. Even in the midst of the exposure scene, it is suggested that the narrator misunderstands the important nature of the conflict. He can even make fun of Micawber: 'And as individuals get into trouble by making too great a show of liveries, or as slaves when they are too numerous rise against their masters, so I think I could mention a nation that has got into many great difficulties, and will get into many greater, from maintaining too large a retinue of words.' This comes at the end of a paragraph wherein David parades his fagged-out worldly knowledge, tiredly minimizing the power of Micawber and missing the real point completely. Micawber has really just separated the two worlds in the novel, his world of comedy from the world of commercial reality. He cannot, it seems, establish his as victorious for the representative David. Even his own restoration is really a res-toration to a position from which he can make no more exposures, and the atypicality and limitations of his triumph become more emphatically insisted on as its inability to influence David is added to its apparent inability really to affect Uriah. We see Uriah, in the end, joined with Littimer in an institution run by Creakle, surrounded by an approving and admiring society. He is obviously poised for a leap back into the commercial fray, no doubt made more cagey by his last experience. The sad conclusion is that neither victory nor happiness is available to David, maybe not to his world, and the triumphant joy is finally cancelled.

Even more deceptive is the humour attending the idyllic courtship and the later marriage of David and Dora. The tone throughout these chapters is tender, protective, and very sad, in consonance with the saddest and most significant of the hero's actions. He says he 'was wandering in a garden of Eden all the while, with Dora' (XXVI), but the truth is that he cannot stay there, nor can he allow her to.

The garden and the lovely child are destroyed, and with them the possibility of comic life.

Dora's position is at the heart of a kind of fragile and tender comedy: 'I heard the empress of my heart sing enchanted ballads in the French language, generally to the effect that, whatever was the matter, we ought always to dance, Ta ra la, Ta ra la! accompanying herself on a glorified instrument, resembling a guitar' (XXVI). But even before the marriage there are shadows on her dedication to dancing; the ominous Miss Murdstone turns up as a 'protector' ('Who wants a protector?' Dora significantly asks, in her comic openness) and Julia Mills is around to play vampire to their joys and miseries: 'though she mingled her tears with mine . . . she had a dreadful luxury in our afflictions. She petted them, as I may say, and made the most of them.' David admits, 'she made me much more wretched than I was before' (XXXVIII). She is a deceptively funny symbol of the secret desire of the world to destroy the happiness of the young and the beautiful: 'Ye May-flies, enjoy your brief existence in the bright morning of life!' (XXXIII). Though she often sounds very much like Micawber and, like him, loves nothing so much as a well-mixed metaphor—'the oasis in the desert of Sahara must not be plucked up idly'—she is actually mean and twisted, and any laughter at her is turned back on us. But surviving and nearly obliterating these shadows is this valid image of Dora as innocence, purity, and love: 'sitting on a garden seat under a lilac tree, what a spectacle she was, upon that beautiful morning, among the butterflies, in a white chip bonnet and a dress of celestial blue' (XXXIII). The butterflies recall the 'preserve of butterflies' in David's own childhood garden, and Dora certainly recalls the boy's equally lovely and fragile mother. David is reaching for an Eden that was once there but can be no longer, not so much because he senses any pattern of incest but because he is not allowed to accept the Micawber values which Dora holds. She does, however, impress them on him for a time; the engagement flies, as it should, directly in the face of prudence. But David, with awful irony, thinks his judgement superior to hers, and even the adult narrator seems to have no real notion of what he has lost: 'What an unsubstantial, happy, foolish time it was!' (XXXIII). Such language simply indicates the extreme distance between the comic reality of the engagement and the narrator's businesslike version of reality. The clash of these two worlds is made clear throughout, as Dora confronts him with the irrefutable logic of comedy:

> 'My love,' said I, 'I have work to do.'
> 'But don't do it!' returned Dora. 'Why should you?'
> It was impossible to say to that sweet little surprised face, otherwise than lightly and playfully, that we must work to live.
> 'Oh! How ridiculous!' cried Dora.
> 'How shall we live without, Dora?' said I.
> 'How? Any how!' said Dora. (XXXVII)

But David is unhappily caught by alternate values, which, ironically, he calls 'the source of my success': 'habits of punctuality, order, and diligence', 'thorough-going, ardent, and sincere earnestness' (XLII), and other such labels of the commercial ant-hill. And he moves to a marriage in which, again and again, he finds that he 'had wounded Dora's soft little heart, and she was not to be comforted' (XLIV). The gentle humour is, thus, deceptive; the clash of the two worlds causes real misery.

It is true that the marriage begins in laughter—the dinner-party at which Traddles is served the unopened oysters, for instance—but as it goes on Dickens insists more and more on the pain. Dora is pushed to acknowledge her limitations in David's world and to plead with him pathetically to relegate her to a low position in it: 'When I am very disappointing, say, "I knew, a long time ago, that she would make but a child-wife!" When you miss what I should like to be, and I think can never be, say, "still my foolish child-wife loves me!" For indeed I do' (XLIV). Still David shoves account books at her until 'she would look so scared and disconsolate, as she became more and more bewildered, that the remembrance of her natural gaiety when I first strayed into her path, and of her being my child-wife, would come reproachfully upon me' (XLIV). But the proper reproaches never really help; David is sensitive, but he is unable to escape his sense of unhappiness and his own limited scale of values. He actually tries to accept Annie Strong's stiff and unimaginative formula as adequate for his own situation: 'There can be no disparity in marriage like unsuitability of mind and purpose', and he adopts her phrase, 'the first mistaken impulses of my undisciplined heart' (XLV), as an important explanation of his existence. As a result, he tries to discipline his wife's wonderful spontaneity and to 'form her mind', accepting the false assumption that life needs moulding to laws, rules, and patterns.

In doing so, David turns his back on comedy and on his wife. She finally admits, 'I was not fit to be a wife' and argues that 'I know I was too young and foolish. It is much better as it is' (LIII). The Edenic Dora is made to wish for death, certainly the final rebuke to those firm 'habits of punctuality'. David has stepped briefly into the role of Murdstone. Beginning in full accord with comic values, he has become their enemy. The novel suggests no criticism of David, no moral judgement against him, only that the society of rich comedy is now far away on the other side of the world, ringing in the last echoes of Micawber's speech but about to disappear completely as a true social possibility from Dickens's novels.

NOTES

[1] To Dudley Costello, *The Letters of Charles Dickens*, ed. Walter Dexter, 3 vols. (London, The Nonesuch Press, 1938), ii. 150, 25 Apr. 1849.

[2] The thematic reading used here is developed further in two articles of mine: 'The Darkness of *David Copperfield*', *Dickens Studies*, i (1965), 65–75, and 'The Structure of *David Copperfield*', *Dickens Studies*, ii (1966), 74–95.

[3] For a reading of the novel which accepts this phrase as an adequate statement of the theme see Gwendolyn B. Needham, 'The Undisciplined Heart of David Copperfield', *Nineteenth-Century Fiction*, ix (1954), 81–107. Several interpretations of the novel which start from an autobiographical premise are also associated with the notion of developing discipline and control; the best is by Edgar Johnson, *Charles Dickens: His Tragedy and Triumph*, 2 vols. (New York, 1952), ii. 677–90.

[4] The discussion most tactfully and fully responsive to the subtlety of this tone is in George H. Ford's Introduction to the Riverside edition of the novel (Boston, Mass., 1958).

[5] *Dickens, Dali and Others: Studies in Popular Culture* (New York, 1946), p. 17. Attacks on the last

two-thirds of the book are as common as praise for the first third, expressing, I rather think, the effectiveness of Dickens's rhetoric, not his failure.

[6] For a fuller discussion of this symbol and other image patterns in the novel see my article, 'Symbol and Subversion in *David Copperfield*', *Studies in the Novel*, i (1969), 196–206.

[7] *The Imagination of Charles Dickens*, London, 1961, p. 114. Others, like G. K. Chesterton, assert that it is impossible really to say anything at all about him: 'All the critics of Dickens, when all is said and done, have only walked round and round Micawber wondering what they should say. I am myself at this moment walking round and round Micawber wondering what I shall say. And I have not found out yet' (*Appreciations and Criticisms of the Works of Charles Dickens* [London, 1911], p. 139). Among the best discussions are those by Bernard Schilling, *The Comic Spirit* (Detroit, Mich., 1965), pp. 98–144, by J. B. Priestley in *The English Comic Characters* (London, 1925), and by William Oddie, 'Mr. Micawber and the Redefinition of Experience', *Dickensian*, lxiii (1967), 100–110.

[8] This point is persuasively made by Douglas Bush, 'A Note on Dickens' Humor', *From Jane Austen to Joseph Conrad*, eds. Robert C. Rathburn and Martin Steinmann, Jr. (Minneapolis, Minn., 1958), p. 88.

[9] 'An Essay on Comedy', *Comedy*, ed. Wylie Sypher (Garden City, New York, 1956), pp. 3–57.

[10] *Dickens, Dali and Others*, p. 67. Douglas Bush rightly remarks that 'one might as well call Jack the Giant-Killer a homicidal maniac' ('A Note on Dickens' Humor', *From Jane Austen to Joseph Conrad*, p. 90).

[11] 'Notes on the Comic', *Thought*, xxvii (1952), 70.

Bert G. Hornback

FRUSTRATION AND RESOLUTION IN *DAVID COPPERFIELD*

Of all Dickens's novels, *David Copperfield* is the most intimately concerned with that finally unmanageable problem, both real and mythic, of ordering a disordered world. In examining this disorder, it includes in its critical focus a representative list of institutions, from school, church, and government to the basic social institution, the family. The larger purpose of the novel transcends this criticism, however, and becomes almost a model working out of Dickens's resolution to the incontrovertible fact of our chaos. In this sense, *David Copperfield* is the most positive of all Dickens's novels, and perhaps his most important work for himself and for us.

Dickens's general thesis, propounded in novel after novel, is that love, which cannot be institutionalized, is the only force capable of ordering this world. In various novels, including both *Pickwick Papers* and *Our Mutual Friend,* there are vain attempts to organize love through the agency of the law. In *Hard Times* Mrs. Gradgrind discovers on her deathbed that "there is something—not an Ology at all—that your father has missed, or forgotten, Louisa" (HT, p. 199). As Mr. Sleary says, love has "a way of [its] own of calculating or not calculating" (HT, p. 293). For Dickens, the "bright old song" is right which says "that oh, 'tis love, 'tis love, 'tis love, that makes the world go round" (OMF, p. 671).

But the world goes round even in the absence of love, and keeps spinning and spinning down into chaos—this is the problem for Dickens. In the early novels he tries to ignore it; in the later ones he keeps reminding himself of it. Miss Flite announces in *Bleak House* that order, which is the archetypal perfection of love, will come only "on the Day of Judgment" (BH, p. 33). In *Hard Times* Stephen Blackpool can't foresee the world's being governed by love, by the rule of "drawin' nigh to folk, wi' kindness and patience," until "the sun turns t' ice . . . till God's work is on-made" (HT, p. 151). This kind of final universal resolution does not take place·at the end of a Dickens novel, of course; though we can expect to find a new beginning

From *"Noah's Arkitecture": A Study of Dickens's Mythology* (Athens: Ohio University Press, 1972), pp. 63–82. An earlier version of this essay appeared in *Studies in English Literature 1500–1900* 8, No. 4 (Autumn 1968): 651–67.

made, both mythically and realistically, we never actually get to the end of the world, to Judgment Day. As I have argued, Dickens's solution in the early novels is to situate those new beginnings in little pockets of love which ignore the old, ruined world about them. He lets the good people establish for themselves retreats in the midst of the greater chaos where they will live on their love for each other, ignoring that pervasive calamity which is the world at large. In *David Copperfield,* however, Dickens finds an alternative to his retreat solution, which changes all the rest of his fiction.

It is obvious from the beginning of Dickens's career that the pocket of love solution is not the right one. Mr. Pickwick determines "on retiring to some quiet pretty neighborhood in the vicinity of London," trusting that he "may yet live to spend many quiet years in peaceful retirement." Mr. Pickwick calls the place his "little retreat," and from it he announces the "dissolution" of the Pickwick Club (PP, p. 796). The happiness he finds in this retirement from the world is promised a continuance which, in the last words of the novel, "nothing but death will terminate" (PP, p. 801). The world of experience, as discovered by the adventuring Pickwickians, is already dead in the fact of Mr. Pickwick's retreat; and that life being gone, there is little of healthy life left. The novel is, fully, *The Posthumous Papers of the Pickwick Club.*

Oliver Twist suffers similarly in its conclusion. In the final chapter, the narrator tries to generate a future for his good people by means of wishful meditation:

> And now, the hand that traces these words, falters, as it approaches the conclusion of its task; and would weave, for a little longer space, the threads of these adventures.
>
> I would fain linger yet with a few of those among whom I have so long moved, and share their happiness by endeavoring to depict it. I would show Rose Maylie in the bloom and grace of early womanhood. . . . I would paint her and her dead sister's child happy in their love for one another, and passing whole hours together in picturing the friends whom they had so sadly lost. (OT, pp. 414–15)

The hiding place for happiness here seems to be in the memories of the past, among the dead rather than among the living. This conclusion is unsatisfactory, not just because it is sentimental, but because it violates life by ignoring it. In *David Copperfield* Dickens attempts to find—or finds and attempts to accept—a much greater and more satisfactory solution. He finds this solution primarily in the career of Tommy Traddles and David himself, each of whom orders reality, not by changing or reforming it, but by comprehending and accepting it in all its complexity. At the end of the novel Traddles is to become a judge; David is a novelist.

There are different kinds of order—physical, for example, and mental, or real and imaginary. The world is in a state of chaos, physically, really; and it cannot be converted to order overnight, or by the concerted goodness and even the hard work of several good men. The effort can be begun, of course—must be begun. But what it takes to begin this impossible task is courage, which comes only with a

critical but sympathetic understanding of the whole problem. Understanding requires mental—"rational" is the word Miss Betsy uses (DC, p. 274)—and imaginative activity. Understanding is itself a kind of order, finally, the kind of order that lets
us see what the whole problem of chaos really is.

The problem of finding and reestablishing order is a qualitative one in *David
Copperfield*, involving the determination of innocence and experience. With the
exception of David himself, the good people of the novel all insist on their innocence; all except David and Traddles try, initially, to refuse or refute experience,
making their worlds thus exclusive and selective. In denying the existence of the
larger, pervasive reality of evil—natural as well as human—they establish for themselves precarious and difficult situations. Their love, then, becomes restrictive and
isolationist, and that larger, responsible love which would establish itself critically
and creatively in the world, however painful this might be, is denied.

The basic unit of love and order, the family, is almost nonexistent in *David
Copperfield*, and it is against this symbolically significant disadvantage that the
characters all react. David himself is a posthumous child, and soon an orphan.
Steerforth has no father, and Traddles is an orphan; Ham and Little Emily are
orphans, and Mrs. Gummidge is a widow. Agnes Wickfield has no mother, Annie
Strong no father; Dora Spenlow's mother is dead, and her father dies midway
through the novel. Mr. Dick has been mistreated and deserted by his family, and
lives with Miss Betsey, who is divorced. Uriah Heep's father is dead, Sophy Crewler's mother dies, and Martha, the Yarmouth prostitute, is an orphan. The only
unbroken family unit in the novel is that of the Micawbers, which struggles against
its own chaotic social incompetence and chronic moral ineptitude to stay whole;
and when they move to Plymouth, they leave behind an orphan servant to be
"disbanded" (DC, p. 174), a metaphysical malapropism for the breaking up of a
home.

In order to overcome the disadvantage of orphanage and to make contact
again beyond its symbolic isolation the characters must create new orders, new
forms in which to live. The largest of these orders and forms are Traddles's, in
marriage and in his career as a lawyer, and David's, in his adjustment and organi-
zation of the whole "family" of the novel in the last chapter, and in his work as a
novelist, as a creative artist. What we see of the orders by which the other
characters live we see through David's imaginative eye; and he represents each of
these attempts at order in terms of one or another of the myths which Dickens
himself has used in his earlier novels to try to resolve the problem of chaos.

Mr. Peggotty tries to establish order for Ham, Emily, Mrs. Gummidge, and
himself in the houseboat, making for them all an artificial home on the edge of "the
great dull waste" of Yarmouth. The first time David visits there he looks out "over
the wilderness, and away at the sea, and away at the river, but no house could /
make out. There was a black barge, or some other kind of super-annuated boat,
not far off, high and dry on the ground" (DC, p. 29). This unimposing Noah's
Ark—such is the obvious translation for that "other kind of super-annuated
boat"—is set up by Mr. Peggotty in opposition to the tides of universal chaos, and

seems to young David, once he knows the place, to be "the most delicious retreat that the imagination of man could conceive" (DC, p. 32). It is only a retreat, however, and it seems safe only to that kind of romantic or childish imagination which foresees nothing but the best of fortunes. David innocently asks Mr. Peggotty if he gave his "son the name of Ham, because [he] lived in a sort of ark" (DC, p. 32). But Mr. Peggotty is not really Noah, and Ham, Noah's son, has no father in this world. Mr. Peggotty is a benevolent bachelor, not a mythological savior; and his "sort of ark" is not protection enough from the real world.[1]

As both David and Steerforth notice on the night of Steerforth's first visit to Yarmouth, the reality of the wilderness world threatens constantly to destroy Mr. Peggotty's simple refuge:

> "This is a wild kind of place, Steerforth, is it not?"
> "Dismal enough in the dark," he said: "and the sea roars as if it were hungry for us. Is that the boat, where I see a light yonder?" (DC, p. 311)

When David returns the next time, on the occasion of Little Emily's disappearance, it is again "a wild night" in the universe, and David has to do "a little floundering across the sand, which was heavy," to get to the houseboat and its light (DC, p. 448). The retreat is a haven, or a lighthouse, perched precariously on shifting sands, surrounded by troubled seas. With the seduction of Emily the retreat fails, and the experiment is ruined. Mr. Peggotty sets out to retrieve Emily, but upon recovering her realizes that he cannot now reestablish the innocent world which has been, and thus the little houseboat is abandoned. The tides of the world have proved too strong; the houseboat-ark is drowned, and Mr. Peggotty takes what is left of his broken family and escapes to never-never land, in Australia. As Mr. Peggotty, Emily, Mrs. Gummidge, and Martha leave, the storm comes again, destroying Ham, Steerforth, and the empty house itself. David finds Steerforth's body on the beach, "on the part where [Emily] and I had looked for shells, two children—on that part of it where some lighter fragments of the old boat, blown down last night, had been scattered by the wind—among the ruins of the home he had wronged" (DC, p. 795).

Experience destroys the houseboat; those of its former inhabitants who escape retreat to Australia, a minor heaven or haven, an unknown place where what should have been can now be, in what pretends to be this life. It is as though Eden has been reestablished. The intrusion of such unreality on the novel is an indication of Dickens's continuing inability to resolve happily and at the same time honestly that which he so much wanted to resolve. Faced with a calamitous world, Dickens's innocents can only be saved by being given "retreats" again; this is the best the imagination can create without completely denying the thesis of experience.

David describes his own technique as a novelist as the "blending of experience and imagination" (DC, p. 665), and generally this is Dickens's technique as well. Unfortunately, even in this most autobiographically based of his novels, Dickens does not always remain as true to his principles as David the novelist seems to, and the realism and moral integrity of his art are sometimes compromised by romantic falsification. The falsification of reality for the sake of innocence is not only a constant temptation for Dickens, it is also the constant endeavor of various characters in the novel. This endeavor is what must be considered first here in order to bring David's response to the difficulties of reality into better focus. The range of the characters' culpability for this unwise insistence upon innocence runs from the positive and only half-comic guilt of Micawber to the comic goodness of Traddles, which ends in his being touted for a judgeship.

Micawber, kinsman to Harold Skimpole in *Bleak House,* reveals the more serious side of the problem of innocence. Micawber is irresponsible, and is in fact a thief, although the one thing he seems to use money for is the punch which generates good fellowship.[2] Mrs. Micawber insists that it is society's duty to employ her husband, and society's responsibility to find a proper use for his talents; one knows, however, that although society is almost always wrong in Dickens's fiction, the Micawbers are at fault here, too. The situation becomes so morally complex for Dickens that in order to resolve Micawber in the novel's London he would have to readjust his whole world, and establish David and Micawber as supports for each other, Micawber becoming the father David wants, and David becoming the child-father Micawber needs. Rather than do this (which would change the focus of the novel entirely) Dickens sends the Micawber family, with Mr. Peggotty and his group, to Australia. There everything works out as it should have in this world, if only life were simple. It is as though Micawber has been read out of the novel's real world and into a storybook world of mythical innocence.

This quest for continuing innocence all begins, in a way, with storybooks: with young David reading *Tom Jones* as "a child's Tom Jones, a harmless creature" (DC, p. 56), with Peggotty insisting from the beginning of the novel until its end on the crocodile book, refusing to let that earlier, innocent world die. Although Peggotty doesn't understand the story about the crocodiles very well—"She had a cloudy impression . . . that they were a sort of vegetable" (DC, p. 16)—and isn't even "quite right in the name" of the things (DC, p. 17); still the story is a proper one for its purpose: the "monsters" "hatch" and populate the world, and then must be fought and defeated, of course, by the "natives" (DC, p. 18). In this storybook version of experience the conflict is falsified for the sake of sentimental innocence, and the natives all live happily ever after.

Young David is constantly meeting such attempts as Peggotty's to exorcise the world of its evil. Miss Betsey Trotwood responds to the mistake of her early marriage by withdrawing from the world and establishing for herself a retreat at Dover where she attempts to reconstruct her own private Eden, much restricted and diminished, but pure. Almost immediately upon David's arrival at Dover she is forced to do battle with the invading reality which constantly threatens to defile that ideal place. At the sight of the intruders she "became in one moment rigid with indignation, and had hardly voice to cry out, 'Janet! Donkies!' "

> Upon which, Janet . . . darted out on a little piece of green in front, and warned off two saddle-donkeys, lady-ridden, that had presumed to set hoof

upon it; while my aunt, rushing out of the house, seized the bridle of a third animal laden with a bestriding child, turned him, led him forth from those sacred precincts, and boxed the ears of the unlucky urchin in attendance who had dared to profane that hallowed ground. (DC, pp. 194–95)

The narrator continues: "The one great outrage of her life, demanding to be constantly avenged, was the passage of a donkey over that immaculate spot" (DC, p. 195).

Miss Betsey's little Eden symbolizes her retreat from life. She has been wronged in marriage and has been unable to face life since. She has withdrawn, and reassumed her maiden name—which is like going back in time "before the Fall." Through her experience with David, however, Miss Betsey is drawn back into life, back into the real world. In returning she compromises her defensive idealism and begins to measure the world according to the wise, sad rule of reality. There are no immaculate green spots in this world; and at its center, in London, as Miss Betsey herself says, the only thing "genuine" is "the dirt" (DC, p. 345). In the end David reports that she "allowed [his] horse on the forbidden ground, but had not yet relented at all toward the donkeys" (DC, p. 858). Miss Betsey comes back to the real world now, and can deal with the fact of evil better than she could before. Still, no donkeys are allowed—and the donkeys, obviously, are evil.[3]

Mr. Dick's response to this disorderly world is one of the most interesting, most complex, and most important, metaphorically and thematically, in the novel. The realization of Dick as a character—and as a writer—gives us one side of Dickens himself. When David first visits Mr. Dick's room as a boy, Dick is at work on the Memorial, and David has "ample leisure to observe the large paper kite in a corner, [and] the confusion of bundles of manuscript" (DC, p. 202). Dick then looks up, greets David cryptically as "Phœbus," and asks:

"How does the world go! I'll tell you what," he added, in a lower tone, "I shouldn't wish it to be mentioned, but it's a—" here he beckoned to me, and put his lips close to my ear—"it's a mad world. Mad as Bedlam, boy!" (DC, p. 202)

Dick recognizes David both as an artist and as a son in that initial address; and he sees that, like Keats's Apollo in the first *Hyperion,* the young David needs to be instructed in the experience of the world if he is to fulfill his destiny in art. According to Miss Betsey, Dick's reason for calling the world mad is his own family situation. His brother has tried to institutionalize him and his sister has married a cruel man who mistreats her. Dick, a compassionate, loving creature, is thrown into a fever by these events, the consequence of which is that oppression which is expressed in the metaphorical intrusion of King Charles's head into his life. "That's his allegorical way of expressing it," Miss Betsey says; "He connects his illness with great disturbance and agitation, naturally, and that's the figure, or the simile, or whatever it's called, which he chooses to use" (DC, p. 205).

Dick speaks his emphatic best in the terms of this metaphor. He is writing a

"Memorial," petitioning the Crown for relief from the grief of his particular family situation. Miss Betsey tells young David that "he is memorialising the Lord Chancellor, or the Lord Somebody or other—one of those people, at all events, who are paid to *be* memorialised—about his affairs" (DC, p. 205). But to memorialize "the Lord Somebody or other" is to memorialize God; and thus Dick's memorial is much more than Miss Betsey assumes it to be. Dick is complaining about the general state of man, and the Memorial is the document which attempts to describe the "Mad as Bedlam" world which Dick sees. King Charles's head is the symbolic expression of Dick's complaint about this "Mad as Bedlam" world, and he says it over and over, impetuously, compulsively, unable to wait for the logic and rhetoric of exposition.

When Miss Betsey loses her fortune, Mr. Dick is put to work to earn money. He tries first to aid his protector with his innocence—"if I could exert myself, Mr. Traddles," Dick says; "if I could beat a drum—or blow anything!" (DC, p. 528)—but innocence will not solve the world's and Miss Betsey's problems. It seems that only something like Carlylean endeavor will do it; and so Mr. Dick is put to work being useful, copying legal documents which Traddles procures for him to earn silver sixpences. Dick produces his copies in an orderly fashion only by keeping King Charles's head out of them, which he accomplishes by writing that grievance over and over into an old copy of the Memorial, exorcising in this way the evil he sees in the world until he becomes so involved in the positive productive activity of copying that he "postpone[s] the Memorial to a more convenient time" (DC, p. 529). As the novel draws to its close, Miss Betsey, her fortune recovered, informs David that Dick now "incessantly occupied himself in copying everything he could lay his hands on, and kept King Charles the First at a respectful distance by that semblance of employment" (DC, p. 836). In the last chapter, which finally brings the time of the story into the present tense time of its writing, Dick is seen as "an old man, making giant kites, and gazing at them in the air, with a delight for which there are no words" (DC, p. 874).

When David was a small boy living at Miss Betsey's house, his first visit to Mr. Dick's room showed him a kite "as much as seven feet high." As David looked at the kite, he saw "that it was covered with manuscript, very closely and laboriously written; but so plainly, that as I looked along the lines, I thought I saw some allusion to King Charles the First's head again, in one or two places" (DC, p. 203). That first kite of Dick's was used to memorialize God, and to get rid of that evil which Dick simply could not comprehend: " 'There's plenty of string,' said Mr. Dick, 'and when it flies high, it takes the facts a long way' " (DC, p. 203). In the end, the people of the novel have resolved their various difficulties with the world, and Dick flies what seem to be blank kites up to heaven. There is still a Memorial to be written, however; the world is not suddenly or at last perfect. But Dick has given over the job of "memorialising" to David, the artist, who presumably can handle the job without losing his sanity, without resorting to King Charles's head.

For Dick, of course, the world now is a satisfactory place. He has David's children to play with, and flies "giant kites" for them. He tells David that the

Memorial—his Memorial—belongs to the future when he will "have nothing else to do" (DC, p. 875). Dick has learned to live with the world by working in it and busying himself with it. Carlyle, it seems, was right. The lesson Mr. Dick has learned is the same lesson that is taught to Miss Betsey: one cannot retire from the world, and either try from that retirement to change it or expect others to change it for one. Perhaps this is the lesson that Dickens is trying to learn, also, through his alter ego David. Innocence is not experience; innocence is both inadequate and irresponsible in the formation of order.[4]

Peggotty is the only character who is allowed to retain her faith in innocence—at least in David's childhood and that particular innocence—and the crocodile book is in her pocket still in the final chapter. To be allowed to retain that past is Peggotty's reward for her goodness, her love, and her strength, and for giving generously of these when others needed her support. David, however, has grown beyond her living memories, and has to look far back to see himself as he was then: "I find it very curious to see my own infant face, looking up at me from the Crocodile stories" (DC, p. 874). He has taken and continues to take Miss Betsey's important advice: "It's in vain, Trot, to recall the past, unless it works some influence upon the present" (DC, p. 347)

Agnes, like Peggotty, would keep the innocent past if she could: "I have found a pleasure," she tells David toward the novel's end, "in keeping everything as it used to be when we were children. For we were very happy then, I think" (DC, p. 840). But living in the past is not the way to make a future, nor is it the way to order life. Finally Agnes is required to give up the past, in which her relation to David was that of "good angel," of "brother," and become his "trew wife," as Mr. Peggotty calls her (DC, p. 866), "the real heroine," as Dickens described her in his notes for the novel.[5] What Miss Betsey calls the important "influence" of that surrendered past—with its happiness and love—is what is matured in the achieved future of the end of the novel.

Miss Betsey, Mr. Dick, and Agnes are all three forced to accept more of reality than they had bargained for. They are all required to come into the world of the real present in order to survive: Miss Betsey from her private Eden, Mr. Dick from his dream of divine intervention to resolve this mess, and Agnes from her sentimental retreat into the past of childhood. Dr. Strong, the teacher and lexicographer, achieves both peace and some sort of productivity for himself in a similar fashion. It is only by coming to terms with his own affairs and seeing the reality of his relationship with his wife and her family, that he can settle down peacefully to his task of ordering all of the world by cataloging and defining its symbols. At the end of the novel he is "labouring at his Dictionary (somewhere about the letter D), and happy in his wife and home" (DC, p. 876).[6]

Only two characters in the novel consistently approach the world with total honesty and courage, and in the end they alone seem capable of leading it. In the end they alone seem to have succeeded in actually mastering it and understanding its full complexity. One, Tommy Traddles, will become a judge. The other, David, is a novelist, an artist. And although Tommy's judgeship is but prospective at the end and David's career as an artist is played down throughout the novel, there are no work or professional assignments in all of Dickens's fiction more significant than these two. David is Dickens's only novelist—although there is an earlier approximation of the artist in the career of young Martin Chuzzlewit as an architect, and Mr. Pickwick was a journalist of sorts. Traddles has the company of but Mortimer Lightwood and Eugene Wrayburn from among Dickens's dozens of legal figures as successful and sympathetically drawn lawyers.

At Salem School Tommy takes out his frustration in tears and skeleton-drawing every time he is abused by Mr. Creakle, every time injustice and disorder impinge upon his idealized conception of the world. He remains an innocent and a sort of idealist throughout the novel, and never, as far as one knows, does he give up his doodling. He literally "draws" the awful reality of the world out of himself onto scraps of paper. Still, Traddles learns and accepts the lessons of experience, though experience does not change him. He maintains his essential innocence; his response to evil in the world never ceases to be compassionate and humanitarian, built on selfless understanding and charity. He achieves something like a Blakean "higher innocence," it seems; and it may well be in response to just this in his character that Dickens establishes Tommy's prospects for a judgeship. In the end Traddles is knowing and well informed about the world, but uncorrupted by this experience. He will order the world in the only legitimate and honest way possible, by simply accepting it as it is, with love.

David's career is quite different from Traddles's, and his calling is, for Dickens, the higher one.[7] In order to discover the meaning of his career we must look first at the full title of the novel, *The Personal History, Adventures, Experience, and Observation of David Copperfield the Younger.*[8] In a way, our calling the novel simply *David Copperfield* is like calling Joyce's first novel *Stephen Hero. A Portrait of the Artist as a Young Man* is a title that would begin to explain Dickens's novel in the same way that it begins to explain Joyce's. David Copperfield is a novelist. One of the points of difference between the character David and the narrator David is that the character David writes novels of social criticism, and is at work on such during the course of the story which the narrator writes, which is, of course, the novel we are reading, *David Copperfield*. The David who writes the novels of social criticism is writing Charles Dickens's career to this point; the David who writes *David Copperfield* seems to represent Dickens's ambition as an artist.

Agnes tells David the character late in the novel, "Your growing reputation and success enlarge your power of doing good; and if I could spare my brother . . . perhaps the time could not" (DC, p. 843). Later, in his letter from Australia, Micawber addresses David as "the eminent author," and asserts the high seriousness of the art of fiction, claiming that the "inhabitants of Port Middlebay" read his novels "with delight, with entertainment, with instruction" (DC, p. 872). David the narrator, however, speaks but little of his occupation, and plays down the mention of his works: "When I refer to them, incidentally, it is only as a part of my progress" (DC, p. 690).

The story of David's "progress" is, in one sense, quite a simple one. As a child,

David is required to relinquish his innocence, and the world which he meets beyond this innocence contains all of the evil which the novel describes. For David, time does not stand still, as it did momentarily in his childhood, in his first innocent infatuation with Emily: "The days sported by us," the narrator recalls, "as if Time had not grown up himself yet, but were a child too, and always at play" (DC, p. 37). Only in Eden was time a child; the real world ever since has been a world of change. So time goes on, and David goes to Salem School, to his mother's funeral, and to Murdstone and Grinby's; he goes through an acquaintance with the Micawbers and, as a consequence of that acquaintance, to pawnshops and to the King's Bench Prison. Finally, his boyhood experience, that first and most subjective part of his "Personal History," reaches its climax in his pilgrim's journey through seventy miles of the world to Dover. The narrator recreates David's consciousness of the ex- perience which precipitated this journey on his first day at Dr. Strong's school: "I was so conscious of having passed through scenes of which they could have no knowledge, and of having acquired experience foreign to my age, appearance, and condition as one of them, that I have believed it was an imposture to come there as an ordinary little schoolboy" (DC, p. 228).

After his schooling is completed, David tries out the law as a profession, but gives it up under stress and never returns to it. He tries escape into childishness—in this novel it is called "Eden" (DC, p. 392), which is the same thing as "Fairyland" (DC, p. 396) and "a Fairy's bower" (DC, p. 543)—with Dora, and discovers not only that he is unhappy but that he and Dora are "corrupting" others through their "want of system and management" (DC, pp. 692, 694). Dora dies as a result of miscarriage, and in the end of the novel David marries Agnes.

This accounting of David's "Personal History," however, is not the novel. Again, we must define the focus of the work, and to do so we must refer again to the full title. In the beginning of the novel our attention is directed toward the "Adventures" of young David because they are his, and David the narrator is telling us about himself as a child in the world. Later, our attention is redirected, and the narrator tells us to look at the world as David grew to look at it, and as it affected him. At this point we read, not of David the character's "Adventures," but of his "Observation," of the "Experience" which has made his point of view—which has made, indeed, his point of view as an artist. What holds the whole novel together is that everything in it belongs to David. The stories of the Peggottys, the Micaw- bers, Miss Betsey, Mr. Dick, and Dr. Strong are all parts of David's comprehension, which is why they have been analyzed here.

The two sides of David's "experience" are, first, his "Personal History and Adventures," and second, his "Observation." His "Observation" includes all the various adventures and experiences of the other characters and sets of characters he meets, and his imaginative interpretation of them. In putting together both of these sides of his "Experience," David comes to an understanding of the world—an understanding, at least, of the large and representative world which this novel describes. It is this understanding and the activity of putting together by which the understanding is achieved, that is David's destiny, David's career as we know it. It is this destiny, then, that establishes the critical place or function in the novel of Miss Betsey, Mr. Dick, the Micawbers, the Peggottys, Steerforth, Littimer, Uriah Heep, Dora, Agnes, and all the rest.

David's destiny is not simply to marry Dora, and then to marry Agnes, and to live happily ever after. What he is required to do is comprehend reality, and in so doing order not only his own life but the world around him as well. David's destiny is the mythical ordering of his "Personal History, Adventures, Experience, and Observations." A more direct way of saying this is to say that David's destiny is the writing of *David Copperfield,* and that this work of his is finally the primary focus of the novel. David's destiny is dependent upon and formed from his understanding of the fates of all the other characters. The association is an intimate one, and David is involved dramatically, organically, personally, and psychologically in their lives. Finally, he *is* his understanding of and response to all these characters and in this he is an artist.

The narrator of *David Copperfield* is correct, initially, in his de-emphasis of his work as a novelist as a relevant matter for this story. The novels which David writes are not in themselves immediately important for *David Copperfield;* that he is a novelist, however, is of the utmost importance, as this gives us our best clue to understanding what the novel is about and what it achieves. As the novel draws toward its conclusion, David and his narrator become one person. Throughout the course of the story the narrator has recreated his own past, taking Miss Betsey's advice "to recall the past" only as "it works some influence upon the present" (DC, p. 347). He engages in what he calls "the blending of experience and imagination" (DC, p. 665) in order to recreate that past in a meaningful way. What he makes of it, of his "Personal History, Adventures, Experience, and Observation," is a comprehensible universe of experience, to which he gives the eponymous title, *David Copperfield.* The largest thing we can say of David is that he is, at this point, his novel; and in this he fulfills his destiny.

In the end, as the two Davids merge into one, David writes this novel. In doing so he fulfills the purpose of the artist, to form order out of chaos, by making the larger world of experience meaningful. He is careful to change, exclude, or falsify none of the reality of the world he creates—and it is for this, for his comprehension and acceptance of his world as it is, that he is so important a character for Dickens.

If the answer to the old question about God's allowing evil to exist in the world is that God understands evil better than we do, and thus allows it, then the artist as a creator is also obliged to recognize the existence of evil, accept it, and understand it. This is not to say that evil must not be judged; Dickens, at any rate, frequently passes judgment upon the world, editorially. David's obligation, how-ever, as Dickens conceives it, is to comprehend, not to judge; anything represented in its proper, full perspective will or should judge itself. Like Mr. Dick, Dickens is himself sometimes impatient with his readers; one of the achievements of David as a novelist is that, at least in this novel, he is never impatient. As a consequence of this, we can accept more easily the whole of the experience—without needing any "authority," for example, for Mr. Murdstone, and readily admitting to the triumph of Uriah and Littimer, and perhaps even believing in the escape of the Micawbers and the remains of Mr. Peggotty's little band into some other world, less critically real, where they can try life over again. Indeed, we must accept this last, however unsatisfactory it may be. We must accept it from David, at any rate, for whom it is simply true; it is only Dickens with whom we may quarrel.

Yet our quarrel with Dickens can only be a minor one. He has achieved in this novel perhaps the climax of his art, and from it will come both the problems and the successes of the last six novels. Here, momentarily, the little pocket of love has transcended itself and achieved a reputable dignity by becoming responsible in and to the world. Reality has claimed almost all of the characters, Traddles and David in a particularly high and full sense, and two significant new "families" are established in the end of the novel.

To make a new "family" is to fit all the people who began the novel in a state of symbolic orphanage into new homes. Traddles does this by accommodating the numerous Misses Crewler after their mother's death, and he will try, as a judge, to accommodate the world. David organizes the various characters out of his past and houses them as his family—Miss Betsey, Mr. Dick, Peggotty, and his wife, Agnes. As a novelist David is more ambitious and, as we can tell from our experience as readers, quite successful. He so orders his "Experience" as to make the world more comprehensible and thus something more than tolerable. Mr. Dick no longer complains, and even the villains—at least two of them, Littimer and Heep—are accommodated. This large family of people, the inhabitants of the world of the novel, all take David's name; they live in and as members of *David Copperfield*.

In a way, David as a novelist is Dickens's wish fulfillment of his own personal and artistic ambitions. At the same time that the novel continues Dickens's romantic attack on the lovelessness of man, on man's inhumanity to man, it also accepts, with neither distortion nor exclusion, the world as it is. It tests the mythic worlds of Eden and Noah's Ark as retreats, finds them inadequate and vulnerable, and opts for hard work and clear sight in the real world instead. That it does this in the name of a novelist who has a "power of doing good," whose audience reads his works "with delight, with entertainment, with instruction" marks the seriousness of the novel's claim for itself. In requiring of its hero a charitable comprehension of the world, *David Copperfield* dramatizes the function of the artist as a lover, and teaches Dickens how to remake the world. Mythically, the novel dramatizes the role of the artist as Noah, and teaches Dickens what his myth of recreation must be in the novels which come after it.

NOTES

Quotations from Dickens's novels throughout are from *The New Oxford Illustrated Dickens* (London, 1947–1958), and their citations appear parenthetically in my text. The following abbreviations are used throughout in referring to the novels:

    BH = *Bleak House*
    DC = *David Copperfield*
    HT = *Hard Times*

MC = *Martin Chuzzlewit*
OMF = *Our Mutual Friend*
OT = *Oliver Twist*
PP = *The Pickwick Papers*

[1] Noah's Ark appears one other time by name, as David sees some boats at Chatham "roofed like Noah's arks" (DC, p. 183) on his runaway trip to Miss Betsey's private Eden at Dover.

[2] "I never saw a man," writes David, "so thoroughly enjoy himself amid the fragrance of lemon-peel and sugar, the odour of burning rum, and the steam of boiling water, as Mr. Micawber did" (DC, p. 412).

[3] Mr. Chillup, the old doctor, never gains this kind of understanding. Late in the novel he remarks to David, "I *don't* find authority for Mr. and Miss Murdstone in the New Testament" (DC, p. 834).

[4] One of the meanings of Harold Skimpole in *Bleak House* is related to this. Through him Dickens settles for himself the make-believe that innocence and childishness are legitimate responses to the world.

[5] John Butt and Kathleen Tillotson, *Dickens at Work* (Fair Lawn, New Jersey, 1958), p. 128. The problem of Agnes's inadequacy as a character is not germane here; however, it is her innocence that causes Dickens to create her as but David's "good angel," "pointing upward"—unless it is David, not Dickens, who cannot see her realistically.

[6] Dr. Strong's plan for ordering the whole of reality by ordering its language alphabetically is destined to fall far short of completion—largely because it is a mythic act, and not merely dictionary-making. Just as love and order will be fulfilled in this world only on "the Day of Judgment" in *Bleak House*, only "when the sun turns t'ice" in *Hard Times*, so the head-boy's calculation "of the time this Dictionary would take in completing, on the Doctor's plan, and at the Doctor's rate of going" is "that it might be done in one thousand six hundred and forty-nine years counting from the Doctor's last, or sixty-second birthday" (DC, pp. 237–38). Along with Mr. Dick and David, Dr. Strong is still another aspect of the personal and professional Charles Dickens, seeking a way to reorder the world through the use of words.

[7] One of Dickens's trial titles was "Mag's Diversions," "mag" being British slang for a chatterer, a talker, a magpie. The title finally chosen takes David's use of words much more seriously.

[8] Cf. Mr. Pickwick's plan for "extending his travels, and consequently enlarging his sphere of observation, to the advancement of knowledge, and the diffusion of learning," and his instructions from the Pickwick Club to forward "authenticated accounts of their journeys and investigations, of their observations of character and manners, and of the whole of their adventures" (PP, pp. 1–2); and Martin Chuzzlewit's "enlarg[ing] his circle of acquaintance; increas[ing] his stock of wisdom; and [multiplying] his own experiences" (MC, p. 278).

Robin Gilmour

MEMORY IN
DAVID COPPERFIELD

There has been a good deal of interest recently in the subject of time and memory in Dickens's work. Both George Ford, in his suggestive essay on 'Dickens and the Voices of Time', and Kathleen Tillotson, in her centenary lecture, have reminded us how time-conscious Dickens was, both as a man and as an artist.[1] What Graham Greene called Dickens's 'music of memory' pervades many of the novels,[2] and as Ford and Tillotson show, in none is it heard with greater distinctness or poignancy than in Dickens's 'favourite child', *David Copperfield*. Readers of *The Dickensian* will not of course need reminding that *David Copperfield* is a novel of memory in a double sense: the 'written memory' of the character David Copperfield as well as the fictional transmutation of many of the memories of Dickens himself. These autobiographical aspects have been explored often enough, and in a sense our awareness of them has prevented a full recognition of the part which memory plays in the structure and meaning of the novel itself—the way in which what Percy Lubbock called 'the long rhythm of Copperfield's memory' gives shape and unity to the book.[3] It is that 'rhythm', with its delicate modulation of past and present, which I should like to examine here: in doing so I want to argue that the remembering consciousness of the narrator is not only a powerful unifying factor, but also—and more interestingly—a source of subtle and ambivalent effects within the novel.

In some respects, notably in its treatment of family life, *David Copperfield* seems closest of all Dickens's works to Victorian middle-class assumptions, and it has suffered accordingly at the hands of twentieth-century critics—'the epitome of Victorian bourgeois morality' is how Angus Wilson, for example, has defined the book's social attitudes.[4] Certainly, looked at from the point of view of the hero's progress through life, the novel does give the appearance of a long day's journey into domestic security and bourgeois prosperity. The closing note of self-congratulation—'I had advanced in fame and fortune, my domestic joy was per-fect...' (ch. 63)—invites Orwell's comment that at the end we are being given the gospel according to Smiles instead of the gospel according to Dickens, and a

From *Dickensian* No. 375 (January 1975): 30–42.

modern reader is likely to sense a similar inadequacy in the novel's ostensible theme: the disciplining of David's 'undisciplined heart'. One can respect the seriousness of Dickens's recommendation of prudence and emotional self-discipline without ever being convinced that this official subject makes contact with the centres of vitality in the novel: these surely lie elsewhere—in the childhood scenes, in the intensity of David's feelings for his mother and Dora, in the liberating imprudence of the Micawbers. Monroe Engel puts the matter well in *The Maturity of Dickens:*

> On the surface, *David Copperfield* asserts the need for prudence and the beauty of success. But the power of the novel comes from its vital rendering of the beauty of incaution and the poignancy of limitation and defeat. In its plot, *David Copperfield* is conventionally Victorian. But essentially and imaginatively it subverts its own conventions.[5]

Engel is surely right to suggest that the deepest, most intimate communication of *David Copperfield* is somehow at odds with its more explicit recommendation of prudence; indeed, if one looks at the world of the novel one can see how pervasive is the experience of imprudence and the 'poignancy of limitation and defeat'. Although David himself progresses through self-help to success, the controlling vision of life in the novel is far from Smilesian. Throughout the book there runs an undercurrent of loss and sadness: there is the death of David's mother at the hands of the Murdstones, the destruction of the Yarmouth household by Steerforth and his own subsequent self-destruction, the betrayed affections of Betsey Trotwood, the crippled lives of Rosa Dartle and Steerforth's mother, the death of Dora. Surrounding these particular defeats is a more general awareness of the process of inexorable change to which all life is subject, a note sounded by the bells of Canterbury Cathedral which tell David 'sorrowfully of change in everything; told me of their own age, and my pretty Dora's youth; and of the many, never old, who had lived and loved and died, while the reverberations of the bells had hummed through the rusty armour of the Black Prince, hanging up within, and, motes upon the deep of Time, had lost themselves in air, as circles do in water' (ch. 52). We are made constantly aware, in reading *David Copperfield,* of 'the deep of Time' and of all the intractable tragic elements in life that cannot be finally understood in terms of the prudential morality of the disciplined heart. This awareness serves to counterbalance the success-story element in the novel, and I would suggest that it is established for us by the rhythm of the narrator's memory.

The characteristic narrative movement in *David Copperfield* is a return from a secure present ('advanced in fame and fortune') to a less secure but more vital and complex past. Although David himself has won through, he is continually drawn back to a remembered world in which others dear to him have not: his successful emergence is tempered by the ties which bind him, in memory, to those who have suffered defeat at the hands of life. For in *David Copperfield* the past exists in dynamic and subversive relationship to the present: it is both something which David outgrows, the background to his success, and also an inner landscape to which he returns compulsively, where the experience of loss and defeat can still be felt and thus modify the position of security towards which the novel tends. And in so far as the past is evoked in its full complexity, the rhythm of memory in *David Copperfield* becomes something more than simple nostalgia: it is an imaginative process which, mediating between different states of being, complicates and enriches the book's total perspective.

One can see an interesting example of the way this happens in a long interpolation Dickens made in the original draft of the first monthly part. After writing Chapter 3, in which David visits Yarmouth and meets little Em'ly, Dickens inserted the passage beginning ' "You're quite a sailor, I suppose?" I said to Em'ly', and ending 'This may be premature. I have set it down too soon, perhaps. But let it stand'.[6] In this inserted passage Em'ly reveals her fear of the sea and her ambition of becoming a lady, and the scene concludes with the striking tableau of her running out along a jagged timber of the jetty on which they are walking:

> The light, bold, fluttering little figure turned and came back safe to me, and I soon laughed at my fears, and at the cry I had uttered; fruitlessly in any case, for there was no one near. But there have been times since, in my manhood, many times there have been, when I have thought, Is it possible, among the possibilities of hidden things, that in the sudden rashness of the child and her wild look so far off, there was any merciful attraction of her into danger, any tempting her towards him permitted on the part of her dead father, that her life might have a chance of ending that day?... There has been a time since—I do not say it lasted long, but it has been—when I have asked myself the question, would it have been better for little Em'ly to have had the waters close above her head that morning in my sight; and when I have answered, Yes, it would have been.

In this way Em'ly is cast from the first in the light of her personal tragedy, and although Dickens does not specify, the nature of her future frailty is indicated: the symbolism of the 'light, bold fluttering little figure', in combination with her confessed aspiration to gentility, suggests that she will be susceptible to someone who can offer to make her a lady; while the sea, with its connotations of mystery and death, seems to prefigure the refuge in oblivion sought by the fallen women of Victorian fiction. The scene is certainly dramatic, but one may reasonably ask why Dickens should have forfeited possibilities of suspense and development in Em'ly's story by so compromising her at the outset. The answer is to be found, I think, in the fact that Dickens's focus falls here, as it does throughout the novel, on the character and reactions of David. The introduction of this future vista into the original draft shows Dickens at work reinforcing his hero's adult perspective with all the pathos of the past. Em'ly will fall in the course of life and David will survive, but not untouched: her loss will also be his, for (as Dickens is at pains to suggest later in the same chapter) he has already started to love her. They will be bound hereafter by the shared experience of their innocence.

Again and again throughout *David Copperfield* the past is brought into this sort of relationship with the present. The rhythm of memory operates continually to uncover and reinforce the bonds of intense feeling between the adult narrator and those he has left behind him in his journey through life. His recollections are extraordinarily intense: for David, as for Dickens himself, the past has a reality of its own, a reality which can at any one moment challenge the authority of the present. Writing in 1855 to his first love, Maria Beadnell, Dickens spoke of the 'changeless Past' in which his memories of her were enshrined: 'Believe me, you cannot more tenderly remember our old days and our old friends than I do. . . . I forgot nothing of these times. They are just as still and plain and clear as if I had never been in a crowd since, and had never seen or heard my own name out of my own house.'[7] David Copperfield shares his creator's emotional and imaginative adherence to a 'changeless Past', and his deepest recollections exist in timeless and antithetical relationship to his present life. Memory intersects the action: a sound, a smell, the return to a familiar place can bring instantly to life a scene or character from the past. When he sees on his daughter's hand a ring similar to the engagement ring he had given Dora, there is a 'momentary stirring' in his heart, 'like pain' (ch. 33). Long after Dora's death the scent of a geranium leaf brings back 'a straw hat and blue ribbons, and a quantity of curls, and a little black dog being held up, in two slender arms, against a bank of blossoms and bright leaves' (ch. 26).

Dickens shows the heightened reality of David's memories in various ways. The early chapters are characterised by a frequent use of hyperbole: the fruit in his mother's garden is 'riper and richer than fruit has ever been since, in any other garden' (ch. 2); recalling his holidays at Yarmouth, it seems to David that he has never since seen 'such sunlight as one those bright April afternoons' (ch. 10). In the same way the incidents of David's childhood are invested by the adult narrator with a significance which dwarfs later events: his mother's funeral is 'yesterday's event. Events of later date have floated from me to the shore where all forgotten things will reappear, but this stands like a high rock in the ocean' (ch. 9). As characters from the past are recalled, they come before David with a reality as immediate as that of his present life:

> Can I say of her face—altered as I have reason to remember it, perished as I know it is—that it is gone, when here it comes before me at this instant, as distinct as any face that I may choose to look on in a crowded street? Can I say of her innocent and girlish beauty, that it faded, and was no more, when its breath falls on my cheek now, as it fell that night? (ch.2)

The obsession with the past shown by the adult narrator is in a sense anticipated by the interest David takes, as a youth, in the scenes and associations of his early childhood. A return to Yarmouth on leaving school gives him the opportunity to revisit Blunderstone, and 'on three or four days that I can at once recall' he makes his pilgrimage to the old house: 'my occupation in my solitary pilgrimages was to recall every year of the old road as I went along it, and to haunt the old spots, of which I never tired. I haunted them, as my memory had often done, and lingered among them as my younger thoughts had lingered when I was far away' (ch. 22).

This concern with time and change is even reflected in the humour of the novel (always an accurate register of Dickens's imaginative pre-occupations) and the prevailing sense of mutation finds comic counterpoint in Micawber's nostalgic addresses to 'the companion of my youth' and in the rhetoric of Julia Mills: ' "Do not allow a trivial misunderstanding to wither the blossoms of spring, which, once put forth and blighted, cannot be renewed. I speak . . . from experience of the past— the remote, irrevocable past" ' (ch. 33).

There are several stages in Dickens's treatment of the past in *David Copperfield*. In the wonderful opening chapters David has not yet developed a consciousness of time, and so exists beyond its influence. At Yarmouth with Em'ly the 'days sported by us, as if Time had not grown up himself yet, but were a child too, and always at play' (ch. 3). Similarly his relationship with his mother has no temporal definition; it precedes and eludes the book's chronology:

> Now I am in the garden at the back, beyond the yard where the empty pigeon-house and dog-kennel are—a very preserve of butterflies, as I remember it, with a high fence, and a gate and padlock; where the fruit clusters on the trees, riper and richer than fruit has ever been since, in any other garden, and where my mother gathers some in a basket, while I stand by, bolting furtive gooseberries, and trying to look unmoved. A great wind rises, and the summer is gone in a moment. We are playing in the winter twilight, dancing about the parlour. When my mother is out of breath and rests herself in an elbow-chair, I watch her winding her bright curls round her fingers, and straightening her waist, and nobody knows better than I do that she likes to look so well, and is proud of being so pretty. (ch. 2)

This is the Eden of early memory, and in its quality of timelessness it is to remain the fixed focus of David's thoughts about his mother. There is a hint of the vanity which will render her susceptible to Murdstone, but essentially she exists for him at a level beneath character and causality, where the seasons change with a flap of the wind and the fruit on the trees is 'riper and richer than fruit has ever been since, in any other garden'. And so it is that when she dies, the intervening misery of her marriage to Murdstone and all the pain this brings to David is cancelled out, and the earliest memory reasserts itself with a new intensity:

> From the moment of my knowing of the death of my mother, the idea of her as she had been of late had vanished from me. I remembered her, from that instant, only as the young mother of my earliest impressions, who had been used to wind her bright curls round and round her finger, and to dance with me at twilight in the parlour. What Peggotty had told me now, was so far from bringing me back to the later period, that it rooted the earlier image in my mind. It may be curious, but it is true. In her death she winged her way back to her calm untroubled youth, and cancelled all the rest. (ch. 9)

David Copperfield shares with Dickens the capacity to partition off his deepest responses and experiences in an area of his being where they remain inaccessible to, or at least unaffected by, the larger process of thought by which he attempts to account for the past. David's mother has an imaginative existence for him in a 'changeless Past', beyond the reach of time and outside the interpretative scope of his history: this pattern is repeated at significant stages throughout the novel, notably in David's attitude to Dora and Steerforth, and it has far-reaching implications for our understanding of his character and emotional growth.

The strength of these early chapters derives from Dickens's capacity to evoke in a particular fiction the deepest associations of common experience, a quality in his genius which led Chesterton to call him 'the last of the mythologists, and perhaps the greatest'.[8] But when David comes to Dover and is at last given a stable home by his aunt, the character of his experience changes. The new beginning he makes there involves a sharp break with the Blunderstone world, a break actively promoted by Betsey Trotwood. From the first, and for the best of reasons, she encourages her nephew to dissociate himself from his pre-Dover past; she changes his Christian name to Trotwood and loses no occasion to criticise the unworldiness of his mother; she refuses to call Peggotty by her Blunderstone name, changing it to 'Barkis', and so on. The result of this persistent and well-intentioned assault on David's earliest emotional loyalties is to place 'a remoteness . . . upon the old Blunderstone life' (ch. 14), and by the time he leaves Dr. Strong's Academy he can already look back to his coming there as to a remote distance: 'That little fellow seems to be no part of me; I remember him as something left behind upon the road of life—as something I have passed, rather than have actually been—and almost think of him as of someone else' (ch. 18).

Aunt Betsey's efforts to turn David into a ' "fine firm fellow, with a will of your own" ' (ch. 19) command our respect, issuing as they do from a generous concern for his welfare and success in life, and a determination that he will not repeat her mistakes. For of course she too has loved unwisely and suffered for it, just as her way of life until David arrives has been framed in conscious reaction to the emotional susceptibility of her own past. (Interestingly, she can never bring herself to reject entirely the handsome but worthless husband she had once loved so passionately.) By encouraging a break with the past of his early childhood, the Blunderstone world (the name is significant), she is trying to wean him away from a too-close identification with his mother and her damaging belief—damaging, that is, in the consequences it has had for David at the hands of the Murdstones—that 'a loving heart was better and stronger than wisdom' (ch. 9). David needs to learn that 'wisdom' and prudence are necessary to the loving heart, but he cannot do so by repudiating a past in which much that is precious is inextricably bound to what is painful; for although he has suffered in the Blunderstone period, he has also known intense joy—his mother's love, the protecting care of Peggotty, the Yarmouth idyll with little Em'ly. One can sense an initial limitation in the ideal of responsible self-advancement for which Betsey Trotwood is the first and perhaps most effective spokesman, in the realisation that the prudence she advocates for David works against a full recognition of the past. Growing older and getting on requires the rejection of 'the old Blunderstone life' and the emotional loyalties associated with it, yet David cannot uproot these loyalties as completely as his aunt would wish and he is continually drawn back, in memory, to the lost world of his childhood. It is significant that one of the first uses to which he puts his new independence on leaving school is, as we have seen, to revisit Blunderstone and 'to recall every yard of the old road as I went along it, and to haunt the old spots, of which I never tired' (ch. 22). This early *recherche du temps perdu* is characteristic of the truant nature of David's memory.

As the novel progresses, one becomes increasingly aware of a discrepancy between the attitude to the past required by David's attempt to discipline his undisciplined heart, and the reality of the past as it is re-experienced in his memory. This discrepancy is especially acute in the case of David's relationship with Dora. As nearly every recent commentator has pointed out, Dora represents a natural choice for David in a way that Agnes never does, because she offers a real link with the past of his childhood and with the intense but submerged associations of the Blunderstone world: like his mother she is a child-wife, doomed to an early death in a world for which she is insufficiently 'firm'. The moral of the disciplined heart, however, requires that their love and marriage be presented from the viewpoint of chastened maturity, with the result that the tone of the Dora passages is usually one of affectionate but ironic nostalgia, as befits an episode poignant in itself but now outgrown: 'What an idle time it was! What an insubstantial, happy, foolish time it was! . . .' (ch.33). But the intensity of real feeling keeps breaking through, and the interesting point about David's attitude to Dora is that, like his attitude to his mother, it leaves the impression of an experience which has *not* been mastered or ever fully outgrown. Here, for example, is a characteristic passage from one of the four 'Retrospect' chapters:

> Once again, let me pause upon a memorable period of my life. Let me stand aside, to see the phantoms of those days go by me, accompanying the shadow of myself, in dim procession.
>
> Weeks, months, seasons, pass along. They seem little more than a summer day and a winter evening. Now, the Common where I walk with Dora is all in bloom, a field of bright gold; and now the unseen heather lies in mounds and bunches underneath a covering of snow. In a breath, the river that flows through our Sunday walks is sparkling in the summer sun, is ruffled by the winter wind, or thickened with drifting heaps of ice. Faster than ever river ran towards the sea, it flashes, darkens, and rolls away. (ch. 43)

True to his mature perspective, David is at pains to distance himself from the recollection—'Let me stand aside'—and the emphasis falls on the insubstantiality of the past: the people are 'phantoms', the procession 'dim', he himself a 'shadow'. The intended effect is of the inevitable passing of time, and with it the ephemeral experience which the passage commemorates. But at the same time there is a contrary impulse at work here which resists this construction on the part of the narrator. It reveals itself in the fact that David's memory of Dora exists in the same timeless region inhabited by the thoughts of his mother: there is the same use of

the historic present tense, the same concentration and confusion of the seasons—
'They seem little more than a summer day and a winter evening'—a similar hyperbole (the Common 'all in bloom, a field of bright gold'), the same quality of an
experience both within and beyond time. Moreover, the language of evocation is
excited and fresh—'bloom', 'bright gold', 'unseen heather', 'sparkling in the summer
sun', 'flashes'—hinting at a vitality curiously incompatible with the attitude David
wants the reader to take towards this recollection; and the effect of 'darkens' in the
last line is not to accustom us to an easy acceptance of change, but to depress with
a sense of emotion deadened before it has been fully realised. While the passage
maintains a surface tone of comfortable nostalgia towards the events described, the
inner movement of the prose drives back into a timeless past of quickened feeling
and unfulfilled promise.

David consistently deprecates himself as a 'lackadaisical young spooney' (ch.
26), but these passages in the novel are touching not so much for the character of
Dora herself as for the intensity of David's feelings for her, an intensity which relates
this episode to the memory of his mother and the Blunderstone world. In the same
way, his memories of Dora serve to enrich his experience, extending and compli-
cating the pattern he seeks to impose upon it. She arouses in him, as Agnes cannot,
an earlier, impulsive, more vulnerable individual, whose capacity to make mistakes
is the function of a generous response to life. The fact that the explicit moral of
David Copperfield lies in an altogether opposite direction, that we are asked to see
both fulfillment and maturity in David's feelings for Agnes—this, I would suggest, is
the central ambiguity of the novel. In a world where others have lost so much,
Dickens reconciles us imaginatively to his hero's success by the implication that he
too has lost something, a capacity for intense feeling, a certain heightened response
to life which is now no longer possible for him. One thinks of Wordsworth and the
'Immortality Ode': 'The things which I have seen I now can see no more'. The deep
imaginative identification with the states of feeling which condition the imprudence
and unworldliness of those characters who have been broken by the world, works
against the tone of mellow acceptance that the adult, domesticated David assumes.
Through the act of memory this contrary process operates to enrich the book's
total perspective, but in the case of Agnes it has the further effect of seriously
weakening the thematic role she supports in the novel.

The trouble with Agnes is that the nature and tendency of her 'wisdom' is
peculiarly hostile to the more complex responses which a reading of *David Copperfield* evokes. Since her function in the scheme of the novel is to embody
prudence, she exists from the first as an enemy of the imprudence towards which
so much of the book's unconscious movement tends. In her relations with David
she adopts Aunt Betsey's name for him, Trotwood, thereby aligning herself with his
aunt in her effort to diminish his Blunderstone identity; and as the chief agent in
Aunt Betsey's attempt to turn him into a ' "fine firm fellow, with a will of your
own" ', she inherits all the unfortunate connotations with which 'firmness' is already
associated in our minds—'Firmness, I may observe, was the grand quality on which
both Mr and Miss Murdstone took their stand' (ch. 4). David's marriage to her spells

the end of his own imprudence, of course, but also the end of his involvement in the imprudence of others, in particular those fallible lives which, by the nature of their failure, suggest the emotional limitations of the success ideal he has embraced; it is significant that before he can marry her, Mr Peggotty, Em'ly, and the Micawbers all have to emigrate to Australia.

The weakness of Agnes and her thematic role is most evident in relation to Steerforth. She is of course right to see Steerforth as David's 'bad Angel': Dickens shows us that she is right, and moreover shows us that David is weak and naive not to see it also—Steerforth's ruthless egotism is fully displayed in his heartless treatment of Mr Mell, the penniless usher at Salem House (ch. 7). What is strange is that Agnes's disapproval arouses so little moral sympathy in the novel as a whole, for Steerforth's seduction of little Em'ly is perhaps the one episode in which the mistaken impulses of David's undisciplined heart are shown to have had painful consequences for others apart from himself. It is his hero-worship which leads him to take Steerforth to Yarmouth in the first place, just as it is his moral blindness—' "You have no best to me, Steerforth . . . and no worst" ' (ch. 29)—which prevents him seeing the obvious signs of his friend's intended treachery. He is indirectly responsible for what happens, yet there is no sign of reproach, let alone self-reproach, in his subsequent reaction:

> What is natural in me, is natural in many other men, I infer, and so I am not afraid to write that I never had loved Steerforth better than when the ties that bound me to him were broken. . . . Deeply as I felt my own unconscious part in his pollution of an honest home, I believe that if I had been brought face to face with him, I could not have uttered one reproach. I should have loved him so well still . . . I should have held in so much tenderness the memory of my affection for him, that I think I should have been as weak as a spirit-wounded child, in all but the entertainment of a thought that we could ever be re-united. (ch. 32)

David's response here is indeed curious, and it gives a clear indication of the kind of novel *David Copperfield* is—or rather the kind of novel that it is not. In another novelist (Jane Austen and Henry James come to mind) the recognition of Steerforth's treachery would have involved David in a radical reinterpretation of his friend's character, the acceptance of personal responsibility for what had happened, and an access of sympathetic respect for the clear-sightedness of Agnes. One thinks of the way, in *Pride and Prejudice*, Elizabeth Bennet's discovery of Wickham's true character alters her response to Darcy. In fact, very little of this re-orientation takes place in *David Copperfield*, and for the good reason that Dickens's imagination is not really engaged (as it will be later in *Great Expectations*) in exploring the processes of moral and emotional self-discovery. There is no real awakening for David's undisciplined heart in relation to Steerforth, because the nature of his response here—as in the case of Dora and his mother—precludes the possibility. The telling phrase is 'I should have held in so much tenderness the memory of my affection for him . . .': what we are witnessing here is a process of imaginative reversion similar in kind to that already noted in the case of David's mother, where death cancels the recognition of change in her character. Instead of dispelling David's illusion, Steerforth's action in fact consolidates it, sealing off the earlier memory in his consciousness. Betrayal comes, significantly, as a kind of death: 'What his remembrances of me were, I have never known . . . but mine of him were as the remembrances of a cherished friend, who was dead' (ch. 32). The fact that we do not criticise David's continuing loyalty to the memory of his friend is in keeping with the retrospective mood of the novel as a whole; it is entirely in character, for in cherishing Steerforth's memory David is really cherishing the state of innocent idealisation which this lost leader had once inspired.

The imaginative loyalty to a past that has not been outgrown which we can see in David's recollections of Dora and Steerforth is not the only respect in which Agnes's prudential role is undermined in *David Copperfield*. This is not the place to enter into a discussion of the part played by Mr Micawber in the scheme of the novel, but it might perhaps be noted in passing that throughout he invests imprudence with the delights of laughter. 'Whenever he is present,' as Q. D. Leavis acutely remarks, 'even in prison or miserably in debt in mean lodgings, there is life, joy, and a defiance of the rules of Victorian good citizenship.'[9] Micawber provides a comic focus for the novel's fascination with the imprudent, the wayward, the exile from respectable society. The result, we can see, is a work which is far from single-minded in the presentation of David's successful progress. Although Dickens brings his novelist-hero to rest in the schematic marriage with Agnes—a marriage which offers the 'reward' of prudent domesticity—at the same time he manages to suggest the losses, the compensations, the imaginative impoverishment which this final position involves. This ambiguity does not destroy the unity of the novel; on the contrary, it gives a coherence and authenticity to the pattern of the hero's development which the overt moral does not supply, for in *David Copperfield* Dickens has dramatised a familiar experience of the Victorian consciousness. One finds a comparable reaction in one of Matthew Arnold's letters to his sister Jane, in which he laments the narrowing of scope and possibility involved in growing older, 'as if we could only acquire any solidity of shape and power of acting by narrowing and narrowing our sphere, and diminishing the number of affections and interests which continually distract us while young':

> The aimless and unsettled, but also open and liberal state of our youth we *must* perhaps all leave and take refuge in our morality and character; but with most of us it is a melancholy passage from which we emerge shorn of so many beams that we are almost tempted to quarrel with the law of nature which imposes it on us.[10]

In *David Copperfield* there is a similar resistance to the claims of 'morality and character', a similar emotional identification with the 'open and liberal' state of youth. For this is not a novel about the disciplining of an undisciplined heart; its real subject is a changed and changing heart, and as such it offers a representative example of the way in which one of the central insights of the Romantic Movement found its way into English fiction. Wordsworth has already been mentioned, and the book's epigraph might well be taken from the 'Immortality Ode':

> Though nothing can bring back the hour
> Of splendour in the grass, of glory in the flower;
> We will grieve not, rather find
> Strength in what remains behind . . . .

What does remain behind for David, of course, is the intensity of his recollective powers. At one stage of the novel Betsey Trotwood remarks that it is in vain to recall the past, 'unless it works some influence upon the present' (ch. 23): David's *recherche du temps perdu* might be described as an effort of the imagination to comprehend the process of change in his heart in order to work an influence upon the present. That influence is no less than to keep the imagination itself alive within the limitations of Victorian domesticity, a process which can only be sustained by vicarious contact with the past. As it is brought into play, memory works subversively in the interests of complexity and emotional vitality: it is the principle by which David Copperfield holds his creative survival. Like Wordsworth, the hiding-places of his power lie in the past. Phiz's final illustration, in which a portrait of Dora hangs over the mantelpiece while Agnes sits with David and their children by the fireside, is emblematic of the reconciliation he has made between past and present, and also for the instinct which compels him to record his 'written memory' (ch. 48).

When Forster praised his friend's book, he paid tribute to 'the generally healthful and manly tone of the story of Copperfield', and then went on to observe that 'the practical man is the outcome of the fanciful youth; and a more than equivalent for the graces of his visionary days, is found in the active sympathies that life has opened to him'.[11] This comment is perfectly sensible and just, and generations of readers have taken a similar meaning from *David Copperfield*. The interpretation for which I have argued need not conflict with the conscious moral of the novel; indeed it is one of the conditions of David's growth that he should move away from the 'open and liberal' state of his youth and take a final refuge in 'morality and character'. When he rationalises the 'old unhappy loss or want of something' as a need for the stable companionship which Agnes can provide, we recognise that this is inevitable, but we know too that she can never compensate David for all that he has lost. Marooned in Victorian domesticity, it is only in the act of memory that he can recover that sense of life's possibilities and complexity which makes him an artist.

NOTES

[1] George Ford, 'Dickens and the Voices of Time', *Dickens Centennial Essays,* ed. Ada Nisbet and Blake Nevius, Berkeley, Los Angeles, and London, 1971, pp. 46–66; Kathleen Tillotson, 'The Middle Years from the *Carol* to *Copperfield*', *Dickensian* supplement, September 1970, pp. 7–19. Michael Slater has also shown how memory becomes a theme of the Christmas Books leading up to *Copperfield*: see his 'The Christmas Books', *Dickensian*, lxv (1969), 17–24.
[2] 'The Young Dickens', *Collected Essays*, 1969, p. 104.

[3] *The Craft of Fiction*, 1921, p. 129.

[4] *The World of Charles Dickens*, 1970, p. 216.

[5] *The Maturity of Dickens*, Cambridge, Mass., 1959, pp. 152–153.

[6] See Butt and Tillotson, *Dickens at Work*, second ed., 1968, pp. 118–119.

[7] *The Letters of Charles Dickens*, Nonesuch Edition, ed. W. Dexter, 1938, ii, 626; letter of 10 February 1855.

[8] *Charles Dickens*, 1906, p. 87.

[9] F. R. and Q. D. Leavis, *Dickens the Novelist*, 1970, p. 87.

[10] *Letters of Matthew Arnold*, ed. G. W. E. Russell, 1895, i, 14; letter of 25 January 1851.

[11] *Life of Charles Dickens*, ed. J. W. T. Ley, 1928, pp. 552, 554.

Norman Talbot

THE NAMING AND THE
NAMERS OF THE HERO

I

In all romances and literary forms descending from romance traditions it is likely that the name—and sometimes the actual process of naming—of the hero will be a major issue. Especially in ancient stories and those embodying ancient elements, the name embodies the truth (or a crucial lie) about the hero and his destiny—indeed it may stand for the identity of the hero. Whether we prefer to think of Tom Jones's "real" name as Allworthy or Summer, the emblematic precision of his usual name is part of the equipment of the book; possibly "Tom Brown" or "Johnny Smith" would have sufficed, but few other names could as readily have fallen between a hero and his inheritance as the inevitable Western "Jones." The romance motif expressed as the baptism, knighting, arming, revealing or proclaiming of the hero is echoed in many works whose overt materials seem a long way from those of the knightly quest.

Charles Dickens is rightly admired for the profusion of brilliantly exact names in his novels, but nowhere is he closer to the arcane implications of mythic naming than in his great novel of the artist as a young man, *David Copperfield*. There can scarcely be a wider range of names and proximate identities (or threats to identity) given to any putative hero, and the issue is so much at the heart of the novel as to make romance comparisons, or even mythic ones, seem not unreasonable. The first sentence of the book helps to indicate this emphasis:

> Whether I shall turn out to be the hero of my own life, or whether that station will be held by anybody else, these pages must show.[1]

Perhaps all autobiographies and pseudo-autobiographies have a similar concern—certainly *The Life and Opinions of Tristram Shandy, Gent.*, with the rival claims to spiritual fatherhood of the brain (Walter), the heart (Toby) and the soul (Yorick),

From *Southern Review* (Adelaide) 11, No. 3 (November 1978): 267–82.

focuses upon the hero's name in a striking way, for the same mock-magical purpose as Betsey Trotwood has on her first appearance. But the question of becoming the hero, autobiographical or not, is largely a matter of self-discovery and self-utilization; in works as different as Malory's *The Book of the Sangreal* and Tennyson's *Gareth and Lynette* we find the central issue of the guest romance to be essentially the discovery and testing of the hero's identity.

David Copperfield may be divided into three plots, each linked to the others more through the presence of David than by anything else. The first plot, of which a great deal has already been said by scores of critics, is that of the child-wife, and entails a changing definition of "Home," whether that is in Suffolk or London. The second plot is essentially concerned with Em'ly and Steerforth, and although parts of it take place in London I call it the "Anglian" plot. The third plot revolves around the machinations of Uriah Heep; it too takes place partly in London, but for convenience I shall call it the "Kentish" plot. The first plot extends the length of the novel, so it entails more name issues than the other briefer plots, but in each of them there is one crucial *good* name and one unhealthy *ill* name given to David. There are also three periods in which a bunch of inaccurate names, confusions of identity and threats of absolute anonymity afflict the hero. The three ill names all try to imprison David in a childish or blissfully childlike state, rendering him impotent where he should be heroically constructive and mature. The home plot has the ill name given by Dora, from the tenderest of motives; fortunately "Doady" is contrasted with the firm public stance of "David Copperfield" (that of an author "making his name"). The other ill names are given by the villains, though very different villains. Steerforth goodhumouredly calls David "Daisy," and Uriah's writhing malice comes up with "Master Copperfield" ("I should say Mister, but the other comes so natural . . ."). The good and stimulating names that lift our hero into a more heroic mould are Dan Peggotty's hearty "Mas'r Davy" and Betsey's (and of course Agnes's) "Trotwood." Noticeably, the healthy names are both slightly comic, but not the worse for that, since both must eventually give way to the baptismal "David Copperfield," when the hero as artist has made it his. On the other hand, the stodgy "disciplined" aspect of David's development needs this comic leaven.

II

From the beginning Dickens elegantly offers us minor key echoes of the portents that should accompany a hero's birth—David is born in a caul, at the stroke of midnight on a Friday; these facts are full of cloudy significance for the wise women of the neighbourhood, but we should rather find the important portent in the presence of the fairy godmother. Admittedly Betsy is a very odd fairy, and even an alarming one, but nonetheless she names and blesses the unborn child. There are certain mistaken assumptions in this naming, to be sure, but it has considerable significance (I would contend that the question of David's sexual identity is not forgotten, and "Trotwood," especially in Agnes's loving and earnest tones, becomes a genuine influence for good upon the young artist). Impatient and haphazard, Miss Betsey Trotwood actually adds to the confusion of nomenclature endemic in Suffolk at the time (the rookless Rookery and the impossible name Peggotty give her grounds for suspicion), but her blessing is by no means inappropriate. Mrs Copperfield needs it more, perhaps, but the malleable David could also have used some insulation against love and deceiving men. Both in himself and through his spiritual half-sister Em'ly, he reposes foolish confidence in Steerforth, and his affections are "trifled with" quite painfully.

Like many a hero, David is born fatherless, but his father does, literally, bequeath him the name we eventually accept as the hero's. When the orphan-hero is doubly separated from his parents, first by the Murdstones and then by his mother's death, something of his own expected identity dies (figured forth in his baby half-brother).

The second stage of David's long journey outward to the self seems like an escape. He is not considered, fortunately, to have any chance of becoming a Murdstone, but when, as "Brooks of Sheffield," he is seen as dangerous to the Murdstone cause, Peggotty takes him off to a different context. The blessedly asexual and compassionate ark of Dan Peggotty is a haven for the vulnerable boy. Lower class and open-hearted, the thorough-built boatman has no connection with begetting or marriage, but only with compassion (as is established by the surprising information about the parentage of Ham and Em'ly and the marital status of Mrs Gummidge). With vigorous naivety Dan Peggotty addresses the little boy as "Mas'r Davy." Unfortunately, the implications of higher social status can also be rather ominous, as in the conversation between Mas'r Davy and Little Em'ly.

> 'You would like to be a lady?' . . .
> 'I should like it very much. We would all be gentlefolks together, then.'
> (p. 85)

We are reminded of this several times in the Yarmouth chapters, and at the first catastrophe of the Anglian plot, when Em'ly's note vows that she will never come back "unless he brings me back a lady" (513). The lower class naming of Mas'r Davy is more effective than is Em'ly's quest for a lady's name, and throughout his connection with Dan Peggotty and the rest the name is used, untouched by reproach in spite of the bitter reflections that Steerforth's conduct could attach to both the name and its class associations.

As David travels to his school he finds himself temporarily threatened by exploitation—like that of the waiter—but also by something more intimate and more savage. A misunderstanding about whether he is a Copperfield or a Murdstone presages the terrible definition of his identity according to the Murdstone logic, represented not only by the choice of school and headmaster but also and mainly by the placard ("beautifully written") placed upon his back and announcing "Take care of him. He bites" (130). Murdstone's instinctive need to destroy David in favour of his own defeated offspring here takes the appropriate form of an attack upon his name and identity. He could not bear to give the terrified and mortified boy the name Murdstone, but forces him in the direction of solitude, anonymity and madness. If the boy were to be known from then on not as "David Copperfield" (or even "David Murdstone") but as "the Biter" or—as some of the early arrivals call him—"Towzer," then he would be almost condemned to death as far as his imaginative potential goes. We do not yet discover what less formal title than "young Copperfield" Steerforth bestows on his protégé, but it is clear that his comment on the earlier naming game, that it was "a jolly shame," is the perfect anodyne (136).

After his mother's death and the inert period at Blunderstone, David's drifting and orphaned personality suffers the deep wound of apparently endless neglect and oblivion, almost crippling to the putative artist. He is a virtually nameless waif in London, trailing clouds of anonymity and alienation: "the young Suffolker" and "the little gent" (someone less aloof might as well have ended up with a mock name as bad as "Mealy Potatoes") are the nearest things to a name he gets, except from the Micawbers. The Micawbers, however, those financial innocents so fascinated by their difficulties that it is clear they would feel lost without them, tend to promote David rather unthinkingly to a premature responsibility. This is not only by comparison with their own genial fecklessness but through requiring him to haggle with pawnbrokers and become an unpaid prison visitor. The nominative sign of this promotion is Micawber's invariably declamatory "Copperfield!" but (like the prospect of something turning up, which fortunately David does not inherit) it is an illusion:

> I think, as Mrs Micawber sat at the back of the coach, with the children, and I stood in the road looking wistfully at them, a mist cleared from her eyes, and she saw what a little creature I really was. (231)

His lack of name, family or connection is one of the most painful aspects of his lonely and betrayed struggle through Canterbury to Dover.

After disposing of the Murdstones, his aunt gives him a new name, a redesigning of the name she gave his non-existent substitute Betsey. In a comic but touching parody of the christening service that she might have dominated had David *been* Betsey, she names him Trotwood Copperfield. Mr Dick is obviously "nature's priest" in this rechristening. "Thus I began my new life, in a new name, and with everything new about me" (271–72). With the comedy somewhat sublimated, his new life and name come under the guardianship of Agnes (his good angel) and the influence of education at Dr Strong's school. However, Canterbury also develops a degraded form of this name, connotative of perpetual childhood, since Uriah can never bring himself to call Trotwood other than "Master Copperfield." Since Trotwood is for a long while half fearful that this title might still be appropriate, it is a quite effective limitation of his self-confidence and the clarity with which he can observe things and people around him.

When Trotwood leaves Kent for East Anglia his raging self-consciousness (hitherto limited to affairs of the heart) would make the label "Master Copperfield" exceptionally painful and accurate. On same road of his anonymous wandering he experiences what, with comic self-pity, he calls "the first fall I had in life" (342). The journey also raises and banishes the terrors of the anonymity of Salem House from Trotwood's conscious mind, but at the Golden Cross he is conclusively fixed in his child form by meeting Steerforth again. His hero's affectionate mockery of everything he does and thinks, his lordly re-disposal of Trotwood's body (much to Trotwood's advantage, certainly), and his bland assumption of superior expertise and wisdom in all things, even the arts, meet no response of resistance from Trotwood's self-respect at all. In view of Steerforth's charm and brilliance, this is hardly to be wondered at, but it is an effective narrative irony that the hard won determination to make his name in the adult world (as when he asks, in his deepest voice, if there are any letters for Trotwood Copperfield Esquire) vanishes immediately that difficult task is removed from him by the angel of his first schooldays. Delighted by the unaffected and tender worship of his protégé, Steerforth takes him over, using a name that, from anyone else, would have been felt most keenly as a reproach:

> 'My dear young Davy,' he said, clapping me on the shoulder again, 'you are a very Daisy. The daisy of the field, at sunrise, is not fresher than you are.' (346)

At Highbury Steerforth's household, especially the superciliously impeccable "pattern of respectability" Littimer and the contortedly acute Rosa Dartle (so sly a parody of naivety in her eagerness to be informed), demonstrate even more convincingly how apposite the name "Daisy" is. As a small innocent glowing prettily among the claws of complex monsters, David of course feels extremely young. This consciousness is later used meticulously by the unholy alliance that has instilled it in Daisy; the Steerforth-Littimer combination is terribly efficient, teaming style with respectability, Adamic charm with satanic subtlety. It is Daisy's pretty ways that attract Steerforth to Yarmouth and the sister-lover of Mas'r Davy's childhood, Little Em'ly. Here we recall a snatch of conversation from Salem House:

> 'You haven't got a sister, have you?' said Steerforth, yawning.
> 'No,' I answered.
> 'That's a pity,' said Steerforth. 'If you had had one, I should think she would have been a pretty, timid, little, bright-eyed sort of girl. I should have liked to know her.' (140)

The casual prurience of the enquiry is heightened by the fact that it is in reply to David's heartfelt gratitude. Later, we find the same assumption that the world owes him its feminine devotion at Highbury, and—in my opinion—in all the scenes where he receives Daisy's shy devotion. In his lordly way, Steerforth is fond of Daisy, but is quite as ready, from mere self-indulgence, to betray him as to foster him.

The Salem House conversation reminds us not only that Em'ly stands in lieu of Daisy's sister but also that David's reaction to Steerforth is in some sense a threat to his own sexual identity. It would be egregious overreading to claim that the novel, or this part of it, is crypto-homosexual, but I believe that the tensions of the relationship involve a dominant male intimacy titillated and eagerly accepted by the shy and blushing passive partner. In other words, Steerforth's interest in Em'ly is not only developed in spite of the betrayal of David's trust that it involves, but also because of it. The feminine nickname "Daisy" becomes a very dangerous plaything when Daisy finds himself aligned with Rosa and Mrs Steerforth (and probably the pretty little maid) in Steerforth's adoring harem. This is verified to some extent by Rosa Dartle's reactions to Daisy; where Mrs Steerforth is content to reject and despise Dan Peggotty for his social class, Rosa lashes out viciously at Daisy. She is supremely conscious of Steerforth not only as villain-hero but also as sexual authority, and it is plain that she has been scarred by him in ways that go deeper than the face. Just as the episode of the harp establishes the razor-edge intensity of her response to Steerforth's physical presence, so does her reaction to Daisy (ostensibly for bringing Dan to the Highbury house) emphasize her involvement with his very existence: "I know that James Steerforth . . . has a false, corrupt heart, and is a traitor. But what need I know or care about this fellow, and his common niece?" (532). Her attacks upon Daisy are almost parallel to her hysterical denunciations of Em'ly and Mrs Steerforth, her female rivals. She feels not only that she is more involved with James Steerforth than anyone else can ever be, but also that these rivals are disqualified by taboo from becoming his true mate: just as Em'ly is guilty of attracting him across the social taboo line, so is Mrs. Steerforth guilty of appealing to him across the incest taboo line—and, I suspect, Daisy across the homosexual taboo line. Since she would stop at nothing to be united with Steerforth herself, she cannot believe that others have any more qualms in pursuing their own single motives (as she conceives them). The mingled vindictiveness and sisterly identification in her care for the bereaved Mrs Steerforth become a constant repetitive cycle of the only feelings worth living for. To paraphrase Steerforth, she has honed herself away, has become her own intensity.

One of the intriguing aspects of the relationship between Steerforth and Daisy connected with sexual tension appears in the early exploitation at Salem House. With the benevolence of divine right, Steerforth has David tell the stories of all the novels and romances he knows:

> 'I tell you what, young Copperfield,' said Steerforth, 'you shall tell 'em to me. I can't get to sleep very early at night, and I generally 'wake rather early in the morning. We'll go over 'em one after another. We'll make some regular Arabian Nights of it.' (144)

This sybaritic image is echoed in David's phrase "it was a tiresome thing to be roused, like the Sultana Scheherazade, and forced into a long story before the getting-up bell rang" (145). Scheherazade's sister notwithstanding, this situation does have reverberations, not least in Steerforth's caliphlike use of Littimer as procurer. His air of being above criticism, of being unquestionably lord of aught that he surveys that is temporarily interesting to him, is part of his charm and the core of his failure.

Daisy's innocence of course is not really effeminate, otherwise the menace of Steerforth's companionship would be at once more obvious and less rich in its implications. It is as a young rake in training that his "Young Innocence" is displayed to Miss Mowcher, in the smooth deception that enables Littimer to use her as a go-between to Em'ly. The ease with which innocence that is unwilling to school itself can lead to corruption of others is not only attested in the famous Chapter 48, "Domestic," but also and equally tellingly in the way the sharp little dwarf is exploited because of the "hot and cold, and red and white, all at once" behaviour of Daisy (525).

In the chaotic period of Mrs Crupp's "Mr Copperfull" and similar errors and oblivions in London, the dazed young proctor scarcely knows who he is. Here Steerforth doubles as the representative of the city's temptations, those in which a young man without firmness of purpose may "lose himself." "My first Dissipation" (Chapter 24) establishes the potential hero's potential to dim rather than brighten in self-knowledge. This eloquent episode summarizes the last of the three near-anonymous stages in David's life, the young man in the big bad city, reminding one of Wordsworth's Luke (in *Michael*). As the drunken Copperfield apostrophizes Steerforth, he is now indeed "theguidingstarofmyexist-ence" (420). Just as Markham loses self in his everlasting impersonal expression "a man . . . ," so Copperfull, free of self-consciousness (in the wrong sense) is aware of himself as if from the outside:

> Somebody was leaning out of my bedroom window, refreshing his forehead against the cool stone of the parapet, and feeling the air upon his face. It was myself. I was addressing myself as 'Copperfield', and saying, "Why did you try to smoke? You might have known you couldn't do it." Now, somebody was unsteadily contemplating his features in the looking-glass. That was I too. I was very pale in the looking-glass; my eyes had a vacant appearance; and my hair—only my hair, nothing else—looked drunk.
>
> . . . .
>
> We went downstairs, one behind another. Near the bottom, somebody fell, and rolled down. Somebody else said it was Copperfield. I was angry at that false report, until, finding myself on my back in the passage, I began to think there might be some foundation for it. (421–22)

Thanks to Agnes, his externalized conscience or "good angel," he "comes to himself," and this dissipation is not repeated, but the state of David's "captivity," his besotted and dazed state of being in love, so that little if anything outside Dora has much reality, has strong similarities to the drunken extraneous self of this episode. It seems possible, by the way, that David was thinking of the "captivity" of the Hebrews when exiled from their true home and identity in Babylon when he uses the title "I fall into Captivity" for Chapter 26.

Dora, the kind of temptation that Daisy and Em'ly seem to have presented to Steerforth (and Clara Copperfield to Murdstone) and the only kind that Miss Betsey Trotwood is unable to equip her own namesake against, infects David with silliness at first sight. This is not unusual when a young man falls in love, but because of her own disposition and training he rapidly gets worse and soon becomes a confirmed case of love-blindness. Her babyish tears and giggles, the play-life which characterizes her, her smug, posturing, self-deceiving father, her love's martyr friend Miss Julia Mills, and her spoiled spaniel Jip, turn David into "Doady" just when the situation as he knows it requires him to be responsible, self-reliant and adult. The chapters focusing on Dora brilliantly intertwine tenderness with extreme exasperation as time and again the adult sexual identity of Agnes just fails to impinge on Doady and he sinks into the Babes-in-the-Wood childishness of his courtship and marriage.

The threat to David Copperfield's identity represented by Doady is partly seen in the mighty allegorical figures his mind establishes and then bathetically falls back from:

> I would sit sometimes of a night, opposite my aunt, thinking how I had frightened Dora that time, and how I could best make my way with a guitar-case through the forest of difficulty . . . (608)

Again, the unconscious precisions of Doady's meditations indicate the almost schizophrenic efforts he makes to avoid judging Dora and his love for her. Such precisions include some simple ambiguities like "but, so far, selfishness was inseparable from Dora . . ." (566), and the more complex sense of wild surmise when his aunt asks questions which imply the totally new possibility that Dora is silly and light-headed. An interesting scene, presaged by the identity threat posed when Dora's aunts think that Traddles is Mr Copperfield, is the first meeting with Dora after Spenlow's death,[2] since there Dora's foolish fears lead her to reveal her tiny pettish spites as directed against the sterling friends Aunt Betsey and Traddles. This scene culminates in her first use of the pet name "Doady"—immediately followed by Doady's explanatory comment "which was a corruption of David" (667), as indeed it was. "David and Dora," already a jingling nursery-rhyme pairing, as of two children playing at house, is all the same more tolerable than "Doady and Dora."

As an author, David acquires a "name" in the specifically public sense, and as an active hero he earns it by working devotedly through the narrow play tunnel of his marriage. A major outward sign of the creative artist as hero is when he turns his autobiographical material to account in his first really significant novel. It is this which has been inhibited by the various childlike names he has survived, and not least by his having "given his name" to Dora in exchange for the "Doady" of baby talk. Just as his spirit sisters Em'ly and Agnes are menaced by the bait of "a good name," one for herself, the other for her father, so David is liberated by his maturely ambitious pursuit of *his* good name as artist.

The limitations of the artist when his opponents are men of action like Steerforth or men of affairs like Uriah Heep are brought out through the interweaving of the Kentish and Anglian plots with the Home plot through Chapters 25–57. Whether his activities in the Home plot are effective or futile, David Copperfield is still capable of seeing and judging his Doady aspect, and he does remain active. However, in both the Anglian and the Kentish stories he remains essentially a passive though passionately concerned observer, identifying strongly with his "sisters," the victims of the two exploiters.

After the chaotic defeat of David's good intentions in "My first Dissipation" there is (not literally but in David's mind) a direct confrontation between the good angel of Kent and the bad angel of Anglia. From that time on, the three plots alternate irregularly until the three climaxes: in Chapter 53 (for the death of Dora, which is the catastrophe of the Home plot), Chapter 54 (for the revelation of Heep's guilt, which is the catastrophe of the Kentish plot) and Chapters 55 and 56 (for the deaths of Ham and Steerforth and the carrying of the news to Highbury, the double catastrophe of the Anglian plot). In Chapter 57 the survivors of the Anglian plot and the Micawbers from the Kentish plot all leave for Australia, and in the opening of the last movement of the novel, when David goes abroad, we have a similar quietude healing the pain of the Home plot. In this case the tumult is past when David returns to England and Agnes, and since he is renewed both as lover and as artist his name is now established.

This takes the double form of fame and gratitude from an admiring public on the one hand, and the perpetuation of David's name through his children on the other. In his children are found not only the names of some of the muses that have inspired his life (Agnes, Betsey Trotwood, Dora, and probably Clara, after his mother and Peggotty) but also his own image. There is a charming reference to the child I assume to be his son David, though there are others:

> I find it very curious to see my own infant face, looking up at me from the Crocodile stories; and to be reminded by it of my old acquaintance Brooks of Sheffield. (947)

Both the rewards of heroes and the ameliorating cycle of human experience are testified to in this image, which would therefore be an alarmingly optimistic one but for the juxtaposed satiric images of the social version of the Desert of Sahara, the ceaseless rehearsal of obsession in Rosa and Mrs Steerforth (who has forgotten his name in order to forget the destruction of her own, 947), and, more closely aligned with the family, the limited changes of the selfless old. It is not a naive impulse towards immobile caricature that keeps, say, Mr Dick almost unaltered, but a subtle testimony to how much everything else but the natural heart *does* change. Only the artist, among those things which (being self-conscious) must alter, can improve, and might earn his name in the way the self-forgetful retain their unspoiled identities.

III

Always, in the major works of Dickens, characters find themselves much more closely involved with each other than they have any right to expect (this is the source of the still reviled "reliance on coincidence" in his plots). However, although this happens in *David Copperfield*, in such episodes as the first visit to Traddles, and especially on the emigrant ship (where Agnes is revealed as having taken a warm sisterly interest in Em'ly, and Micawber and Dan Peggotty become allies), there are some striking exceptions. The villains of the Anglian and Kentish plots may never

meet, except in David's mind. Indeed, though both have efficient and totally obe-
dient unjudging assistants (Littimer and Mrs Heep) they are really very solitary and
self-imprisoned people. More surprisingly, though, their respective opposites and
antagonists—the active surrogates to David in the two plots—also never meet, nor
do they ever meet the villains of the other plot. Ham, embodying the rather
simpering and ignorant lower class version of David's naivety (exactly calculated to
arouse Steerforth's contempt and irritation), never meets anyone not directly
connected with the Anglian plot, let alone Micawber or Heep. Micawber's pompous and wild gestured self-importance conceals imperfectly his improvident good
nature; he is a vulnerable and ludicrous version of David's innocent and enthusiastic
concern for others, his potential for magnanimity, and exactly the kind of legal and
financial gull and self-deceiver that Uriah would most like to exploit, tyrannize over
and despise. The villains are both oblivious to the true strengths and delights of their
antagonists' personalities, or (to be more exact) they see in David what they are
blind to in its lower manifestations.

It is true that Steerforth passes Micawber outside David's rooms in Chapter
28, and is highly amused by David's description of him, vowing that "he was a man
to know, and he must know him" (486)—it is also true that Traddles might have
linked them, but Steerforth has no interest in renewing acquaintance with Traddles.
There are tantalizing gestures of this kind associated with Littimer, too. Earlier in the
same chapter that respectable man interrupts and blights the merry gridiron operations at which Micawber was presiding, and later he is found in the cell adjoining
Uriah's, his only parallel as a model prisoner. But these only serve to remind us of
how scrupulously the villains, their antagonists and their styles are separated through
the whole book.

There is, however, one excellent example of Dickens's use of non-logical
recognition which tantalizingly suggests their parallel roles. David dreams of Heep,
after his first day at school, in a way that links the two plots and aligns the two
villains with admirable subtlety:

> [I dreamed] about him, for what appeared to me to be half the night; and
> [dreamed] . . . that he had launched Mr Peggotty's house on a piratical expe-
> dition, with a black flag at the masthead, bearing the inscription 'Tidd's Prac-
> tice', under which diabolical ensign he was carrying me and little Em'ly to the
> Spanish Main, to be drowned. (293)

As a prophetic dream from a very young artist may well do, this confuses two
things that the merely rational mind would consider unalike, the glamorous tyranny
of the seamanlike Steerforth and the sly practices of Uriah. However, the threat to
both David and his two soul sisters (here conflated to one) is real, and the piratical
swashbuckling of Steerforth is not really much more than a step from the diabolical
theft of a good man's house by Uriah.

No such parallel is made between these two villains (the destructive namers
of David) and Dora, the unintentional threat to his development. However, in
David's reactions to their degrading names for him we do have a grading of them.

Steerforth's affectionate but dismissively mocking "Daisy" is gladly and openly accepted by David, like so much else from his brilliant mentor; he is tenderly reluctant
to accept Dora's "Doady" once he realizes that it is a wrong and emasculating name;
Uriah's elaborate writhings of apology for tying "Mister Copperfield" back to "Master Copperfield" only make it less acceptable, though it clings infuriatingly to all their
transactions (there is an excellent scene where David uses the name Uriah, "spontaneous"). In most other respects Dora's name for him, though limiting, is quite
dissimilar to the others: her pen-holding is a ritual of apology for not being able
otherwise to help him grow beyond "Doady" into "David Copperfield, Author,"
whereas the others, however much they are attracted to David, consciously try to
keep him ignorant and undeveloped for their own purposes. This is for reasons of
sexual rivalry, but also because of a profound sense that he is their spiritual superior
and a reproach to them. Perhaps Steerforth's text might be

> .. .and under him
> My genius is rebuked, as it is said
> Mark Antony's was by Caesar.   (Macbeth of Banquo,[3] *Macbeth* III.i.55–57)

and Uriah's

> He hath a daily beauty in his life
> That makes me ugly.   (Iago of Cassio, *Othello* V.i.19–20)

The simplicity that Steerforth sees but can only mar is in all the open-hearted
Anglians, and the generosity that makes Uriah so conscious of his own malicious
meanness can be found in the Strongs and the Wickfields as well as in the Micawbers, Traddles, and David.

To be more specific, Steerforth is attracted not only by the innocent responsiveness of Daisy but also by his creative potential. What was a utilizable talent for
the schoolboy caliph when Daisy was playing Schererazade seems to inspire an
unconscious jealousy in the lordly young man (who is still a spoiled child to whom
everything comes too easily). Subtly Dickens delineates a proud and vigorous
nature touched and secretly humiliated before the achieved and creative openness
of his admiring young friend. At the risk of overstatement, we may say that
Steerforth seduces Em'ly partly as if he were raping and destroying the imagination
of Daisy.

Uriah is Steerforth's opposite in that everything comes to him through unre-
mitting, stretching and twisting effort. His servility and charmless grovelling can
never make him loved or respected. He both loves and helplessly hates Master
Copperfield, and the very blatancy of his tactics results in Master Copperfield
responding with a revolted fascination, sometimes almost like a bird before a snake.
Like Steerforth, Uriah can at times dominate David's imagination almost exclusively,
but soon the artist can turn and respond elsewhere. When we see Uriah, cornered
and revealed, addressing his vindictive snarls at Master Copperfield rather than at
the architects and executives of his defeat, Traddles and Micawber, it reminds us
that all his major machinations, culminating in his attempt to change the name of

"your Agnes" to "my Agnes" (641), are largely the product of his knowledge that Master Copperfield is his rival, and that to frustrate any growth into Mister Copperfield, or especially David Copperfield, Author, is his primary objective. At times it seems that Uriah's longing to degrade Agnes, and his hatred of mankind in general, are almost trivial by comparison. The perverted and convoluted logic that discovers Master Copperfield as the secret manipulator of his defeat has always seen him as the true opponent, even from the first few days in Canterbury. This essential opposition causes all the ambitious wiles of the young lawyer to be redirected for more destructive purposes; he feels it imperative to bring down the creative potential, the instinctive, undisciplined and wholly proper pride of the younger author, to his own level. With "pride that licks the dust" he finds his humility become malevolence, not merely self-interest or lust.

It has of course been recognised that the names David and Uriah echo the story of King David and Bathsheba (II Samuel) and that that echo is a sharp irony in itself. Agnes is named for Bathsheba in the form given her by Nathan's rebuking parable, "the one ewe lamb" (II Samuel 12.1–14). However, in spite of the greasy covetousness and lechery of the phrase "my Agnes," Agnes could never be Heep's, whatever happened to Master Copperfield. Again, it would be macabre in the extreme to connect the deaths of Dora's child and Dora herself with the guilt (if any) of the David-Agnes relationship. However, there are connections between the biblical and the Canterbury stories, at least in Uriah's mind. Uriah always avoids the name David, but feels the rule of this English King David over a harem of adoring women is a standing affront to his own unlovely self-consciousness, knowing he is adored only by one unlovely woman. He sees David worshipped by his Aunt Betsey, by Peggotty, and by Agnes above all; we can be sure too that he sucks up all available information about Clara Copperfield, Little Em'ly and Dora with even more avidity than usual. Uriah, plunged into the fieriest state of envy, must have been made all the more passionate by his perception that Master Copperfield has childishly taken over these hearts without even thinking about it. Master Copperfield's relationship with Agnes, especially, remains dangerously presexual for the duration of Uriah's plotting—David seems content to remain Master Copperfield in that area because he is Doady elsewhere. However, this only makes matters worse for Uriah's world view—how galling to realize that your enemy and spiritual opposite, so overpoweringly successful, does not even notice that the contest is going on!

Like the Biblical Uriah refusing to go down to his own house and lie with Bathsheba but lying at David's door, Uriah has worked out exactly how humbly he ought to proceed (in terms of the battlefield) before he unburdens himself to Master Copperfield. It is impossible for him to be spontaneous, uncalculating or artless, even when he tells the truth. The grotesquerie of the parallel with II Samuel is brought out especially well by the repulsive sight of Uriah sleeping before David's fire, just as the earlier Uriah had slept at the door of King David. This Uriah has become so adroit at abasing himself that, like envious malice, the prone posture "comes natural" to him. It is comically apposite that his uncertainty about initial h-sounds extends to the pronunciation of "heart" as "art," for his heart is indeed all craft or sullen art. His heart, like Iago's, is totally disciplined, especially to the hatred of all who are superior to him. Like Iago again, he has long realized ("we had such a lot of betters!" 639), that everyone around him is his better. Yet always he hates the finest best.

Gracefully, this superiority, and even an echo of the Bathsheba story, is an issue in the Anglian plot too. Just as Uriah's vicious servility brings out the innate royalty of spirit in King David Copperfield ("Master" in Dan Peggotty's sense, not Uriah's), so Daisy's uncalculated response to Steerforth emphasizes the greatness of potential and the consequent greatness of the betrayal in his hero. Just as Uriah sees Master Copperfield surrounded by adoring women (though not quite as many as Saul's wives), so Daisy sees Steerforth adored in Highbury and realizes he must always be so adored wherever he goes. Daisy, as the representative of the trustful, dutiful and respectful Uriahs, Dan Peggotty and Ham, realizes that they have but their one ewe lamb; Littimer makes a thoroughly respectable Joab to effect their deprivation. If Uriah's heart is all art, Steerforth's is all careless ease and self-indulgence, a royalty of nature and blessedness before God that becomes an unthinking tyranny of temperament and whim. If Master Copperfield seems to Uriah to behave as if Agnes is his by divine right, so does Steerforth seem to behave in the eyes of Rosa, Dan and Ham Peggotty, and all judges less partial than Daisy.

It is curious that both Uriah and Steerforth, the one as consciously below David as the other is consciously above him, feel the need to give him a "conditioning" or involuntary excuse for their past and future conduct and their moral situation. In Chapter 39, just before his first blatant declaration of intent to Mr Wickfield (so elegantly contrasting with Agnes's selfless advice to Trotwood about the effective wooing of Dora's aunts), Uriah gives a famous account of his foundation school upbringing (639). Standing in the little unassuming ark he is about to wreck, Steerforth had long before lamented his unguided state to his "gentle Daisy"—though for once he addresses him without mockery as "David."

'David, I wish to God I had had a judicious father these last twenty years! . . . I wish with all my soul I had been better guided! . . . I wish with all my soul I could guide myself better!

. . . .

At odd dull times, nursery tales come up into the memory, . . . I believe I have been confounding myself with the bad boy who "didn't care", and became food for lions—a grander kind of going to the dogs, I suppose. What old women call the horrors, have been creeping over me from head to foot. I have been afraid of myself. . . . it would have been well for me (and for more than me) if I had had a steadfast and judicious father!' (380–81)

Since we have had abundant evidence that David's lack of a father, and even the provision of an appallingly steadfast stepfather, does not destroy the ability in him to care for others, we find this excuse less than completely effective. Ham is also immediately available for comparison. However, just as is the case with Uriah's more celebrated account of his upbringing, this passage has the merit of indicating how little the speaker has grown beyond the limitations of his childhood. In Steerforth's case we remember the hurling of the hammer at Rosa; "A promising young angel I must have been!" is Steerforth's wry comment (353), and the description remains valid, not only in that he is, as Agnes realizes, Trotwood's evil angel, but also in that he still shows flashes, just as at Salem House, of his potential to be the brightest of the angels. Interestingly, although the treacheries in the two houses that David loves and which at different times adopted him are parallel in many ways, the successful treachery (by transferring the designing function to the instrument Littimer) never makes the fallen angel seem calculating. Steerforth's "air of easy patronage" may conceal hypocrisy and vicious self-interest, but it is not in itself an illusion. In strict contrast, Uriah is never able for a moment to conceal from the rest of the human race his essential ugliness of spirit, whatever else he conceals.

Appropriately, both villains have a strong influence upon David's education, since both attempt to trap him in his childlike state, just as they are trapped respectively in their destructive self-will and servile malice. Steerforth casually and brilliantly dominates Salem House whenever he has a mind to, alternately liberating and limiting David's creative potential, protecting the small boy or abetting Creakle's ignorant tyranny as the mood takes him. He calls out David's story-telling talent or dismisses the well-meaning Mr Mell according to how things suit with him. Uriah has no control over the second stage of David's education, naturally, but he has a strong resentment of it from the first. He endeavours to make Trotwood ashamed of his opportunity to learn Latin, but then retreats in disorder from the magnanimity with which Trotwood offers to teach him in turn. Later his vindictive and obscene attempt to destroy the happiness of Dr Strong and his wife is based as much upon his awareness of David's love and gratitude for his old teacher as upon his loathing of the lofty cad Jack Maldon, his hatred of women or his urge to isolate Agnes from all help. His implication of Master Copperfield in his accusation is an especially cruel blow, to which a physical blow cannot serve as reply. Just as Steerforth plays upon the most vulnerable parts of David's character and friendships, so Uriah unerringly picks as his victims those David loves. In distinction to the creative artist's blending of the responsive heart and the disciplined mind, both villains exaggerate the miseducation of their own sensibilities. Uriah's constant professions of humility not only half conceal but entirely exacerbate his loathing of Master Copperfield and all the potential in mankind. Steerforth's charming and easy dominance of the imagination must either make him into the bad boy who "didn't care" for anything at all or make his infantile self-love totally unschoolable and constantly destructive. Although David is essentially passive in both plots (Dan and Ham are the active sufferers in the Anglian plot, Micawber and Traddles the righteous exposers of villainy in the Kentish one), he is nonetheless seen as the natural opposite of both villains, for almost opposite reasons.

A detailed study might be made of the art associations of the chief characters. One could compare the artless artistry of Steerforth (whenever he cares to try) with the earnest efforts of Daisy, whether later toiling with shorthand or earlier spinning romances in the lazy ear of his hero. The art of writing is paralleled both to legal copying—a major industry in the Kentish plot, with Uriah contrasted with Mr Dick, Mr Micawber and Sophy Traddles—and to the guiltier, less circumscribed imitations of forgery and fraud. Dora's inability to read cookbooks or do more than hold pens makes for similar contrasts, but gives an effect of pathos to the treatment both of the young author and of his helpless wife; for Dickens, pathos and tenderness are creative and positive emotions, by the way, not mawkish, inhibiting ones. The art theme, however, might most eloquently be used to compare the still, quiet guidance of the Agnus Dei church window with the fussy sentimental trilling of Dora's guitar and the vacuous rhetoric of Miss Julia Mills. Just as David's arrival at the status of successful novelists parallels his begetting of an indefinite (but substantial) number of children, so does his early period of struggle parallel his artistic and his emotional recognitions. Indeed, the very concept of "making a name for himself" cannot be separated from the concepts of signing one's name, giving one's name, and passing one's name onto the future.

It is commonly acknowledged that Dickens, given the need to name his villains and ludicrous characters in a way that would not offend his readers (whatever their names might be), took enormous care to provide exactly the right name for each character. In conspicuous examples throughout his writing, ranging from the adoption of pseudonyms by a hero in *Our Mutual Friend* or the process of finding names for orphans in *Oliver Twist* and *Little Dorrit* to crucial issues like the appositeness of the title *Dombey and Son* or the invention of a past for the name Bounderby, we find intensified care for the significance of names. In his various attempts to discover the right name for the hero (as listed in a footnote to the Penguin edition, 951) we see a serious concern to involve the necessary art and nature connotations in a name worth battling over. There can be no example, even in Dickens, of such powerful interchanging and contrasting names (and absences of names) at the centre of a novel—at the disciplined heart, as it were. Nor can I recall any story, myth or legend in which attempts to give the hero the wrong name (attempts by his allies as well as his conscious or unconscious opponents) remain so much a focus of the whole narrative, from before his birth to the final world-wide acceptance and celebration of his true name.

NOTES

[1] *The Personal History of David Copperfield*, ed. Trevor Blount, Penguin Books, 1966, p. 49. Further page reference to this edition are in the text.
[2] Dora's father is her true begetter; irresponsibly bedecking both of them with outward proofs of prosperity, he eventually is discovered to have not enough identity to put his name to a will. Disappearing or inadequate fathers have much to answer for.
[3] Steerforth compares himself to Macbeth, and Daisy to "a reproachful ghost" confronted by Banquo's ghost, of course, and draws attention to the "mongrel time, neither day nor night" and the "Devil's bark of a boat" that he has usurped the soul of, in a brilliantly rich lament, 379–81. The beauty and acuity of Dickens's use of Shakespeare (as of the Bible) has not always been properly acknowledged.

Mark M. Hennelly, Jr.

"THE THEME OF THIS INCOMPREHENSIBLE CONUNDRUM WAS THE MOON"

Long time in search of knowledge did I range
The field of human life, in heart and mind
Benighted; but, the dawn beginning now
To re-appear, 't was proved that not in vain
I had been taught to reverence a Power
That is the visible quality and shape
And image of right reason; that matures
Her processes by steadfast laws; gives birth
To no impatient or fallacious hopes,
No heat of passion or excessive zeal,
No vain conceits; provokes no quick turns
Of self-applauding intellect; but trains
To meekness, and exalts by humble faith;
Holds up before the mind intoxicate
With present objects, and the busy dance
Of things that pass away, a temperate show
Of objects that endure; and by this course
Disposes her, when over-fondly set
On throwing off incumbrances, to seek
In man, and in the frame of social life,
Whate'er there is desirable and good
Of kindred permanence, unchanged in form
And function, or, through strict vicissitude,
Of life and death, revolving. Above all
Were re-established now those watchful thoughts
Which, seeing little worthy or sublime
In what the Historian's pen so much delights
To blazon—power and energy detached
From moral purpose—early tutored me
To look with feelings of fraternal love

From *Studies in the Novel* 10, No. 4 (Winter 1978): 375–96.

Upon the unassuming things that hold
A silent station in this beauteous world.

—*The Prelude* (1850), XIII, ll. 16–47[1]

Just before Dora's death in *David Copperfield* (1849–50), David revisits Canterbury and remarks: "the towers themselves, overlooking many a long unaltered mile of rich country and its pleasant streams, were cutting the bright morning air, *as if there were no such thing as change on earth*. Yet the bells, when they sounded, *told me sorrowfully of change in everything*" (p. 742, italics mine).[2] His apparent ambivalence here addresses a central issue in this novel, as well as in all of Dickens's novels, namely the problematic clash between changelessness and change, that is, between Being and Becoming, the One and the Many. In fact, a rough count reveals well over a hundred such specific references and over three hundred if combined with synonyms and antonyms like "vicissitudes," "loss," "time," "same," "permanent," "constant," "adapt," and "alter." When that wise-lunatic Mr. Dick Babley greets David with "Ha! Phoebus! . . . How does the world go?" (p. 202), his epithet and central question hit, as usual, upon a half-truth since the sun is one of Dickens's primary metaphors for this clash and since David certainly embodies the unchanging characteristics—intelligence, static resilience, daylight ("Daisy" or Day's eye) innocence—of a solar hero in quest of metaphysical knowledge. On the other hand, David is also "The moonstruck slave of Dora" (p. 474); and it is his lunar madness which he must learn to reconcile with its sunny counterpart. The moon's waxing and waning values include imaginativeness, dynamic growth, and dark experience. Unintentionally symbolizing this duality, David twice considers the paradox of how to "round the square" (p. 487), that is, the "venerable riddle of my childhood, to go 'round and round the house, without ever touching the house'" (p. 474). He concludes, and this playful metaphor is the key to the present reading of *David Copperfield*, that "I believe the theme of this incomprehensible conundrum was the moon" (p. 474).

Following Coleridge's famous definition of the Imagination, Morse Peckham has demonstrated that the Romantic paradox resolving symbolic lunar and solar contraries is an identical conundrum;[3] and it is this Romantic riddle reconciling change with permanence, temporal beauty with eternal truth, that is one of Dickens's primary interests in the novel. I mean *Romantic* here, however, not in terms of the often cited influence of Carlyle; but as our epigraph from *The Prelude* suggests, *Romantic* in the Wordsworthian sense of imitating the simple purity of Natural Forms, "the unassuming things that hold / A silent station in this beauteous world" (ll. 46–47).[4] Indeed, those thirty-one lines from Book Thirteen, published in the same year as *David Copperfield*, include all the major nuances of Dickens's conundrum of change. Consequently, after outlining relevant past readings of the novel and the thematic significance of this riddle of "the melancholy glory of the moon" (p. 199), we will discuss more fully the way it interrelates and informs the narrative technique, the fairy tale-Romance structure, and the overlapping image patterns of polarized Nature, retreats-invasions, and youth-age.

Pertinent critical reactions to *David Copperfield* fall into two related camps; and both are relevant to, and somewhat reconciled by an understanding of the problem of change. The first views the novel as the most classic example of what James E. Marlow terms "the two horns of Dickens's dilemma both in life and art. On the one hand, he wished to reconcile mankind (and, undoubtedly, himself) to the world; on the other, he felt the need to escape from the world."[5] These readers discover a maddening, because irreconciled, counterpointal movement in the novel, what A. O. J. Cockshut calls "two almost opposite qualities,"[6] and James R. Kincaid labels "a basic dualism, a split between the comic world of the imagination, and the threatening and hostile world of practical or commercial 'reality.' "[7] This tension between what we can call simplistic and usually pastoral permanence and complex and normally urban, chaotic change overlaps into the second critical camp which emphasizes the transitional place of *David Copperfield* in Dickens's canon. Here it is not so much that Dickens consistently fails to reconcile permanence with change, but that his earlier novels celebrate comic worlds of eternally-sunny springtime, *loci amoeni* like Dingley Dell; while his more mature works focus on the tragic, lunar effects of temporal institutions like Chancery, Marshalsea, and Coketown's factories. *David Copperfield* bridges the sacred and profane—although usually it is looked upon as rooted most firmly in the former, as Dickens's swan song to unending youth. Philip Hobsbaum, for instance, claims this book is "the last novel of his apprenticeship" and his final "protest at facing life";[8] and the Leavises see it as the last of the "happy endings."[9] However, G. K. Chesterton's commentary is an important qualification to this usual view; for he finds that *Dombey and Son* is the end of Dickens's immature phase, while *David Copperfield* is the beginning of his darker, more mature vision: *Dombey* "is the last farce. . . . And in a sense his next novel may be called his first novel. But the growth of this great novel, 'David Copperfield,' is a thing very interesting, but at the same time very dark, for it is a growth in the soul."[10] At least implicit, then, in the critical disagreement over the novel is the question of whether Dickens dramatizes a fictional world of permanence, or a world of change, or both. And if both, are they reconciled or irreconciled? I hope to show not only that both worlds are reconciled, but also that their respective concern with changelessness and change helps coordinate the major image patterns and themes in *David Copperfield*. If Dickens does agree with Wordsworth that the child is father of the man, and if this Romantic equation bridges the gap between eternal innocence and mutable experience, then the job of a comprehensive reading of the novel is to try to provide the solution to its conundrum of change.

David Copperfield's riddle regarding "the swarm of life" (p. 845) teases both the novel's characters and readers out of thought because, like Wordsworth's "Power" in *The Prelude*, it "Holds up before the mind intoxicate / With present objects, and the busy dance / Of things that pass away, a temperate show / Of objects that endure" (ll. 29–32). The question then is: Is reality protean or permanent? and similarly, does human happiness demand adaptive change or adamant resilience? As far as I can discover, the only reader to deal directly with this central issue in Dickens is Dianne F. Sadoff in her essay on "Change and Changelessness in *Bleak House*"; and her assumptions reflect the critical debate over Dickens's two voices. Implicitly assuming that to change is the mature thing to do and to remain the same is regressive escapism, Professor Sadoff declares that "Obsessive change and obsessive changelessness conflict throughout the novel [*Bleak House*] because Dickens feels divided about these opposing values." She concludes that "Because he cannot decide whether change means healthy growth or loss, frustration, and separation, Dickens and his characters vacillate between experiencing those alternatives, and as a result he and they always confront change with trepidation."[11] This persuasive study, however, fails to understand Dickens's real point, which is, to use the diction of our opening questions, that reality is *both* protean *and* permanent and that consequently humanity itself must sometimes adapt but at other times remain resilient. Put more precisely, Dickens consistently believed, and *David Copperfield* dramatizes this belief, that first of all the external world is in flux, but there is a primordial and permanent pattern to that flux, and secondly the individual must conform to this changing flux, but still remain impervious to the kind of wholesale adaptation that would destroy his very individuality. As a man speaking to men, Joe's household words to Pip regarding mutability and mature, steadfast acceptance of it, suggest Dickens's simple, Wordsworthian celebration of such natural piety: "Pip, dear old chap, life is made of ever so many partings welded together, as I may say, and one man's a blacksmith, and one's a whitesmith, and one's a goldsmith, and one's a coppersmith. Diwisions among such must come, and must be met as they come" (*Great Expectations*, ch. 27). Moreover, like Wordsworth in "Elegiac Stanzas," Dickens repeatedly compares physical and psychological change, the "winter of despair" or the "spring of hope" (*A Tale of Two Cities*, Bk. I, ch. 1), and frequently demands that the numinous transcend phenomena. Thus, David "gradually fell . . . to tracing prospects in the live-coals, and to thinking, as they broke and changed, of the principal vicissitudes and separations that had marked my life" (p. 830); while in an earlier conversation with Dora: "I was not aware of any change having taken place in the weather. It was in the state of my own feelings" (p. 394). And as we will observe, Dickens is remarkably fertile and flexible in diagnosing attitudes toward external and internal change and changelessness, in demonstrating the reciprocity and, finally, identity between solar and lunar values. For example, Uriah Heep's satanic malice is reflected in his eyes ever glowing like "two red suns . . . either just rising or just setting" (p. 221); but the growing mystery of his saturnine "power" over David is revealed in his apparition "looking flabby and lead-coloured in the moonlight" (p. 574). Lunar change finally unites with solar permanence in David's profession of his love for Agnes: "I have been through the darkness that is past. Whatever betides, whatever new ties you may form, whatever changes may come between us, I shall always look to you, and love you, as I do now and have always done" (p. 843).

In terms of external changelessness versus change, Dickens's early title for the novel, *The Copperfield Survey of the World as It Rolled*, appears to suggest his belief in a world of process; and in a primary sense *David Copperfield* is certainly like the Chinese *I Ching,* a Book of Changes, a canto to mutability. For example, apropos of the death of David's mother, Mrs. Creakle and Mr. Omer deliver thematic statements that underscore the difficult lesson that the individual must not delude himself into believing that he can change a changing world; he can only hope to change himself in adapting to the hard times around him: " 'You are too young to know how the world changes everyday,' said Mrs. Creakle, 'and how the people in it pass away. But we all have to learn it, David; some of us when we are young, some of us when we are old, some of us at all times of our lives' " (p. 123); and "fashions are like human beings. They come in, nobody knows when, why, or how; and they go out, nobody knows when, why, or how. Everything is like life, in my opinion, if you look at it in that point of view" (p. 126). Thus there are "very agreeable change[s]" (p. 19) which allow David to "seek the restoration of my peace in change" (p. 769) after Dora's death; but there are also those "dread surprise[s]"—the "prospect of change and separation" (pp. 441–42), like the death of Barkis and loss of Emily. As Dr. Strong understands, however, all change is "unavoidable change . . . in the sequence of time" (p. 657); and houses like Mrs. Steerforth's, which remains in a "changeless state" (p. 665), are doomed to decay and dementia; for change is a principle of life, and lack of change is death. But that very "sequence of time" itself supplies an enduring pattern to the change; and Dickens's attentive reader is well aware that he also champions such unchanging externals as Agnes's home at Canterbury, which remains always "unchanged" (p. 838); or better, any disagreeable change there is only transitory or illusory: "All the little changes that had crept in when the Heeps were there, were changed again. Everything was as it used to be in the happy time" (p. 838). As a matter of fact, David's farewell to the reader is one which, like Wordsworth's, attempts to reconcile "the busy dance / Of things that pass away" with "objects that endure": "Oh Agnes, oh my soul, so may thy face be by me when I close my life indeed; so may I, when realities are melting from me like the shadows which I now dismiss, still find thee near me, pointing upward!" (p. 877).

In *David Copperfield,* there are fewer truly good but static characters who do not change internally, like Little Dorrit who is "always without change" (Bk. II, ch. 4), than the general reader might suspect; but as those histrionics of Agnes's final posture suggest, she apparently is one of the few. Indeed she approaches Wordsworth's "Power / That is the visible quality and shape / And image of right reason; that matures / Her processes by steadfast laws" (ll. 19–22); as David affirms, "She did not once show me any change in herself. What she always had been to me, she still was; wholly unaltered" (p. 857). In the final scene with the returning Dan Peggotty, however, even her sober serenity is transfigured to an emblem of playful Dora: "I never saw Agnes laugh so. . . . she could not leave off laughing" (p. 869). And unlike both Murdstone and David, whom Dickens similarly satirizes for trying to "change" their child-brides, Agnes alone can preach for a gradual "change" in David's hero-worship of Steerforth: "you can . . . change any sentiment that has become a conviction to you" (p. 368); and David is auspiciously the only "cause of . . . bright change in her attentive face" (p. 567). Another such character whom

David and Dickens both seem to condone is Clara Peggotty who, after presumably confronting change in her marriage to Barkis, "was just the same as ever" (p. 146). Usually, however, Dickens condemns such total inflexibility. For example, beneath his "inconstant humour" (p. 800), Steerforth remains basically "unchanged" (p. 301), that is, his constant vacillation is the mark of his lack of mature growth; and the final catatonia of his mother reflects her son's petrified heart: "the figure was unchanged, and looked unchangeable" (p. 801). Similarly, Heep and Creakle's declaration that Uriah in prison "was changed" and "quite changed" (p. 854) ironically reveals that his renewed "umbleness" is "perfectly consistent and unchanged" (p. 856). The inability to adapt to change maturely is questioned most seriously with Dora; and Jip's identical problem is talismanic of his mistress's since he "positively refused to adapt himself to circumstances" (p. 603). Implicitly, Dickens even seems to disapprove of Ham who, though always "honourable and manful" (p. 314), passively stagnates after his loss of little Emily; as Mr. Peggotty suggests, "Ham was just the same . . . wearing away his life with kiender no care nohow for 't" (p. 676). On the other hand, though Dickens sometimes criticizes internal change, he ordinarily champions it, as long as it does not betray stabilizing personality traits such as Agnes's repeated triple virtues of "goodness, peace, and truth" (p. 232) or Aunt Betsey's echoing and finally fulfilled wish that David develop the enduring virtues and become "persevering, self-reliant, self-denying" (p. 776). Thus, while little Emily rightly criticizes herself to Ham: "I'm often cross to you, and changeable with you, when I ought to be far different" (p. 339), David's approval of "What a change in Mrs. Gummidge in a little time!" (p. 458) is a clearer reflection of Dickens's usual sympathies, though again Mrs. Gummidge's reformed selflessness significantly is characterized by stable, unending perseverance: "She persevered an equable cheerfulness in the midst of her sympathy, which was not the least astounding part of the change that had come over her" (p. 459). Consequently, Dickens's paradox is that characters must adapt to change, yet they must also develop personality traits which will help them endure change.

But to understand more fully Dickens's reconciling attitude toward change and permanence, we must take a brief, closer look at these qualities in three pivotal foil characters—Dan Peggotty, Mr. Micawber, and Dr. Strong. On the one hand, the always "rough and ready" Peggotty in "conviction remained unchanged" (p. 714) in his fidelity to Emily; and thus David certainly is correct in pointing out at their final meeting that "Time has changed me more than it has you" (p. 867). On the other hand, Mr. Peggotty does change in a way which becomes exemplary for David and thematically crucial for Dickens. As he confesses to Martha, the fall of Emily has taught him that innocence and experience, or virtue and vice, are *not* self-exclusive qualities: "God forbid as I should judge you. . . . You doen't know half the change that's come, in the course of time, upon me" (p. 684). The case of Mr. Micawber is more instructive since for the first half of the novel, he remains, like David, "not a bit changed" (p. 406); or in his own idiom, "I am *in statu quo*" (p. 406). And as David learns, Micawber's temperament, having "undergone many vicissitudes" (p. 530), is consistently mercurial. Moreover, when Mrs. Micawber first writes

David that "Mr. Micawber is entirely changed" (p. 624) and then writes Traddles of
the resulting "change in Mr. Micawber's conduct, of his wildness, of his violence"
(p. 703), his fortunate fall into the depths of external and internal cataclysm renders
him a foil for David's analogous fall. Furthermore, Micawber's final recovery and
"adaption of himself to a new state of society" (p. 802) become a model for David's
own self-renewal through change. Lastly, the absent-minded Dr. Strong seems to
be Dickens's weakest personification of inert and thus unearned benevolence. To
young David even the plant life around Strong's school is "symbolical to me of
silence and retirement" (p. 228); in fact, David consciously identifies with the
pastoral permanence of Canterbury: "I wondered the place was so little changed,
until I reflected how little I was changed myself " (p. 564). Strong's well-intentioned
creation of a similar, hothouse cloister for his child-wife Annie is double-edged since
it denies the possibility of her natural growth and thus covertly comments upon
David's protection of Dora; as Strong admits, "I regarded myself as a refuge, for
her, from the dangers and vicissitudes of life" (p. 618). The "late change" (p. 662)
in the Doctor is thus realistic and even redemptive because it ultimately places his
marriage in a much more open and equitable state than before Heep's warped
revelation of the Jack Maldon affair. His thematic acceptance of both change and
non-change consequently casts implicit suspicion upon the lack of productive change
in David's first marriage and also provides one of the clearest examples of Dickens's
solution to the conundrum of change. As Strong confesses to Annie, "If any unavoidable change has come, in the sequence of time, upon our married life, you are
not to blame. The fault is mine, and only mine. There is no change in my affection,
admiration, and respect" (p. 657).

    Wordsworth's formula for poetry—"emotion recollected in tranquility"—is an
accurate description of Dickens's first-person, narrative technique, which itself is
another barometer of thematic change. David himself affirms: "this narrative is my
written memory" (p. 817); and J. Hillis Miller has seconded the motion: "*David
Copperfield* . . . is before everything a novel of memory."[12] Significantly, David's
very act of recollection is the last change in his developing, adapting personality: "I
set down this remembrance here, because it is an instance to myself of . . . how
some main points in the character I shall consciously develop, I suppose, in writing
my life, were gradually forming all this while" (p. 168). Not until the protean flux of
his past experience can be permanently ordered and structured by his recording
act of memory can David finally understand that change is "natural." Thus his return
from Switzerland to the inn where years before he had chanced upon Steerforth
"recalled, at first, that so-different time when I had put up at the Golden Cross, and
reminded me of the changes that had come to pass since then; but that was natural"
(p. 820). Like Wordsworth in *The Prelude*, David's "spots of time" also "retain / A
renovating virtue" (XII, ll. 209–11), so that with this last memory, "I had recovered
my spirits" (p. 820). Consequently, as implied earlier, David's searching memory
discovers order both in external process, what his maturing recollection once
describes as "all the colours of my life were changing" (p. 861), and in his own
confused, internal transformations, those "shifting quicksands of my mind" (p. 819).
As William H. Marshall perceptively argues, this technique is a kind of dramatic

monologue enabling David to understand "with increasing clarity what he has written earlier in his manuscript, but at any stage he is still in the process of becoming."[13] Consequently, as the Wordsworthian "train" of associations surrounding the "changeless state" of Steerforth's house suggests, Dickens's art of memory in *David Copperfield* is one of his most notable Romantic strategies, "blending" together solar "experience" and the lunar "imagination": "my mind could not go by it and leave it, as my body did; and it usually awakened a long train of meditations. . . . mingled with the childish recollections and later fancies, the ghosts of half-formed hopes, the broken shadows of disappointments dimly seen and understood, the blending of experience and imagination, incidental to the occupation with which my thoughts had been busy, it was more than commonly suggestive" (p. 665).

The structure of the novel depends upon two ancient forms which both make generous use of riddles of metamorphosis, the fairy tale and the Romance.[14] Generally speaking, *David Copperfield* begins in the changeless, solar world of the fairy tale and concludes in the realm of the Romance, many of whose lunar adventures signalizing mature growth are internalized in the more modern, Romantic genre of the *Bildungsroman*.[15] In fact, while he convalesces in Switzerland after Dora's death, David clearly heralds the end of his fairy-tale existence and the beginning of his Romance-quest to redeem his own personal wasteland. He feels "a hopeless consciousness of all that I had lost—. . . the whole airy castle of my life; of all that remained—a ruined blank and waste, lying wide around me, unbroken, to the dark horizon" (p. 813). At the outset the hero, embodying the fear-fulfilling paranoia of fairy-tale orphans, sees himself as Tom Thumb, "the boy in the fairy tale" (p. 27), that is, as Oedipal David battling a series of repressive Goliaths like Murdstone and Creakle.[16] Consequently, he seeks the womblike security of pre-lapsarian Edens where no serpent of mutability has yet reared its head. As he remarks of his puppy love for Dora, "it would have been a happy fate to have been struck immortal with those foolish feelings, and have strayed among the trees for ever!" (p. 485). But Bruno Bettelheim's remarks are necessary to qualify the repeated criticism that Dickens himself is half in love with this· easeful and eternal Fairyland:

> Dickens understood that the imagery of fairy tales helps children better than anything else in their most difficult and yet important and satisfying task: achieving a more mature consciousness to civilise the chaotic pressures of the unconscious. . . . In childhood, more than in any other age, all is becoming. As long as we have not yet achieved considerable security within ourselves, we cannot engage in difficult psychological struggles unless a positive outcome seems certain to us, whatever the chances may be for this in reality. The fairy tale offers fantasy materials which suggest to the child in symbolic form what the battle to self-realization is all about, and it guarantees a happy ending.[17]

Such an analysis describes David's response to the adventure tales of Fielding and Smollett and the fairy-tale worlds of the *Arabian Nights* and *Tales of the Genii* since "whatever harm was in some of them was not there for me; *I knew nothing* of it. . . . It is curious to me how I could ever have consoled myself under my small troubles (which were great troubles to me), by impersonating my favorite characters in them—as I did—and by putting Mr. and Miss Murdstone into all the bad ones—which I did too" (pp. 55–56). After several such projections polarizing innocence and evil, "like a great fairy story" (p. 273), changeling David finally paves the way for his growth from fairy-tale playmate or orphan to Romantic pilgrim when he reveals to Dora that, after their marriage, he must work by the sweat of his brow. He consequently finds himself projected not as the victim but perpetrator of change: "I felt like a sort of Monster who had got into a Fairy's bower" (p. 543).

Once on his "pilgrimage" or Romance-quest on the recurrent image of "the road of life" (p. 268), David begins to understand that "some better change was possible within me" (p. 814).[18] As in the traditional Romance, the goal of David's quest is the renewal of both the wasted, diseased kingdom back home and his own sympathetically-wounded self; and this dual rebirth is earned only through the symbolic goal of new magical insight or self-knowledge, what our epigraph describes as "Long time in search of knowledge did I range / The field of human life" (ll. 16–17). In fact, even before his journey David begins to feel "like a shipwrecked wanderer come home" since Agnes's "old house . . . freed from the presence of the Heeps, seemed purged of a disease" (p. 781). Then, "After some rest and change" (p. 816) in Switzerland, "My health, severely impaired when I left England, was quite restored. . . . and I hope I had improved my store of knowledge" (p. 817); and "change . . . gradually worked in me, when I tried to get a better understanding of myself and be a better man" (pp. 817–18). Finally, David begins to solve his own private riddle, "the most secret current of my mind," and to "penetrate the mystery of my own heart" (p. 817) regarding Agnes. The novel's two structures ultimately coalesce when Agnes's "favorite story . . . of a wicked old Fairy in a cloak who hated everybody" (p. 866) introduces the arrival of that other Romance "pilgrim," once on his own "solitary journey" (p. 589), Dan Peggotty. This resolution of the solar fairy tale and lunar Romance is reflected most thematically in Mr. Omer's final wisdom accepting that period "when a man is drawing on to a time of life, where the two ends of life meet" (p. 735).[19]

Three related clusters of natural images support this structural resolution of solar permanence and lunar change; these are images of seasonal progression, the ripening process, and what Joyce calls the "everchangingneverchanging" sea. H. K. Browne's cover-design for the first serial publication of David Copperfield highlights the Echoing Green, a traditional icon of cyclic change from life, through death, to rebirth; and this cycle of the "growing season" (p. 389) provides a barometer reflecting both the changing maturation of the hero but also the permanent consistency within that very change. As Morse Peckham has written regarding this general Romantic formula, "Nature is the source of both disturbance and equilibrium, of disorientation and orientation. . . . Hence romanticism leads directly to the realism of Dickens . . . ";[20] and as Wordsworth in the last book of The Prelude proclaims of those "higher minds" that "from their native selves can send abroad / Kindred mutations" to Nature: "Them the enduring and transient both / Serve to exalt" (XIV, ll. 90–101 passim, my italics). David, too, must learn to accept and finally, perhaps, even "exalt" the bittersweet modality of "the varying seasons of the year" (p. 78). Like his creator, mature David certainly believes in the valuable innocence of Wordsworth's "simple creed / Of Childhood" from the "Immortality Ode." For example, after recalling the Yarmouth waiter's deceit against his younger self, David insists that "the simple confidence . . . and natural reliance of a child" are "qualities I am very sorry any children should prematurely change for worldly wisdom" (pp. 69–70). His youthful, springtime innocence, however, is too much in the sun; for, unaided by autumnal experience, it wishes that "bright with the light of innocence," he and Emily could "live among the trees and in the fields, never growing older, never growing wiser" (p. 147). To become experienced and well-seasoned, it must answer to the conundrum of "the wild moon [which] seemed to plunge headlong, as if, in a dread disturbance of the laws of nature" (p. 786) during the "late in September" night of Ham and Steerforth's deaths.[21] And Dora's illness also begins in "autumn" (p. 65). But the novel itself, following its structural models, opens in the "March" (p. 3) springtime, albeit an early, cold springtime, of fairy-tale innocence and concludes "one night in [the] spring" (p. 866) of Romance-rebirth, what in our epigraph Wordsworth calls "the dawn beginning now / To re-appear" (ll. 18–19). Thus David must learn that every "time came in its season" (p. 437) and that those "summer days . . . filled with my boyish enchantment" (p. 646) inevitably pass away when the autumn "wind changed" (p. 506) since "Weeks, months, seasons, pass along. They seem little more than a summer day and a winter evening" (p. 626) and since "wind" is the usual harbinger of seasonal mutability in the novel. Consequently, when David symbolically accepts the season of Steerforth's drowning, "where Death was already," as "a mellow autumn day . . . when the ground was perfumed by fallen leaves, and many more, in beautiful tints of yellow, red, and brown, yet hung upon the trees" (p. 796), he has almost reached his own harvesttime of mature growth. When "great Nature spoke to me; and smoothed me to lay down my weary head upon the grass, and weep as I had not wept yet, since Dora died!" (p. 815), the seasons of innocence and experience, of solar and vernal birth and of lunar and autumnal death finally become one and the same cyclic continuity for him, the rhythmic systole and diastole of Nature's eternal heartbeat. Then, like Lazarus, whom he identifies with, David is "raised up from the dead" (p. 14).

Closely related to this seasonal metaphor is the image of the ripening, blossoming self, what Dan Peggotty finally describes as David's "own sweet blooming self" (p. 867). Echoing Shakespeare's recurrent belief that "Ripeness is all," *David Copperfield* returns repeatedly to this natural trope in order to underscore the fact that the mature personality must unite its adaptation to seasonal transformation with the permanent power of blooming or self-recovery, what *The Prelude* calls the "Power" (and we have identified this with Agnes) "that matures / her processes by steadfast laws" (ll. 22–23). And this mature state is the condition of the "disciplined heart" or "mind of the heart" (p. 623).[22] Thus Gradgrind finally learns in *Hard Times* that "there is a wisdom of the Head, and . . . there is a wisdom of the Heart" (Bk. III, ch. 1); and as our epigraph suggests, Wordsworth's ripened "knowledge" reconciles "heart and mind" (1. 17). Discipline, or the Head, is a solar value usually symbolized by the color *brown,* the permanent result of exposure to Time or the sun's rays; while the Heart is a lunar quality suggesting acceptance of growth or vernal change and ordinarily symbolized by the color *green.* Again, maturity demands a brown-green personality; and this paradox or riddle is characteristically dramatized after Dora's death when David's "undisciplined heart is chastened heavily" as "The bright moon is high and clear" (p. 768). Once David returns from Switzerland and is seasoned like Mr. Peggotty—"burnt dark by the sun" because he had "wandered through all varieties of weather" (p. 583) in search of Emily—Traddles's repeated greeting is a symbol of his newly-ripened personality: "How brown you are! How glad I am" (p. 823); and "You are so extremely brown, my dear Copperfield! God bless my soul, how happy I am!" (p. 824). Thus prefiguring later "brown" or fully mature heroes like Woodcourt, that "brown, sunburnt gentleman" (*Bleak House,* ch. 46), and Clennam, that "brown, grave gentleman" (*Little Dorrit,* Bk. I, ch. 14), David finally achieves time-tested and -tempered endurance. And yet, in a sense, he still strikes the reader as "the greenest and most inexperienced of mortals" (p. 301). But this blossoming power is his eternal salvation and sadly lacking in a character like Julia Mills who sells out to the Head and finally has "no green growth near her; nothing that can ever come to fruit or flower" (p. 875). Micawber's characterization of Mr. Dick finally celebrates this green power of self-recovery: "It has been my lot . . . to meet, in the diversified panorama of human existence, with an occasional oasis, but never with one so green, so gushing, as the present!" (p. 709).

Thus, natural growth throughout the novel is a norm for human development; and David wistfully reflects on the ideal maturity of "fruit clusters on the trees, riper and richer than fruit has ever been since" (p. 15). As Aunt Betsey knows, however, immature, "Little Blossom" Dora "is a very tender little blossom, and the wind must be gentle with her" (p. 638). When David feels "that a baby-smile upon her breast might change my child-wife to a woman" (p. 698), Dora's psychological, more than physical ripening process is lethal because this sensitive plant cannot endure the winds of change and growth: "the blossom withered in its bloom upon the tree!" (p. 700). Uriah Heep, conversely, ripens but into a blighted, mutant form; and David, reflecting on his cankerous condition, concludes: "I had seen the harvest, but never thought of the seed" (p. 575). Thus for Micawber Heep becomes "The canker . . . in the flower" and "The worm . . . at his work" (p. 702); and again depending on a metaphor expressing the destruction of natural growth, Uriah admits his designs on Agnes have been premature, that he "plucked a pear before it was ripe" (p. 580). Yet David, unlike Dora and Uriah, ultimately survives the changing climate of the "growing season" and does not become stunted or rotted by the extreme conditions of either sun or moon, brown or green, Head or Heart, though he nearly follows Miss Lavinia Spenlow's regressive parody of "mature" love: "Such is the mature fruit. Sometimes a life glides away, and finds it still ripening in the shade" (p. 597). Finally, though, David steps into the sun and tells Agnes of "my love for her, and the trouble in which it had ripened to be what it was" (p. 862).

Reflecting on the expected completion of *David Copperfield* during his up-coming visit to the sea, Dickens wrote Forster: "I hope to go down to that old image of Eternity that I love so much, and finish ... to its hoarse murmur." And almost finished, Dickens wrote again: "I am within three pages of the shore; and am strangely divided ... between joy and sorrow."[23] Significantly, the sea rolls through *David Copperfield* as a cosmic image of life in all of its varied and divided, lunar and solar dimensions—changing and unchanging, destroying and creating, a thematic image of both love and lovelessness.[24] As the controller of the changing "variation of the tide" (p. 40), the moon naturally correlates with the sea in David's memory as the "silvery light upon the sea" (p. 738); and yet at Dover their combined image poses the enduring riddle of his future and forms an indelible association with his dead mother: "I remember how I still sat looking at the moonlight on the water, as if I could hope to read my fortune in it, as in a bright book; or to see my mother with her child, coming from Heaven, along that shining path" (p. 199). The memory of this teasing conundrum finally returns (p. 845) to round off the novel's structure, though Agnes has gradually replaced Clara as David's lunar goddess. The sea, then, is also an emblem of solar steadfastness, "that old image of Eternity," as its per-sonified association with the enduring Mr. Peggotty and Ham suggests: "they were both as grave and steady as the sea itself: then lying beneath a dark sky, waveless—yet with a heavy roll upon it, as if it breathed in its rest—and touched, on the horizon, with a strip of silvery light from the unseen sun" (p. 456). The real significance here, however, is that, like "the great voice of the sea, with its eternal 'Never more!'" (p. 670), lunar and solar energies finally combine to reflect unity-in-diversity. The "silvery light" can denote either, or both where they coincide on that mystic "shore where all forgotten things will reappear" (p. 131).[25] For the present, though, it is enough to see that the Eternal Sea is also the "sea of per-plexity" (p. 545) and that sea changes are not only external but also the internal "flowing water" of David's own consciousness, "The silent gliding on of my existence—the unseen, unfelt progress of my life" (p. 265). At the death of Ham and Steerforth, while "Something within me, faintly answering to the storm without, tossed up the depths of my memory and made a tumult in them" (p. 789), the sea, like that "pageantry of fear" in "Elegiac Stanzas," becomes for David an emblem of cosmic and personal destruction, a "chang[ing]" chaos, a "rending and upheaving of all nature" (p. 788), that precedes his own final rebirth.

As Menelaus learns during his wrestling match with the shape-shifting, sea god Proteus in the *Odyssey* and as Stephen Dedalus learns during his internal struggle with "seaspawn" and "seawrack" in the "Proteus" chapter of *Ulysses*, the only way to master fluctuations in "the deep of Time" (p. 743) is to adapt and conform to them, allowing their energy to transform one's character so that the individual finally becomes resilient to change. In *David Copperfield*, the fishermen at Yarmouth, where "the town and the tide had ... been quite so much mixed up" (p. 28), provide this model of adaptive resilience for David. Ham performs, in Mr. Peg-gotty's words, "rough sarvice in rough weather" (p. 588); and as Daniel says of himself, "water, ('specially when 'tis salt) comes nat'ral to me" (p. 867). At Barkis's death, Mr. Peggotty's natural empathy with the sea gives him the mythic under-standing, which he passes along to David, of the relationship between the human and the natural, between the loss and recovery of tidal change: "People can't die, along the coast . . . except when the tide's pretty nigh out. They can't be born, unless it's pretty nigh in—not properly born, till flood" (p. 445). Thus the beacon light in Dan's symbolic *boat-house*, like that in the "Evening-Star" of Wordsworth's *Michael* whom he so closely resembles, becomes an emblem of his well-weathered "readiness" (or ripeness) to lead others through the tempests of change, to find eternal similitude in temporal dissimilitude.

This repeated metaphor of "buffeting of rough seas, and braving of hard weather" (p. 426) with rocklike endurance, relates finally to the theme of love in the novel. As Annie Strong puts it in a secularized version of the founding of the Christian Church, "my love was founded on a rock, and it endures!" (p. 663); or as David implies when he first establishes the image, the loving memory of his moth-er's death "stands like a high rock in the ocean" (p. 131). Dickens's point here is crucial and complex. Wordsworthian love of Nature leads to love of man because the combination of change and permanence residing in natural models urges one, as we have heard, "To look with feelings of fraternal love / Upon the unassuming things that hold / A silent station in the beauteous world" (ll. 45–47). Thus not only does mature love demand the rock-hard endurance of *both* partners through the changing waters of life; but love also demands their fluid and joint adaptation to permanent absolutes such as loss itself and ultimately death since "There can be no disparity in marriage like unsuitability of mind and purpose" (p. 660). Without the adamantine perseverance and discipline of the rock, love becomes "rather spongy and soppy" like "the great dull waste" (p. 28) along the river and thus also like Uriah Heep's "damp fishy fingers" (p. 574) which grasp after Agnes's heart and home. And such imagery (usually related to the river rather than to the sea) links with the moral and physical disease of Martha's prostitution and the riverside environs of her attempted suicide-by-drowning: "a melancholy waste" of "ooze and slush" and "corruption and decay" (pp. 679–80). This "polluted stream" also contaminates Emily's London rooms and, sympathetically, her diseased love for Steerforth since the place is filled with "rot, damp, and age" and is "miserably decayed and dirty" (p. 717). Rosa even calls her "a piece of pollution picked up from the waterside" (p. 720). The contagion element implied in this metaphor of water-pollution is expressed most clearly by Agnes's father: "My natural grief for my child's mother turned to disease; my natural love for my child turned to disease. I have infected everything I touched" (p. 578); but it also spills over into David's comic, though crucial, diagnosis of his and Dora's love, which he finally realizes is not "founded on a rock": "The fact is my dear . . . there is a contagion in us. We infect every one about us. . . . We are positively corrupting people" (pp. 693–94). Both the fact that he was born with a caul, or protection against the water, and Quinion's "Brooks of Sheffield" joke on David suggest, however, that he must also reject the opposite temptation of being too rocklike, or adamantine as steel, in love; Dora even sobs that he is a "hard-hearted thing" (p. 693). Several minor characters personify this inflexibility and lack of fluid change, most notably Miss Murdstone, that "metallic lady" with her "hard steel purse" (pp. 47–48) and stony name, who externalizes her brother's philosophy of "Firmness" (p. 49) in love, which itself petrifies the ripening growth of childbrides. Throughout the novel, hard cash or money, like this "hard steel purse," is the antithesis of fluid love; and that is why Mr. Peggotty refuses the Judas-payoff of Mrs. Steerforth and why even Martha rejects Dan's offer of money. Rosa Dartle, who has been "hammered" into hardness by Steerforth's sadomasochistic love, is another flinty character, one "inflexible as a figure of brass" (p. 720) who "brings everything to a grindstone" and has "worn herself away by constant sharpening. She is all edge" (p. 294). And finally the obdurate Mrs. Steerforth, who represents monolithic class barriers against love and whose own love cannot accept her son's "inconstant humour" (p. 800), eventually transforms into a marble statue, "for she sat like a stone figure" (p. 798).

The next image pattern revolves around the polar motifs of retreats and invasions. Again, I think past criticism has misunderstood Dickens's meaning by stressing both the moral value of hard work in the changing world of the invaders and the corollary need for abandoning the static world of the retreat. For example, Bert G. Hornback concludes that the novel "tests the mythic worlds of Eden and Noah's Ark as retreats, finds them inadequate and vulnerable, and opts for hard work and clear sights in the real world instead."[26] And if read superficially, Dickens's 1858 letter to Wilkie Collins seems to agree with such a view: "Everything that happens, everybody that comes near ... shows beyond mistake that you can't shut out the world; that you get into a false position the moment you try to sever yourself from it; and that you must mingle with it, and make the best of it, and make the best of yourself in the bargain." However, these significant remarks actually condemn only those recluses, like Miss Havisham, who are *totally* "resolved to shut out the world, and hold *no* communion with it."[27] For complete enjoyment of "the world," the individual also must agree with Mr. Dick that "it's a mad world. Mad as Bedlam" (p. 202) and with the understanding of Miss Mowcher: "What a world of gammon and spinach it is" (p. 329). The novel consequently assures the reader, especially through Tommy Traddles, that the most well-adjusted personality accommodates both the changing and progressive world of work and the unchanging and retreating world of play.

David Copperfield is literally riddled with symbolic, often playful retreats which are finally invaded by threats of loss or change: Aunt Betsey's "hallowed ground" which the psychologically-related triumvirate of donkeys, boys, and her husband all "had dared to profane" (p. 195); Mr. Dick's kiteflying and Memorial which are attacked by King Charles and decapitating madness; Dr. Strong's "old secluded garden" (p. 228) which is besieged by the Old Soldier, Jack Maldon, and marital trials; Mrs. Gummidge's retreat with Dan Peggotty which is upset by her memory of the "old 'un"; the "Goroo" man's "slop-shop" which is beleaguered by "boys, who continually came skirmishing about the shop" (p. 185); and of course David's fairy-tale marriage to Dora which is invaded by thieving servants and ultimately by "the Angel of Death" (p. 769) itself. Although someone like Miss Mills, who further retreats behind the philosophy of "Blood" after her marriage, remains a "Voice from the Cloister" (p. 489) forever, the many distractions of the playful retreat are usually replaced by a major symbolic conversion to "one," or a "single purpose" or "work," which redeems the regressive personality. Steerforth's warlike hammer repulsing love is replaced by Omer and Joram's peaceful hammer of loving work; and Peggotty's "work box," with its emblems of measuring changes in time and space, is the recurrent symbol of adaptive work: "the old insensible work box, yard measure, and bit of wax candle . . . that had now outlived so much" (p. 803).[28] Thus, Mr. Dick becomes an amanuensis who "incessantly occupied himself in copying everything" to earn money for Betsey; Martha searches for Emily; Mrs. Gummidge guards the window lantern and soothes Dan, "not the least astonishing part of the change that had come over her" (p. 459); and Micawber works for the exposure of Heep and salvation of Wickfield. When his Aunt Betsey loses her fortune and before he has passed totally through his fairy-tale stage, David's "whole manner of . . . thinking was changed"; and he determines to "turn the painful discipline of my younger days to account, by going to work with a resolute and steady heart" (p. 520). Thus he works through his symbolic "forest of difficulty" until "a complete change had come on my whole life" (p. 520). Again, in Switzerland "After some rest and change, . . . [David] fell to work" and "worked early and late, patiently and hard" (p. 816). However, not until he *writes at home* with his playing wife and children, does he finally follow the thematic example of Traddles who himself, after invading that apparent sweatshop of industry, Commons, discovers only "the dreamy nature of this retreat" (p. 352), which he immediately transforms through real work. Traddles consequently amalgamates work and play by *living in his office* with his merry wife and her young sisters; and this continuity bridges the gap between the change of work and the changelessness of play: "I am in a most enviable state. I work hard and read Law insatiably. I get up at five every morning, and don't mind it at all. I hide the girls in the day-time, and make merry with them in the evening" (p. 828).

Dickens's next to final image in *Oliver Twist* is a *memento mori:* "Everything told of life and animation, but one dark cluster of objects in the centre of all—the black stage, the cross-beam, the rope, and all the hideous apparatus of death" (ch. 52). His final image, however, is of the well-harmonized society, one linking and reconciling youth and age: "thus linked together a little society, whose condition approached as nearly to one of perfect happiness as can ever be known in this changing world" (ch. 53). Dickens's attitude here, which introduces our final image pattern, is one that persists through all of his novels and especially in *David Copperfield;* that is, the seasoned personality must never regress to the eternal green fields of youth and forget about the final changes of aging and death; but on the other hand, it should not dwell morbidly on the grim reaper. Rather, the "mind of the heart" accepts all change with a persevering and adapting *joie de vivre,* which is personified in a community combining the best of older and younger generations. As Mr. Omer describes this acceptance, "I find my breath gets short, but it seldom gets longer as a man gets older. I take it as it comes, and make the most of it. That's the best way, ain't it?" (p. 304). *David Copperfield*, a novel which seems to be a paean to childhood, actually is punctuated with repeated reminders of "that great Visitor, before whose presence all the living must give place" (p. 438). For example, Omer's rheumatic cough, Traddles's skeletons—"those symbols of mortality" (p. 91), Mrs. Gummidge's thoughts of the "old 'un," Mr. Dick's obsession with King Charles's decapitation, the hammering of coffin construction, which taps "the tune that never *does* leave off " (p. 306), and finally the numerous deaths in the novel (*ten* by my count) all portend that last great transition. Related to these is the image of aging which pursues almost all the characters and is another reminder of natural change. For instance, Betsey remarks that her husband "was a fine-looking man when I married him," but at his death "he was sadly changed" (p. 782); and David must remind his wife that Jip suffers not from laziness, but "he has a worse disorder than that. Age, Dora" (p. 698). Even the irrepressible, "young butcher" (p. 266) at last ages into an "ancient enemy" (p. 743). Although George Ford sensitively comments that "The passage of time is rarely specified; it is felt"[29] in *David Copperfield*, still such passages, along with the imagery of seasonal cycle, do help to specify the time "fading away in the light of a young moon" (p. 325). Further, the characters' reaction to the ultimately-terminal aging process is an index to their maturity or lack of it. For example, little Emily feels a "dread of death" (p. 444); and on a cancelled proof sheet, Mr. Wickfield deplores the aging process: "He talked of the time that had glided away since I first dined with him, and the change that had stolen imperceptively upon myself and Agnes. He felt sometimes that he was changed too, he said, and not for the better."[30] On the other hand, Traddles champions the mature aging of Micawber's personality during his battle with Heep: "he is a most untiring man when he works for other people.... he must be, virtually, about two hundred years old at present" (p. 774). Early in life, David admits that he and Emily blithely "made no more provision for growing older, than we did for growing younger" (p. 37); later at the death of Steerforth, his despair pushes David to the opposite extreme: "all the world seemed death and silence" (p. 801). He finally ages, however, toward the *working* example of Peggotty, "An old man now, but in a ruddy, hearty, strong old age" (p. 866), an example most thematically proclaimed by the coughing but still hammering Mr. Omer: "a man must take the fat with the lean; that's what he must make his mind up to, in this life.... the way I look at it is, that we are all drawing on to the bottom of the hill, whatever age we are, on account of time never standing still for a single moment. So let us always do a kindness, and be over-rejoiced. To be sure!" (pp. 733, 735).

And as indicated above, the best way "to be over-rejoiced" about life is to become a working, playing member of a cooperative society of young and old, mutual friends, that well-integrated family which makes up the thematic subject matter of *David Copperfield*. As Carlyle's Teufelsdröckh suggests, the natural world is the best model for this society in which duality dissolves into primal unity: "Yes, truly, if Nature is one, and a living indivisible whole, much more is Mankind, the Image that reflects and creates Nature, without which Nature were not."[31] *The Prelude* more simply advises:

> ... to seek,
> In man, and in the frame of social life,
> Whate'er there is desirable and good
> Of kindred permanence, unchanged in form
> And function, or, through strict vicissitude,
> Of life and death, revolving.   (ll. 34–39)

A "social life" reconciling the young and old, the steadfast innocence of the sun and the maturing experience of the moon, does not appear in the families of Creakle, Steerforth, Heep, or Murdstone, whose latest girl-wife is characteristically "subdued and broken" (p. 833). It does appear, however, in Omer and Joram's family, in the Chillips, Strongs, and the Australian emigrants who practice "perfect good will and harmony" (p. 779) aboard a ship loaded with resolved generations, "From babies who had but a week or two of life behind them, to crooked old men and women who seemed but to have but a week or two of life before them" (p. 810). Again, though, Traddles's blooming family has the greatest influence on David: "If I had beheld a thousand roses blowing in a top set of chambers, in that withered Gray's Inn, they could not have brightened it half so much. The idea of those Devonshire girls, among the dry law-stationers and attorney's offices...!" (pp. 829–30). And the final, imitative happiness which David shares with his own family transcends the orphan's fairy-tale world of self-defensive paranoia with the suffering but loving world of Romance. Here, a well-integrated self and well-integrated society both mirror unity-in-diversity. And such an ending reflects a philosophy which basically remained unchanged throughout Dickens's career. As he reminds us of Martin Chuzzlewit, "So low had Eden brought him down. So high had Eden raised him up" (ch. 33); or as he concludes in his first novel, "There are dark shadows on the earth, but its lights are stronger in contrast" (*Pickwick Papers,* ch. 37).

Our age cannot blame Dickens because it chooses to view the existential and clinical "dark shadows" in stronger contrast—at least his vision understood that both finally make up the ambience of life. As Edgar Johnson remarks of *David Copperfield*, if the ultimate triumph of "the good and the brave" seems "a simple philosophy, it might be asked whether the belief that evil always carries off the victory is so much more worldly-wise."[32] Or as G. K. Chesterton brilliantly puts it, "the book is true to life" because "It is not only both realistic and romantic; it is realistic because it is romantic."[33] Our belief throughout this essay is not simply that *David Copperfield* reconciles the light and dark shadows, or lunar change and solar permanence, but that its imaginative alchemy actually dissolves their apparent diversity and re-creates a primary unity.[34] Thus, sometime after David's original allusion to that "incomprehensible conundrum," he remembers it again and symbolically understands its true relevance as he becomes "painfully aware of [himself] being a much better answer to the old riddle than the original one" (p. 487). And in Dickens's climactic lunar image, the contraries of change and changelessness, fairy tale and Romance, finally unite as the pronoun shift from first to third person reveals that David, the narrating man, and David, the growing child, are also one: "We stood together in the same old-fashioned window at night, when the moon was shining; Agnes with her quiet eyes raised up to it; I following her glance. Long miles of road then opened out before my mind; and, toiling on, I saw a ragged way-worn boy forsaken and neglected, who should come to call even the heart now beating against mine, his own" (p. 863).

NOTES

[1] *Wordsworth's Prelude,* ed. Ernest de Selincourt (Oxford: Clarendon Press, 1926), pp. 447, 449. All future references to Book Thirteen are noted within the text.

[2] This and subsequent references to *David Copperfield* are to the Oxford Illustrated Dickens edition (London: Oxford Univ. Press, 1947). Citations from Dickens's other novels are from popular paperback editions and are indicated in the text simply by chapter number.

[3] Peckham's two most important essays have been combined under the general title "Toward a Theory of Romanticism," in *Romanticism: Point of View, Second Edition,* eds., Robert F. Gleckner and Gerald E. Enscoe (Englewood Cliffs, N. J.: Prentice-Hall, 1970), pp. 231–57. The essays originally appeared as "Toward a Theory of Romanticism," *PMLA,* 66 (1951), 5–23 and "Toward a Theory of Romanticism: Reconsiderations," *Studies in Romanticism,* 1 (1961), 1–8.

[4] For the most relevant past discussion of Dickens and Wordsworth, see James E. Marlow, "Memory, Romance, and the Expressive Symbol in Dickens," *Nineteenth-Century Fiction,* 30 (1975), 20–32 pass. Carlyle remains, of course, a significant influence though past discussions have, in fact, dealt mainly with the impact on Dickens of Carlyle's "work ethic," rather than his Romanticism. See, for example, Samuel G. Barnes, "Dickens and Copperfield: The Hero as Man of Letters," in *The Classic British Novel,* eds., Howard M. Harper, Jr., and Charles Edge (Athens: Univ. of Georgia Press, 1972), pp. 85–102, and Richard J. Dunn, "David Copperfield's Carlylean Retailoring," in *Dickens the Craftsman: Strategies of Presentation,* ed. Robert B. Partlow, Jr. (Carbondale and Edwardsville: Southern Illinois Univ. Press, 1970), pp. 95–114.

[5] Marlow, p. 21.

[6] *The Imagination of Charles Dickens* (New York: New York Univ. Press, 1962), p. 115.

[7] *Dickens and the Rhetoric of Laughter* (Oxford: Oxford Univ. Press, 1971), p. 165.

[8] *A Reader's Guide to Charles Dickens* (New York: Noonday Press, 1973), pp. 125 and 123.

[9] *Dickens the Novelist* (New York: Pantheon Books, 1970), p. 43.

[10] *Charles Dickens,* with an introduction by Steven Marcus (New York: Schocken Books, 1965), p. 189.

[11] *Victorian Newsletter,* 43 (1974), 7, 10. See also Barbara Hardy's more general analysis of the conversion experience, or "The Change of Heart in Dickens' Novels," *Victorian Studies,* 5 (1961), 49–67. This fine essay makes the same assumptions regarding the value of change.

[12] *Charles Dickens: The World of His Novels* (Cambridge: Harvard Univ. Press, 1965), p. 152. The interested reader should consult Miller's entire discussion which often focuses on Wordsworthian resonances in the novel; see pp. 150–59. See also Marlow's discussion of Dickens and memory, and Robin Gilmour, "Memory in *David Copperfield,*" *Dickensian,* 71 (1975), 30–42.

[13] "The Image of Steerforth and the Structure of *David Copperfield,*" *Tennessee Studies in Literature,* 5 (1960), 57.

[14] See also Kincaid's discussion of structure, pp. 165ff., and his essay "The Structure of *David Copperfield,*" *Dickens Studies,* 2 (1966), 74–95.

[15] For a treatment of the novel as *Bildungsroman,* see Jerome H. Buckley, *Season of Youth: The Bildungsroman from Dickens to Golding* (Cambridge: Harvard Univ. Press, 1974), pp. 28–43. For discussions of the fairy-tale motif, see Harry Stone, "Fairy Tales and Ogres: Dickens' Imagination and *David Copperfield,*" *Criticism,* 6 (1964), 324–30, and Michael C. Kotzin's more general study, *Dickens and the Fairy Tale* (Bowling Green: Bowling Green Univ. Press, 1972).

[16] For a different reading of the Biblical name, see E. Pearlman, "David Copperfield Dreams of Drowning," *American Imago,* 28 (1971), 394–95.

[17] *The Uses of Enchantment: The Meaning and Importance of Fairy Tales* (New York: Alfred A. Knopf, 1976), pp. 19, 39.

[18] In terms of the importance of the Romance for Dickens, Marlow relevantly remarks that "Romance became for Dickens a way to fuse the contradictory impulses of acceptance and escape, of 'usefulness' and evasion. And Romance was, for him, inextricably tied to memory," p. 23. On the general significance of the Quest-Romance, the reader should also consult Harold Bloom, "The Internalization of the Quest-Romance," Yale Review, 58 (1969), 526–36, and a series of articles I have written on the relationships between the Romance-form and nineteenth-century prose fiction in England: "Waverley and Romanticism," Nineteenth-Century Fiction, 28 (1973), 194–209; "Dracula: The Gnostic Quest and Victorian Wasteland," English Literature in Transition, 20 (1977), 13–26; and "The Time Machine: A Romance of 'The Human Heart,'" forthcoming in Extrapolation. Also relevant to our discussion is Northrop Frye's analysis of the basic "contrast of cadences" in romance. These penseroso and allegro motifs are analogous to lunar and solar values. See The Secular Scripture: A Study of the Structure of Romance (Cambridge and London: Harvard Univ. Press, 1976), p. 83 and pass.

[19] See M. H. Abrams's relevant summary of this primary Romance structure in Natural Supernaturalism: Tradition and Revolution in Romantic Literature (New York: W. W. Norton, 1971), p. 255.

[20] Peckham, pp. 254–55. For other discussions of Dickens's Romanticism, see Marlow pass. and Dunn, pp. 108–11.

[21] The most relevant discussion of the themes of innocence and experience is Bert G. Hornback's Noah's Arkitecture: A Study of Dickens' Mythology (Athens, Ohio: Ohio Univ. Press, 1972), pp. 63–82; see also A. E. Dyson, "David Copperfield: The Favorite Child," in The Inimitable Dickens (London: St. Martin's Press, 1970), pp. 119–53, and Vereen M. Bell, "The Emotional Matrix of David Copperfield," Studies in English Literature, 8 (1968), 633–49.

[22] For discussions of this theme, see Gwendolyn Needham, "The Undisciplined Heart of David Copperfield," Nineteenth-Century Fiction, 9 (1954), 81–107, and Joseph Gold, "The Disciplined Heart," Charles Dickens: Radical Moralist (Minneapolis: Univ. of Minnesota Press, 1972), pp. 175–84.

[23] Edgar Johnson, Charles Dickens: His Tragedy and Triumph (New York: Simon and Schuster, 1952), 2 vols., II, 676.

[24] For other discussions of water imagery, see Pearlman, E. K. Brown, "David Copperfield," Yale Review, 37 (1948), 661–62, and especially Roseless Robinson's general study, "Time, Death, and the River in Dickens' Novels," English Studies, 53 (1972), 436–54. Leonard F. Manheim discusses the "caul" symbolism in his early but relevant treatment of the hero-myth in the novel, "The Personal History of David Copperfield: A Study in Psychoanalytic Criticism," American Imago, 9 (1952), 21–43.

[25] Interestingly, Joseph Campbell's treatment of the mythic theme of "The Wisdom of the Yonder Shore" enlightens this enigmatic allusion in a way which reinforces our point that Sun and Moon are One. See The Mythic Image (Princeton: Princeton Univ. Press, 1974), pp. 313–29.

[26] Hornback, p. 82.

[27] Sept. 6, 1858; quoted by Harry Stone in Charles Dickens' Uncollected Writings from Household Words 1850–1859 (Bloomington: Indiana Univ. Press, 1968), II, 596, italics mine.

[28] For a valuable discussion of the "work" theme in the novel, see Barnes.

[29] In his Introduction to the Riverside edition of the novel (Boston: The Riverside Press, 1958), p. xiii.

[30] Reprinted in the Riverside edition, p. 675.

[31] Sartor Resartus, ed. Charles Frederick Harrold (New York: Odyssey Press, 1937), pp. 246–47.

[32] Johnson, pp. 699–700.

[33] Chesterton, pp. 193–94, 195.

[34] In discussing mythological symbology, Erich Neumann repeatedly points out that "the archetype of the hero myth is often a sun myth or . . . a moon myth. . . . The hero is sun or moon." Again, "the dragon-slaying hero who represents the sun on its 'night sea journey,' or in other cultures the moon, is the archetypal exemplar and guiding figure of all historical heroes." See Origins and History of Consciousness, trans. R. F. C. Hull (Princeton: Princeton Univ. Press, 1954), pp. 149, 337.

John P. McGowan

DAVID COPPERFIELD: THE TRIAL OF REALISM

In March 1850, when *David Copperfield* was still eight installments from completion, the first issue of *Household Words* appeared. In "A Preliminary Word" to his new magazine, Dickens pledges to "tenderly cherish that light of Fancy which is inherent in the human breast" and to "show to all, that in all familiar things, even in those which are repellent on the surface, there is Romance enough, if we will find it out."[1] It would be impossible to prove that this championing of fancy is the result of the experience of writing *David Copperfield*, but the timing of the defense is suggestive. In this essay I will discuss the nature of *David Copperfield*'s realism and, subsequently, the problems the attempt to write a realistic novel presented to Dickens. My general contention is that the failure of this novel's realism gave Dickens a new appreciation of fancy's claims, and led to the aesthetic of fancy articulated by Dickens for the first time in "A Preliminary Word" and defended by him throughout the rest of his career, most notably in *Hard Times*.

In a recently published book, Robert Newsom, starting from the reiteration in the preface to *Bleak House* of "A Preliminary Word"'s promise to reveal the romance in familiar things, discusses that novel's "play . . . between the empirical and the fictional."[2] While touching on issues I discuss here, Newsom's view is much more dialectical, focusing on the relation of fiction to the real, whereas I wish to discuss the existence of realism and fancy side by side in a novel in which they both exist even though they contradict one another. The difference between our arguments is related, at least in part, to Newsom's discussing a novel written after Dickens's explicit statement of the aesthetic of fancy and my discussing a novel written before that statement.

The distinction between realism and fancy with which I shall begin is a simple one. Realism is that literary mode which stresses language's ability to repeat or represent accurately in words the world of things, whereas fancy focuses on the difference between the world of objects and a linguistic world, thus emphasizing what imagination adds when it undertakes to describe the world "out there." In

From *Nineteenth-Century Fiction* 34, No. 1 (June 1979): 1–19.

Adam Bede, George Eliot states the realist's desire simply to describe the world as it is. She recognizes that the novelist might use fancy to "refashion life and character entirely after [her] own liking," but informs the reader that she will "avoid any such arbitrary picture."[3] Jacques Derrida, among contemporary theorists of language, has discussed most fully what the user of language adds when he describes the world in words, and my discussion will depend on issues Derrida has made familiar: representation, repetition, and the difference between words and things.[4] *David Copperfield* presents the distinction between realism and fancy as follows:

> When my thoughts go back now, to that slow agony of my youth, I wonder how much of the histories I invented for such people hangs like a mist of fancy over well-remembered facts! When I tread the old ground, I do not wonder that I seem to see and pity, going on before me, an innocent romantic boy, making his imaginative world out of such strange experiences and sordid things.[5]

"Fancy" is confronted with "fact" here, just as it will be in *Hard Times,* but in this case the narrator's sympathy is with fact. Fancy is all right for the child, especially if he needs to retreat from a world of "sordid things" which he cannot change. But for an adult, for a narrator who wishes to present the facts about his life clearly and accurately, fancy only threatens the integrity of his narrative. David must sift through his memories, separating fact from fancy. The only crime which David ever admits is that he was "romantic"; at the end of his narrative, he will attribute the troubles of his adult life to following the dictates of a childish, "heedless fancy" (62). David's progress leads him from a childhood "romanticism" toward a staunch reliance on and, at times, stoical acceptance of "the reality principle," a movement thematized as the maturation of an "undisciplined heart."[6] Or, at least, that is the way David likes to present his progress. As we shall see, fancy has more to do with David's story than he, as a realistic narrator, is prepared to admit.

A realistic narrative must establish what is indisputably "real." In *David Copperfield* this privileged position is accorded to immediate perceptual experience, primarily the visual and the aural. The second chapter of the novel, entitled "I Observe," establishes the primacy of the visual. The chapter begins: "The first objects that assume a distinct presence before me, as I look far back, into the blank of my infancy, are my mother . . . and Peggotty . . ." Seeing things is the way in which they are established as "objects," as separate from the perceiving self, yet present to that self, as immediately real as it is.

Memory is another kind of seeing, as the phrase "look far back" in the passage just quoted indicates. If memory's "seeing" is not merely metaphorical, but as accurate as the original seeing, then the narrative as a "written memory" (58) will simply record the discoveries of that looking back. And David takes pains to characterize himself as an exceptionally observant person throughout his life. "I looked at nothing, that I know of, but I saw everything, even to the prospect of a church upon his china inkstand, as I sat down—and this, too, was a faculty confirmed in me in the old Micawber times" (27).

The primary reality of the visual is asserted by contrasting it to the fanciful in a passage which gathers together several of the novel's most central concerns.

> One Sunday night my mother reads to Peggotty and me in there [the room in which his father's funeral was held], how Lazarus was raised up from the dead. And I am so frightened that they are afterwards obliged to take me out of bed, and show me the quiet churchyard out of the bedroom-window, with the dead all lying in their graves at rest, below the solemn moon.
>
> There is nothing half so green that I know anywhere, as the grass of that churchyard; nothing half so shady as its trees; nothing half so quiet as its tombstones. The sheep are feeding there, when I kneel up, early in the morning, in my little bed in a closet within my mother's room, to look out at it; and I see the red light shining on the sun-dial, and think within myself, "Is the sun-dial glad, I wonder, that it can tell the time again?" (2)

The visual fact of the quiet churchyard is presented to the child to quell the fanciful fears awakened by the story. The clarity of daytime vision is contrasted to the fancies of nighttime, romantic visions developed in the dark when nothing real can be seen. The return of the sun at dawn means the return of the outside world to the child—and this daytime world of consciousness and visual perception is the world of time. Only with the sunrise does time begin, as the question to the sundial indicates. David clearly associates consciousness with the ability to see things. "I felt so sleepy, that I knew if I lost sight of anything, for a moment, I was gone" (2). Consciousness is that condition in which we remain aware of the outer world, and the most important awareness is visual.

Yet, interestingly enough, the reality which so completely dominates David's childhood vision, the landscape which seems more green, more shady, more quiet than anything else, is the churchyard, with its reminders of death, particularly the gravestone which marks the father's resting place. David is quieted down by being assured that the dead remain dead, that the story of Lazarus is not real.[7] In a world of objects present to his sight, the child is fascinated by the object—a tombstone— which is a memorial to an absent object. This passage already suggests the limits of a reliance on a purely visual apprehension of reality. A historical world has a depth which cannot be comprehended by the purely visual; things which are absent, which cannot be seen now, have a bearing on the significance of that which is seen in the present moment. But, at this early stage in the narrative, explicit awareness of this complication is avoided, while David celebrates, as Wordsworth was wont to do, the union of the child with his immediate surroundings.

Aural perceptions do not receive as much attention as visual ones, but they are also classed among immediate perceptions of the real, establishing contact between the self and the outside world. Hearing is most important when sight is deprived; in normal cases, hearing is simply linked with seeing, since we hear as well as see the person speaking in front of us. However, when locked into his room after biting Murdstone, David has to rely entirely on hearing to gain information of the outside world. "I listened to all the incidents of the house that made themselves

audible to me; the ringing of bells, the opening and shutting of doors, the mur-
muring of voices, the footsteps on the stairs; to any laughing, whistling, or singing,
outside, which seemed more dismal than anything else to me in my solitude and
disgrace" (4). Hearing, like seeing, involves a perception of the present moment; a
nearby sound is heard in the moment in which it is made. But since seeing is
primary, when we cannot see what is making a sound we need to interpret the
noise in order to understand who or what caused it. Thus aural perception, when
unaccompanied by the presence of the causal agent to sight, already implies a
distance from the external world, albeit a spatial, not a temporal, distance. The
primacy of sight rests on its exclusion of all such distance, its immediate union of self
and world.

The clarity of daytime vision is often contrasted to the confusion of dreams,
but this is not the case in David's narrative. Several chapters in the first half of the
novel end with his falling asleep, and with a short account of his dreams.[8] The last
page of chapter 7 is fairly typical: "I had many a broken sleep inside the Yarmouth
mail, and many an incoherent dream of all these things. But when I awoke at
intervals, the ground outside the window was not the playground of Salem House,
and the sound in my ears was not the sound of Mr. Creakle giving it to Traddles,
but was the sound of the coachman touching up the horses." The dreams in the
novel break down into isolated perceptions, in this case both visual and aural, having
no plot, and usually being simple repetitions of the images of the day just past.
Focusing on the imagistic content of dreams assures their "incoherence" in terms of
narrative structure. This places dreams in an odd position, epistemologically, in the
novel. Dreams are "realistic" insofar as they present aural and visual images, and as
such, the dreams in the narrative are usually easily recognizable as representations
of David's experiences. However, dreams are nonrealistic, "fanciful," insofar as
these images float free of context, notably narrative context.

This odd position of dreams is tied to the narrative's commitment to the
factual as opposed to the fanciful quality of memory; it is important to David as
narrator that the memories presented in the narrative be established as accurate.
The images of memory are, in several ways, obviously akin to those of dreams, so
the narrative takes pains to establish the perceptual accuracy of both. The difference between memory and dream is that memory can construct a coherent
narrative account by which its images are organized temporally.

Dream images and memory are most obviously alike in the way they differ
from the images of sense perception. Hume has offered the traditional distinction
between the two types of images by calling those of dream and memory "ideas"
and those of sense perception "impressions." Hume's insistence that impressions
are always more "lively" than ideas is questionable, since a vivid dream or memory
is often more pronounced than a weak sensory perception.[9] David offers his own
counter example to Hume, when he writes of Traddles: "His honest face . . .
impresses me more in the remembrance than it did in the reality" (41). This ability
of memory to see details clearly, perhaps even more clearly than at the moment
of original perception, is crucial to the narrative's insistence on its accuracy.

"Ideas" (in Hume's sense) are suspect because they do not rely on the object's presence, whereas an "impression" is generated by an object present to the perceiver. The problem with second-order images, those "ideas" formed in the object's absence, is that their faithfulness to the thing represented is not immediately verifiable; these ideas might be fanciful. In *David Copperfield*, that fancy alters or remakes the world in imagination is assumed, but the narrative tries to keep memory, and even dream images, out of fancy's camp. Of course, some dream distortion is admitted, but since dream images are similar to those of memory, the clarity of dreams is stressed in order to help establish the reliability of memory.

Thus, when David comes to narrate "an event in my life, so indelible, so awful" that his whole narrative has been directed toward it, he combines dream and memory to assert the faithfulness of his narration to the original:

> For years after it occurred, I dreamed of it often. I have started up so vividly impressed by it, that its fury has yet seemed raging in my quiet room, in the still night. I dream of it sometimes, though at lengthened and uncertain intervals, to this hour. I have an association between it and a stormy wind, or the lightest mention of a sea-shore, as strong as any of which my mind is conscious. As plainly as I behold what happened, I will try to write it down. I do not recall it, but see it done; for it happens again before me. (55)

Determined to validate the accuracy of his narrative, David appeals to the perceptual situation in which the object is present to the viewer. Memory can "see" so clearly that David can insist that the original event is not temporally distant, not permanently lost in the past; it exists in the present and, because present, is seen. "I do not recall it, but see it done; for it happens again before me." In this instance, there is no temporal absence; the event has been present in dream and memory to David throughout the years since it took place.

This is the "realism" for which David's narrative strives: a point where the images of memory are overwhelmed by the lost object's return to presence, to immediate perception. By locating the real in immediate sensory perception, David can only assert the "reality" of his memory when it yields to such immediacy. Ideally, the images of memory, and the words David uses to convey those images, are transparent, opening toward an apprehension of the event which was their genesis—an apprehension that is the same as having actually witnessed the event.

"Realism" is the attempt to guarantee that all representations are exact copies of the original; that words serve as simple, faithful, and transparent denominations of things; that meaning is something which exists separate of words and which is made manifest by words. Realism is essentially hostile to time; its most fundamental desire is to regain the past, to repeat that past exactly in the present, denying that anything is lost irrevocably. This demand for the lost object's return to presence is the repudiation of all representations, all substitutes, in favor of the thing itself. It is the impossibility of this desire, recognized dimly, as we shall see, in David's narrative, even while he strives to fulfill it, which leads to Dickens's absolute abandonment of realism in the celebration of "Fancy" in the 1850's.

Realism's hostility to time, its attempt to deny death, is one reason Dickens eventually abandons it; another is its hostility to words. The realist aspires to silence, the mute apprehension of actual things. David evidences some of the realist's mistrust of words, of their tendency to get between the perceiver and that which is to be perceived. In search of a transparent style, David often expresses his belief that metaphorical and rhetorical flourishes crowd out the real. A simple instance occurs in one of his attempts to be "serious" with Dora. He tells her: "We infect everyone about us" and then comments on this way of stating his "meaning." "I might have gone on in this figurative manner, if Dora's face had not admonished me that she was wondering with all her might whether I was going to propose any new kind of vaccination, or other medical remedy, for this unwholesome state of ours. Therefore I checked myself, and made my meaning plainer" (48). Figurative language is directly contrasted with making one's meaning "plain," and David, as usual when he is explicit about the type of language he prefers, chooses the latter. (Of course, his narration as a whole is full of metaphors, just as it has a "style," but these are not explicitly acknowledged.)

David's "transparent style" is implicitly compared with Micawber's use of language throughout the novel. Style as tyranny, as the imposition of one's particular point of view on another, is represented by Micawber—and is why that comic figure is as threatening a father figure as Murdstone. Micawber's extravagance, both financial and linguistic, is dangerous in its subjection of other people. Traddles "loans his name" to Micawber (28); this ominous phrase combines the linguistic and the financial, placing Traddles within the world Micawber has constituted for himself to serve his own purposes. David must avoid Traddles' mistake, must hold on to his own name, and forge a style of his own. The Micawbers belong to the warehouse world, a world to which David is introduced by Murdstone, and from which he must escape.

Both Murdstone and Micawber try to impose a certain world upon the child, a world most easily identified by its language; Murdstone's puritanical vocabulary is as distinctive as Micawber's florid style. David must reject both as inadequate; the process of his maturation is, in part, the process of developing his own style. However, that style is never recognized as one. Rather, the narrative acts as if its own style were transparent, with no tinge of self. The Murdstone and Micawber languages are idiosyncratic and hence objectionable. Their styles are personal and imply a refusal to participate in the human community, but David, using "ordinary" language, establishes a "pure" communication with others, one which simply states what has happened.[10]

The most complete denunciation of words and their use to obscure meaning, to prevent a clear apprehension of the real, comes in a discussion of Micawber's language. This passage is worthy of the third book of Locke's *Essay concerning Human Understanding* in its plea for a plain style in which words are fitted to things.

Mr. Micawber had a relish in this formal piling up of words, which, however ludicrously displayed in his case, was, I must say, not at all peculiar to him. I have observed it, in the course of my life, in numbers of men. It seems to me to be a general rule.... We talk about the tyranny of words, but we like to tyrannise over them too; we are fond of having a large superfluous establishment of words to wait upon us on great occasions; we think it looks important, and sounds well. As we are not particular about the meaning of our liveries on state occasions, if they be but fine and numerous enough, so, the meaning or necessity of our words is a secondary consideration, if there be but a great parade of them. And as individuals get into trouble by making too great a show of liveries, or as slaves when they are too numerous rise against their masters, so I think I could mention a nation that has got into many great difficulties, and will get into many greater, from maintaining too large a retinue of words. (52)

A remarkable passage, in which we find a writer complaining that we have "too large a retinue of words," many of which are superfluous. Our extravagance with words, which leads to a disregard of "meaning," is declared to be a "general rule," but the form of David's critique makes it clear that he feels he avoids the worst abuses. Micawber's use of language, marvelous as it is, is finally seen as abusive, and he is banished to Australia.

Yet this hostility to words is not consistently maintained throughout the narrative, and in considering David's attitudes toward language we shall discover the implicit critique of realism found in this novel which struggles to be realistic. Even Micawber will be found to have a legitimate place in those instances when the novel relies on, rather than bemoans, the difference between words and things.

The first indication of this difference is the child's fascination with the physical properties of words. David's reliance on sensory perception insures that words, as peculiar sensory experiences, will interest him. Spoken words can be heard, but not seen; written words can be seen, but not heard. David experiences the material existence of the spoken word when trying to communicate with Peggotty through the keyhole after he has been locked in his room for biting Murdstone. "I was obliged to get her to repeat it, for she spoke it the first time quite down my throat, in consequence of my having forgotten to take my mouth away from the keyhole and put my ear there; and though her words tickled me a good deal, I didn't hear them" (4). This experience suggests that when the material qualities of words attract our attention, we begin to lose our sense of what the words mean. The word's existence in itself as a material thing conflicts with its function as a sign of something else.[11]

David is also fascinated by the appearance of the written word. "To this day, when I look upon the fat black letters in the primer, the puzzling novelty of their shapes, and the easy good-nature of O and Q and S, always seem to present themselves again before me as they used to do" (4). Written letters "present themselves" to the viewer as objects in their own right, as physical things which have form and color. The struggles to learn shorthand repeat this preoccupation with the physical shapes of signs, as well as suggesting that when the signs' novelty wears off, we become less aware of their physical presence and more willing to see them only in terms of what they are meant to represent. "The most despotic characters I have ever known; who insisted, for instance, that a thing like the beginning of a cobweb, meant expectation, and that a pen and ink sky-rocket stood for disadvantageous." Of course, if the fact that the sign looks like a sky-rocket is emphasized, its standing for disadvantageous will seem absurd. These "arbitrary characters" become "despotic" at the moment when David looks at them as if they were not arbitrary, as if their physical appearance were a clue to their conventional meaning as signs (38).

When handwriting is involved, however, physical appearances are not so arbitrary. How a person writes is as important an indication of his or her character as what he or she writes. David is able to guess accurately the characters of Steerforth and Traddles simply by examining their carved signatures on an old door at Salem House (5). Peggotty's letters are incomprehensible in all the ordinary senses of the word, but their physical appearance is "more expressive . . . than the best composition" (17). Jack Maldon and Mr. Dick are implicitly contrasted within a few pages of each other in terms of their writing skills, with Maldon's "numerous mistakes" placed alongside Mr. Dick's "extraordinary neatness" (36). When Traddles' Sophy suppresses all her femininity to write "masculine" legal script, it serves as final proof of her self-denying character. A person's handwriting becomes a kind of "objective correlative," an outward manifestation of his personality. This same connection does not apply to the printed word, since its appearance is completely arbitrary and impersonal. The printed word's physical appearance will only distract us from its sense.

David's naïve perceptual experience of letters and words as physical objects, while conforming to his tendency to privilege sensory perception, involves the recognition of the word's essential difference from the thing. And this essential difference must undermine literary realism. There can be no exact repetition; a repetition in words or in memory is a repetition by representative, a repetition with a difference. David's narrative hedges on this point; it both accepts and denies that repetition always carries a difference within it. David, as we have seen, insists that an exact repetition is possible when he narrates the events surrounding Ham's and Steerforth's deaths. But other experiences, particularly the failure of his first marriage, will lead David to question the possibility of exact repetition.

The hostility which realism directs toward a differential vision of language is, as I suggested above, a hostility to time. If there is a difference between the word and the thing, then the word marks the place of the thing's absence. Where the word is, the thing once was. The word re-presents the thing in the present, but the thing itself is lost. Difference is loss—and if only the word, not the thing, can be called to presence, the difference is not only loss, but death. What cannot be repeated is dead. The narrative is obsessed with the fleeting nature of all experience, especially moments of happiness. One of the most perfect moments in the novel is the happy scene following Emily's acceptance of Ham, a scene interrupted by David and Steerforth entering Mr. Peggotty's boat. As David finishes describing the scene, he adds: "The little picture was so instantaneously dissolved by our going in, that one might have doubted whether it had ever been" (21). The brute facts of time and change, carrying the message of death (whose symbol is the sea), seem to overwhelm all human constructions. Peggotty's boat is a refuge from the sea, but it is destroyed in the storm which kills Ham and Steerforth. The dissolution of that happy scene points toward the larger dissolutions in the novel; the narrative can only reconstitute the scene in words. Words can never die, can always be said again, but things and situations do not enjoy the same immunity to time.

The child, in a world of immediate perception, also lives in a world of an eternal present. "As to any sense of inequality, or youthfulness, or other difficulty in our way, little Em'ly and I had no such trouble, because we had no future. We made no more provision for growing older, than we did for growing younger" (3). Realism wants to restore the child's world, resenting language for its destruction of the world in which all there is is completely present; language introduces a world in which reality is dispersed over time and space, with only a small fragment of the totality present to us in any particular moment. Most of reality is only present to us in words which represent absent objects. The eternal and full present of the child is lost, and mourned.

Both the psychologist and the theologian will recognize the narrative's presentation of that loss. The child loses his mother, and is expelled from a garden "where the fruit clusters on the trees, riper and richer than fruit has ever been since, in any other garden" (2). David's first marriage must be seen as an attempt to regain this lost paradise,[12] with Dora slated to play the role of the lost mother. But a repetition of that earlier happiness is impossible, and David comes to admit, uneasily to be sure, that loss is inevitable. "What I missed, I still regarded—I always regarded—as something that had been a dream of my youthful fancy; that was incapable of realisation; that I was now discovering to be so, with some natural pain, as all men did" (48). The "disciplined" David gives up the "dream of . . . youthful fancy" that time and death can be overcome, accepting Agnes, the bride whose habitual gesture of "pointing upward" (64) links her with a peaceful acceptance of death.[13] But the dream of a perfect and eternal present is not renounced without suggesting that life is a prison. Describing the death of his and Dora's child, David writes: "The spirit fluttered for a moment on the threshold of its little prison, and, unconscious of captivity, took wing" (48). Imprisoned in time, men are barred from eternal union with the dearest objects of perception.

Once the historical nature of experience is accepted, language is not only necessary, but can be recognized as the source of many benefits. Even if words do, at times, confuse rather than clarify, they alone make meaning possible. The child David sees Murdstone's visits to his mother, but remains completely innocent of their meaning. "No such thing came into my mind, or near it. I could observe, in little pieces, as it were; but as to making a net of a number of these pieces, and catching anybody in it, that was, as yet, beyond me" (2). Immediate perception is always of "little pieces" because it only registers what is present. Meaning can only be grasped when the connections between disparate events are explored; most of these events are, necessarily, no longer perceptually available. Language is the "net" in which the various pieces supplied by perception are caught and put together. Words grant us access to absent events, particularly events distanced in time from the present.

The limits of sight, which is the child's only reliance, are evidenced in David's inability to see anything through the telescope (2). The child, living in the present, is unable to use his past to discover patterns which would allow him to understand what is about to happen in the future. His exile in the present means that his perception of its objects is especially intense and particularly innocent, but his understanding of the present's relation to a whole sequence of events, by which its meaning is constituted, is limited.

Language also grants the ability to share these grasped meanings with others, to make significance available to a community. The whole subplot of the Strongs' marriage makes this point: open statements of one's feelings form the basis of love and community. David learns the same lesson in his courtship and marriage of Dora. His secret engagement only leads to trouble, while his openness with Dora's aunts makes the marriage possible. Once married, he is oppressed by all the things he cannot talk about with his wife. "That it would have been better for me if my wife could have helped me more, and shared the many thoughts in which I had no partner; and that this might have been; I knew" (48). The community established by language is an important consolidation for what has been lost in entering the realm of language, of history. David's narrative tries to create with the reader that ideal openness of expression which he also achieves in his second marriage. Since the experiences of individuals vary, only language can establish a community in which one can share what has been present to him by representing it in words to another.

Furthermore, and this is the crucial point, in representation, in the repetition of his history in the "now" of writing, David can discover its significance.[14] When the past is relived and memory used to recognize the present's novelty (its difference), the "mistaken impulses" of the past can be overcome. Aunt Betsey sums up the novel's whole message concerning repetition and memory when she states: "It's in vain, Trot, to recall the past, unless it works some influence upon the present" (23). The difference between the original and its repetition is a saving difference, one that is not to be lamented. Realistic, exact repetition is obsessional, leaving no room for growth or progress; repetition with a difference is liberating. David's fear of exact repetition is apparent in his reaction to the story of Lazarus; he does not want the resurrection of the dead, but only the memory of the dead. His father's tombstone is a comforting and significant monument in the child's world, but a returned father is a terrifying thought. In more obvious cases David does not as readily admit his desire that the past remain dead except in memory. (As I have noted, at times he explicitly desires the opposite.) But even while regretting his mother's fate, David's narrative shows his becoming reconciled to the fact of loss, learning to accept the substitutes time offers him. David writes: "how blest I was in having such a friend in Steerforth, such a friend as Peggotty, and such a substitute for what I had lost as my excellent and generous aunt" (22).

French psychoanalyst Jacques Lacan has noted the movement from object to object in the "chain of desire," each object existing as a substitute for (as a signifier of) the original lost object, generally the mother. For Lacan, repetition is both inevitable and impossible: inevitable in that we always focus our desires on objects which recall the original object; impossible because the original object will never return and never be replaced. This movement of desire is precipitated by our continual reinterpretation of our desires; only this ability to revise our desires moves us from one object to another. Neurosis is defined as obsessive fixation on a particular object, as acute nostalgia. (By this definition, David's love for Dora is neurotic.) Therapy functions to aid the patient's movement from one object to another; in therapy the patient repeats his past not only in the narration of old memories but also in the transference relationship, and through this repetition is able to reinterpret the past and form new desires on the basis of this reinterpretation.[15]

The relevance of this account to *David Copperfield* is clear. David must accept the fact of loss and the substitute time offers him. Comedy is possible when a writer is able to affirm this process of substitution, is able to affirm the changes time brings and the various new objects he desires. (We should note that these new objects function as words, since they are always not only themselves but also signs of the original object. Thus the new objects always carry the mark of difference, of death, since they remind us of the loss of the original object even while consoling us for that loss.) This affirmation requires the renunciation of realism (the insistence that the representative *be* the thing) and implies the acceptance of difference, of death. Time offers new possibilities to the novel's hero, but these can be seized only if he is reconciled to living in situations which are not the same as those of his past. Language becomes crucially important because it is the field of reinterpretation, the space in which that which is similar yet different appears and allows the movement away from the lost past.[16] Words, in their difference from things, necessarily change the world in the act of representing it.

The Strongs' marriage offers a minor instance of this crucial act of reinterpretation. When Dr. Strong says: "Much that I have seen, but not noted, has come back upon me with new meaning" (42), he echoes a very similar statement made earlier by David: "And now, I must confess, the recollection of what I had seen on that night when Mr. Maldon went away, first began to return upon me with a meaning it had never had, and to trouble me" (19). The Strongs' difficulties point out the dangers of misinterpretation and also indicate that the significance of the past is not fixed, but altered by the understanding of it developed in the present.

David's narrative recognizes the special role that stories and art play in this task of reinterpretation. After the first time he ever goes to the theater, David is "filled with the play, and with the past—for it was, in a manner, like a shining transparency, through which I saw my earlier life moving along." The play's ability to cause him to recall the past is in no way linked to any resemblance between it (he has seen *Julius Caesar*) and that past, but, it would seem, results from the play's existence in a realm a step removed from reality. Memory takes place in time, but it is also a way of stepping back from complete immersion in the present. Art stands in a similar relation to the present, and seems to invite David to run his eye over the whole of his experience. And the state of mind produced by the play gives David the "confidence," which "at another time [he] might have wanted," to speak to Steerforth when he sees him that night at the hotel (19).

Stories not only evoke the past but point toward a future as well. From his childhood readings, David derives "visions" of other times and places which appear "as if they were faintly painted or written on the wall" of his room (10). In the retreat from time (even while it is within time) which is the space of art, the future, as well as the past, can be written. And it is this writing that David's narrative of his "personal history" undertakes.

A more direct liberation into the future by way of story is David's repetition, while working in the warehouse, "again, and again, and a hundred times again . . . [of] that old story" of his birth and Aunt Betsey's part in it. He focuses on his mother's belief that his aunt had touched her hair "with no ungentle hand," a belief which "might have been altogether my mother's fancy, and might have had no foundation whatever in fact" (12). However, as Dickens will insist throughout the 1850's, this element of fancy is precisely what makes stories liberating. Whether this part of the story is true or not, the reader never discovers; it is enough to know that David acts upon that interpretation, running away to Dover—and that this "fancy" is repeated after his arrival. "It might have been a dream, originating in the fancy which had occupied my mind so long, but I awoke with the impression that my aunt had come and bent over me, and had put my hair away from my face, and laid my head more comfortably, and had then stood looking at me. The words, 'Pretty fellow,' or 'Poor fellow,' seemed to be in my ears, too; but certainly there was nothing else, when I awoke, to lead me to believe that they had been uttered by my aunt, who sat in the bow-window gazing at the sea" (13). Whether this incident is fact or fancy is irrelevant to its allowing another interpretation of Aunt Betsey's character, one which gives David hope, and which furnishes support for his new beginning.

Aunt Betsey insists that the past must be recalled to influence the present when relating her own "past history" (23), finding in her neglect of David's parents a reason to aid him. Part of David's recovery after Dora's death is attributed to his writing a semiautobiographical story (58). When reinterpretation and the acceptance of substitutes for the desired objects of the past are affirmed, writing and its ability to represent, to repeat, are also affirmed. David fluctuates between accepting the difference inherent in writing and its repetition and struggling to overcome that difference to "see" his past as if it were present. At times, this fluctuation results in an appreciation of fancy which looks forward to the fifties, but at other times it leads to a characterization of fancy as childish that is worthy of Mr. Gradgrind. Fancy is aligned with difference, and the narrative cannot lose its suspicion that reinterpretations are in some way unreal and, as unreal, are just words, not a very good consolation for the lost object.

David's uneasiness with the place of fancy leaves the most complete demonstration of the power of the word to Mr. Micawber. In his denunciation of Uriah

Heep, Micawber, characteristically, depends on language to provide him with the energy necessary to carry out his arduous task. The name Heep, repeated time and again, carries within it all the reasons for Micawber's activities, and is called upon whenever he requires fresh inspiration. David describes Micawber's reliance on the word: "With this last repetition of the magic word that had kept him going at all, and in which he surpassed all his previous efforts, Mr. Micawber rushed out of the house" (49). By a significant displacement, Micawber is able to practice the repetition which David is uneasy about, and by means of that repetition Micawber causes Heep's downfall and the Wickfields' liberation, a feat the novel's hero has been unable to effect. In Micawber the narrative recognizes the necessity of repetition, even while remaining unable to endorse it unconditionally or to recognize explicitly its own act of repeating in words the narrator's past.

The words in art, in repetition, is magic; by merely talking about it the past can be changed, a change which must also influence the present. This is the basis of the "talking cure" developed by Freud; a reevaluation of the past in words can successfully cure the patient's present illness. Literature often demonstrates its faith in a similar magic; it is not surprising that Dickens should examine this possibility in a novel in which he was writing about a past he had long kept repressed. In union with an audience who will endorse his transforming words—the readers to whom the novel appeals in its opening sentence—the writer can change the world. In *David Copperfield*, Dickens is shy of this power, afraid that the writer's changes are "fanciful," but in subsequent years, as his disillusionment with the "real" England grows, he will rely more and more on "fancy" as an escape from that England, and as a possible means of changing it.

NOTES

[1] *Household Words*, 30 Mar. 1850, p. 1.

[2] *Dickens on the Romantic Side of Familiar Things: Bleak House and the Novel Tradition* (New York: Columbia Univ. Press, 1977), pp. 149–50.

[3] *Adam Bede* (New York: Dutton, 1923), Bk. II, ch. 17.

[4] See especially *Of Grammatology*, trans. Gayatri Chakravorty Spivak (Baltimore: Johns Hopkins Univ. Press, 1976).

[5] *David Copperfield*, New Oxford Illustrated Dickens (London: Oxford Univ. Press, 1948), ch. 11. Subsequent references to this edition of the novel are given parenthetically in the text by chapter number.

[6] Almost every critic who writes on the novel discusses the theme of the "undisciplined heart." The best essay is still Gwendolyn B. Needham's "The Undisciplined Heart of David Copperfield," *Nineteenth-Century Fiction*, 9 (1954), 81–107. James R. Kincaid's reading of the novel in *Dickens and the Rhetoric of Laughter* (Oxford: Clarendon Press, 1971), ch. 7, is an important qualification of Needham's essay. Basically, Kincaid argues, and my discussion follows him on this point, that David's movement to discipline is, at the very least, an ambiguous one, if not completely lamentable. The realistic narrator is priggish in his suspicion of fancy, as evidenced by his uneasiness with Micawber.

[7] Mark Spilka, "*David Copperfield* as Psychological Fiction," *Critical Quarterly*, 1 (1959), 295, reads David's reaction to the Lazarus story as a fear of the father's return, a fear about to be realized in Murdstone's appearing to end the close union David enjoys with his mother. Jack Lindsay, in his *Charles Dickens: A Biographical and Critical Study* (London: Andrew Dakars, 1950), p. 34, sees the churchyard (a prominent image in Dickens's early memories, as well as in David's and Pip's) as "both the lost Eden,

and the dark spot of the death-wish." This would be another explanation for the child's fascination with the dead father, and yet his strong wish that the father remain dead.

[8] Chapters 6, 7, 8, 14, 19, 24, and 25 all mention David's dreams on the last page of each chapter.

[9] See David Hume, *An Inquiry concerning Human Understanding*, ed. Charles W. Hendel (Indianapolis: Bobbs-Merrill, 1955), pp. 26–27.

[10] This negative description of Micawber emphasizes his similarity to Pecksniff, but since *David Copperfield*, as we shall see, both recognizes, albeit dimly, and makes use of Micawber-type language, Micawber is treated more kindly (banished to triumph in Australia rather than caned) than the earlier extravagant talker.

[11] Sigurd Burckhardt, *Shakespearean Meanings* (Princeton: Princeton Univ. Press, 1968), ch. 2, offers one of the clearest accounts of the emphasis on material existence of words in poetry. Rhymes in poetry "call attention to the purely sonant nature of words. They aid the poet in weighting the balance on the side of sound and thus giving words body, which simply as signs they lack" (p. 27). The essential characteristic of poetic language for Burckhardt is that it calls into question the normal acceptance of the "transparency" of language by opening up a disturbing distance between the word and the thing, a distance which reminds us that word and thing are not one and the same.

[12] In Hablot K. Browne's illustration of David's meeting with Dora at her aunts' house, a copy of *Paradise Regained* is prominently displayed on the book shelf.

[13] Agnes "points upward" both at Dora's death and when David anticipates his own death in the novel's last sentence. Alexander Welsh discusses in detail Agnes's connection with death in *The City of Dickens* (Oxford: Clarendon Press, 1971), ch. 13.

[14] David, addressing the reader, often refers to the "now" of writing. For example: "The reader now understands, as well as I do, what I was when I came to that point of my youthful history to which I am now coming again" (ch. 4).

[15] This summary of one aspect of Jacques Lacan's theories is not specifically drawn from any particular essay or text. But see Lacan's *The Language of the Self*, trans. Anthony Wilden (Baltimore: Johns Hopkins Press, 1968), with Wilden's notes and commentary, for a general overview of Lacan's work.

[16] My discussion of David's relation to death and loss should be placed alongside Robert E. Lougy's excellent article, "Remembrances of Death Past and Future: A Reading of *David Copperfield*," in *Dickens Studies Annual*, VI (Carbondale: Southern Illinois Univ. Press, 1977), 72–101. Lougy discusses several scenes on which I also focus: in particular, the child's fear of the father's return and David's narration of Ham's and Steerforth's deaths. Lougy, however, is more interested than I in how the deaths of others serve to illustrate to David his own mortality, and he portrays David as attempting to avoid this lesson. Also, Lougy sees the novel's ending as a retreat from the more honest confrontations with death in its earlier episodes. My differences from Lougy are, I trust, clear. I wish to emphasize how language itself carries death within it, and also how language offers certain compensations for the consciousness of loss and death which it introduces.

Iain Crawford

SEX AND SERIOUSNESS
IN *DAVID COPPERFIELD*

If David's struggle between his wayward emotions and the endeavor to discipline his heart has become a commonplace of *Copperfield* criticism, much recent writing on the novel has focused on those aspects of its narrative which go beyond the limitations of this basic dichotomy.[1] Despite this, the stance which David the narrator adopts towards the materials out of which he constructs his "written memory" has remained problematic, and this has led to wide divergencies of opinion on the ultimate state of his erstwhile undisciplined heart and, consequently, on the nature of his activities as editor of his life's story. I would argue here that, while overtly describing his progress through life in terms of those characteristically Victorian orthodoxies of earnestness and self-help, David in fact adopts such cultural desiderata as an acceptable and, for him, essential alternative to the sublimated sexual emotions which appear as a continual sub-text in his narrative. This strategy is principally evident in the contrast which emerges between the recurrent patterns of narrative motif into which he, apparently unwittingly, organizes his perceptions of the key figures in his life and the more overt account he gives of the parallel discoveries of his love for Agnes and vocation as a writer. It is this contrast between willed idea and insistent desire which surely offers the truest image of David's emotional development, and the unresolved discrepancy between the two that remains with him argues against suggestions that his narrative is a successful act of purgation or that, as Jerome Buckley has put it, he "transcends his miseries and bears few lasting scars."[2]

That David is engaged in a reconstruction of his past through memory has been frequently argued, most effectively by Robin Gilmour,[3] though it is also to be noted that he himself gives some indication of being aware of this process. One instance of this tendency is to be seen in the references he makes to eighteenth-century picaresque fiction, a love of which he shares with his creator. While the influence of this genre is apparent throughout the novels of Dickens's early career, none of them refer to it so frequently or directly as does *David Copperfield*, and

From *Journal of Narrative Technique* 16, No. 1 (Winter 1986): 41–54.

on a number of occasions David himself likens some event in his story to an incident in *Roderick Random* or *Robinson Crusoe* (see, for example, 54, 382, 423).[4] Just as he had drawn comfort from his collection of books in the period after his mother's remarriage (48–9), so too in later life they offer him an imaginative alternative to some unpleasant event in the real world. Perhaps the most revealing instance of this is to be seen during his visit to Micawber in the King's Bench. In contrast to the excitement his contemporary, Pendennis, shows on a similar occasion, David responds with characteristic mildness and reduces the impact of what he sees by likening it to Roderick Random's imprisonment (142), thus making the suffering appear less immediate and, by association with the happy outcome of Roderick's story, suggesting the hope of eventual release. David himself is well aware on this occasion of his tendency to fictionalize:

> I set down this remembrance here, because it is an instance to myself of the manner in which I fitted my old books to my altered life, and made stories for myself, out of the streets, and out of men and women; and how some main points in the character I shall unconsciously develop, I suppose, in writing my life, were gradually forming all this while. . . . When my thoughts go back, now, to that slow agony of my youth, I wonder how much of the histories I invented for such people hangs like a mist of fancy over well-remembered facts! When I tread the old ground, I do not wonder that I seem to see and pity, going on before me, an innocent romantic boy, making his imaginative world out of such strange experiences and sordid things! (144–45)

What he is perhaps less conscious of is the possibility of this becoming a habit throughout his narration, and it is precisely the subjective patterns into which he unwittingly organizes his account that give the deepest insight into his nature and which reveal most about his motivations in the retelling of his personal history.

Nowhere is this more the case than in his description of the ways he perceives the people who come into his life. As is Dickens's usual practice, the characters of *David Copperfield* are delineated in terms of a restricted range of their physical features, hands, hair, and eyes being the most important—a selection which may owe as much to Dickens's interest in its theatrical potential as it does to Victorian prohibitions against description of the human, and especially the female, body. What is innovatory in *Copperfield*, however, is the extent to which such apparently formulaic description is itself revealing of the perceiving and narrating consciousness which records it. David's inner emotional life is revealed through such description, and it can be observed that his subjects divide into two broad groups: dark, powerful figures who will their dominance upon him; and charming but pliable characters to whom he is attracted.

Although we are given very few details of David's own appearance, what we do know casts significant light upon his relationships with the other characters in his account. He is chubby (77), small for his age as a child (138), and as a young man, retains a certain fresh innocence (246). This latter quality is particularly important, for it is part of a softness and even a pliability which frequently allow other people to dominate him, something true not only of his encounters with his social inferiors (the waiter at the Golden Cross [243–44] or Littimer [278, 291], for example), but also of the major relationships in his life. As Sylvère Monod has appropriately suggested, there is a certain femininity to David,[5] something also evident in certain of Browne's illustrations, most notably Plate XVIII, "I Fall into Captivity." However, we should neither laugh off this soft weakness as David appears to do nor should we allow it to conceal from us the fact that, from very early in life, his physical responses to others are both complex and clearly discriminating.

All of his relationships, for instance, are strongly defined by physical contact. Through touch David expresses much of that personal warmth which is one of his most attractive features. Both during his childhood and later, he and Peggotty frequently embrace (54, 119, 262), a detail which is given an appropriately comic tone by the repeated references to her explosive buttons. A similar expressiveness marks his relationships with Steerforth (245) and Betsy Trotwood (587–88), as well as those with such other characters as Wickfield and Dr. Strong, and it may well be the case that no other Dickensian hero is so defined by touch as is David. The importance of this motif in Dickens's conception of his hero is indicated by his care to include it when David parts from Steerforth for the last time, "Never more, oh God forgive you, Steerforth! to touch that passive hand in love and friendship. Never, never more!" (373), a detail deliberately prepared for in the number plan (765). This emphasis, and the striking parallel it coincidentally finds in Tennyson's recollections of his great lost friendship, may well be indicative of the cultural value touch held for the Victorians, but it is also to have a particular meaning within the novel.

For David similarly reveals his feelings of animosity through motifs of physical contact, most notably with Murdstone and Uriah Heep. From his first childhood meeting with Murdstone, David expresses hostility and reveals his fear of being replaced in his mother's affections: "He patted me on the head; but somehow, I didn't like him or his deep voice, and I was jealous that his hand should touch my mother's in touching me—which it did. I put it away, as roughly as I could" (15–16). As is the case with his fictionalizing of his experience, David reveals far more awareness of his emotional life when recollecting events from his childhood; as the narrative approaches closer to the point from which he writes, he becomes less able to distinguish perception and motivation. Such is certainly the case in his description of Uriah where he reveals a rather more complex set of responses than he had shown in the fairly simple opposition of acceptance and rejection that characterizes his depiction of Murdstone.[6] Few characters in all Dickens are so insistently and repetitively described as is Uriah Heep, and references to his hands make up an important part of David's response. Not only are they clammy and fishlike (202, 519), but they never stop moving, whether it be to rub his chin or, in a superbly grotesque detail, to cover the pony's nostrils after apparently breathing into them (187–88). David can resist neither the fascination these hands have for him nor Uriah's power to dominate him manually (325, 441, 489) and, through his repeated references to this and other aspects of Uriah's appearance, he gives

ample evidence of the way he is "attracted to him in very repulsion" (328). Moreover, it is a measure of the complexity of response that *Copperfield* calls for that,
where every reader will sympathize with David's biting of Murdstone's hand (50),
his striking of Uriah (579) evokes only the feeling of shame and faint self-disgust he
himself experiences.

The sexual undercurrent in David's description is even more evident in his
observation of hair and eyes. He tends to see people in highly pictorial terms,
frequently associating them with one particular image which he retains in his memory like a snapshot, a habit which is especially true of those images of his mother
which he stores away and draws upon in times of trouble. One of the most
important of these pictures is saved from that single peaceful holiday afternoon:

> I crept close to my mother's side according to our old custom, broken now
> a long time, and sat with my arms embracing her waist, and my little red cheek
> on her shoulder, and once more felt her beautiful hair drooping over me—
> like an angel's wing as I used to think, I recollect—and was very happy indeed.
> (96)

The security and protection he thus gains are essential to him and surely make up
part of that "fanciful picture" of his mother which sustains him on the road to Dover
(160). However, she also offers him another kind of femininity in the sexual
attractiveness of her hair, something which she takes pride in and of which he is well
aware, even as a child:

> When my mother is out of breath and rests herself in an elbow-chair, I watch
> her winding her bright curls round her fingers, and straitening her waist, and
> nobody knows better than I do that she likes to look so well, and is proud of
> being so pretty. (13)

Curls are also to be an important part of his later description of Dora's girlish charm
(460) and, as has often been remarked, in her David rediscovers aspects of his
mother and comes to a temporary solution of his Oedipal conflicts. There are,
however, certain key differences, for where his mother had offered him security as
well as sexual attraction, Dora fulfills only the latter need. Both women, though, fall
victim to his tendency to see people in static terms: when Mrs. Copperfield's
sexuality becomes more than the latent attractiveness he had appreciated, and she
actually remarries, their relationship loses its idyllic quality and they can only recapture it, fleetingly, on that one holiday occasion. Dora has even more to complain
of, since, as far as David is concerned, she so far fails to evolve that he can only solve
his emotional needs by transferring his affections to Agnes.

During his childhood, David is also offered a dominating masculine ideal which
contrasts strongly with both his mother's delicate femininity and the gentleness of
his own character. Murdstone is, as even David admits, an attractive man and he
brings the best out of Mrs. Copperfield (16). Although he may in both appearance
and activity resemble the Captain Murderer figure of fairy-tale,[7] there is no denying
his sexual vitality:

Several times when I glanced at him, I observed that appearance with a sort of awe, and wondered what he was thinking about so closely. His hair and whiskers were blacker and thicker, looked at so near, than even I had given them credit for being. A squareness about the lower part of his face, and the dotted indication of the strong black beard he shaved close every day, reminded me of the waxwork that had travelled into our neighbourhood some half-a-year before. This, his regular eyebrows, and the rich white, and black, and brown, of his complexion—confound his complexion, and his memory!—made me think him, in spite of my misgivings, a very handsome man. I have no doubt that my poor dear mother thought him so too. (19)

How engaged such writing is when set beside the stilted tones of his later description of Agnes! For David's reaction here is made up of fascination and resentment, both at the knowledge of the threat of being displaced in his mother's affections and the knowledge of being unable to do anything about it. Even years later when he and Murdstone meet again in London he cannot prevent himself noticing the older man's still imposing masculinity (407), and it is evident that he never fully escapes from Murdstone's hold. That such details of physical description are integral to their relationship is apparent, and Dickens's own conscious awareness of this as a narrative strategy is perhaps indicated by the various references to Murdstone's appearance which are to be found in the number plans as well as in the running title later added to chapter two of the Charles Dickens edition, "The Gentleman with Black Whiskers."

The sexual connotations of hair are also apparent in other less than entirely benign characters. Steerforth's curls (75), together with his nice voice, fine face and easy manner, suggest that luxuriant sensuality which is central to his personality. Uriah's cadaverously cropped head and lack of facial hair (187) are essential details in David's communication of the sense of horror his would-be rival creates in him. It is to be noted, however, that Uriah's desire for Agnes is by far the most vivid rendering of lust in the novel, if not in all Dickens. Beside it even the Steerforth-Emily elopement has very little force. Uriah's feelings for Agnes are far more powerfully urgent than David's and, although such lust lacking quality is typical of the Dickensian hero, the discord between David's statements of feeling and his actual displayed emotion and the further contrast with the equal temper of Uriah's unheroic heart create serious confusion among the novel's scale of sexual values. While it is probably true, as Ross Dabney has said, that "Dickens makes sexual relationships real only when they are horrible to contemplate,"[8] the result is a major dilemma within the novel, the implications of which become further apparent in David's observations of people's eyes.

The contrast between dominated and dominating characters which David first reveals in his patterns of reference to touch and hands is substantially developed through ocular detail, for eyes, as Dickens remarks in *Bleak House,* are the window to the soul, and there is little question but that they offer one of the sharpest insights into David's emotional world. A particularly revealing instance of this is to be found in color coding; it soon becomes apparent that David has a special partiality for things blue. Both Emily and Dora are blue-eyed (121; 549) and this is a detail to which David habitually refers when describing them (632, 552, 609, 655). He is easily captivated by them both and they share a certain delicate beauty and light charm, something which is emphasized by further instances of this formulaic color tagging. Just as Dora will be nicknamed "Little Blossom" by Betsey Trotwood, so too Emily is described by Mr. Omer as "a little piece of blue-eyed blossom" (376). Dora is often seen in or associated with blue ribbons (337, 467, 538); Emily ties a blue ribbon round Minnie Joram's neck on the night of her elopement (392—the color is specified in the running title added for the Charles Dickens edition), and the association of the color with sexuality is later to be reiterated by her poignant recollections of the blue Mediterranean waters (498, 576).[9] Emily's set of blue beads (27) is matched by the ring of blue forget-me-nots David later buys Dora (417), a detail which offers a finely delicate insight into the complexity of David's feelings for her, since he also records the pang he feels when seeing a similar ring on his daughter's finger years later (418). Such parallels serve to bring out delicately the links between the two girls in David's mind, and also, perhaps, through the greater frequency and precision of reference to Dora, which of them matters most to him. Other references to the color blue reinforce its significance to David as an emblem of his romantic fantasy and also help cement that link between the character and his creator, for blue was also Dickens's own favorite tone.[10] After the blue-eyed charms of Miss Larkins have smitten him in schoolboy days (229–32), for example, he is to be drawn to yet another charmer in the person of the Steer-forths' pretty maid with her blue ribbons (367). The narrative pattern of reference revealed through David's descriptive habits thus extends to become a significantly unconscious mode by which he reveals much about his responsiveness to sexual attraction.

A contrasting pattern is, however, revealed through his account of a group of characters who exercise a very different kind of hold over him, almost hypnotically capturing and subduing his personality by the sheer force of their own, and it is perhaps no surprise that his portrayal of their ocular power parallels his observations of their hands and hair. Thus Murdstone, for example, fascinates the young David with eyes from which the boy can hardly tear his gaze during that ride to Yarmouth:

> He had that kind of shallow black eye—I want a better word to express an eye that has no depth in it to be looked into—which, when it is abstracted, seems from some peculiarity of light to be disfigured, for a moment at a time, by a cast. Several times when I glanced at him, I observed that appearance with a sort of awe, and wondered what he was thinking about so closely. (19)

We are hardly surprised when, a little later, David testifies to the mesmeric hold his step-father has over him (39). As Fred Kaplan has argued, the relationship between mesmeric operator and passive subject is a recurrent one in Dickens's fiction and is invariably associated with sexuality,[11] which is clearly the case with David. For, just as Murdstone's hypnotic eyes haunt him, so too do Uriah's red suns of orbs (190) and, even more revealingly, Rosa Dartle's:

> So surely as I looked towards her, did I see that eager visage, with its gaunt black eyes and searching brow, intent on mine; or passing suddenly from mine to Steerforth's; or comprehending both of us at once. In this lynx-like scrutiny she was so far from faltering when she saw I observed it, that at such a time she only fixed her piercing look upon me with a more intent expression still. Blameless as I was, and knew that I was, in reference to any wrong she could possibly suspect me of, I shrunk before her strange eyes, quite unable to endure their hungry lustre. (368)

Like Murdstone's black eyes, these fix him helplessly and no other woman in the novel exercises such a hold over him. Even by his susceptible standards, his first reaction to her is unusually intense, "I felt myself falling a little in love with her. I could not help thinking, several times in the course of the evening, and particularly when I walked home at night, what delightful company she would be in Buckingham Street" (304). It is perhaps just as well that he does not see too much of her, since in both this curious comment and in his later reaction when she brings forward Littimer, "The air of wicked grace: of triumph, in which, strange to say, there was yet something feminine and alluring: with which she reclined upon the seat between us, and looked at me, was worthy of a cruel Princess in a Legend" (569), she evokes responses in him that he would find difficult to reconcile with his feelings for either Dora or Agnes.

Agnes provides the one exception to this broad dichotomy of response revealed through David's recording of motifs of physical depiction. She is given almost no physical presence in the novel at all: when she and David touch (312, 718), there is nothing at all sexual in the contact and it is curiously lacking in life beside his other encounters; the one descriptive detail that he does insist upon—that of her "clear calm eyes" (419)—has a similarly neutral effect; and, as Michael Steig has shown,[12] even Browne's illustrations give her very little substance in the text. In this, of course, she is to be contrasted with most of the other women in David's story, but, if he is so alive to the physical attractiveness of almost every woman he encounters, why does he so ignore this aspect of femininity whenever he mentions Agnes? Indeed, it is remarkable that, while almost every woman in the novel reciprocates his attention and frequently displays almost maternal protectiveness towards him—Peggotty, Betsey Trotwood, Mrs. Micawber, and the publican's wife in London (138–39) are all instances of this phenomenon—Agnes's feelings for him remain consistently vague, undefined, and almost vapid.

She can perhaps best be understood if she is seen as a variation upon a type of femininity that Dickens idealizes throughout his fiction, that of the earnest heroine, although I would argue that David's use of the ideal of earnestness constitutes an essential narrative stratagem in his resolution of the dilemmas posed by that emotional nature which is revealed through his patterns of physical observation. The earnest heroine, who has much in common with the bride from heaven

Alexander Welsh has described,[13] is the single most important feminine stereotype in Dickens, first appearing in the form of little Nell and present as late as *Our Mutual Friend* in the person of Lizzie Hexam. Typically, she is meek, devoted, self-sacrificing and largely sexless, and she is frequently subjected to both threats from the villain of the plot and a dilemma of choice between a more or less inadequate father and the new claims of the youthful hero. Her essential moral quality is that Victorian seriousness of purpose, dedication and rectitude covered under the term earnestness, which is also a characteristic to which the heroes of Dickens's later novels become increasingly responsive and which they themselves display more and more.

Agnes is clearly the example par excellence of this type, and finally she finds it quite impossible to be anything other than earnest in all she does. Her embodiment of the quality overshadows all other physical and emotional characteristics:

> There was always something in her modest voice that seemed to touch a chord within me, answering to that sound alone. It was always earnest; but when it was very earnest, as it was now, there was a thrill in it that quite subdued me. I sat looking at her as she cast her eyes down on her work; I sat seeming still to listen to her; and Steerforth, in spite of all my attachment to him, darkened in that tone. (313)

Whenever Dickens falls back from description of speech to that of voice it can usually be said that this is *faute de mieux* and Agnes is no exception. Moreover, the writing here is over-insistent and has none of the convincing delicacy David evinces with almost every other major character he describes—even Uriah Heep is rendered with a complexity of response that originates from a highly delicate sensibility. Throughout his depiction of Agnes, in fact, David insists upon her earnestness to an extent which renders it largely unpalatable and, unlike, for example, Florence Dombey or Amy Dorrit, she does not embody the quality in herself as much as she depends upon his perceiving it in her. In part, this stems from the fact that she has very little to do in the plot other than to sit and wait for him, but it is also related to her role as his spiritual mentor:

> She filled my heart with such good resolutions, strengthened my weakness so, by her example, so directed—I know not how, she was too modest and gentle to advise me in many words—the wandering ardor and unsettled purpose within me, that all the little good I have done, and all the harm I have foreborne, I solemnly believe I may refer to her. (443)

Though one's hackles may justifiably rise at such a misplaced anticipation of Sidney Carton, what is more important here is to note the extent to which Agnes's earnestness is not defined as an independent quality but takes its sole meaning and value from its significance for David himself:

> Whatever contradictions and inconsistencies there were within me, as there are within so many of us; whatever might have been so different, and so much better; whatever I had done, in which I had perversely wandered away from

the voice of my own heart; I knew nothing of. I only knew that I was fervently in earnest, when I felt the rest and peace of having Agnes near me. (484)

Read in isolation, this might well lead one to assume that David has been guilty of grave moral transgression. He seems, indeed, to be casting himself in the role of the reformed picaresque hero so prominent in eighteenth-century fiction and in such Dickensian characters as Martin Chuzzlewit.

Whatever the limitations of Agnes's presentation, and however much we may question the narrative strategies by which David depicts both her and his life before it came under her influence, there is no doubting the fact that Dickens means us to take it all entirely seriously and, while his Victorian readers may have demurred at the actual presentation of Agnes's character, they certainly found little to object to in her idealized nature. Within the context of David's presentation of his emotional life, however, this stress upon earnestness takes on a specific meaning and has a vital function to perform. For earnestness, or rather the lack thereof, is the criterion by which he exorcises from his life the two characters who touch most deeply upon his deepest emotional being, Steerforth and Dora. Steerforth, while cast by the plot in the conventional and rather peripheral role of villainous seducer, is central to the emotional tides of the novel and exerts considerably more sway over its hero than do either of the heroines. David's very real but largely unacknowl-edged sexuality finds its principal outlet in his attraction to and vicarious identifi-cation with his Byronic doppelganger, and this does much to explain his inability to voice outright condemnation of the seduction of Emily. In startling contrast to this, however, the woman on whom his choice eventually falls has no difficulty in rejecting Steerforth unreservedly and in terms which are astonishingly powerful under the circumstances—a brief glimpse across a theatre (312–14). Agnes's out-burst is surely a case of moral over-kill, for not only is it based upon the most superficial of encounters but also, at this stage of the plot, Steerforth has done nothing to merit such reprobation. Even if his purposelessness and lack of moral ballast, together with the attraction he holds for David, do make him a dangerous character and afford some justification for his being cast into the outer darkness, this does not account for Agnes's reaction here.

With Dora, though, the case is far more complex, since not only is it David who rejects the unsuitable character but also he does so through a subtle sustained presentation of her lack of the very quality he most prizes in his future partner. Thus, although Dickens may at first sight appear to be dealing with an issue he had faced in *Dombey and Son,* namely that of the difficulty of reconciling unwordly earnestness with depiction of the heroine as a woman capable of sexual response, what he is also doing is making this opposition central to his characterization of the two heroines, building it into the very structure of the novel. For Dora is anything but earnest in the way Agnes is and in the way upon which David comes to place an increasing amount of stress as his narrative progresses. She is entirely girlish and her light charm is aptly caught in her nickname of Little Blossom. This, however, is not to say that she is anything other than utterly serious in her love for David and, while one would hardly wish to make any great claims for her personality, it is clear that she gives him all that is in her power to give. Moreover, and as Michael Slater has effectively argued,[14] Dora manages to reconcile within herself the limitations of her conventional upbringing and an instinctive emotional understanding that David clearly lacks. He, however, consciously measures her against a standard of earnestness by which she will inevitably be found wanting:

> I did feel, sometimes, for a little while, that I could have wished my wife had been my counsellor; had had more character and purpose, to sustain me and improve me by; had been endowed with power to fill up the void which somewhere seemed to be about me; but I felt as if this were an unearthly consummation of my happiness, that never had been meant to be, and never could have been. (552)

Not only does David seem quite unaware of the self-pitying quality of his halting prose and of his evading any responsibility for creating the situation in which he finds himself, but he also reveals an entirely characteristic need to depend upon somebody else for support—though he may use the language of self-help, his self, he appears to feel, is best helped by the efforts of others. Neither he nor Dickens seems aware of the inadequacies of his response to his wife or the horrifying convenience of her dying to make way for Agnes, but Dora at least has some revenge in one of her last remarks to her husband: "I loved you far too well, to say a reproachful word to you, in earnest—it was all the merit I had, except being pretty—or you thought me so" (657). Whether David could affirm a similar fidelity in his love for her seems questionable.[15]

Nevertheless, both he and Dickens seem quite confident that Dora was an unfortunate mistake and, while it was good to have loved, it was even better to have loved and lost. David's presentation of her inadequacies is, moreover, given further and considerable support by his subsequent treatment of the theme of earnestness and the role he accords it in the development of both his character and his career as a novelist. Thus, on a number of occasions he is called upon to supply a certain want in his character:

> "Some one that I know, Trot," my aunt pursued, after a pause, "though of a very pliant disposition, has an earnestness of affection in him that reminds me of poor Baby. Earnestness is what that Somebody must look for, to sustain him and improve him, Trot. Deep, downright, faithful earnestness."
>
> "If you only knew the earnestness of Dora, aunt!" I cried.
>
> "Oh, Trot!" she said again; "blind, blind!" and without knowing why, I felt a vague unhappy loss or want of something overshadow me like a cloud. (430)

The fact that such an apparently blameless piece of morality emanates from an entirely attractive, if rather eccentric character only helps to authenticate it and to obscure the extraordinary quality of her "blind, blind!" Yet although David appears to be candidly admitting a failing in himself, what he is surely also doing is subtly preparing his defenses for that later depiction of Dora's inadequacies as a wife. For it may be seen that while, here, "earnestness of affection" is cited to his credit, Dora is soon to be reproved for her lack of a more general kind of earnestness. A little over a hundred pages later (552) and when Dora has become his wife, David will closely echo his aunt's use of the language of self-improvement but will also omit any compensatory reference to Dora's earnestness of affection in his repetition of Betsey's emphasis on his need for sustaining help. Poor Dora thus loses out on both occasions and it is hard not to feel that she has become the victim of David's shifting criteria, while the reader, unaware of the change in emphasis, is lulled into unconscious acquiescence with the nature of David's argument.

David himself has no doubt of his own redemption through earnestness and he attributes all his worldly success to the quality:

> The man who reviews his own life, as I do mine, in going on here, from page to page, had need to have been a good man indeed, if he would be spared the sharp consciousness of many talents neglected, many opportunities wasted, many erratic and perverted feelings constantly at war within his breast, and defeating him. I do not hold one natural gift, I dare say, that I have not abused. My meaning simply is, that whatever I have devoted myself to, I have devoted myself to completely; that, in great aims and in small, I have always been thoroughly in earnest. I have never believed it possible that any natural or improved ability can claim immunity from the companionship of the steady, plain, hard-working qualities, and hope to gain its end. There is no such thing as such fulfillment on this earth. Some happy talent, and some fortunate opportunity, may form the two sides of the ladder on which some men mount, but the rounds of that ladder must be made of stuff to stand wear and tear; and there is no substitute for thorough-going, ardent, and sincere earnestness. Never to put one hand to anything, on which I could throw my whole self; and never to affect depreciation of my work, whatever it was; I find, now, to have been my golden rules. (518)

The moving and dignified character of such writing and the fact that it is, to a real degree, a superb testimony to an in many ways admirable ideal which lies at the heart of Victorian culture should not blind us to its implications for David's personality and narration. For he clearly does believe that there is such a thing as fulfillment on this earth, only its name is Agnes and not Dora—to whom he certainly did not devote himself completely. Nevertheless, it is evident that he comes to make the concept of earnestness his most important criterion in judging both himself and others and uses it, above all, to justify transferring his affections from Dora to Agnes.

The often-discussed question of David's credibility as a novelist is relevant here, since it is closely related to the issue of his imaginative life, and through it, to his attitude to the two heroines. David is clearly highly imaginative; even as a child he constructs fictions that enable him to cope with the miseries of his existence. Whatever we may come to feel about the uses to which he puts his imaginativeness in that re-ordering of his life which the narrative constitutes, it is abundantly clear that such a capacity is essential to his whole being as a novelist, and it is Dora who, more than anyone else, most appreciates this aspect of David, paying tribute to it by describing him as "full of silent fancies" (553). By contrast with such delicate sensitivity, Agnes can only call his writing work and emphasize its value to society (698, 721–22), thus aligning herself with David's own comments upon the linked values of earnestness and work. However, if Dora realizes the importance of David's imaginative life, this is not to say that she possesses anything of the quality herself, and, had he made the point, this would have been a far more effective line of attack for Dickens than his condemnation of her inability to have the meals cooked on time. Unfortunately, such criticism would also have drawn attention to Agnes's even greater lack of silent fancy and to the deficiencies of David's (and, in this novel at least, Dickens's) whole conception of women.

This implicit opposition of the values of earnestness and sexual love is not confined to David's presentation of the twin heroines, for he also applies it in his consideration of Emily's elopement. Steerforth is not an earnest character, although he does express a curious "dark kind of earnestness" (275) as his thoughts wander amidst images in the fire—almost as if, once again, he offers an inverted model of David's ideals. So too, Emily herself, despite looking so "extraordinarily earnest and pretty" (123) as an innocent child, "wants heart" when she grows up and is easily tempted away from the earnest and hard-working Ham (227, 287, 629) by Steerforth's charm and the chance to become a lady without any need to ascend upon David's ladder of earnest endeavor. Mr. Peggotty's sole ambition from this point on is his earnest commitment to bring her home (620) and, while there may be something faintly disturbing in such devotion to his niece, there can be no doubting that David is making an equation between earnestness and the values of the family and domesticity, with the corollary that these are disrupted by the undisciplined sexuality of the eloping couple. His refraining from expressing overt condemnation of them may be thus accounted for, since he passes tacit judgement upon their actions by suggesting their aberration from such fundamental norms of the Victorian social world and yet also remains free to voice his own personal feelings of sadness and loss.

The whole question of the discipline that is involved in the ideal of earnestness is one which raises fresh problems and carries implications that David again fails to appreciate. Not only is his insistence upon the undisciplined nature of his youthful heart subject to the limitations we have already seen, but it also brings him into rather unfortunate parallel with his much-resented step-father. Just as both he and Murdstone court their future wives with a delicacy and charm emblemized by symmetrical references to geraniums (18, 338),[16] so too both come to find fault with their want of firmness once they are married and both are relieved of their inadequate spouses by illnesses and death—and illnesses, incidentally, which in both cases have their origins in pregnancy. It is as if, in both cases, some monstrous revenge is being wreaked upon the delicate femininity of these women who, not proving able to satisfy their husbands' criteria of personal strength, are punished through that uniquely female capacity, the gift of life. However, where there is no question of Murdstone's own personal strength, David is in many ways a weak character and there is something decidedly inconsistent in his complaining of a lack of resolution in others. If he does indeed discipline himself by the later stages of the novel and thus make himself worthy of Agnes, we may well feel that he has achieved this strength at the expense of many of the less controlled, more spontaneous emotional qualities he possesses and at the price of sacrificing much of his memory of Dora to an ideal which seems seriously deficient in humanity. Earnestness, as it is presented in *David Copperfield,* is a narrowing, exclusive quality which has none of the human warmth or spiritual depth it usually bears in Dickens's novels and we should surely resist David's (and Dickens's) attempts to persuade us to accept it as an unquestioned ideal by which the relative worth of the various figures in his story is to be measured.

There is much in *Copperfield* which lies outside this dichotomy into which David structures his emotional life, and it is part of the novel's greatness that it contains characters and values quite inimical to the orthodox beliefs its hero comes to voice and which he uses so subtly in his direction of the reader's response to the course of his life. Indeed, that same retrospective mode of narration which David uses to re-align certain events in his past with the priorities of his later life also allows and, in fact, obliges him to present that past in truthful immediacy. As Robin Gilmour has aptly put it, there is "a discrepancy between the attitude to the past required by David's attempt to discipline his undisciplined heart and the reality of the past as it is re-experienced in his memory,"[17] and it is this distinction which leads David to give weight to comic and imaginative values that find little place in his and Agnes's scheme of earnestness but which do enrich the narrative immeasurably. The outstanding individual example of this tendency would be Wilkins Micawber, but, more generally, the novel is colored by emotions which, though recollected in the tranquillity of life with Agnes, go far beyond the limitations of her view of the world and humankind.

It is perhaps no wonder that Freud so liked *David Copperfield:* "Every child at play," he wrote, "behaves like an imaginative writer, in that he creates a world of his own or, more truly, he rearranges the things of his world and orders it in a new way that pleases him better . . . "[18] David, of course, does precisely this throughout his narrative, re-ordering the events of his past life so that they and the emotions associated with them may be either excluded from the present or only revived in a controlled form. But if, as Matthew Arnold thought, the novel is "an all-containing treasure-house of English middle-class civilization,"[19] this is not to say that it is simply "the epitome of Victorian bourgeois morality."[20] For no fiction is perfect, the treasure-box turns out to be Pandora's and, in opening it, David and Dickens indicate limitations in the very ideals they mean to champion. Like the speaker of the dramatic monologue, David betrays a deeply imaginative insight into those fundamental cultural norms of Victorian society which his life's story claims to uncritically embody. Whether Dickens himself was aware of how much he had given away is debatable, but that he had not finally resolved the issues raised in *Copperfield* is evident from his returning to many of them throughout the 1850s and, above all, from his re-working of many of David's themes in what is perhaps his finest novel, *Great Expectations.*

NOTES

[1] See, for example, Stanley Friedman, "Dickens' Mid-Victorian Theodicy," *Dickens Studies Annual,* 7 (1978), 128–50, or Gordon D. Hirsch, "A Psychoanalytic Reading of *David Copperfield,*" *The Victorian Newsletter,* 58 (Fall 1980), 1–5.

[2] *Season of Youth* (Cambridge, Mass.: Harvard University Press, 1974), pp. 17–18.

[3] "Memory in *David Copperfield,*" *The Dickensian,* 71 (1975), 30–42.

[4] All references are to the Clarendon edition of the novel, ed. Nina Burgis (Oxford, 1981), and will be included in the text.

[5] *Dickens the Novelist* (Norman, Oklahoma: University of Oklahoma Press, 1968), p. 323.

[6] Uriah is usefully discussed by Michael Irwin in his *Picturing: Description and Illusion in the Nineteenth Century Novel* (London: George Allen and Unwin, 1979), pp. 78–81.

[7] See Gillian M. V. Thomas, "The Miser in Dickens's Novels and Nineteenth Century Urban Folklore," Diss. University of London 1972, p. 27.

[8] *Love and Property in the Novel of Dickens* (London: Chatto and Windus, 1972), p. 69.

[9] Dickens's own proximity to the characters of this novel is again evident in his comment to Maclise: "If you ever have occasion to paint the Mediterranean, let it be exactly that colour. It lies before me now, as deeply and intensely blue." Quoted in Forster, *The Life of Charles Dickens,* ed. J. W. T. Ley (London: Cecil Palmer, 1928), p. 331.

[10] See both the previous note and also Michael Slater, "David to Dora: A New Dickens Letter," *The Dickensian,* 68 (1972), p. 162.

[11] *Dickens and Mesmerism: The Hidden Springs of Fiction* (Princeton: Princeton University Press, 1975), p. 188.

[12] *Dickens and Phiz* (Bloomington and London: Indiana University Press, 1978), p. 130.

[13] *The City of Dickens* (Oxford: Clarendon Press, 1970), Part III.

[14] *Dickens and Women* (London: J. M. Dent & Sons Ltd., 1983), p. 248.

[15] Rebecca Rodolf, "What David Copperfield Remembers of Dora's Death," *The Dickensian,* 77 (1981), 32–40, reads this scene perceptively, though from a point of view more sympathetic to David than mine.

[16] Also, of course, Dickens's favorite flower. See, for instance, Mamie Dickens's *Charles Dickens, by His Eldest Daughter* (London, 1885), p. 103.

[17] Gilmour, p. 36.

[18] Quoted by Vereen M. Bell, "The Emotional Matrix of *David Copperfield,*" *Studies in English Literature,* 8 (1968), 633–49.

[19] *Irish Essays* (1882); reprinted in Philip Collins ed., *Dickens: The Critical Heritage* (London: Routledge and Kegan Paul, 1971), p. 269.

[20] Angus Wilson, *The World of Charles Dickens* (1970; paperback edition, Harmondsworth: Penguin Books, 1972), p. 216.

Chris R. Vanden Bossche

FAMILY AND CLASS IN *DAVID COPPERFIELD*

> "Why Rookery?" said Miss Betsey. "Cookery would have been more to
> the purpose, if you had any practical ideas of life, either of you."
> —*David Copperfield*, chapter 1, p. 5

Aunt Betsey's question about the name of the Copperfield home creates a division between two sets of values. Mr. Copperfield had tried to set himself up as a country gentleman by calling his home Blunderstone Rookery; to Aunt Betsey, this idea is as empty as the rooks' nests out in the yard. To the rookery, she opposes her own practical middle-class domesticity, represented by cookery. The rhyming conjunction of rookery and cookery never occurs again in the novel, but the two words do re-appear. Coming as it does, on the eve of David's birth, Betsey's comment directs the search for social legitimacy that constitutes the course of his career. Cast out of the Rookery, losing his family, he seeks to re-establish his identity by finding a new family and a new meaning for rookery. Like his father, he seeks the legitimacy of the country gentleman, and, in the subtitle of his autobiography, claims the title "David Copperfield the Younger of Blunderstone Rookery." But, by the time he completes his search for family and identity, the meaning of rookery has changed a great deal because he has accepted the values of cookery.

Dickens' novels always demonstrate the linkage between class and family, and *David Copperfield* can be read as a story of the triumph of the middle-class family.[1] Like so many novels, *David Copperfield* depicts a search for a family, but the family finally discovered sets this novel apart from eighteenth-century novels and even from an earlier Dickens novel like *Oliver Twist*. In *Twist*, as in *Tom Jones* or *Humphrey Clinker*, the orphan discovers his social identity, his place in the world, by discovering his familial origin.[2] Only within the notion of the aristocratic family does origin matter because this family defines itself in terms of lineage.[3] Oliver's notoriously correct English accent is his patrimony. Even so, when he discovers his

From *Dickens Studies Annual* 15 (1986): 87–109.

parentage, his social origin, he also recovers his birthright and, most importantly, a complex of family relationships that reveal that Rose Maylie is his aunt: "A father, sister, and mother, were gained, and lost, in that one moment."[4] Even though the novel insists upon Oliver's basic human value, it finally affirms that that value rests upon his social origin; Jack Dawkins and Charley Bates, for whom no such discovery is possible, cannot escape from the den of thieves into middle-class respectability. *Great Expectations* returns to the same issues, but has Pip discover that his origins are criminal, that the basis for his status as gentleman is not owing to his natal origin (the motif of misidentification at birth), but to crime and money. It carries out what *David Copperfield* commences, an analysis of the naturalization and legitimation of social status.

David Copperfield establishes an intermediate position between these two novels. Whereas Oliver moves with naive certainty from his childhood in the workhouse into the middle-class world of the Brownlows, David Copperfield, though born and raised in a gentleman's home, never feels certain that he belongs among gentlemen as we are constantly reminded by his fears that servants and other social inferiors can see through his pretenses to that estate. Discovery of social position in family origin has become just as impossible as it is to be in *Great Expectations*. David already knows where he was born and who his parents were, but this is of little use to him in his future life. Nor does the novel reveal an original family or crime; it is not a novel of origin but of destination. In this regard it may be considered every bit as devastating in its critique of society as *Great Expectations*. While the substitution of social destination for social origin still aims to naturalize social status, legitimizing middle-class self-making, this novel also provides us with reasons to doubt that David has always been destined by providence to achieve this end.

David Copperfield begins with an initiatory loss of family and status, and its plot portrays David's quest to regain social legitimacy through the discovery of a family. In the process, he discovers three types of families, which while presented as alternatives, define a complex structure of class relations in which no single one could exist without the others. Only his journey through the first two makes it possible to enter the family he discovers at the novel's end. These three family types correspond to the three major loves in his life: Emily, Dora, and Agnes.

I

The novel's retrospective narration, the story told from David's destination as middle-class novelist and contented family man, reinforces the notion that *David Copperfield* is a novel of destination. This provides us with a way of understanding why the happy ending of *David Copperfield* differs from many other Dickens novels in that the family resides in London, not in a pastoral setting. For, in a significant way, the pastoral, though not depicted, makes the final scene of domestic bliss possible. In order to explain why, we must go back to the domestic and pastoral idylls of Blunderstone and Yarmouth presented in the beginning of the novel.

Blunderstone, before Murdstone arrives, is a self-enclosed community composed of David, his mother, and Peggotty. The idyllic nature of his childhood there is largely retrospective; indeed, it is already so in his childhood. The opening chapters, though presented as comedy, portray a series of childhood anxieties: Aunt Betsey's frightening arrival on the night of his birth, his fears of the ghost of his father, even a tyrannical Peggotty.[5] And already in chapter two Murdstone intrudes upon the scene. The most idyllic scene occurs only after he has been sent away to school (chapter eight), a brief moment that David describes as a last taste of his idyllic childhood, but this former life is already a creative memory, the product of his resistance to Murdstone and Creakle.

His idyllic representation of this moment places it in the same space as Yarmouth. David presents his first visit to Yarmouth as an extension of the early childhood idyll into a timeless dimension. He gives it special force precisely because his visit means the end of that life; he has been sent there to be out of the way while Murdstone usurps his place. The idyll of Blunderstone is limited to the domestic sphere, but Yarmouth is full-blown pastoral, a lively pre-industrial community that, as Peggotty says, is "the finest place in the universe" (DC, 3, 25). David describes it as Edenic: timeless, classless, and innocent of the knowledge of good and (future) evil. The immediacy of the sea—the Peggottys live in a boat that has often sailed on it and that now lies on the sands close by it—makes this place seem a part of nature. Dickens' representation makes us want to call it a village rather than a city in order to emphasize what seems to be its natural order; the model is not the industrial midlands, but the agricultural village, its principal activity, fishing, like farming, being the provision of food. Furthermore, it does seem to be classless; the fishermen have no masters, and we see neither boat-owners nor the merchants who take the fish to market. Finally, both the boat-house and the town possess that element of neatness and busy snugness, that elementary but unfussy order, that so often characterizes idyllic spaces in Dickens. The very smallness of the boat-house makes it a child's paradise, as does the ingenuity and simplicity of its conversion to that purpose. And the town, crammed full of "gas-works, rope-walks, boat-builders' yards, ship-wrights' yards, ship-breakers' yards, caulkers' yards, riggers' lofts, [and] smiths' forges" would seem to be the Wooden Midshipman of Dombey and Son unpacked into its more lively pastoral origins (DC, 3, 25).

Yarmouth represents David's first desperate attempt to find a family, the loss of which is symbolized by his displacement by Murdstone. When he first enters the boat-house, which becomes his fundamental emblem of the domestic idyll, "the perfect abode" (DC, 3, 26), he sees a family that does not really exist. In an ironic reversal of the discovery of father, mother, brother, and sister that closes novels like Oliver Twist, David finds that the occupants of the boat-house whom he sees as husband, wife, son, and daughter do not fit his preconceived categories. Yet he continues to identify them as a family precisely because their solidarity comes from the communal relationships that motivate Mr. Peggotty to gather this group to-

gether under his roof, not simply from the fact that they share the same dwelling
or name. By falling in love with little Emily, David expresses his desire to enter into
this family that, because it remains outside of time, will remain an essential stage in
his search for family. Even when he begins to feel his class difference and can no
longer desire Emily herself, she and her family represent one aspect of the family
he would ultimately create for himself.

But in making Yarmouth an idyll, he blots out all the problematic elements of
the place: the sea, representative of its naturalness, also signifies death, and has
"drowndead" two fathers and a husband in this group alone. (Later, we will be
introduced to Yarmouth's other principal family, that of Omer and Joram the
undertakers.) David's sense of equality is illusory for he is treated with deference,
and Emily wants to be a lady, demonstrating her own recognition that Yarmouth
exists in a class-bound society. David's failure to recognize these problems only
emphasizes the fact that he wants to make Yarmouth an idyll. He never wants the
real Yarmouth life, but a life that would fulfill his desires. It represents something
that he desires and remains always as a representation, for he already expresses his
distance from Yarmouth when he complains of its dreary flatness upon first arriving
there (DC, 3, 24). In fact, his experiences there make him conscious for the first
time of his own social position and, as much as anything, cause him to resist the loss
of social status incumbent upon being sent to the bottle factory.

This new awareness of social status, more than Murdstone's shove down the
social scale, makes David feel he has been deprived of any secure and legitimate
social position. David's anxiety has a real social basis, for social mobility runs in both
directions: even as many were arriving in the middle and upper classes others were
being proletarianized, their position as lower gentry threatened by the changing
structure of economic relations. David does not mind the work so much as the
degrading company it forces him to keep, and the passage in which he describes the
"secret agony of [his] soul" as he "sunk into this companionship," with its disparaging
comparison between Mick Walker and Mealy Potatoes on the one hand and
Traddles and Steerforth on the other, betrays a well-developed class consciousness
(DC, 11, 133). Indeed, the passage shows such emphatic disregard for his fellow
workers that, taken from their point of view and not that of the boy suffering the
angst of social displacement, it comes as a shocking display of class violence. Yet he
never recognizes the similarity between his alienation from the Peggottys and from
these boys, and continues to idealize the Peggottys' condition even as he deplores
the warehouse.

II

London represents David's exile from home, the city being the antithesis of
the pastoral idyll. There he identifies not with his fellow mistreated workers, but
with the Micawbers, who feel, like David, that they have been displaced from their
proper social station. Just as David has lost his family, Mrs. Micawber claims to have

lost hers. The Micawbers are a comic version of the aristocratic family David idealizes, the Steerforths. Mrs. Micawber constantly refers to her "family" in order to insist upon her pretension to gentility in the face of their actual situation (*DC,* 11, 136; 12, 146; 17, 222–223; 57, 689–691). But the Micawbers are never able to ally themselves with her always absent and therefore functionally fictitious family. We believe so much in their social status that we readily accept that Mr. Micawber's attempts to enter commerce as a corn factor and a coal seller are inappropriate. His (great) expectations that "something will turn up" are a parody of the plot in which the orphan's true identity finally returns him to his proper place in society. This adult orphan still awaits the return to social origins no longer possible in this novel, and, in the meantime, remains a bankrupt. Resisting a decline, whether real or imagined, into the status of middle-class tradespeople or the working class, the Micawbers insist that they belong to and are destined for the gentry just as David clings to the images of Blunderstone and his upper-class school chum, Steerforth.

When, after he has completed his schooling in Canterbury, he takes a journey to "look about" for a profession, he soon encounters the image of his desire, Steerforth, who introduces him to a new family that represents social legitimacy, the next family that David seeks to enter. The Steerforths, like the Peggottys, are fragmented, a bachelor, widow, and orphan, but here the fragmentation divides the family, as every member fights against the others. Nonetheless, whereas Mr. Peg-gotty immediately disabuses David of his vision of a family, the Steerforths insist that they are one. Family here does not represent communal values, but social status. Rosa speaks for her family when she asks if it is true that the Peggottys, because they are mere rustics, have no feelings (*DC,* 20, 251), and Mrs. Steerforth speaks from this point of view when she insists that it would be impossible for her son to marry Emily (*DC,* 32, 400). Most significantly, Rosa insists that only a real family, one that lays claim to that title through its legitimate lineage, can have a home; to her, only the Steerforth home, not the Peggotty home, is laid waste by the elopement of Emily and Steerforth (*DC,* 50, 614–615). These attitudes, along with their style of living, cause us, like David, to associate them with the aristocracy even though they apparently possess no titles. This family merely asserts its social status by claiming to be a special kind of family. David always seems shocked by their attitude, but he never rejects the Steerforths or submits them to the comic satire with which he represents the same pretensions of the Micawbers. He seems unaware that his sense of the Peggottys as unselfconscious country folk lies very close to the Steer-forths' view of them as simply insensitive.

Although he takes the Steerforths as his model, he does not fall in love with Rosa Dartle, though he considers the possibility, but with another apparent rep-resentative of the gentry, Dora Spenlow. Aware that his social situation locks him out of the Steerforth world, he nonetheless aspires to it and accepts a career at Doctors' Commons upon Steerforth's assurance that they "plume themselves on their gentility there" (*DC,* 23, 293). Mr. Spenlow lives up to this characterization, claiming that "it (is) the genteelist profession in the world" (*DC,* 26, 331), and David's determination to fall in love with his daughter before he has ever met her indicates that he desires the social legitimacy of gentility as much as Dora's charms. Indeed, Dora's charms themselves simply signify her social status: flirtatiousness, silliness, guitar playing, even curls, all mark her class identity. Almost immediately, David fantasizes living with her in Highgate, the neighborhood where the Steer-forths reside, and which he associates, therefore, with gentility.

David's representation of this stage of his career satirizes the aristocratic economy that he had embraced in order to signify his allegiance to that class. His amorous exploits are marked by these aspirations, and, like Steerforth, who can afford to buy a boat and take jaunts whenever he wishes, he becomes wasteful in his pursuit of Dora. Entertaining extravagantly, which incurs Agnes's disapproval, he spends a large portion of his allowance to become a dandy, buying shoes that are, like Dora's housekeeping, uncomfortable. He wastes time seeking a chance encounter with Dora, and when he is not doing that he is pursuing a career in Doctors' Commons where the principle of gentility is allied to the most wasteful of legal operations. With Aunt Betsey's bankruptcy, he undergoes a major transformation. Still motivated, as before, by the goal of attaining Dora, he embraces a totally different economy as a means of attaining her, replacing the show of indolence with dreams of industry. The time he had spent wandering the streets in search of Dora, he now spends as Doctor Strong's secretary, in his spare time working at shorthand to produce a surplus of literal and symbolic capital for his future.

But how can we explain this sudden abandonment of gentility in favor of what would seem to be the more mundane claims of the middle class? When he had previously been threatened with social displacement, it was precisely the aristo-cratic model that had motivated his escape. When he decided to flee London and the warehouse, he turned to Peggotty only for a loan, feeling that she could do no more than this for him. Betsey Trotwood, his father's aunt, had been his only hope for restoring his social status.

Though he feels he has succeeded, Dover and Canterbury do not represent gentility but the middle class. David encounters all the virtues of middle-class life there: Aunt Betsey's common sense and prudence, Dr. Strong and Annie's com-panionability, and, above all, the domestic virtues of Agnes Wickfield. He encoun-ters tradespeople and professionals—teachers, lawyers, clerks, butchers—not gentry. Corresponding to the chance meeting with Steerforth that led him to choose Doctors' Commons, his chance encounter with Traddles now provides another model for his new means of attaining Dora. Although David always regards him with condescension, Traddles's steady accumulation of furniture and other capital—each step in his professional progress is a "pull"—in order to marry his Sophy parallels David's more melodramatic visions of self-improvement. Whereas, earlier, David had prided himself on Dora's accomplishments relative to Sophy's, he now seems to wish she had more of Sophy's household experience. Dora, for her part, almost instinctively fears both Traddles and Betsey Trotwood as represen-tatives of an alien way of life (*DC*, 41, 513–514). In Mr. Spenlow he comes to see economic failure caused by the attempt to emulate gentility. Indeed, the middle-class economy defines itself as a rejection of the style of living that it considers a wasteful economy. But this sets up a comic conflict between David and Dora, the occasion of their first dispute in their courtship, and, as he himself points out, their first marital discord. The conflict arises when David announces to Dora that he has become poor, and asks her if she would try to learn about accounts and read a cookery book. We can recognize that in making this suggestion he is drawing on what he learned at Dover, because cookery was first introduced into the novel by Aunt Betsey.

Considering his objectives, David would undoubtedly have given Dora one of the many cookbooks aimed at "the middle class of society."[6] Eliza Acton's *Modern Cookery in All Its Branches*, considered the first cookbook especially designed for the middle class, appeared in 1845 and remained the most popular cookbook until the appearance of *Beeton* in 1861. Alexis Soyer's popular *The Modern Housewife or, Ménagère* (1849), published the same year as *Copperfield*, specifically claimed to aim at the "moderate scale" of the middle class, "leaving the aristocratic style entirely to its proper sphere."[7] Along with the cookery books came a panoply of domestic manuals. The title of the most famous of the nineteenth-century cook-books, Isabella Beeton's *Book of Household Management* (1861), expresses the claims of cookery books themselves to provide much more than mere recipes. This book, which combined features found in many earlier ones, sold more copies than any Dickens novel. Other manuals—corresponding to our popular "how-to" books—offered specific domestic advice on the "servant problem," health, child-rearing, budget management, accounting, and all aspects of housekeeping, as well as the more edifying moral economy laid out in Sarah Ellis's tetralogy, also aimed at the middle class, *The Women, The Daughters, The Wives*, and *The Mothers of England* (1839, 1842, 1843, 1845).

While the contents vary widely, all of these books align themselves with what their authors prefer to call "domestic economy," the science of creating a "com-fortable" home.[8] Nearly all of the domestic manuals instruct wives on how to budget their income and how to keep accounts of what they spend so that they can stay within their budget. Micawber understands the middle-class rule of domestic economy well. His famous advice, "Annual income twenty pounds, annual expen-diture nineteen six, result happiness. Annual income twenty pounds, annual ex-penditure twenty pounds ought and six, result misery" (*DC*, 12, 150) merely repeats a commonplace of the manuals regarding the basic budgetary process.[9] But Micawber finds this "advice so far worth taking" that he "has never taken it himself" (*DC*, 12, 149) because he lives within the aristocratic economy, and like Dora, cannot really comprehend this middle class one.[10]

The principle of economy extends far beyond income and expenditure. Even the style of cooking comes under this heading since the menus and recipes usually eschewed a complex style, beyond the capabilities of the serving staff of a middle-class household, in favor of fresh ingredients, simply and sensibly prepared. Beeton standardized measurements and provided precise information on how many peo-ple each recipe would serve and how much it would cost to prepare. Class distinction can even be found in the basic rules of cooking: "The object, then, is not only to *live*, but to live economically, agreeably, tastefully, and well" (p. 39). Beeton distinguishes her middle-class audience from the working class by awarding them a diet that goes beyond mere subsistence while at the same time proscribing excess; no scrap of food, right down to the drippings, can be wasted.[11] As Soyer's Mrs. B. insists, "I managed my kitchen and housekeeping at a moderate . . . expense compared with some of my neighbors, who lived expensively, but not so well as we did" (*The Modern Housewife*, p. 1).

If the novel represents Yarmouth as the scene of the tragic fall (both in terms of nostalgia for the lost pastoral realm and its destined effacement through the seduction of Emily, linked together by David's class awareness and his complicity with Steerforth), David's courtship of and marriage to Dora belongs to its comic-satiric strand. Writing from the point of view of his final allegiance to the middle class, David makes himself as well as Dora and the Micawbers the object of gentle but insistent satire. Yet he does not satirize their ambitions or their desire for a special social position, only what he now deems to be a wasteful and irrational economics. From the time of his "conversion," when he rejects the aristocratic economy, the center of the comic scene shifts from his own antics to Dora's inability to comprehend domestic economy, presenting the comedy of her "irrational" and "impractical" response to housekeeping (*DC*, 37, 461; 41, 516).

Dora's failure can be keyed precisely to a lack of understanding of domestic economy. As the domestic manuals demonstrate, this economy is not only monetary, but spatial, temporal, emotional, and moral. In fact, Dora does not make extravagant purchases, except perhaps the pagoda, and her housekeeping never seems to endanger their overall budget. Rather, David feels "uncomfortable" because she is so inefficient. The pagoda bothers him, not because of its expense, but because it wastes the very limited space of their cottage, as does the rest of the dining room clutter. Because "nothing ha[s] a place of its own," Traddles must squeeze himself in at the table amidst Dora's flower-painting, the guitar case, and the irrepressible Jip. Contrast this with the tranquility of the Wickfield drawing room, or with the Wooden Midshipman where each navigational instrument has its own box perfectly fitted to it, the ultimate expression of the adage "a place for everything and everything in its place" (see Warren, p. 45). Similarly, Dora wastes time because she cannot command her servants to get dinner ready on time, not because she is simply indolent. And, although she does not get into debt, she does waste money because she does not know how to market, choosing lobsters that are all water and unrecognizable joints of mutton, and buying a "beautiful little barrel" of unopened oysters, making her choice on aesthetic rather than economic grounds (*DC*, 44, 548). Because she does not know enough about cooking, her roasts turn out burnt or underdone; because she does not keep her accounts, tradespeople overcharge her for butter and pepper and servants charge cordials to her; and because she does not keep the pantry locked, the servants steal from her. Had she been able to endure the cookery book, it would have advised her on all of these matters.

If David finds Dora impractical and irrational, she finds his insistence on early rising and hard work "nonsensical" and "ridiculous" (*DC*, 37, 464). Since Dora's sense of economy is so totally foreign to his, it is only appropriate that the cookery book makes her head ache and ends up a play thing for Jip. In it she would have found the same complaints made by David without his mitigating charms. When he decides that she is already "formed" and simply will never comprehend his understanding of economy, he gives in to their warnings that the education of daughters is crucial to their future abilities as wives and housekeepers, crucial precisely because it will form their attitudes towards home and family.

Dora's absolute incomprehension of David's pride in his poverty comes from a completely different code of behavior corresponding to an aristocratic economy. These economic codes do not correspond, however, to actual economic differences between classes. This representation of the different economies originates from middle-class sources and a view of the national economy in which the symbolic, political, and economic capital of the aristocracy was felt to be steadily declining as that of the middle class was just as surely accumulating. Dora's code demands her total ignorance of money, while David would impose one that makes the housewife the keeper of the account book. From David's point of view, Dora lives within an open-ended economy that has driven her father to bankruptcy, an economy that employs leisure talents, like guitar playing and flower-painting, to represent its success by displaying the extent to which one can appear not to have to economize. For Dora, allegiance to this code is absolutely necessary if she is to marry, as her father had obviously planned, into the gentry. Whenever she endeavors to act the role of the middle-class housekeeper, however, she soon becomes weary, bored, and frustrated. Her most serious attempt at housekeeping is simply "make-belief . . . as if we had been keeping a baby-house for a joke" (*DC*, 44, 553). This childish and playful attitude towards housekeeping is entirely in keeping with her training and her other talents. She cannot work hard because her identity is formed by a notion of delicacy and ornamentation and her ability to charm with these talents.

The writers of the domestic manuals would have blamed all the problems of Dora's household on her, and on her parents for failing to make her better able to cope with them. Sending a daughter to school was itself suspect since the daughter would likely fail to learn household skills, and might furthermore learn values that would make her unwilling to do so. They argued that education should prepare young women for the role of housewife, both through training in domestic skills and by inculcating the sense of self-effacement necessary to motivate them to always consider the comfort of others.[12] Manuals like *Economy for the Single and Married*, for those like Dora and David whose income ranged between £50 and £500, complain that the education of women "in the middle classes" is "simply *ornamental*," rendering them "indolent, useless, and a disgrace to their connexions."[13] Nor was this attitude limited to these manuals; Ruskin criticized the middle class for bringing up their girls "as if they were meant for sideboard ornaments."[14] So we should not be surprised when David complains of Dora that she "seemed by one consent to be regarded like a pretty toy or plaything" (*DC*, 41, 515–516).

Because female education had for some time focussed on the "refined ac-complishments" identified with leisure activities (drawing, playing the piano, and French conversation), it is criticized for failing to prepare young women for their role as middle-class wives. Sarah Ellis bluntly charges that this sort of education is meant to reinforce the values of the aristocracy, its products learning, "for the future guidance of their future lives, the exact rules by which the outward conduct of a *lady* ought to be regulated" but not conduct appropriate to their own station in life (*Wives*, pp. 164–165). Ellis does not object because she regards this sort of education as pretentious social-climbing but because she believes in the moral superiority of middle-class life. While arguing that the schools fail to prepare young women for domestic duties, she and her fellow writers seem more concerned with the bad moral economy of a system in which these girls lose "the influence of household life and know as little how to cook a dinner as to cure a cold."[15] Consequently, Catherine Beecher, in a *Treatise on Domestic Economy*, suggests that less time be spent at school and more in domestic employments (p. 26), an argument undoubtedly welcome to those who could hardly afford to send their girls away to school anyway (Branca, pp. 45–46). The ideal, of course, is the wife who combines housekeeping efficiency with more refined accomplishments; after all, part of her role of creating a comfortable environment is aesthetic, and Soyer's Mr. B. is proud of his wife who was "first acquainted with the keys of the store-room before those of the piano" (p. 4).[16]

For the purposes of defining one's class status, the moral economy outweighs the economic one. David never complains about the actual economic consequences of Dora's housekeeping; despite the examples of the Micawbers and Mr. Spenlow, he seems confident that his industry will keep them ahead of their creditors. In portraying the comic "Ordeal of Servants," David stresses his public humiliation rather than the financial cost. On their comfortable income (already when they get married he is apparently making £350 which would put them at the top of the middle-class income level),[17] he is not as concerned with the loss of money itself as with the public display of wastefulness. He is ashamed, a feeling that he expresses obliquely when he complains that their housekeeping "is not *comfortable*" (*DC*, 44, 544, emphasis added). The domestic manuals, like David, are much concerned with comfort, whether it be comfort of shoes or the home; through the notion of comfort, the more mundane aspects of domestic economy are transferred to the moral sphere. In *How I Managed My Home*, Mrs. Allison's friend Bertha insists on finding a way to dispose of stale bread because she is concerned with the moral, not the negligible monetary, significance of wasting it. At this point, domestic econ-omy becomes socially significant as well because one's commitment to its morality signifies one's values and class loyalty. David does not care about the physical discomforts of Dora's housekeeping so much as the "something wanting" that pervades his life, the emptiness of that signifier, "David Copperfield the Younger of Blunderstone Rookery," which was to have been filled up by his marriage to Dora, but persists throughout it (*DC*, 48, 594). He learns that Dora's gentility is only another empty signifier, and this ultimately generates his desire for the homemaker, the woman designated upon her first appearance in the book, when still a child, as a "housekeeper" (DC, 15, 191).[18]

III

The cookery books and household manuals that would only have hurt and baffled Dora would tell Agnes what she already knew. If she read them, she would not go to them for information but for reinforcement of her identity in a world that had always based social legitimacy upon values other than her own. By implicitly telling women that they should educate their daughters to be home-makers, not idle and decorative, these books created an opposition to the aristocracy that helped define the new realm of the domestic.

The domestic manuals also dealt with the "servant problem," and David and Dora's "Ordeal of the Servants" must be understood in the context of books like Home Difficulties; or Whose Fault Is It? A Few Words on the Servant Question (1866).[19] The solution of the manuals is that good wives must start out by being good servants (Warren, pp. iv–vi, 52–55, 67). Agnes, who has dedicated herself to maintaining the comforts of her father's home since childhood, is the ideal woman to replace Dora.

The basket of keys is the sign of the housekeeper's household authority, and Agnes, like Esther Summerson, wields them with confidence and skill. The keys are symbolic scepters of their sovereignty, yet their subjects, the servants, are seldom permitted on stage. Although she must have them, Agnes seems to have no servants in her house, and there is no mention of them in the household described at the end of the book. She has no servant problem because she is herself a housekeeper. She and Esther wave their keys like magic wands that produce order and comfort through selfless devotion alone. (When Aunt Betsey moves into David's quarters after her financial failure, Agnes noiselessly transforms his rooms so they resemble her Dover home [DC, 35, 440].) In her attempt to be domestic, Dora takes charge of the keys, but for her the magic does not work; although she goes "jingling about the house," the places to which the keys belong are left unlocked—an invitation to the servants to steal—and the keys become, like the cookery book, a plaything for Jip. Murdstone had forced David's mother, who was equally incompetent, to hand her keys over to Jane Murdstone (DC, 4, 42). In effect, when David transfers his affections from Dora to Agnes, and already when he feels that emptiness in his life that only Agnes can fill, he does the same thing.[20]

Out of the creation of the domestic idyll, David hopes to erect his new social identity. In turning the home into an idyll, in marrying the angel in the house, he seems to find an alternative to both the working-class family and the aristocratic family, but, at the same time, the identity of the middle class depends on his belief in these other family forms against which he defines the superiority of his own. His narrative creates an entire mythology of the family, a history and a geography, through which one can distinguish family forms. It accounts for the creation of the middle class by distinguishing between past and present forms of both the gentry and the working class.

The aristocracy represents social legitimacy because it had once deserved its powerful position. To come from a "good family" means that you belong to the ruling class, but also suggests ethical superiority. But the aristocracy's moral and literal bankruptcy—represented by the financial failure of Spenlow and the moral one of Steerforth—forces it to relinquish this position. The world of the Micawbers and Doctors' Commons gives way to that of Betsey Trotwood, Tommy Traddles, and David Copperfield.

Similarly, he splits the working class between Yarmouth and London, a geographic distinction that corresponds to the historical realities of urbanization. But, while urbanization and industrialization are historical facts, nineteenth-century representations of these social phenomena create a history that does more to justify and legitimate the middle class than explain the condition of the working class. Just as the middle class finds the basis for its power in the precedent of the aristocracy, it finds the model for the home in the pastoral image of the rural working class—the Peggottys—while distinguishing itself from the nearby urban proletariat—the rookeries inhabited by the likes of Mealy Potatoes and Mick Walker. Like David's depiction of Yarmouth, these depictions of the communal family, extremely common in the nineteenth century, usually present it as a lost pastoral idyll. The notion of the communal values of the extended family forms the basis for the values of domesticity, and sets the middle class family apart from the urban working class with which it co-existed.[21]

Embracing the home and the *work* ethic, David attempts to reproduce the communal values represented by the older working class while asserting his difference from the new one. His family performs the communal function that the Peggottys, driven apart by the course of events, can no longer perform. In order to claim this realm for the middle class, Gaskell and others depict the pastoral ideal as something that is passing away if not altogether vanished. David, of course, spatializes this by representing the passing order of things in terms of rural Yarmouth, the future as his own London. But he also deals with it temporally, and Dickens himself seems to have preferred things that are "old-fashioned rather than old."[22] While he frequently satirizes affection for "the good old days," he sentimentalizes "old-fashioned" Paul Dombey, and makes old-fashioned furnishings a part of the charm of Bleak House. Old-fashionedness does not belong to the past, to be exhibited in museums; it belongs to the present, an anachronistic transcendence of history. This old-fashionedness sets apart both the Peggotty family, as part of the passing rural era, and the home of the Wickfields, with its "quaint" diamond panes, its "wonderful old staircase," "old oak seats," and "old nooks and crannies" filled with "queer" furnishings (*DC*, 15, 190–191). When David Copperfield senses a distance between himself and Emily, he suggests that the Yarmouth order of life is no longer viable in the modern world he inhabits, but also asserts that it can be recovered in middle-class domesticity.

The middle class absorbs the pastoral, the family as communal unit of production. While the homeless contemporary working class must constantly struggle to survive, the middle-class domestic sphere reconstitutes the lost sense of community. Agnes with her brood of children, gathered around David, reproduces Mr. Peggotty's generosity in gathering in orphans and widows in his boat-house.

Consequently, the conclusion of *David Copperfield* does not require a pastoral setting. The home becomes the urban version of pastoral, a bit of the country within the city.[23] Esther's room in old-fashioned Bleak House represents its own idyllic nature in pastoral scenes of "ladies haymaking, in short waists, and large hats tied under the chin" (p. 116). As the title of Ruskin's "Of Queens' Gardens" suggests, the middle-class family specifically associates itself with the pastoral ideal embedded in this representation of the family; the home "is the place of Peace; the shelter, not only from all injury, but from all terror, doubt, and division" and in "so far as the anxieties of the outer life penetrate into it, and the . . . hostile society of the outer world is allowed . . . to cross the threshold, it ceases to be home" (p. 122, emphasis added).[24] It is a garden of Eden kept by a queen, a refuge for those kings who, as the companion essay's title ("Of Kings' Treasuries") suggests, spend their days in the counting house.

The home, as pastoral refuge of communal labor, depends on the selfless devotion of the housekeeper. The warlike economic forces that threaten the family pervade the male domain outside the home, and the threshold between inside and outside is a place of social transformation. Just as David refuses to see the Peggottys as part of the modern working class, allied to Mealy Potatoes and Mick Walker, he seeks to evade the problematics of this division between domestic and commercial worlds that even affects the form of his narrative. David needs the city even as he idealizes the country, and this produces a tension between the commercial act of writing his history and the domestic realm that he records through that act.

IV

If the family and its domestic milieu enables the middle class to define a neat structure of classes and social relationships, of upper and lower, inside and outside, these structures themselves cannot entirely enclose society, and they are not able to put everything neatly into place. After defining the roles of men and women through the opposition of home and workplace, Ruskin runs into difficulties, his argument self-destructing in the nearly indecipherable tangle of metaphor that concludes his essay.[25] Both the division into private and public domains, and the even more fundamental division of urban and pastoral upon which it depends, produces disturbing contradictions that may make us feel less than content with the final vision that David offers us.

The home as an enclosed and protective space can also be stifling. The boat-house appeals to young David because its scale is closer to his, its rooms are so neat and snug, its curving walls resembling the womb. And if one of the prime functions of the home is to isolate one from the outside world, what better means than the self-contained boat at sea? Even on land, it lies on the shore apart from the town, giving it a suburban aspect transferable to a cozy cottage in Highgate. The appeal of the ship as home certainly has much in common with our fascination with life on spaceships and space stations. But, as Fredric Jameson has pointed out, this pleasure runs against the almost certain monotony of sensory deprivation, isolation, and the limited society of a small space crew.[26] In transforming his pastoral idyll into a domestic one, David builds his home around one of those women whom Alexander Welsh calls "angels of death," a woman who reminds David of a saint in a stained glass window.[27]

The division between the private home, peaceful sphere of the angelic woman, and the public world, sphere of conflict and the economic activity of the man, also betrays fundamental contradictions and discontinuities. The problem of gender, dividing the world into masculine and feminine spheres, becomes a problem of the binary division itself that creates an ambiguous threshold between the two domains, the necessity of crossing this threshold constantly threatening the division itself. Ultimately, we find that the realms are interdependent and implicated within one another: try as Wemmick (of *Great Expectations*) may to rigidly separate Walworth from the City, the walls around his castle possess an all too ominous resemblance to those of the Newgate prison. Recent analyses of the family have argued persuasively that by accepting this separation of home and commerce we fail to see the way in which they reinforce one another.[28] Beneath this opposition of home and commercial world lies their basic identity: the desired reconstitution of the home as idyllic unit of production.

The notion of "domestic economy" itself should remind us that the home is a site of commercial activity, but, at the same time, it also implies its distinctness from the non-domestic economy. The idyllic portrayal of the home implies the concept of unalienated labor, a labor of love rather than necessity. For the nineteenth century, labor, which is always alienated and performed within the warlike conditions of the marketplace, must take place outside of the home if the home is to maintain its idyllic status. Women's work within the home has wrongly been considered non-work simply because child-rearing and housekeeping, which have important economic functions, are not remunerated with wages. But if we consider the ideological necessity that the home remain unpolluted by the alienated labor of the marketplace, we can begin to see an underlying reason for this attitude.

The notion of unalienated labor suggests that work is not really work because one's relationship to it is fundamentally different than that of the factory worker. This accounts for how the domestic manuals treat housework. Their insistence on self-sacrifice and consideration for others suggests that women perform their work out of love, without any motive of profit (see Ellis, *Women,* II, chapters 1–4). This also accounts for why the actual work of housekeeping is disguised by descriptions of the basket of keys, descriptions that conceal the real work. Ellis proscribes bustling about in a manner that makes your housekeeping obtrusive, and Eliza Warren advises the wife to conceal all signs of her labor before her husband returns from work.[29] Not only do Agnes's servants remain invisible, so does the scrubbing, dusting, and mending that she or they must perform.

This desire to find an unalienated form of labor that does not participate in the violence of the marketplace and can resume its place within the home defined as unit of production produces further discontinuities when the husband crosses the threshold. In *Dombey and Son,* Dickens had presented the problematics of the separation of home and work in the separation between Dombey's house and his "firm." David attempts to reunite them when he rejects the work assigned to him by that advocate of "firmness," Edward Murdstone, in favor of writing, a more genteel profession that seemingly enables him to regain control of the means of production as an author who can work at home. Traddles too combines work and home, in the reverse direction, when he "unprofessionally" moves his family into his law office.

The work ethic, that David embraces so fervently, evokes the pastoral ideal embodied in Caleb Garth of *Middlemarch* and the beehive of activity in the village of Yarmouth, but not washing bottles in London.[30] The difference between washing bottles and writing novels is not just the wages, but where one works, the warehouse or home. Working as a secretary he earns about four times as much (£70) as he did in the warehouse, but the symbolic payoff is much greater than if he had earned the same amount at a menial occupation. For, at the same time that he believes he will find his place through hard work, he believes that only the elect can reach it. Although this paradox employs the theological language of Calvinism, which urges hard work yet insists that salvation cannot be earned, the problem need not be considered in the theological terms it borrows; it belongs to economics, and extends to the nature of domestic economy.[31] In secular terms, domestic economy legitimizes the middle class: the work ethic displays its superiority to the wasteful aristocracy while the theory of the elect, translated as unalienated labor, distinguishes their labor from that of the factory operative. This legitimation is essential in a world in which unrestricted self-making—the ability of just anyone to achieve "respectability"—would destroy the class structure that the middle class only wishes to re-arrange.

The paradox of the work ethic, however, produces discontinuities within the role of the writer. Even as the writer himself enters the home, writers are represented in terms of the woman who crosses into the marketplace: the philanthropist and the prostitute. In "Of Queens' Gardens," Ruskin argues that the only appropriate activity outside the home for middle-class women is philanthropy, as an extension into the public realm of their domestic duties of securing "order, comfort, and loveliness" (p. 136). Philanthropic endeavors, like the home, are non-profit organizations, motivated by selfless regard for others. Women who profit by their economic activity prostitute themselves. In contrast to Agnes and Esther, we have Nancy (of *Oliver Twist*) and Martha Endell. Or Edith Dombey, whose marriage of convenience is clearly marked as prostitution.

Dickens, and David, would like to think that authors too are philanthropists. Dickens works at producing the excess of language that will give joy to his readers as Sleary's circus does, and he attacks social misery with the same aims as the philanthropists. While completing *David Copperfield* he started his weekly *Household Words,* with its obvious allusion to hearth and home, as a vehicle for social reform. During this time he was also helping Angela Burdett-Coutts establish an institution for "fallen women," advising that these women should be trained in home-making.[32] His instinct that these women must yearn for a home suggests that he identifies with them as well in their role as "street-walkers." Significantly, David does most of his street-walking during his extravagant courtship of Dora, and only walks through London when led there by a street-walker (he apparently also walks to think about his writing, like Dickens, but sticks to the suburbs). Martha, whose last name, Endell, suggests the end of life in the dell, has left the rural idyll of Yarmouth to become an urban street-walker in London. Writers, whatever their intentions, must sell their work, and it, like the banknote, is mere paper.

These divisions of pastoral/urban and private/public also produce discontinuities between David Copperfield and Charles Dickens, between the world of the novel's domestic fiction of wedded bliss and its excluded domestic frictions. We find in this novel a clue to some of Dickens' desires: his desire for social legitimacy and his distaste for Catherine Dickens' reported indolence. But, whereas David Copperfield achieves the comfortable home with surprising ease once he sets his mind to it (compared to Traddles for example), Dickens found himself at this time distressed by an apparently loveless marriage (Johnson, p. 494). His home was not comfortable, yet what would he have done with an Agnes even if she were able to bear up to being constantly pregnant while managing the household better than Catherine Dickens did? (Perhaps Dickens did acknowledge the impossibility of his desire by associating Dora's fatal illness, which causes her to remain inactive, with childbirth.)

Dickens was always most at home when he was at work. His compassionate portrayal of prostitutes, as well as his interest in philanthropic endeavors to aid them, suggest his strong identification with the symbolic anti-domestic impulse that they represent. Rather than bringing his work into the home, he constantly fled to Broadstairs and Brighton, even to the Continent, more at home in the streets where he gathered material for writing and worked through its problems, and where he could carouse with friends in a most undomestic way. "Nurses, wet and dry; apothecaries; mothers-in-law; these, my countrymen, are hard to leave," he wrote in tongue-in-cheek response to an invitation from Stanfield, Maclise, and Forster in 1844: "But you have called me forth, and I will come" (Johnson, p. 494).

Because the author works for joy and not merely to accumulate capital, he paradoxically produces an excess within the literary work that defies domestic economy. The parsimony of Dickens' miserly characters must be contrasted with his own extravagance with words and with David's ability to produce both comedy and melodrama. Yet, though David Copperfield returns his work to the home, he does not bring the rest of the family into the workforce as Mr. Peggotty had done; Agnes's role is to take care of the house, and Dora's assistance with the pens—a parody of the family as unit of production—comes only as compensation for her inability to keep house. Furthermore, the form of David's autobiography reinforces the division of the world into public and private realms, constraining the autobiography within the realm of the domestic and private (he never meant it to be published on any account) while excluding his writing activity and its unwritten *Kunstlerroman.* The excess involved in artistic production might endanger the household economy; to discuss his writings would be to bring his commercial activity into the home. If Dickens' fictional autobiography, representing his progress towards achieving middle-class status, reduplicates the cookery books, his novels would seem to belong to another realm.[33]

NOTES

Two individuals deserve special acknowledgement for the assistance they have given me with this essay. It owes much to a series of discussions with John O. Jordan, and I refer the reader to his essay in *DSA* 14 for a view of *David Copperfield* in many ways complementary to mine. This essay also incorporates many suggestions from Laura Haigwood.

[1] My discussion of the Victorian family is indebted to a number of sources. In addition to the social history of the family to be found in the works of Aries, Goode, Laslett and others (see below), I am especially indebted to those who have studied the family as an idea or ideology. Among the latter are Leonore Davidoff, Jean L'Esperance, and Howard Newby, "Landscape with Figures: Home and Community in English Society," in *The Rights and Wrongs of Women,* edited by Juliet Mitchell and Ann Oakley (Harmondsworth: Penguin, 1976); Jeffrey Kirk, "The Family as Utopian Retreat from the City: The Nineteenth-Century Contribution," *Soundings: An Interdisciplinary Journal,* 55 (1972), 21–41; and Patricia Branca, *Silent Sisterhood: Middle Class Women in the Victorian Home* (Pittsburgh: Carnegie-Mellon University Press, 1975). On the developing history of the word family, see Raymond Williams, *Keywords* (London: Croom Helm, 1976), pp. 108–111, and Jean-Louis Flandrin, *Familles, parenté, maison, sexualité dans l'ancienne société* (Paris: Hachette, 1976), pp. 10–15. Finally, on the sociology of cookery, see Jack Goody, *Cooking, Cuisine, and Class: A Study in Comparative Sociology* (Cambridge: Cambridge University Press, 1982).

[2] As one of the most familiar plots of romance, this plot precedes the novel by centuries. But this only further reaffirms the argument that this form of discovery of family is linked to the aristocracy, for whom romances were initially written.

[3] The history of the word "family" demonstrates this. Its earliest meaning indicated household, but by the Renaissance, it was defined in terms of lineage and descent, as in the term "the royal family." See Williams and Flandrin above.

[4] *Oliver Twist,* edited by Peter Fairclough (Harmondsworth: Penguin, 1966), p. 463.

[5] *David Copperfield,* edited by Nina Burgis (Oxford: Clarendon Press, 1981), chapter 2, pp. 13–14. Chapter and page will hereafter be cited in the text.

[6] *The Housewife's Guide; or, a Complete System of Modern Cookery* (1838). Cited in Eric Quayle, *Old Cook Books: An Illustrated History* (New York: Dutton, 1978), p. 164. These books often were specific about their audience, and others were implicitly designed for the middle class. They first began to appear around the turn of the century. See Maria Rundell's *A New System of Domestic Cookery; Formed upon Principles of Economy, and Adapted to the Use of Private Families* (1806), which she claimed was unlike anything available in her early years.

[7] I cite the first American edition (New York: D. Appleton & Company, 1850), p. 6. Soyer also wrote *The Gastronomic Regenerator* (1846), aimed at his Reform Club Clientele, and a *Shilling Cookery for the People Embracing an Entirely New System of Plain Cooking and Domestic Economy* (1854).

[8] See Isabella Beeton, *The Book of Household Management* (1861; facs. rpt. New York: Farrar, Straus, and Giroux, 1969), pp. iii, 17.

[9] See, for example, Beeton, who cites Judge Haliburton as writing: " 'No man is rich whose expenditure exceeds his means, and no one is poor whose incomings exceed his outgoings' " (p. 6). See also Soyer, pp. 1–6, and Catherine Beecher, *A Treatise on Domestic Economy* (1841; facs. rpt. New York: Schocken, 1977), pp. 41, 176. Beecher's American version of domestic economy, despite its emphasis on the needs of American women, follows the English manuals in its basic principles.

[10] On the more positive side, his exuberance and wasteful extravagance demonstrate his adherence to the economics of unlimited expense. This is what endears him to us, of course, and is clearly allied to the comic excess that makes him so important in James Kincaid's reading of the novel in *Dickens and the Rhetoric of Laughter* (Oxford: Clarendon Press, 1971), pp. 162–191.

[11] See Mrs. Eliza Warren, *How I Managed My House on Two Hundred Pounds a Year* (London: Houlston and Wright, 1864), p. 50.

[12] See Ellis, *Wives*, vol. 2, chapters 1–4, on "Domestic Habits."

[13] By "One who 'makes ends meet' " (London: C. Mitchell, 1845), p. 44. See also Soyer, who uses almost exactly the same language (p. 338).

[14] "Of Queens' Gardens," in *The Works of John Ruskin*, edited by E. T. Cook and Alexander Wedderburn (London: George Allen, 1905), 18, 132.

[15] *The Hand-Book of Woman's Work*, edited by L. M. H. (London, 1876), pp. 6–7, cited in Branca, p. 24.

[16] Consequently, the manuals don't positively discourage education. Ellis even argues for it rather vigorously. Mrs. Allison, of *How I Manage on £200 a Year*, sees with chagrin that her heroic friend Bertha has managed the perfect combination while she has let her own skills in music slip away.

[17] I presume that "when I tell my income on my left hand, I pass the third finger and take the fourth to the middle joint" (*DC*, 43, 535) means that he is making £350, a reasonable, though extremely fortunate, increase from the £70 per annum with which he began as Dr. Strong's secretary (*DC*, 36, 446). Branca argues that the middle-class income ranged between £100 and £300.

[18] The fact that Agnes and her housekeeping double, Esther Summerson, take up their duties when so young corresponds to the need for early formation of character, since household economy comes about not merely through mathematical calculation but as a result of identification with the values of domestic economy.

[19] See N. N. Feltes's excellent essay, " 'The Greatest Plague of Life': Dickens, Masters, and Servants," *Literature and History*, 8 (1978), 197–213; Branca, pp. 30–35; and Leonore Davidoff, "Mastered for Life: Servant and Wife in Victorian and Edwardian England," *Journal of Social History*, 7 (1974), 406–428.

[20] The comparison between Dora and Clara has been noted frequently, but one must also make distinctions. Murdstone marries Clara in order to "form" her (*DC*, 4, 100); David is confused about why Dora is formed in such a way to make housekeeping impossible. Jane Murdstone is the frugal housekeeper carried to the negative extreme, always suspecting the servants of plots and keeping a parsimonious eye on all goods, in contrast to the benign talents of Agnes and Sophy Traddles. At the same time, this depiction is also relevant to problems inherent within domestic economy that will be discussed below.

[21] In fact, extended families are just as likely to be found today as in the past. See John Goode, *World Revolution and Family Patterns* (London: Free Press, 1963), and Peter Laslett, *Household and Family in Past Time* (Cambridge: Cambridge University Press, 1972). My point is that this history of the family reflects the nineteenth-century view of the family. Numerous writers, including Ruskin, Carlyle, and Engels, evoke an idealized view of the extended family as do the works under discussion. A central document, one on which Engels drew, is Peter Gaskell's *Artisans and Machinery: The Moral and Physical Condition of the Manufacturing Population with Reference to Mechanical Substitutes for Human Labour* (London: John W. Parker, 1836); Gaskell's analysis of the problems of industrialization and urbanization focusses on their effects on the family. For an argument that the extended family increased in importance, rather than decreased, see Michael Anderson, *Family Structure in Nineteenth Century Lancashire* (Cambridge: Cambridge University Press, 1971).

[22] *Bleak House*, edited by Norman Page (Harmondsworth: Penguin, 1971), p. 116.

[23] Kirk Jeffrey, discussing the American family, makes this clear when he compares the family to nineteenth-century utopian ventures. The utopians often did attempt to reproduce what was felt to be an older, more communal social structure, which usually meant a rural setting as well as experimentation with social structures, and Jeffrey argues that the formation of the nucleated family was a similar venture accommodated to the needs of urban life.

[24] This passage has become the *locus classicus* of discussions of the importance of the home to the Victorian middle class, but in most cases the analysis simply accepts the Victorian explanation of the division between home and world rather than trying to discover its structural significance. The following is a far from exhaustive list of those who cite the passage: Walter E. Houghton, *The Victorian Frame of Mind* (New Haven: Yale University Press, 1964), p. 343; Carol Bauer and Lawrence Ritt, *Free and Ennobled: Source Readings in the Development of Victorian Feminism* (Oxford: Pergamon, 1979), p. 16; Jenni Calder, *The Victorian Home* (London: Batsford, 1977), p. 10; Susan Casteras, *The Substance or*

the Shadow: Images of Victorian Womanhood (New Haven: Yale Center for British Art, 1982), p. 14; Erna Olafson Hellerstein, Leslie Parker Hume, and Karen M. Offen, eds., Victorian Women: A Documentary Account of Women's Lives in Nineteenth-Century England, France, and the United States (Stanford: Stanford University Press, 1981), p. 278; Christopher Wood, Victorian Panorama: Paintings of Victorian Life (London: Faber and Faber, 1976), p. 59; Eli Zaretsky, Capitalism, The Family, and Personal Life (New York: Harper, 1976), p. 51.

[25] Kate Millett partially untangles it in "The Debate over Women: Ruskin vs. Mill," in Suffer and Be Still: Women in the Victorian Age," edited by Martha Vicinus (Bloomington: Indiana University Press, 1972), pp. 121–139.

[26] Fredric Jameson, The Political Unconscious: Narrative as a Socially Symbolic Act (Ithaca, N.Y.: Cornell University Press, 1981), pp. 217–218.

[27] Alexander Welsh, The City of Dickens (Oxford: Clarendon Press, 1971), chapter 11.

[28] Eli Zaretsky, p. 27 and passim; Rayna Rapp, "Household and Family," 175–178, in Ellen Ross Rapp and Renate Bridenthal, "Examining Family History," Feminist Studies, 5 (1979), 174–200; and Michele Barrett, Women's Oppression Today: Problems in Marxist Feminist Analysis (London: Verso, 1980), chapter 6, "Women's Oppression and 'the Family'."

[29] Sarah Ellis, The Wives of England (London: Fisher, Son, & Co., 1839), pp. 239–240, and Eliza Warren, A Young Wife's Perplexities (1886), p. 35, cited in Calder, p. 111.

[30] On the relationship between family and pastoral in Middlemarch, see Anthony G. Bradley, "Family as Pastoral: The Garths in Middlemarch," Ariel, 6:4 (1975), 41–51.

[31] For a very useful discussion of the work ethic in Dickens, see Welsh, pp. 75–84. The relationship between Evangelical religion and middle-class values is explored in Catherine Hall, "The Early Formation of Victorian Domestic Ideology," in Fit Work for Women, edited by Sandra Burman (London: Croom Helm, 1979), pp. 15–32.

[32] Edgar Johnson, Charles Dickens: His Tragedy and Triumph, 2 vols. (New York: Simon and Schuster, 1952), II, 714–718, 593–594, 621.

[33] To a certain degree this process of exclusion reverses Dickens' own practice. While David excludes his novels from his domestic autobiography, Dickens excludes his domestic life from his novels. At this point, one could follow another trajectory than that I have followed here, and examine how Dickens attempts to differentiate his representation of the family from that found in the domestic manuals and social histories. Placing himself outside of the novel's domestic realm by injecting it with humor, sentiment, and linguistic excess, just the converse of David's attempt to put his art outside of his autobiography, Dickens attempts to distinguish the economy of his novel from the taut economies of the middle class. But this division between the novelistic and the domestic is tenuous at best, and in Eliza Action's cookery book, Dora would have found a recipe for "Ruth Pinch's Beef-Steak Pudding." The cookbook writers were quick to employ the means of the novelist, recognizing its appeal to the housewife: Soyer's book is in the form of an epistolary novel, Eliza Warren's domestic advice is written as an autobiographical narrative, and Isabella Beeton originally published her cookbook in twenty-four monthly parts. This sort of analysis has been carried out in other discussions of Dickens; see David A. Miller, "Discipline in Different Voices: Bureaucracy, Police, Family and Bleak House," Representations (1983), 59–89, and Catherine Gallagher, "The Duplicity of Doubling in A Tale of Two Cities," Dickens Studies Annual, 12, edited by Michael Timko, Fred Kaplan, and Edward Guiliano (New York: AMS Press, 1983), pp. 125–145.

Edwin M. Eigner

DAVID COPPERFIELD AS ELEGIAC ROMANCE

Mortality and gentility, two concepts central to an understanding of *David Copperfield*, have become the subjects of important, recent studies of the nineteenth century. Philip Mason's *The English Gentleman: The Rise and Fall of an Ideal* (1982) and Robin Gilmour's *The Idea of the Gentleman in the Victorian Novel* (1981) both pay considerable attention to the works of Dickens, and Garrett Stewart's *Death Sentences: Styles of Dying in Victorian Fiction* (1984) uses *David Copperfield* as one of its primary texts. The themes appear to have little in common with one another and to require, indeed, quite different sorts of critical approaches, but still another recent book, *Elegiac Romance* (1983) by Kenneth A. Bruffee, although it deals with neither Dickens nor his times, provides nevertheless a way of discussing the pervasive Victorian aspiration toward gentility and the obsessive nineteenth-century preoccupation with the fear of death as they relate to one another in *David Copperfield*, the central novel in Dickens' career.

Most simply described, an elegiac romance is a first-person retrospective narration recounting the death of a romantic figure who has captured the imagination of the less heroic narrator. A few examples are *Moby-Dick, Heart of Darkness, The Great Gatsby,* Thomas Mann's *Doctor Faustus,* Ford Madox Ford's *The Good Soldier,* Salinger's "Seymour: An Introduction," R. P. Warren's *All the King's Men* and Saul Bellow's *Humboldt's Gift,* but Bruffee's impressive list of eighteen well-known novels and twice as many shorter pieces offers convincing proof that we have to do here with an important fictional construct, full of significance to some of our best writers. By virtue of the *apparent* heros, these works descend, according to Bruffee, from medieval exemplary romances. However, the down-to-earth writing styles and the self-effacement typical of the narrators, who, although they always turn out at last to be the true heroes, characteristically begin with the sincerely avowed purpose only of coming to terms with their grief by discovering its meaning, connect these important novels and stories with the non-didactic, unpretentious elegiac mode.

From *Dickens Studies Annual* 16 (1987): 39–60.

As the examples indicate, this apparently self-contradictory form belongs mainly to our own century. Moreover, *David Copperfield* is far too long and complex a novel to be summed up in terms of such a discreet and so relatively simple a genre. There is a great deal more in Dickens' novel than can be explained by it, or indeed by any single critical approach. It remains, nevertheless, that when we focus on the narrator's relationship with James Steerforth, *David Copperfield* displays most of the characteristics of an elegiac romance and can be profitably read as such.

Indeed, the novel's opening sentence—"Whether I shall turn out to be the hero of my own life, or whether that station will be held by anyone else, these pages must show"—is a sentiment that might almost have been spoken by Marlow or Nick Carraway or John Dowell or Gene Forrester of *A Separate Peace* or any of the other elegiac romance narrators who struggle to recapture, through their writing, the sense of identity and personal worth they lost through their ambiguous relationship with the hero. It is late in the novel, for instance, before Jack Burden of *All the King's Men* is ready to concede that "This has been the story of Willie Stark, but it is my story, too. For I have a story" (435); and Salinger's Buddy Glass castigates himself in the last paragraph for his "perpetual lust to share top billing with" his dead brother.

The role of David Copperfield in the novel that bears his name is similarly confusing. As Lawrence Frank writes, "Steerforth threatens to usurp our interest" (67), and, more significant, he threatens also to usurp the interest of the narrator. At times David appears to be writing an autobiography, and the complexities of the character self-revealed, either consciously or unconsciously, have proved fascinating to such acute critics as Barry Westburg and Sylvère Monod. At other times, he seems to operate merely as a window, an insignificant observer, reporting the far more interesting doings of the Heeps, the Strongs, the Peggottys, Micawbers, and Steerforths, and to be so uninteresting in his own right as to have led such a great Dickens enthusiast as George Bernard Shaw to conclude that David "might be left out of his biography altogether but for his usefulness as a stage confidant, a Horatio or Charles his friend: what they call on the stage a feeder" (31).

In *Charles Dickens: The World of His Novels*, J. Hillis Miller puts these two David Copperfields together in a way that will be useful to our discussion. Miller writes that "David has, during his childhood of neglect and misuse, been acutely aware of himself as a gap in being. . . . The center of David's life . . . is the search for some relationship to another person which will support his life, fill up the emptiness within him, and give him a substantial identity" (156–157). This is the quest of all the twentieth-century elegiac romance narrators, who, again like David, discover at the death of the other person that by attempting to complete themselves in this questionable fashion they appear to have lost themselves entirely. They then proceed, like David, to recount the story of the tragic loss, to elegize the heroic dead man, to puzzle over the meaning of the gut experience they have survived, and in the process, hopefully to free themselves of the fallen hero's quest, perhaps indeed of all heroic questing, and, in the end, to find their own true identities, to become, indeed, the heroes of their own lives, or to reject, once and for all, the romantic notion of heroism (Bruffee, 49–50).

David Copperfield had sought in his friendship with the arch-gentleman, James Steerforth, just such an identity-giving relationship as Miller describes, the intellectual companionship he somewhat peevishly complains of having missed in his marriage to Dora and which Dickens himself felt he had never been able to find. Friendships and would-be friendships abound in the novel. Murdstone begins his acquaintance with David by saying, "Come! Let us be the best friends in the world!" (16), and while David is wisely on his guard from this quarter, he usually welcomes the friendships that are constantly offered him throughout the novel. He "soon became the best of friends" with Mr. Dick (185), and he responds so positively when Mr. Wickfield refers to him as "our little friend" (189) that he soon finds himself "feeling friendly towards everybody" (192), including even the sinister Uriah Heep, who much later in the novel insists on the friendship then established:

> "This is indeed an unexpected pleasure! [says Heep]. To have, as I may say, all friends round Saint Paul's, at once, is a treat unlooked for! Mr. Copperfield, I hope I see you well, and—if I may umbly express myself so—friendly towards them as is ever your friends, whether or not." (637)

David's substitute father, Mr. Micawber, refers to Uriah as "your friend Heep" (224) or "our friend Heep" (482). Poor Micawber, embattled though he is, perceives friends everywhere, even in the razor he sometimes thinks of using to cut his own throat (224). He regards David as "the friend of . . . [my] youth, the companion of earlier days!" (348); and Mrs. Micawber tells David "You have never been a lodger. You have always been a friend" (149). David thinks himself "blest . . . in having . . . such a friend as Peggotty" (273), and, of course, his relationship with Agnes Wickfield sails under the flag of a "pure friendship" (737) until the very conclusion of the novel.

But it is, of course, Steerforth whom we and the narrator think of as "the friend" in the novel *David Copperfield*. Young David fastens onto this friendship as firmly and immediately as he does because, in the first place, Steerforth appears in his life at the moment when he is in most need of confirming his very nearly lost human identity. David's stepfather has beaten him like a dog, and David has responded, doglike, by biting his tormentor's hand. Now he walks around with a dog's sign tied to his back—*"Take care of him. He bites"* (67). In this state he is carried before Steerforth, "as before a magistrate," who enquires into the facts of the case and concludes "that it was 'a jolly shame;' for which," as David states, "I became bound to him ever afterwards" (72). Later on in the novel, when an older but still socially insecure David has been assigned a bed in "a little loft over a stable," Steerforth gives him a suitable, human identity once again. "Where," he demands of the innkeeper, "have you put my friend, Mr. Copperfield" (245). And David is immediately translated into a more genteel room "with an immense four-post bedstead in it, which was quite a little landed estate" (246).

Just what Steerforth sees in David besides an admiring plaything is perhaps somewhat more difficult to explain. Like most of the elegiac romance heroes Kenneth Bruffee describes, Steerforth does not reciprocate the affection entirely. At their reunion in London, for instance, David is overcome. " 'I never, never, never was so glad! My dear Steerforth, I am so overjoyed to see you!' " Steerforth is more restrained: " 'And I am rejoyced to see you, too!' he said, shaking my hands heartily. 'Why, Copperfield, old boy, don't be overpowered!' And yet he was glad, too, I thought, to see how the delight I had in meeting him affected me" (245–246). After their final parting, David concedes that Steerforth's "remembrances of me . . . were light enough, perhaps, and easily dismissed" (388).

Like most romance heroes, Steerforth is too self-absorbed for satisfactory friendship, but, as his mother assures David, "he feels an unusual friendship for you" (253), and he is uncharacteristically solicitous of David's good opinion. " 'If anything should ever separate us,' " he says at their parting, " 'you must think of me at my best. Come, let us make that bargain' " (373). George Bernard Shaw's belittling identification of David as a Horatio turns out to be inspired criticism. There is a great deal of Hamlet in James Steerforth, or at least he fancies so. Steerforth is broodingly suspicious of action, and he is cynically unable to direct his abundant energy to any goal except winning because he fails to see the value of any other goal. " 'As to fitfullness,' " he says, " 'I have never learnt the art of binding myself to any of the wheels on which the Ixions of these days are turning round and round' " (274). He even feels troubled by " 'a reproachful ghost' " (273), and he misses the presence of " 'a judicious father' " (274). The Hamlet-like James Steerforth wears David Copperfield in his heart of hearts because he thinks David, whom he nicknames Daisy, is free of the romantic passions which govern *him*, and because, like Hamlet and such elegiac romance heroes as Lord Jim, Jay Gatsby, Willie Stark of R. P. Warren's *All the King's Men*, and the mad editor of Nabokov's *Pale Fire*, he needs desperately to be understood aright and to have his story told. " 'I don't want to excuse myself;' " Lord Jim says, " 'but I would like to explain—I would like somebody to understand—somebody—one person at least' " (69). And on his deathbed, Willie Stark of *All the King's Men* tells his flunky and future biographer, " 'It might have been all different, Jack. . . . You got to believe that,' he said hoarsely. . . . 'You got to,' he said again. 'You got to believe that' " (400).

David Copperfield becomes a novelist, a storyteller, because that was the identity James Steerforth, who had an equal need of justification, gave him when they were children back at Salem House School. Previously, in the lonely days at the Rookery, David sat upon his bed in solitude and read, as he says, "as if for life" (48). Now in his new friend's bedroom, to which David "belong[s]" (80) and where he feels "cherished as a kind of plaything" (81), Steerforth proposes that they "make some regular Arabian Nights of it" (79). David, as official storyteller to Steerforth, likens himself to "the Sultana Scheherazade" (80), who, of course, *told* stories for her life.[1]

Later on, when David becomes what he calls "a little laboring hind" (132) and feels in danger once again of losing both his class and his human identity, he makes use of this resource Steerforth had taught him when he tells "some astonishing fictions" (143) to the Orfling who works for the Micawbers. And, at the end of the novel, he will tunnel out from his grief for Steerforth by writing a story. It is significant that when David mentions working on his "first piece of fiction" he finds himself coming by accident "past Mrs. Steerforth's house" (567). And, while it is perhaps too much to say that the one surviving work of our fictional novelist may be a life of James Steerforth, curiously titled *David Copperfield*, it *is* true that when Dickens shortened his complex novel into an evening-long public reading, he omitted almost everything in the novel which did not relate to Steerforth, and he ended the reading with Steerforth's death.[2]

Kenneth Bruffee, whose book on elegiac romance is subtitled *Cultural Change and Loss of the Hero in Modern Fiction,* sees his genre as the most recent phase of a long tradition. In the medieval quest romance, he writes, our attention is directed "exclusively to the task and character of the aristocratic seeker, the knight ... [whose] story is always courageous and serious ... seldom ironic." In the second phase, invented by Cervantes, "the whole story becomes ironic," because the knight must now share the stage with Sancho Panza, and "the reader is never allowed to feel quite sure whose values Cervantes means us to share: the knight's or the squire's. . . . For the first time in the quest romance tradition, the conventions and values of feudal life, courtly love, and [the] heroic knightly quest receive serious criticism in the light of everyday experience" (32). In the modern or elegiac romance phase, as Bruffee sees it, the irony disappears once again as the squire, after a tremendous struggle, rids himself of his obsession with his hero, and in so doing, utterly rejects the corrupt values of the society that the hero represents, including the concept of heroism itself.

It follows from this line of thinking that an individual elegiac romance will become significant when the values of the romantic hero that obsess the narrator and that he finally comes to reject are of deep cultural importance. Thus Jay Gatsby and Lord Jim can be said to embody the false dreams of the societies they represent. It is not enough, therefore, simply to explain the psychological reasons for David Copperfield's decision to lose himself, so to speak, in James Steerforth. We must ask ourselves what social values Steerforth represents, and how he may be regarded not only as David's personal hero, but as a significant hero of the Victorian age, perhaps as *the* significant hero. When we have done this, we may also be able to see why he is so important to David, and why David must ultimately outgrow him.

Ellen Moers writes in her study of *The Dandy* that with Steerforth "Dickens for the first time draws a character whose 'aristocratic' temperament, manners, and attitudes play a major part in the novel. Steerforth the wicked seducer [of little Em'ly]," she writes, "is merely a repetition of immature melodrama [such as Dickens had frequently made use of in earlier novels], but Steerforth the schoolboy hero of David Copperfield is Dickens's first attempt to deal with a problem that would bedevil him in maturity" as he dealt with such ambiguous, gentlemanly characters as James Harthouse, Henry Gowan, and Eugene Wrayburn (229–230). It is not quite accurate to say that there had been no admirable or admired gentleman in Dickens before Steerforth, but it is true, nevertheless, that in *David Copperfield,* for the first time in Dickens, the idea of gentility, represented by such a problematical figure, becomes the obsessive goal of the principal point-of-view character.

David's background may account for his social ambitions. Early in the novel Little Em'ly distinguishes between herself and David by noting, "your father was a gentleman and your mother is a lady" (30). David does not contradict her, but the reader knows that his mother was a governess, not a lady, before her marriage and that, as David's Aunt Betsey has pointed out, she and her husband "were not equally matched" (7). Perhaps David, like Dickens himself, was sensitive on this score of a servant ancestry, for, in contrast to such earlier heroes as Nicholas Nickleby and Oliver Twist, he behaves like a boy, and later on like a man, who is shamefully uncertain of his own position in society. His difficulty with servants, who almost always refuse contemptuously to accept his authority, is one of the great comic strands of the novel. When David's stepfather, who has told him that he is "not to associate with servants" (103), condemns him to become a laborer, David is devastated mainly at the loss of his social position:

> No words can express the secret agony of my soul as I sunk into this com-panionship; compared these henceforth every-day associates with those of my happier childhood—not to say with Steerforth and Traddles and the rest of those boys; and felt my hopes for growing up to be a learned and distin-guished man, crushed in my bosom. (133)

Later when he is rescued and again finds genteel companions at Dr. Strong's school, "My mind ran upon what they would think, if they knew of my familiar acquaintance with the King's Bench Prison" (195). And still later he becomes morbidly afraid that his enemy Uriah Heep will discover these secrets from Micawber, and publicly taunt him with them, as indeed Heep does, when he calls Micawber, "the very scum of the world—as you yourself were, Copperfield, you know it, before anyone had charity on you" (640).

David's extraordinary sensitivity on the score of Heep has been noted by several critics, and usually interpreted, mistakenly, I believe, as an unconscious revelation of class consciousness on Dickens' own part. Thus, A. H. Gomme writes:

> [Heep's] writhings are real enough, but it is impossible at times to avoid a feeling of special pleading against him, of Dickens with a knife in Uriah. . . . It is made a point against him that not only does he pretend to a humiliation he does not own, but that he has a coarse accent and drops his aitches. . . . That . . . snobbery in Dickens as well as in David . . . becomes vicious in the scene in which David is obsessed by Heep's physical repulsiveness. (176)

In Great Expectations, where Pip feels a similar repulsion to the lower-class Orlick and where Orlick responds with the same enmity, readers have no trouble dis-tinguishing between the class attitudes of the character and those of the author. The confusion exists in David Copperfield partly because it is an elegiac romance, while Great Expectations is not, and because what Barry A. Marks has called the writing time of a story, the months or years during which we are to suppose the narrator is putting his experience on paper so that he can "seek and express an under-standing of it,"[3] is consequently more important. Pip-the-narrator at least believes that he has already achieved his wisdom, his maturity, his sense of his own identity long before he begins writing his autobiography. Thus he is able compassionately to condemn his own childish snobbery and to make us understand that neither he nor Dickens shares it. David Copperfield-the-narrator is in the *process* of learning about himself as he writes his own (or is it James Steerforth's?) life story, and since he does not yet understand his own class consciousness, his obsession with gentility, the blindness appears also to be that of Dickens, the creator of David-the-narrator as well as David-the-character, neither of whom is yet free of the hero-worship of Steerforth and a thralldom to the false values of gentility he represents.

David-the-narrator's excessive hatred of Uriah Heep is also understandable in terms of the behavior of David-the-character, which, if given an unfavorable construction—the sort of critical construction a Heep internalized in David's own psyche might put upon it—is not very easily distinguishable from the actions of Heep himself. In *Dickens and the Invisible World,* Harry Stone has written that Uriah personifies "David's most aggressive and covetous thoughts" (222). Certainly the two characters, both poor boys, are similarly determined to rise in the world. Keith Carabine believes that "Heep embodies and deflects those elements of David which . . . [he needs to] deny—namely his ambition and his sexuality" (161). And it must be admitted that as far as ambitious sexuality is concerned, neither David nor Heep is especially scrupulous in the business of secretly courting the daughter of his wealthy employer. Carabine sees Heep as "a rival and a double" of David's (161–162), and Harry Stone calls our attention to the Uriah-David rivalry over Bathsheba in the Bible, where, of course, King David, and not his subordinate Uriah, is the clear sexual aggressor. In light of this confusion and this combination of roles for Heep, we should note that David sees Uriah, as indeed Pip sees Orlick, in disgustingly phallic terms. The thought of his Agnes "outraged" by this "red-headed animal" makes David positively "giddy," so that Uriah "seemed to swell and grow before my eyes" (326).

Nevertheless, the aggressiveness and the aggressive sexuality of David or Heep are nothing when compared to these same qualities in Steerforth, a character David strives to exculpate as strongly as he works to incriminate Uriah. Steerforth, after all, succeeds in *his* seductions, and while he obviously disdains the tawdry business of rising in the world, he is clearly as determined as Heep is to win at any price:

> "Ride on! [he says] Rough-shod if need be, smooth-shod if that will do, but ride on! Ride over all obstacles, and win the race!"
> "And win what race?" said I.
> "The race that one has started in," said he. "Ride on!" (364)

Dickens, who had already risen high enough by the time he was writing *David Copperfield* to enroll his eldest son at Eton, but who found himself still possessed by an excess of competitive energy, may have been as much or more disturbed by

Steerforth's gratuitous aggression, when he saw it reflected in his own character, than he was by Uriah's self-help ambition.

Another servant who aspires to marry a woman David loves and against whom there is almost as much special pleading as there is against Heep is Steerforth's man, Littimer. Why, after all, should David hold Littimer more guilty and in so much greater contempt than he does Steerforth in the business of Little Em'ly's seduction? And what is so outrageous, after all, in Littimer's desire to marry Em'ly when Steerforth has cast her off? Is he not, as he represents himself, "a very respectable person, who was fully prepared to overlook the past, and who was at least as good [socially] as anybody the young woman could have aspired to in a regular way" (511)? As George Orwell says in defense of Heep, "Even villains have sexual lives" (41). It appears that, just as David prefers to revile Heep instead of himself for the sexual fantasies both of them cherish regarding Agnes, he also prefers, in the matter of Em'ly's seduction, to hate the servant Littimer rather than the gentleman Steerforth.

And David is not the only one who indulges this preference. Littimer (I almost said poor Littimer) is everybody's scapegoat. Miss Mowcher, who also, after all, assisted in the seduction, prays, "May the Father of all Evil confound him [Steerforth] . . . and *ten times more* confound that wicked servant" (395). Rosa Dartle, whom Steerforth had previously seduced, holds Littimer in such deep contempt after the Little Em'ly business that she will not permit him to address her (395). Steerforth insults him (572), and even Little Em'ly, meek though she is, tries to murder him (571). Daniel Peggotty, who can keep his powerful emotions under control when speaking of Steerforth, the man who has abused his hospitality and ruined his niece, boils over with rage whenever he thinks of "that theer spotted snake . . . may God confound him!" who tried, from his own point of view, at least, to make an honest woman of her (619).

What all these characters have in common with one another and with David is an absolute fascination with James Steerforth and the gentility he represents. Miss Mowcher is an indefatigable name-dropper, and Rosa is a sycophantic dependent. Daniel Peggotty may seem a much more self-respecting character, but he is so charmed by Steerforth from the moment of their first meeting at David's school that we can feel pretty sure he was more of an ally than Littimer in the business of his niece's seduction, albeit, of course, an unwitting one. Not only did he talk Steerforth up on every occasion—

> "There's a friend!" said Mr. Peggotty, stretching out his pipe. "There's a friend, if you talk of friends! Why, Lord love my heart alive, if it ain't a treat to look at him!" (122)

—but it was he who first started Em'ly dreaming of becoming a lady when she was a small girl, wearing "a necklace of blue beads," which must have been a present from him.[4]

David's attraction to gentility is at least as strong as his need for friendship, and genteel people draw him out as easily as servants repel him. He finds his schoolmaster's daughter "in point of gentility not to be surpassed" (79), and Micawber impresses him "very much" at their first meeting with his "certain indescribable air of doing something genteel" (134). Both David and his biological mother come close on a number of occasions to acknowledging Peggotty—"that good and faithful servant, whom of all the people on earth I love the best" (113)—as his true mother (11, 13–14, 17, 53), and at one point Peggotty asserts her claim to act as David's motherly protector—"who has such a good right?" she asks—and she assures David "that the coach-fare to Yarmouth was always to be had of her for the asking" (212). But to accept Peggotty as his mother would mean an end to his dreams of gentility. Even Steerforth tells David that it is with Peggotty that he "naturally belong[s]" (265). And yet in his moments of deepest depression as "a little laboring hind" in London, he "never in any letter (though many passed between us) reveals the truth" to Peggotty (139), and when his situation becomes intolerable, David chooses to take his chances with Aunt Betsey, whom he has never seen and about whom he has heard nothing in the least bit encouraging, rather than come home to Peggotty, although he has to write a lie to Peggotty to get his Aunt's address and to borrow enough money to get to Dover in genteel fashion (151). As one critic writes, "David's walk to Dover is as irrepressible an assertion of individuality and the will to succeed as Heep's faith in his father's words, 'be 'umble, Uriah . . . and you'll get on' " (Carabine, 160). He also has a lot in common with Pip of *Great Expectations.* "I never could have derived anything like the pleasure from spending the money Mr. Dick had given me," David writes, "than I felt in sending a gold half-guinea to Peggotty, per post . . . to discharge the sum I had borrowed of her" (211). For David, as later for Pip, cutting the old, shameful though legitimate ties, is as important as weaving the new, highly questionable connections to the world of gentility.

With the help of his chosen mother, David, again like Pip, seems to have his fairy-tale wish of great expectations fulfilled. He gets a new name, becomes an heir, and is educated at a school for gentlemen. And when, like the hero of a fairy tale, he sets out into the great world to choose a genteel profession for himself, the first significant person he encounters, of course, is his old idol, the archetypal gentleman, whom he once chose over the skeleton-drawing Tommy Traddles and whom he soon acknowledges, in preference to Agnes Wickfield, as the guiding star of his existence (308). The profession David chooses, both at the suggestion of his lady Aunt, who wishes "to provide genteely" for him (299), and on the recommendation of his gentleman friend, could not be better suited to the goal he has set for himself. "A proctor is a gentlemanly sort of fellow," Steerforth tells David in a cancelled passage (293), and in a passage which was allowed to stand, Steerforth says, "On the whole, I would recommend you to take to Doctors' Commons kindly, David. They plume themselves on their gentility there" (293). So, in effect, it is Steerforth's advice that makes David a gentleman, just (and just as ambiguously) as it later makes Little Em'ly a lady.

Returning to the Em'ly plot and Daniel Peggotty's part in his niece's seduction, we can see just how Dickens connects his two themes of death and gentility, for it was Em'ly's concern to prevent her uncle's death that was the first cause of her dangerous ambition to become a lady. As she told the young David,

> "We would all be gentlefolks together, then. Me, and uncle, and Ham, and Mrs. Gummidge. We wouldn't mind then, when there come stormy weather— Not for our own sakes, I mean. We would for the poor fishermen's, to be sure, and we'd help 'em with money when they come to any hurt.... I wake when it blows, and tremble to think of Uncle Dan and Ham, and believe I hear 'em crying out for help. That's why I should like so much to be a lady." (30–31)

This passage, one of the most poignant and meaningful in the novel, shows that for Dickens gentility was not only a question of social ambition or snobbish pride, but a life and death matter. In *Oliver Twist,* if you are not a gentleman, like Oliver, you are literally starved to death in the workhouse or hanged as a criminal. In *Bleak House* you are helplessly "moved on," carrying the plague that kills you. In *Great Expectations* the social alternatives are presented with a stunning simplicity: you can either be a hound (a gentleman) or a varment; if you do not run with the hunters, you must inevitably and unsuccessfully run from them. In *David Copperfield,* according to Little Em'ly's experience, if you are not a lady, all the men around you will be "Drowndead." On the night of her elopement with Steerforth, David, who is attending the death of Barkis, has "leisure to think ... of pretty little Emily's dread of death" (379).

Steerforth and the gentility he both stands for and appears to offer, for he is ready "to swear she was born to be a lady" (284), seems to provide an escape from death and the grief death causes. I believe that Steerforth stands for something similar in David's mind also, and that this is why David is initially fascinated by Steerforth and so unwilling to condemn him even after he has been found unworthy. Steerforth the gentleman is thus the false cultural hero of Victorian England, the romantic knight whom the narrator of one of the century's most significant elegiac romances must reject for himself and his age, so that he and his readers can find their true identities in the face of their otherwise overwhelming and paralyzing fear of death.

Saul Bellow's *Humboldt's Gift,* perhaps more than any of the other works on Kenneth Bruffee's list, demonstrates that elegiac romance, like pastoral elegy, provides an opportunity for a serious inquiry into the general question of death. The subject had always fascinated Dickens, but nowhere more powerfully than in *David Copperfield,* where the narrator is, after all, a "posthumous child" (2), and where his story includes the deaths of his mother, his infant brother, the previous tenant of his London rooms, his aunt's estranged husband, his beloved nurse's husband and her nephew, his own first child, who is stillborn, his first wife, her father and even her dog, and, finally, his own best friend and alternate identity. Moreover, David's childhood sweetheart is an orphan, motivated, as we have seen, with the dread of death; his first wife's mother is dead; and so is the mother of his second wife, who has been brought up in a mausoleum, haunted by a father, overcome with what he calls "disease(d)" and sordid "grief" (493–494). As Garrett Stewart has noted, *David Copperfield* is the only work "before *Malone Dies* that has invented a new word for death (drowndead, and)...the novel has, beyond this, far more than a word to add to the idea of death as a test of wording" (73).

If we are at first surprised at this quantity of deaths, it is perhaps because so few of them are actually rendered in the novel, so few of them directly witnessed by the narrator. I take this suppression to be in itself significant, for *David Copperfield* is a novel of suppressions, especially suppressions of death. Thus, Stewart suggests that Doctor Strong has been unable to get past the letter D in his unfinished dictionary because he cannot confront the word death. David apparently, or Dickens, cannot stand the sight of it, and so the writer who had sent Victorian England into profound mourning in his previous novel with the death of Paul Dombey and was to electrify them in his next book with the death of Jo the crossing-sweeper, shows David present at the dying moments only of the dog, Jip, and of the comic figure, Barkis. Moreover, both experiences are immediately overshadowed by so-called "Greater Loss[es]" (380), which David does not directly witness, the death of Dora and the elopement of Em'ly, who asks her family to "try to think as if I died when I was little and was buried somewhere" (386). When David remembers the last time he saw his mother alive, he writes, "I wish I had died. I wish I had died then with that feeling [of being loved?] in my heart!" (94). And soon his wish is symbolically fulfilled, although he has typically missed even his own death scene: When he describes his mother and his brother in their coffin, he thinks "The little creature in her arms was myself" (115).

David denies on the very first page of the novel that he was "privileged to see ghosts and spirits," but all the characters he subsequently introduces are referred to as "shadows" on the last page. Earlier he called them "phantoms" (541). The novel abounds with references to the ghosts in *Julius Caesar, Macbeth,* and especially *Hamlet.* Indeed, no other work of Dickens is so specter-ridden. The recollection of his unhappy youth, he writes, came upon David "without...invocation...like a ghost, and haunted happier times" (129), and after Steerforth's death David entered, what he calls "a long and gloomy night...haunted by the ghosts of many hopes, of many dear remembrances, many errors, many unavailing sorrows and regrets" (608).

As the presence as well as the denial of all this death in the novel would indicate, David Copperfield's reaction to death is both profound and ambiguous. "If ever a child were stricken with sincere grief," it was David at the news of his mother's death, yet he felt "distinguished" by it in the eyes of his schoolmates "and walked slowly" (107). When Mr. Spenlow dies David has "a lurking jealousy...of Death...[which might push him from his] ground in Dora's thoughts" (475). But, on the whole, he has a nightmare dread which dates back to his association with the best parlor and Peggotty's account of his father's funeral there. The story of "how Lazarus was raised up from the dead" so frightened him as a child that his mother and Peggotty were obliged to take him out of bed and show him the quiet churchyard out the bedroom window, "with the dead all lying in their graves at rest, below the solemn moon" (12). It is, of course, his own death David fears. When he returns from his first trip to Yarmouth and thinks that his mother is dead, he feels as though he "were going to tumble down" (36), and this is precisely his sensation later on when he hears of Mr. Spenlow's death—"I thought it was the office reeling, and not I" (474). Spenlow, whose posthumous son-in-law David will soon become, is another character paralyzed at the thought of death. He has been psychologically unable to make out a will. But the subject of death is as fascinating to David and the others as it is horrifying. The death-dreading Em'ly goes to work for an undertaker, and David ends his search for a genteel profession by binding himself apprentice to a probate attorney.

Barry Westburg argues that David's stepfather, Mr. Murdstone, is the personification of Thanatos himself. Westburg writes:

> When David is told, "You have got a Pa!" he says, [that] "Something . . . connected with the grave in the churchyard, and the raising of the dead, seemed to strike me like an unwholesome wind." [Later,] when two of his associates greet Murdstone they say, "We thought you were dead!" He is dark of dress, skin, and whiskers and professes a mortifying religiosity. . . . Murdstone is the resurrection of death itself, of life's primal antithesis. (46)

And as we have seen, it is Murdstone who initiates the friendship theme in the novel. " 'Come! Let us be the best friends in the world!' said the gentleman, laughing. 'Shake hands!' " (16).

David offers Murdstone only his left hand, but to Steerforth, the second gentleman of the novel, he gives both hand and soul wholeheartedly, and with Steerforth he does become "the best friends in the world." It is a strange substitution, as profoundly ironic as Little Em'ly turning to this same gentleman-sailor as a protection against being "drowndead." the warnings come quickly in both cases. On the first evening, Steerforth entertains Em'ly with "a story of a dismal shipwreck" (269), and David, who is introduced to Steerforth "under a shed in the playground" (72), spends *his* first night sitting with Steerforth in the bedroom, thinking of ghosts. We have previously seen that Steerforth gives David a life-saving, artist's identity at school, but we should note that if David is Scheherazade in the relationship, Steerforth is the Sultan, who may choose to spare, but whose more usual course is to execute his brides after the wedding night.

Michael Slater has suggested that the invention of Steerforth, "handsome and captivating, entrancing company, yet ultimately shallow, selfish and cruelly frivolous . . . enables Dickens to create David's Maria (Beadnell) figure, Dora Spenlow, untouched by the unhappy memories of the way in which his real-life original had tormented and ultimately failed him" (62–63). Dora, who dominates the second half of the novel almost as powerfully as Steerforth had the first, and whose plot was the only one besides Steerforth's that Dickens kept for his public reading of *David Copperfield*, is, with her attractive vivacity and gentility, yet another ironically fragile safety-net against death. David's association of Dora with life and gentility becomes comically clear in his shocked horror when his landlady likens his love for the doomed "Little Blossom" to the passion of a dead lodger, David's predecessor, for a working-class girl. "I must beg you," David says, expressing far more than snobbery, "not to connect the young lady in my case with a barmaid, or anything else of that sort, if you please" (341).

But it is more frequently to Steerforth directly that David, like Em'ly, looks for salvation. David refers to Steerforth as his "protector" (307). Steerforth, David says, "was a person of great power in my eyes" (76), power which I submit David believes will save him from the dominance of Murdstone and the spell of death, as, indeed, at their reunion at the London inn it rescues David from his "small bed-chamber," which David describes as "shut up like a family vault" (243). Em'ly seems actually to expect something like a rebirth through Steerforth, hoping for the day when "he *brings me back* a lady" (386, my emphasis). That this appearance is delusive goes perhaps without much saying—Steerforth is himself "drown-dead"—but *In Memoriam,* and a host of important literary works glorifying the gentleman give evidence that it was the culture's delusion as well as David's and Em'ly's. Robin Gilmour believes that Pip's great expectations represent "some of the deepest hopes, fears, and fantasies of Dickens's class and generation" (118), and Arnold Kettle writes that the "day-dream nature . . . of Steerforth, the By-ronic superman, aristocratic self-confidence and all, is revealed in the novel as no arbitrary personal 'weakness' in David's character, but as an important and com-plex social psychological problem of nineteenth-century England" (72–73). He seems, according to Lawrence Frank, "to have stepped out of David's dreams as the dazzling figure David wishes and fears to become" (92). "Steerforth was a myth," according to Garrett Stewart, "generated out of the . . . suspension of moral consciousness into which David was betrayed by his adolescent identifi-cation with his idol as the incarnated dream of invincible vitality and charm" (78); i.e., of life and gentility.

After Steerforth rescued David from the vault-like room above the stable at the Golden Cross Inn, David, who had just seen a performance of *Julius Caesar,* "fell asleep in a blissful condition, and dreamed of ancient Rome, Steerforth, and friend-ship, until the early morning coaches, rumbling out of the archway underneath, made me dream of thunder and the gods" (247). Steerforth is, of course, the principal god in question, but David's and Em'ly's hope that he will confer some of his immortality on them does not reckon with the fact that he regards them and all servants and the children of servants as belonging to a different species from himself. Their "feelings," he assures one of his schoolmates, "are not like yours" (86), and when a member of his own class asks him if the Peggottys and people of that sort are "really animals and clods, and beings of a different order," he allows "with indifference," that "there's a pretty wide separation between them and us" (251). When Steerforth dismisses Ham Peggotty as "a chuckle-headed fellow," David, who has been vaguely worried about Steerforth since the latter's gratuitous humiliation of their unoffending schoolmaster, Mr. Mell, finds it possible, or perhaps necessary, to convince himself that his friend and protector is only hiding his sympathies for the poor by making a joke (271). Obviously Em'ly is capable of the same kind of self-delusion, until Steerforth unmistakably shows how he regards her by trying to arrange a marriage for her with his own servant.

Both David and Em'ly have passed through a sort of fairy-tale experience, which can be called the motif of the bad wish granted and which Dickens employed to structure a number of his novels, most obviously *The Haunted Man, Little Dorrit,* and *Great Expectations.* In such works the beneficent fairy, who is sometimes only implied, makes the wish come true so that the hero can learn its falseness and try to save himself by unwishing it. David and Em'ly both wished for gentility through Steerforth, and they both seemed about to have the desire fulfilled, but only so that, like Pip and the others, they might discover in time that the ambition was unworthy.

Em'ly began the necessary redemptive business of reversing the destructive wish when, after recovering from the fever which followed her flight from Steerforth and Littimer, she told the Italian children not to address her as " 'pretty lady' (*bella donna*) as the general way in that country is, and . . . taught 'em to call her 'Fisherman's daughter' instead" (622). Then she became a servant at an inn in France. And finally, after her arrival in England, she walked from Dover to London, literally reversing David's earlier painful and heroic march to gentility.

David's way back is more difficult because he has invested still more of himself even than Em'ly has in Steerforth and what he represents. She has been Steerforth's mistress and has lost her good name; but David, like the narrator of the twentieth-century elegiac romances, has allowed himself to become Steerforth's double, and it is not too much to say that he has lost his soul. After the seduction of Little Em'ly, which occurs at the precise center of the novel, David declares his cherished friend dead. He claims that Steerforth "fascinated me no longer" and that "the ties that bound me to him were broken" (388). Steerforth disappears physically from the next seven numbers of the novel, but his name recurs regularly in each monthly installment. And like Tennyson to the dead Hallam's door, David keeps returning during these pages—"in an attraction I could not resist" (445)—to the garden under Steerforth's window. After the drowning, which takes place in the next to last number, David mourns for Steerforth as a potential hero "who might have won the love and admiration of thousands, as he had won mine long ago" (696).

Robin Gilmour writes that "there is no real awakening of David's undisciplined heart in relation to Steerforth" because "Dickens's imagination is not really engaged [in *David Copperfield*] as it will be later in *Great Expectations* in exploring the processes of moral and emotional self-discovery" ("Memory," 39). I have been arguing a greater similarity between the two novels in question. According to my reading, David and Pip are alike not only in regard to their social ambition and the fear of death which sparks it in both instances, but, to an even larger extent, in the burden of guilt they share. Pip is made to feel guilty about being an orphan, about being a boy, about being a laborer, and he makes himself guilty by wishing himself into becoming a snobbish, persecuting gentleman. In the last third of *Great Expectations,* Pip suffers various kinds of symbolic death, which have been seen as ritual attempts to expiate that guilt, to unwish the bad wish that had caused it. But in respect to guilt, David, I think, surpasses even Pip. As the projections on Littimer and Heep indicate, he feels guilty about his social background, about his ambition to rise above it, and about his sexual nature, which Dickens frequently saw as both motivation and means for social advancement. He even feels guilty about distrusting the perfidious Steerforth. More legitimately, perhaps, David appears to blame himself for his part in the seduction of Little Em'ly and for unconsciously wishing his unsatisfactory wife to death.[5] And the writing of *David Copperfield* can be seen as *David's* ritual attempt—the elegiac ritual, this time—to clear himself of this enormous load of guilt.

Elegy would seem to be a promising means of expiation in this case because the sins were all connected with the fascination for the dead Steerforth. It was David who introduced little Em'ly to her seducer and, according to John O. Jordan, gave her to Steerforth in an unconscious attempt to gain his idol's approval and thus rise in social class (69–70). Even the unsatisfactory wife recommended herself in the first place as a tangible representation of the Doctors' Commons gentility Steerforth had advised David to pursue. If David can come to terms with Steerforth through the act of writing *David Copperfield*, then he will perhaps have found the absolution he requires and will perhaps have unwished *his* evil wish.

And the ending of *David Copperfield*, which finds the hero comfortably married and the father of a growing family, might suggest that David's elegy has been more effective than the ritual expiations of Pip, who in the original version of *Great Expectations* remains a wanderer and a childless bachelor. Lawrence Frank believes that David has succeeded where Pip later fails, because at the end of *David Copperfield*—"at the successful end—one has come into possession of one's own story. At the end David's story stands in chronological and thematic coherence" (92), whereas Pip recoils "from his own imaginative achievement," glorifying Joe as he had previously falsified Miss Havisham (181). But I am not convinced that either hero really succeeds in overcoming his obsession with death, and Pip is, at least, a great deal clearer about the social significance of his guilt than David ever consciously becomes.

Nor, finally, am I certain that David Copperfield ever frees himself from his fascination for Steerforth, even after he has described the latter's death and supposedly ended the elegy. At the conclusion of the novel David has become a gentleman who keeps a respectful servant, and he has reached this station by exercising the identity of the storyteller which Steerforth has conferred on him as a schoolboy. *Steerforth's Gift,* Saul Bellow might have named the novel. There would be nothing wrong with this ending if the story that came before it had been in all respects an elegiac romance. But it seems to me that *if* David has attained the more significant "station" he wondered about in the first sentence of the novel, if he has, in fact, become the hero of his own life, he has done so not by acknowledging his alternate identity and then letting it go, like the narrator in Conrad's "The Secret Sharer," not, as Frank maintains, by recognizing "the failings of Steerforth without rejecting what is redeeming in him," thus acknowledging "the ambiguity of his own moral condition in which good and bad intermingle" (72). Rather, he asserts his identity at the conclusion by rigorously suppressing even the name of his rival.

David Copperfield, like most of Dickens' novels, was originally published in eighteen equal, monthly parts and a bonus nineteenth installment of one and a half times the normal length. Steerforth's death is recounted in the eighteenth number. The final "double-number," seven chapters long, one-thirteenth of the entire novel, contains the most gratifyingly protracted set of curtain-calls in all of Dickens. Everyone is brought back for a final round of applause. Mr. Peggotty comes all the way from Australia so that we can learn not only about Em'ly, Martha, Mrs. Gummidge and the Micawbers, but even about Mr. Mell, whom we had long forgotten, and Mr. Creakle's son, who never appeared in the novel except to be briefly mentioned. Dickens even reminded himself in the Number Plan not to forget Aunt Betsey's donkeys. Most of the dead are recalled, including James Steerforth, whom David "mourns for" (696), but whom in this single case, he consistently avoids naming.

There are plenty of opportunities in the last seven chapters for David to write the name of Steerforth—he recollects the meeting at the Golden Cross Inn (702), he has an interview with Littimer, who mentions his master only through a reference to "the sins of my former companions" (730), and finally, in the last chapter, he encounters James's mother, whose name he also suppresses and who, in retaliation perhaps, has "forgotten this *gentleman's* [David's] name" (749, my emphasis). It has required considerable ingenuity on David's part to avoid writing the name of the character who has dominated so much of what has gone before. Perhaps Steerforth, the only major character in the novel without a counterpart in Dickens' biography and thus the only pure product of his imagination, is too powerful a force to be laid to rest, but an elegy which fails to commemorate does not legitimately permit a final shift of attention to an elegist, who free now for "fresh woods and pastures new," can become a true hero of his own life.

I mentioned earlier that death scenes are scarce in *David Copperfield*— another important suppression—and that the only death scene of a human being at which David is himself present is that of Barkis. The last words of the dying man, "Barkis is willin'," are a reference to the private joke he shares with David, but, coming at this precise moment, they also express a willingness to face death, which the miserly Barkis had been previously reluctant to do.[6] The most obvious and significant suppression in the novel occurs in an earlier speech of Barkis's:

> "It was as true," said Mr. Barkis, "as turnips is. It was as true," said Mr. Barkis, nodding his nightcap, which was his only means of emphasis, "as taxes is. And nothing's truer than them."

David has long since completed Barkis's suppressed thought, when he said "it is as certain as death" that greed and cunning will overreach itself (650), but he used this lesson not to redeem himself, but to cast into the teeth of his old scapegoat, Uriah Heep.

Garrett Stewart believes that David has "put his dead back together again" and has thus succeeded, where such suppressing characters as Mr. Dick and Doctor

Strong failed, in completing "an articulate memorial or record" (80). I question whether he has even conceded that his dead are in fact dead. David-the-narrator tells us that he has been dreading "from the beginning of the narrative" (673) to recount the death of Steerforth, and when the doctor tells him of the approaching death of Dora, David-the-character "cannot master the thought of it" (656). This reluctance and inability is caused, perhaps, by the young David's failure, as Lawrence Frank would have it, to confront his mother's death. "Part of David," Frank writes, "has never left that room [at the Rookery], has remained within it, gazing longingly in dread and yearning at the graves in the churchyard" (66). If so, then it is unlikely that he ever does learn to make this confrontation, for his remembered image of Steerforth dead, like the image Peggotty leaves him of his dead mother, is of a child sleeping.

At least one critic shares my sense of disquiet at the ending of *David Copperfield*. Judith Wilt writes:

> the final pages seem to picture a "tranquility" achieved with "a better knowledge of myself" and Agnes. Yet the tranquility is a strange one.... David, in his last paragraph, imagines in the mirror of the future the hard-won "realities" melting from him "like shadows which I now dismiss." Further, this Prospero pictures Agnes, not joining him in a final Reality, but rather "pointing upward" where the restless heart rests at last. Perhaps. (305)

The ambiguity suggests that the fear of death remains potent enough with David Copperfield, and perhaps also with Dickens, to prevent proper dismissal of the concept of gentility and of the gentleman who, as both the author and the narrator of this most penetrating study of death and gentility must surely know by now, cannot afford them the least protection.

NOTES

[1] Sylvia Manning notes that "David's ability to tell stories is a saving social asset: his 'good memory' and his 'simple, earnest manner of narrating' win him a special position of storyteller to Steerforth." She goes on to say that "Just as the Sultana Scheherazade, whose image presides over the episode, told stories for her very life, her young successor David told them to save his sheltered niche—to save his boy's life—in the isolated world of Salem House" (331–332).

[2] Samuel Clemens, who attended one of these performances, wrote that Dickens' reading of the storm scene "in which Steerforth lost his life was so vivid and so full of energetic action that the house was carried off its feet, so to speak" (175).

[3] Marks, whose article anticipates Bruffee's by several years, does not distinguish between kinds of retrospective narrators, or between authors who attempt to discover meaning through this technique or discipline and those who use it merely as a device for "engaging the reader in order that he might be led to believe what he might otherwise have merely understood" (375). This last distinction seems crucial to me, and I could wish Bruffee himself had confronted it more directly. Romance asserts. Elegy seeks rather to discover.

[4] In Hugh Walpole's fine scenario for the 1930s film version, we actually see Mr. Peggotty, played by Lionel Barrymore, give the necklace to Em'ly and tell her it comes from France.

[5] Perhaps the most persuasive of the critics who have argued this point is Carl Bandelin, "David Copperfield: A Third Interesting Penitent," but Christopher E. Mulvey and Harry Stone also make strong cases for David's guilt.

[6] George Anastaplo, writing on *A Christmas Carol*, argues that avarice should be regarded as "a determined attempt to fence oneself off from death" (127).

WORKS CITED

Anastaplo, George. *The Artist as Thinker: From Shakespeare to Joyce*. Chicago: Swallow Press, 1984.

Bandelin, Carl. "David Copperfield: A Third Interesting Penitent." *Studies in English Literature 1500–1900* 16 (1976), 601–611.

Bruffee, Kenneth A. *Elegiac Romance: Cultural Change and the Loss of the Hero in Modern Fiction*. Ithaca, N.Y.: Cornell University Press, 1983.

Carabine, Keith. "Reading *David Copperfield*." In *Reading the Victorian Novel: Detail into Form*. London: Vision Press, 1980.

Clemens, Samuel. *The Autobiography of Mark Twain*. Ed. Charles Neider. New York: Harper, 1959.

Conrad, Joseph. *Lord Jim*. New York: Holt, Rinehart and Winston, 1965.

Dickens, Charles. *David Copperfield*. Ed. Nina Burgis. London: Oxford University Press, 1981.

Frank, Lawrence. *Charles Dickens and the Romantic Self*. Lincoln and London: University of Nebraska Press, 1984.

Gilmour, Robin. *The Idea of the Gentleman in the Victorian Novel*. London: Allen and Unwin, 1981.

———. "Memory in *David Copperfield*." *Dickensian* 71 (1975), 38–42.

Gomme, A. H. *Dickens*. London: Evans, 1977.

Jordan, John O. "The Social Subtext of *David Copperfield*." *Dickens Studies Annual* 14 (1985), 61–92.

Kettle, Arnold. "Thoughts on *David Copperfield*." In *Review of English Studies* N.S. 2 (1961), 65–74.

Manning, Sylvia. "*David Copperfield* and Scheherazade: The Necessity of Narrative." *Studies in the Novel* 14 (1982), 327–336.

Marks, Barry A. "Retrospective Narrative in Nineteenth-Century American Literature." *College English* 30 (1970), 366–375.

Mason, Philip. *The English Gentleman: The Rise and Fall of an Ideal*. New York: William Morrow, 1982.

Miller, J. Hillis. *Charles Dickens: The World of His Novels*. Cambridge, Mass.: Harvard University Press, 1958.

Moers, Ellen. *The Dandy: Brummell to Beerbohm*. New York: Viking, 1959.

Monod, Sylvère. *Dickens the Novelist*. Norman: University of Oklahoma Press, 1968.

Mulvey, Christopher E. "*David Copperfield*: The Folk-Story Structure." *Dickens Studies Annual* 5 (1976), 74–94.

Orwell, George. "Charles Dickens." In *Dickens, Dali and Others*. New York and London: Harcourt Brace Jovanovich, 1973.

Salinger, J. D. *Raise High the Roofbeam Carpenter and Seymour: An Introduction*. New York: Bantam Books, 1981.

Shaw, George Bernard. "Epistle Dedicatory" to *Man and Superman*. Harmondsworth: Penguin, 1983.

Slater, Michael. *Dickens and Women*. London: J. M. Dent and Sons, 1983.

Stewart, Garrett. *Death Sentences: Styles of Dying in Victorian Fiction*. Cambridge, Mass.: Harvard University Press, 1984.

Stone, Harry. *Dickens and the Invisible World: Fairy Tales, Fantasy, and Novel-Making*. Bloomington: Indiana University Press, 1979.

Warren, Robert Penn. *All the King's Men.* New York: Bantam Books, 1981.

Westburg, Barry. *The Confessional Fictions of Charles Dickens.* DeKalb: Northern Illinois University Press, 1977.

Wilt, Judith. "Confusion and Consciousness in Dickens's Esther," *Nineteenth-Century Fiction* 32 (1977), 285–309.

Virginia Carmichael
NOM/NON DU PÈRE IN DAVID COPPERFIELD

Victorian novels are remarkable for missing parents who, in most cases, are not missed. Their absence usually functions as a fictive device allowing the hero or heroine maximum freedom in the task of constituting himself or herself as subject in society. The main characters are spared the experience of the loss of the parents, and they proceed directly to the task of establishing themselves as vocationally, socially and maritally defined subjects. Becky Thatcher, Dorothea Brooke, Emma Woodhouse, and Jane Eyre have to establish themselves in the world without maternal or parental support, and their actions, even though sometimes wrong-minded or compensatory for parental absence, are also explicit responses to present reality and future plans. Dickens's protagonists however, and especially David Copperfield, are often preoccupied with "that old unhappy loss," and appear to be as involved with attempting some sort of recovery from their pasts as with achieving an identity in the present.[1] As David struggles toward maturity, he re-enacts precisely the backward-looking and repetitive struggle of a child-becoming-adult whose original family triangle was insufficient. This working-through occurs in his fragmented, flawed, or partial identification with surrogate father and mother figures and alter egos; his repeated involvement with men who are unsuccessfully attempting to find themselves vocationally; and his selective memory for and repetitive participation in triangular structures of sexual competition.

Leonard F. Manheim gives us a multi-faceted classical Freudian reading of *David Copperfield,* also noting similarities between David's life and the mythological pattern of the hero as analyzed by Otto Rank; J. Hillis Miller points out that this is the first of Dickens's novels "to organize itself around the complexities of romantic love"; and Dianne Sadoff analyzes the Oedipal work of the text.[2] The Oedipal material is certainly there, but there are also elements of the text that suggest a reading that is culturally and critically more inclusive in its complexity than a psychological or mythological interpretation. In Lacan's understanding of the individual's development, the third term that interrupts the dual and immediate relationship

From *ELH* 54, No. 3 (Fall 1987): 653–67.

between mother and child is language, or the Symbolic Order, represented by the "name of the father," and the pun in French, *le nom du père,* also comprehends the "no of the father," *le non du père,* by which the child's desire of the mother is prohibited by the father. The symbolic father, through his naming/claiming authority in a patriarchal linguistic order, both institutes and denies the child's desire as he propels him or her out of infancy into the social order of language. *David Copperfield* is a novel of search for *beein',* Yarmouth dialect for "home," and this pun nicely resonates with Lacan's by suggesting David's search for both social vocation and sexual bonding. His two tasks of expressing himself through mature work and love are enormously complicated by the violence with which the name and no of his particular father are uttered. What is universally an agonizing transition from the pre-linguistic Imaginary Order to the Symbolic Order of language becomes for David the repetitive struggle of his recorded life.[3]

It is possible to read the plot and character development in the traditional psychological terms of an individual's search for identity, but the language, the narrative structure and structures, and the sustained imagery all suggest a reading that considers David's development in terms of his desire to experience and express the Imaginary in a Symbolic Order of differential value. Such a reading also makes possible a consideration of the reciprocal relation between the particular individual and his or her society. As Fredric Jameson suggests, if we can convincingly establish identity between the image content and the Lacanian Imaginary, then we can analyze the interaction between the Imaginary and the Symbolic, thus adding another critical dimension to our interpretation.[4] We can discover whether the writing necessarily works to transform the Imaginary, or whether the Imaginary opens a momentary space for itself through its expression in the Symbolic. Such an analysis of *David Copperfield* suggests the extent to which David is being mastered as he writes, and the extent to which his writing itself bespeaks a problematic accession to the Symbolic realm, not only for David, but also for Charles Dickens as he wrote David writing.

Even the more successful half of David's search—for vocation—is characterized by puzzling encounters with language, beginning with the multiple and confusing names he is given by surrogate parents and friends (Copperfield, Murdstone, Daisy, Trotwood, Doady) and continuing into associations with people whose relationships to language are troubled by a prevailing need to deal with the past. With the exception of Mr. Peggotty and Ham, every man with whom David feels friendship or hostility or identity is someone explicitly practicing a particular relationship to language in an attempt to master his world. Their pathologies of expression reveal an attitude toward present reality skewed by long-held illusions or by past preoccupations with issues of dominance and sexuality. Micawber's bombastic language and unnecessary letters (Aunt Betsey thinks he dreams in letters) are, as R. L. Patten notes, his "real medium of being."[5] Mr. Dick's compulsive writing of the King Charles Memorial is his way of managing intrusive desires and failures from the past; Dr. Strong's life's work is a continual delimiting of meaning in the Dictionary he is compiling; Mr. Wickfield has spent his life rationally reducing his experience and emotions to sole motives with his "one inch-rule" (909); Uriah Heep strives for dominance—with his mother's help—by perverting meaning, as his father taught him, through a practice of manipulative hypocrisy and dishonesty; Steerforth utterly corrupts all meaning and relationships in an amoral and socially destructive way; and only "plodding" Traddles moves along in his present world, limited in his achievements as a writer by what he recognizes as a failure of imagination. David, who is trying to discover by writing his life whether he is its hero or not, manages through discipline, earnestness, patience, and imagination to develop a felicitous and fruitful relationship to language. His laborious learning of shorthand, which he undertakes in order to find work, becomes also a means of defining in a fairly sophisticated way his relationship to the arbitrary and powerful system of meaning in which he resides. He ultimately matures into a level of competence as a successful writer that satisfies him vocationally.[6]

We don't have to take David's word for his success; we have the book we are reading as evidence of his, and Dickens's, imaginative mastery of the symbolic realm of language. But if we take his words—instead of his word—and the images, configurations, and story he remembers and constructs with those words, we discover something more troubled in the other half of his search, toward sexual bonding. This struggle is instituted by the no of the father and characterized by a triangulation of desire that occurs and collapses repetitively in David's life and the lives of his friends. David's selective memories are of course motivated by his particular entry into life as a "posthumous child" (50). Since he begins life in a triangle collapsed by the death of his father, he is able to continue for a while in an exclusive relationship with his child-like mother; his birth is marked by a sign (a caul) of this extended connection with his mother. Even as a child he already vaguely understands the effect of the missing father, for he has nightmares that his father might rise again, Lazarus-like, and interrupt his dual relationship with his mother. He tells Emily that "my mother and I had always lived by ourselves in the happiest state imaginable, and lived so then, and always meant to live so; and how my father's grave was in the churchyard" (84–85). When he returns from this first trip to Yarmouth to be told, "You have got a Pa," he responds, "Something—I don't know what, or how—connected with the grave in the churchyard, and the raising of the dead, seemed to strike me like an unwholesome wind" (92). Mr. Murdstone's entry into the family establishes the first familial triangle for David, and his hostility toward this intruder is natural. But because of the inadequacy of Clara and Mr. Murdstone as maternal and paternal participants in this structure, David is not to be allowed or enabled to work his way through and out of the triangle into maturity. Neither Clara nor Mr. Murdstone can tolerate the presence of the third person. Clara now embraces David "hurriedly and secretly, as if it were wrong," and must let go of David's hand before she can take her husband's arm (97). Murdstone's no to David's desire of his mother is a totally excluding one; he will not tolerate *any* show of affection for her son on Clara's part. And furthermore, by refusing David the word of "welcome home" by which, as David says, "[I] might have been made another creature, perhaps for life" (96), that is, by withholding the naming/claiming of the father, Murdstone effectively shuts David out of the mediation of the family process.

From the time of Murdstone's arrival, David experiences himself as "a somebody too many" (174), betrayed by his mother and rejected by his father. His biting of Murdstone's hand results in his physical expulsion from home, and he begins his journey of self-definition without benefit of parents. But, as he notes later in his writing, "the things that never happen are often as much realities to us, in their effects, as those that are accomplished" (891). He has been rejected by the father who has denied him a mother, and because of the nature of Murdstone's no, denying not only the sexual but even the nurturing mother, the desire instituted by that no is radically divided, leaving David attempting to recover split images of the Imaginary mother of immediate relationship. He carries with him the compelling imaginative presence of the nurturing mother on whose shoulder he had rested his head with "her beautiful hair drooping over me—like an angel's wing" (165), a spatial image that recurs in various configurations in his future relationships with women. But he will also remember her "from that instant, only as the young mother of my earliest impressions, who had been used to wind her bright curls round and round her finger, and to dance with me at twilight in the parlour" (186), that is, as the sexual mother of prohibited desire. And so we see David beginning a dance of his own as he attempts to recover what he has lost, led on by this split image from the past, unwittingly replicating in various configurations the particularly violent triangulation that instituted his loss. In what he notices in his world, and in the imaginatively projected or real forms through which he relates to the people of his world, David encounters and experiences different versions of triangulated desire, always attempting to achieve some sort of mastery over this structural obstacle to the recovery of the desired mother.

The Murdstone triangle was not David's only experience with competitive triangles by the time of his mother's death and his departure from home. He has noticed the rivalry that exists because Clara Copperfield perceives Peggotty as a threat to her love for David; Peggotty is, in Clara's words, "my most inveterate enemy" (94). Miss Murdstone, with her "hard steel purse" (97) and her appropriation of the keys, inserts herself as a third rival for control into the relationship between Peggotty and David, between Clara and David, and between Murdstone and Clara. In fact, one reason David is a somebody too many is that there is already a closed triangle between Miss Murdstone, Mr. Murdstone, and Clara, with Clara as the exploited child. By the time of his mother's death, David has also begun his attraction to and identity with alternative figures who can in some way substitute and compensate for his loss and feelings of deprivation. While Clara is his child-like mother of desire, Peggotty gradually becomes his substitute mother of nurture, giving him food, money, acknowledgment, and affection. Mr. Peggotty's household provides him with an ideal father figure and a young lover, Emily. And when he is sent away to Salem House and falls under the sway of Steerforth's "protective" and powerful personality, he tells us, without noting the connection, that Steerforth is the only student who can stand up to Mr. Creakle, who has turned out his own son for protesting the father's abuse of the mother. Steerforth becomes a compensatory alter ego and hero for David by virtue of his ability to stand up to the abusing father, a task David found himself inadequate to perform except at the cost of exclusion and loss.

After his mother's death, when he is home again anticipating nothing but abuse and neglect, he realizes that in some sense he is at a crossroads: he sees that he can grow up as "a shabby moody man, lounging an idle life away, about the village," or he can "go . . . away somewhere, like the hero in a story, to seek my fortune" (188)—like the heroes David has heard about in his "only and . . . constant comfort" (106), his books. So by the time David is subjected to what he perceives as the degradation of working at Murdstone and Grinby, he has already discovered the creative potential of surrogates and substitutes, alternative identities, and the imaginative authorship of one's life. After his brief and not untroubled, but somehow happy, stay with the Micawber family, he has made his choice: he will begin his quest as hero of his own life, and he will begin by "tell[ing] my story to my aunt, Miss Betsey." He chooses Aunt Betsey because, even though he thinks of her as a "dread and awful personage,"

> there was one little trait in her behaviour which I liked to dwell on, and which gave me some faint shadow of encouragement. I could not forget how my mother had thought that she felt her touch her pretty hair with no ungentle hand; and though it might have been altogether my mother's fancy . . . I made a little picture, out of it, . . . It is very possible that it had been in my mind a long time, and had gradually engendered my determination. (232)

It is this little picture that guides David through the nightmare journey he makes on foot, deprived of food, shelter and clothing, to her house, and he doesn't know whether he dreams or wakes when he believes that in putting him to bed the night he arrives, Aunt Betsey bends over him, puts his hair away from his face, and lays his head more comfortably.

David's choice of Betsey is felicitous, for he finds a substitute mother both nurturing and disciplining, a "somewhat masculine lady, with a strong understanding" (668), without the complications of sexuality. Betsey has removed the possibility of sexual triangulation by putting "the tender passion—all that sort of sentiment [David's euphemism for sexual desire], once and forever, in a grave, and fill[ing] it up, and flatten[ing] it down" (757). She lives in a non-sexual companionship with Mr. Dick, another figure with whom David is able to identify. From this point on, with Aunt Betsey's guidance, support, and wisdom, and his own earnestness, David is able to progress steadily, Aunt Betsey's financial failure notwithstanding, in his search for vocational and even social identity. But it is precisely in the realm of his identity with Mr. Dick that he is left to his own painful, repetitive and divided search: the realm of sexual desire. As Sadoff notes, Mr. Dick is suffering from "the prohibitions visited upon a desiring boy."[7] His obsession with King Charles's beheading is the product of his own guilty desire for his sister and felt impotence in protecting her from an abusing husband. Mr. Dick, like David, was rejected from a triangle in which he as a child was unable to protect the desired other from a threatening rival. As Betsey tells David, the King Charles story is Mr. Dick's "allegorical way of expressing it. He connects his illness with great disturbance and agitation, naturally, and that's the figure, or the simile, or whatever it's called, which he chooses to use" (261). David's way of expressing "it," or coming to terms with "it," is by means of the various triangles—dynamic, or collapsed and static—he keeps working through, either as an intensely interested observer, or as a constituting participant. This "it" Betsey uses without a clear antecedent David defines repeatedly during his search for romantic, sexual bonding as that "old unhappy loss or want of something" (713), "something that had been a dream of my youthful fancy, that was incapable of realization" (765): "it" is desire of the irrecoverable mother.

With the exception of the three familial structures in which David participates as an included and valued member—those of Peggotty and Barkis, Aunt Betsey and Mr. Dick, and the Micawbers—he experiences a proliferation of flawed, corrupted, or imagined triangles, all of which have been engendered by an original collapsed triangle, and which are characterized by displaced Oedipal relationships. Steerforth, who laments the absence of "a steadfast and judicious father" (381), has a mother whose claim upon her son is total and exclusionary:

> My son, who has been the object of my life, to whom its every thought has been devoted, whom I have gratified from a child in every wish, from whom I have had no separate existence since his birth,—to take up in a moment with a miserable girl, and avoid me! (531)

If David is trying to become the hero of his own life, he has indeed found a dark double in Steerforth; it is because of his problematic attraction to and identity with him that so much destruction is wrought on the people David loves and admires. Steerforth's seduction of Emily disrupts and triangulates the bondings of David and Emily, David and Steerforth, Ham and Emily, Peggotty and Emily, Peggotty and Steerforth, Rosa and Steerforth, and Steerforth and his mother. Uriah Heep, who has also lost his father, lives in a collapsed triangle with his mother—"We are much attached to one another" (292)—and together they practice their destructive version of "umbleness" as a means of acquiring a position and a wife for Uriah. He is the only person who is able to disrupt the Micawber relationship, not in a sexual triangulation, but in one having to do with power, money, and authority. He imagines David as his rival in his plans for Mr. Wickfield as well as for Agnes, and he intrudes himself into the Strong marriage to proclaim the existence of another imagined triangle, to the grief of both Dr. Strong and Annie. Annie comes to Dr. Strong from the collapsed triangle brought about by her beloved father's death, but she comes under the cloud of her mother's exploitative and corrupt "love" for her daughter. The Strong marriage has in fact been arranged by Mrs. Markleham, who "pretended, in consulting her own inclinations, to be devoting herself to her child" (716). She betrays her real intentions, however, after Annie has innocently agreed to the marriage, by explaining:

Doctor Strong will not only be your husband, but he will represent your late father: he will represent the head of our family, he will represent the wisdom and station, and I may say the means, of our family; and will be, in short, a Boon to it. (298)

Mrs. Markleham thinks she has sold her daughter for profit into this marriage, and the way she perceives the relationship enables the destructive speculations about Annie and Jack Maldon. It is Mr. Dick who becomes for the Strongs "what no one else could be—a link between them" (689), resolving the destructive imagined triangle into the loving and secure relationship that exists between Annie and her "husband and father" (724).

Though these three characters—Steerforth, Heep and Mrs. Markleham—embody David's experience with moral corruption, Annie, Mrs. Micawber, Mrs. Wickfield, Mr. Wickfield, Agnes, Traddles, Sophy, and Dora are also the products of collapsed triangles. Mrs. Micawber always knew her father to be "too partial" (842) to her, resulting in his rejection of her when she married Mr. Micawber. Mr. Wickfield's wife, who marries against her father's wishes, and is renounced by him, dies from grief over that triangulation, and Wickfield's response, just like that of Mrs. Steerforth, is to attach all his affection and life's energy to his daughter:

My natural grief for my child's mother turned to disease; my natural love for my child turned to disease. I have infected everything I touched. . . . I thought it possible that I could truly love one creature in the world, and not love the rest; I thought it possible that I could truly mourn for one creature gone out of the world, and not have some part in the grief of all who mourned. (642)

He understands that his love for Agnes "was a diseased love" (915), another mutually damaging misapprehension of the "economy of love."[8] Traddles is the disinherited nephew of a guardian-uncle who turned against him and married his housekeeper, and Sophy is the victim of another exploiting mother who, unable to assume her own familial responsibilities, tries to restrain Sophy from marrying Traddles. From this group only Traddles and Sophy, perhaps because of their ability to deal with present reality, are able to move from limiting and even destructive familial relationships into what we perceive through David's eyes as realized domestic and sexual harmony.

For David, however, the journey to this state is neither so direct nor so successful. He is still searching in the present for the dancing mother with the bright curls, and the moment he first sees Dora Spenlow he recognizes her:

All was over in a moment. I had fulfilled my destiny. I was a captive and a slave. I loved Dora Spenlow to distraction!

She was more than human to me. She was a Fairy, a Sylph. . . . I was swallowed up in an abyss of love in an instant. There was no pausing on the brink; no looking down, or looking back; I was gone, headlong, before I had sense to say a word to her. (450)

In David's description of his transports of romantic love throughout the next several hundred pages, he indicates no awareness of the ways in which he reveals this love as an illusory attempt to recover his lost mother. He is swallowed in the "abyss" of this love; he could "drown" in it (535); it is an "insubstantial, happy, foolish time" (550); the "idea"—not the real experience—of Dora is his "refuge in disappointment and distress"; and her "image" is his "consolation" (534). Their courtship is filled with elements of a fairy tale: Mr. Spenlow is the dragon of Wantley, who devours children, and David feels as though he were wandering in a "garden of Eden" with Dora (452). Not only does Miss Murdstone magically reappear as Dora's companion and "protector," as she had been Clara Copperfield's, but Dora herself shakes her curls, dances, and is a child, just like his mother: "Her childish way was the most delicious way in the world to me" (603). The only qualification to David's rapture is a feeling that comes over him when Aunt Betsey asks him if Dora is silly or light-headed: "Without knowing why, I felt a vague unhappy loss or want of something overshadow me like a cloud" (565), and that night he dreams a series of dreams of deprivation and distress, followed by one of Dora dancing incessantly, "without taking the least notice of me" (566). His inability to understand the connection between the feeling of loss and deprivation from his mother and his present experience with the childish Dora allows him to believe that in his courtship and marriage with Dora he will recover the relationship represented by the image, that he will achieve Imaginary immediacy in his present world. And not surprisingly, since his original desire of the mother was interrupted and punished by an intruding third figure, David's courtship is an ongoing proliferation or even paroxysm of imagined triangles.

The David–Dora–Mr. Spenlow and David–Dora–Miss Murdstone triangles are real; both Mr. Spenlow and Miss Murdstone want Dora to themselves and David out of the figure. But he is unable to experience any other person except as a rival; only the asexual Miss Mills, who suffers the permanent scarring of a "misplaced affection" (544), escapes his jealousy. "What a state of mind I was in! I was jealous of everybody" (452): the old grey-headed great-grandfather with whom Dora is speaking when David meets her ("I was madly jealous of him" [451]); "Red Whiskers" at Dora's birthday picnic; the little dog Jip, who "was mortally jealous of me" (455), and "who barked madly all the time" (549) during David's declaration of his idolizing "worship" of Dora. (It was a new fierce dog in the kennel at Blunderstone Rookery barking madly at David that marked Murdstone's intrusion into David and Clara's relationship.) During his courtship David perceives—with humor, but also with terror—what he construes as rivalry for him between Peggotty and the dread Mrs. Crupp, and also between Aunt Betsey and Mrs. Crupp. But most telling, and most reminiscent of his youthful desire to have his mother all to himself, is David's response to Mr. Spenlow's death:

> What I cannot describe is, how, in the innermost recesses of my own heart, I had a lurking jealousy even of Death. How I felt as if its might would push me from my ground in Dora's thoughts. How I was, in a grudging way I have no

words for, envious of her grief. How it made me restless to think of her weeping to others, or being consoled by others. How I had a grasping, avaricious wish to shut out everybody from her but myself, and to be all in all to her, at that unseasonable time of all times. (621)

David is not talking about a relationship between himself and another person; he is rather revealing the Imaginary dimensions of his desire to recover an original and irrecoverable unmediated relationship, a dual relationship that was once "all in all."

David's feeling about his marriage to Dora, however, is not one of "all in all," but instead is characterized by a sense of insufficiency, of something lost. So in an inversion of the triangle with a rival that threatens his attachment, he introduces Agnes as the third person in an attempt to compensate for the insufficiency of his attachment. As soon as he and Dora had become secretly engaged, David wrote a letter marked by its tone of denial:

I entreated Agnes not to regard this as a thoughtless passion which could ever yield to any other, or had the least resemblance to the boyish fancies that we used to joke about. I assured her that its profundity was quite unfathomable, and expressed my belief that nothing like it had ever been known. (551)

While he is writing this letter, his memory of Agnes "soothe[s] [him] into tears"; in all the "agitation" in which he has been living, he experiences Agnes as one of the "elements of [his] natural home," the place where his heart finds "its refuge and best friend" (552). Since David first met Agnes and associated her with the stained-glass window, she has provided an external completion for David's lack of self-reliance; she has been "an influence for all good" (288). He keeps insisting that he does not love her, "no, not at all in that way" (289)—sexually that is—but that all that is good and moral in him is attributable to her: "I seem to want some faculty of mind that I ought to have. You were so much in the habit of thinking for me . . . and I came so naturally to you for counsel and support, that I really think I have missed acquiring it" (630–31). Although he insists that Agnes is his beloved sister, she is also the other half of the desired mother, the nurturing mother, the approving, sustaining mother whom both David and Dora draw into their child-like relationship to form a stable triangular familial structure following Mr. Spenlow's death: as he tells Agnes after Dora's death, "when I loved her—even then, my love would have been incomplete, without your sympathy" (936). Aunt Betsey wisely refuses to be drawn into any such parental role, insisting instead that David and Dora establish their marriage as two adults. But self-sacrificing Agnes, who has been in love with David since meeting him, is quite willing to provide the soothing comfort and approval he and Dora so desperately need throughout their predictably troubled marriage. During this marriage, however, which is "the realization of my boyish day-dreams," in which "nothing is real" (694, 695), while he is patiently but futilely struggling to enlist Dora's help in their life together, David begins to be troubled by the recurrent feeling of "the old unhappy loss or want of something" (713, 722, 734,

765, 885). This much-repeated phrase expresses the futility of David's attempting to recover the image, rather than searching for a viable metonymic substitute for the irrevocably lost mother.

David's narrative has been "proceed[ing] to Agnes, with a thankful love" (672), since he became engaged to Dora, and when his child-wife "falls asleep"—dies—on Agnes's "bosom, with a smile," he first awakes

> to a consciousness of her [Agnes's] compassionate tears, her words of hope and peace, her gentle face bending down as from a purer region nearer Heaven, over my undisciplined heart, and softening its pain. (840)

David has lost the dancing mother of desire, but he awakens from this loss to find another mother—the comforting one—bending over him in the same spatial relationship as that of the image he has carried with him all his life, of little David and Clara, with his head on her shoulder and her hair "drooping over [him] like an angel's wing" (165). With his "good angel" Agnes's encouragement, he goes away for an extended period of time during which he "[is] left alone with my undisciplined heart . . . [with] no conception of the wound with which it had to strive." Healing and wisdom come "but little by little, and grain by grain" (885). During this time David grieves for "all that had been shattered—my first trust, my first affection, the whole airy castle of my life" (886). But most critical for his ability to begin a marriage with Agnes upon his return to England, he mourns "for the wandering remnants of the simple home, where I had heard the night-wind blowing, when I was a child" (886), the remnants that had powerfully lived on in his mind as memories and images, pulling him always toward the recovery of a child-like state instead of toward a more present reality.

The transcendentally ideal marriage David finally appears to achieve with St. Agnes is, however, a problematic resolution of David's search for sexual bonding. In his relationships with women he has been attempting to recover the split image of his desire, instituted and divided by the no given and the name withheld by Murdstone. David's passion for Dora was sexual, and he explicitly insists that his feelings for Agnes are not; Agnes is like a sister to him, and she evokes for him again and again his specific image of the nurturing mother. We can see in this splitting a reflection of the Victorian tendency toward idealization of the non-sexual woman and degradation of the sexual one, and that cultural dichotomization was undoubtedly also at work in Murdstone's and Clara's inability to deal with a desiring child. They had their own individually and socially instituted prohibitions and desires regarding sexuality and the politics of possession and dominance. Once the splitting of desire was so effectively accomplished in David by his particular initiation into the Symbolic realm, he found ample reinforcements and expressions of this division and repression in his larger world. And although at the end of his writing of his life he asserts complete contentment at last with Agnes, the imagery and the triangulated structures of the narrative, as well as the transcendental language, betray this ending's tone of resolution, showing David still firmly imprisoned in the illusions of the Imaginary realm.

But at what costs? What fragmentation has been exercised on the Imaginary by David's inevitable but unnecessarily violent emergence into the Symbolic Order? At this point we need to consider Charles Dickens writing David's writing and recognize the fictive resolution he was attempting on David's behalf as a compensation for a felt insufficiency in his own life. Dickens wrote this novel when he was 37, married, with eight children. "Why is it," he exclaimed in later life, "that as with poor David, a sense always comes crushing upon me now, when I fall into low spirits, as of one happiness I have missed in life, and one friend and companion I have never made?"[9] In killing off the insufficient Dora, and in providing David with that "one friend and companion" which he himself had never found, he, like David, attempts to give fictive expression to the recovery of the Imaginary; instead both have produced a narrative text in which the Imaginary is radically bifurcated and transformed by the telling. The image of sexual love is first split into mutually exclusive images of sexuality and love, and then the image of sexuality is transmuted into death, and the image of love, deprived of its body, is abstracted into virtual transcendence. Through the work of this text, devoid of irony, and with no dimensions of the tragic, the desire for sexual love ends in death and abstraction. The questions I leave open are to what extent were Dickens and David writing as they had been written, perpetrating in the telling the very denial and division of desire they were attempting to reverse and reconcile, and secondly, to what extent is Dickens through his literary work uncritically reinstituting and passing on the name and the no of the father?

NOTES

[1] *David Copperfield*, ed. Trevor Blount (New York: Penguin Books, 1966), 713. All citations are from this edition.

[2] Leonard F. Manheim, "The Personal History of David Copperfield: A Study in Psychoanalytic Criticism," *The American Imago* 9 (1952); J. Hillis Miller, *Charles Dickens: The World of His Novels* (Cambridge: Harvard Univ. Press, 1959), 150; Dianne F. Sadoff, *Monsters of Affection: Dickens, Eliot & Brontë on Fatherhood* (Baltimore: The Johns Hopkins Univ. Press, 1982).

[3] In Lacan's topology the Symbolic Order is primary, since it is the only means of "thinking" the other two orders. The Imaginary stands for the pre-linguistic experience of unmediated dual relationship with the (m)other, and the Real, according to one of Lacan's formulations, is "what resists symbolization absolutely" (quoted in Jameson, 384). The Individual's accession to the Symbolic Order of language gives him/her a capacity for mediation and articulation of the other two realms, as well as the experience of being a subject separate from others. These terms represent not so much a progression of discrete states as the revisionist Lacanian dialectic that is the movement of "the subject in his reality" (*Écrits*, 196), an extension through displacement that can only asymptomatically approach the Real. Individual development makes it possible, however, to speak of relatively successful or failed acquisitions of the Symbolic; a person unable to construct subjectivity in his or her experience of the language of the other may tend to deal with the Real in terms of the Imaginary, as in the imaged fantasies of neurosis. See Jacques Lacan, *Écrits: A Selection*, trans. Alan Sheridan (New York and London: W. W. Norton & Company, 1977); Anthony Wilden, *Jacques Lacan: Speech and Language in Psychoanalysis* (Baltimore and London: The Johns Hopkins University Press, 1968); Anika Lemaire, *Jacques Lacan* (Brussels: Pierre Mardage, 1977); and Fredric Jameson, "Imaginary and Symbolic in Lacan: Marxism, Psychoanalytic Criticism, and the Problem of the Subject," *Yale French Studies: Literature and Psychoanalysis* 55/56 (1977): 384.

[4] Jameson, 376.

[5] R. L. Patten, "Autobiography into Autobiography: The Evolution of *David Copperfield*," *Approaches to Victorian Autobiography*, ed. George P. Landow (Athens, Ohio: Ohio Univ. Press, 1979), 276.
[6] I am indebted in part for this analysis to Manheim, 21–43, and to Sadoff, 10–64.
[7] Sadoff, 46.
[8] Manheim, 29.
[9] Edgar Johnson, *Charles Dickens: His Tragedy and Triumph*, revised and abridged (New York: The Viking Press, 1952), 415.

Alexander Welsh

YOUNG MAN COPPERFIELD

Strictly speaking, the "great fairy story" of Copperfield's life commences only after he meets Agnes Wickfield, Mr. Wickfield, and Uriah Heep in chapter 15, attends a new school, and makes "another Beginning." I have deliberately put off until last consideration of the early experiences of the hero because the perspective of memory places them last. Memory looks backward; earliest experiences are farthest away in time; and from this perspective childhood comes after adulthood. Dickens did not begin a life of writing by writing *David Copperfield*. He wrote this version of his childhood when he was thirty-seven and pretty well had to accept that he was the hero of his own life.

We do not know when Dickens discovered or decided that his experience in the blacking warehouse was traumatic. A reasonable assumption is that he did not recognize it as such before the writing of his autobiographical fragment and of *Copperfield*. I have pointed out that some of the language of the fragment came to him earlier in New York, when he was suffering from blows to his adult ego. To imagine that his recollection and estimate of a childhood experience was continuous from the time of occurrence goes against all that we know of ourselves and what psychoanalysts tell us of the analytic situation, which in this case can be thought of as the time of writing; and though we remain ignorant of the course of Dickens's memory, we are told that Copperfield's memory, at least, was intermittent. At the time of his second beginning in life, that soon-to-be-famous writer thought little about his childhood and recent past. The experience at Murdstone and Grinby's warehouse could not have seemed traumatic then, because the "misty ideas" and "visionary considerations" of youth intervened:

> Misty ideas of being a young man at my own disposal, of the importance attaching to a young man at his own disposal, of the wonderful things to be seen and done by that magnificent animal, and the wonderful effects he could not fail to make upon society, lured me away. So powerful were these

From *From Copyright to Copperfield: The Identity of Dickens* (Cambridge, MA: Harvard University Press, 1987), pp. 156–72.

visionary considerations in my boyish mind, that I seem, according to my present way of thinking, to have left school without natural regret. The separation has not made the impression on me, that other separations have. I try in vain to recall how I felt about it, and what its circumstances were; but it is not momentous in my recollection. I suppose the opening prospect confused me. I know that my juvenile experiences went for little or nothing then; and that life was more like a great fairy story, which I was just about to begin to read, than anything else.[1]

Thus in musing over a particular lacuna in his memory, Copperfield realizes that his juvenile experiences meant little to him at the time. He did not look backward but forward. Only latterly has he felt that early hardship shaped his character, therefore, and this belated response was undoubtedly true for Dickens as well: only during early middle life, when he had time to question his identity, did he formulate the autobiography that the early chapters of the novel enclose. Like Copperfield, he would sit down to write his story but not without indirectly acknowledging, through Copperfield, that youth—"that magnificent animal"—had little time for suffering. After taking the world by storm, after traveling to America, after writing *Chuzzlewit* and *Dombey* and reflecting on memory itself in the Christmas books, Dickens thought back on his childhood and singled out the episode of the blacking warehouse. With this investment in his childhood experience he thus confirmed in advance the theories of Steven Marcus and Edmund Wilson, and in this way of thinking in general he anticipated Freud.

In other words, however we interpret the narrative of the blacking warehouse and its revision in the novel, we have to address the question of why Dickens composed the narrative—both why he recalled the episode and why an experience of childhood suited his purposes. Since he has not told us why, in so many words, some reasoned presumptions have to be made. The first, which I have stressed all along, is that he had resolved the uncertainties about his identity that he experienced after completing *Barnaby Rudge* and that came to a crisis during the journey to America. Though the crisis was mild enough according to the evidence of his daily life, it was amplified and worked out through the writing of *Martin Chuzzlewit, Dombey and Son,* and the Christmas books. Second, if we can believe John Forster, he was stimulated by his friend's curiosity to write something about his experience, which had generated enough distress between the child and his parents to cause them to pretend it had never happened. Third, precisely because Dickens now felt secure and certain of his vocation, he could take satisfaction in contemplating such wrongs and misfortunes that he had overcome—as a hero overcomes his enemies. The more bitterly he could taste the memory of wrongs, the more credit, at this distance, he could extract from them. He virtually spelled out this motive in the meditations of Redlaw, in *The Haunted Man.* Fourth, he determined to exploit this contemplation of the past in a more ambitious fiction, the autobiographical novel. His motive here was mainly opportunistic, the motive of a professional writer: he had his plot and characters and was ready to begin. But

Dickens's elaboration of his memories and his situation of *the* traumatic event in childhood are too much like a fairy tale, on the one hand, and the Oedipus complex, on the other, for us to discount the possibility of a broad cultural motive behind the direction the story took. This motive can be thought of as the need to justify a rise in the world, so desired by the sons of the nineteenth century. Rather than the spur of ambition in the child, the incident can be seen as the justification of ambition in the adult. Both the imputation of general passivity and the displacement of conflict to childhood worked well for men of that era, whether they were novelists of genius, founders of psychoanalysis, or far more commonplace individuals. We may begin to see how this is so by reconsidering *David Copperfield* and the Oedipus complex as well, from a point of view as culturally neutral as possible.

Fairy tales themselves have a way of situating in childhood incidents that are both traumatic and somehow good for people to experience, if only at second hand. The epoch that Dickens believed to be crucial in his own life, disguised as the Murdstone and Grinby's episode in the novel, is only a part of this story. Some general characteristics of fairy tales adopted in the early chapters of *Copperfield* include the splitting of parents into more than one representation, the helplessness and relative passivity of a child-hero, and the courage and stamina of the child—notwithstanding his or her weakness in the face of the adult world. Stepparents abound in fairy tales because real parents appear to a child in opposite guises, as providers of care and governors of behavior. Not surprisingly, they are fictively multiplied into "good" and "bad" parents, as well as into parents who seem one thing and act another. In *Copperfield* the child's actual father appears only by repute, as a man rather gently susceptible to women and a bestower of books. His mother appears as a beautiful child-wife,[2] all too susceptible to men. The one parent is out of the way before the action commences and the other soon after, and they are replaced by the cruel and rigorous Murdstones (who naturally turn up later in charge of Dora or bending other brides to their will). But the child's Aunt Betsey and nurse Peggotty are kindly grotesque parents, showing love beneath rough exteriors, and the Micawbers are kindly helpless parents—rather like children themselves—who have an agreeable way of treating a boy as their equal. Many children, in real life, experience the pleasure of encountering such foster parents—persons with whom they may be only slightly acquainted but who treat them respectfully, without the contradictions so apparent in actual parents.

Children *are* nearly helpless to begin with, and for a good number of years after birth. This is one of the crucial facts of human experience, which Dickens realizes with profound memory of his own childhood and great good humor in the early chapters of his novel. (The inclusion of these memories makes the novel seem much more modern than Thackeray's *Pendennis,* which begins with the hero's coming of age and his first courtship.) It is the relative vulnerability of the child, a reflection forced upon us by Dickens, that speaks to the idea that we are all in some sense helpless before the circumstances of modern life. An advantage of the fairy-tale approach to this idea is that the helplessness of a small person can be exaggerated and thereby discharged in tears or laughter. Perhaps the most extravagant (and purely make-believe) instance of helplessness in *Copperfield* is the episode in which the waiter, in the inn at Yarmouth, consumes David's ale and his dinner for him as casually as if that were the function of waiters everywhere. Childhood confers such rapidly changing awareness that mental as well as physical differences from adults are readily apparent, and comprehension in the child normally outstrips the capacity to respond to adults. So in the coach journey to London that follows the waiter episode, David is mercilessly squeezed between adult passengers whose mistaken merriment further prevents him from eating supper, through sheer embarrassment; or David half understands and half does not understand, as we gather from his recall of the conversation and his repeating it to his mother, the sexual meaning of the talk among Murdstone and his men friends, in the course of which the stepfather-to-be concedes the boy's sharpness by referring to him in code as the cutler "Brooks of Sheffield" (2.20). The sheer rapaciousness of the adult world—according to this account of it—the narrator conveys as a kind of joke upon himself when a child; his recall of the past repeatedly features moments in which bewilderment and insight converge, and thus constitute growth and learning in the ways of the world. The narrative, finally, is replete with a sense of the child's overcoming helplessness and fighting back. The novel as a whole will celebrate the survival and success of Copperfield, but even early on the reader can relish the sinking of a hero's teeth into Murdstone's murderous hand, or the secret credit in the sign of shame that he is required to wear at Creakle's school: *"Take care of him. He bites"* (5.67). The sign is a portent as well as a stigma. "Take care" can mean either beware or cherish, and it comes to mean both.

It is no wonder that many readers have found these early chapters of *David Copperfield* the best in the book. Dickens did here what few other writers could do; his recall of what it is like to be a child is extraordinary; and this portion of the book has seemed authentic. William Spengemann, for example, argues that the autobiographical fiction of the early chapters is somehow more genuine than the fictional autobiography of the later chapters.[3] To some degree, obviously, this judgment depends on the hindsight shared with readers since the publication of Forster's *Life*. Because Dickens incorporated the substance and even whole paragraphs of his autobiographical fragment here, the validity of the first part of the novel seems confirmed. "I know enough of the world now," the chapter on Murdstone and Grinby's begins, "to have almost lost the capacity of being much surprised by anything; but it is matter of some surprise to me, even now, that I can have been so easily thrown away at such an age." That fresh concession about the way of the world shows that Dickens could already see the experience in perspective, but he let his hero continue, actively paraphrasing and quoting from the fragment. "A child of excellent abilities, and with strong powers of observation, quick, eager, delicate, and soon hurt bodily or mentally, it seems wonderful to me that nobody should have made any sign in my behalf." He either had the language of the fragment by heart or it lay on the desk before him as he made Copperfield write:

> No words can express the secret agony of my soul as I sunk into this companionship; compared these henceforth every-day associates with those

of my happier childhood—not to say with Steerforth, Traddles, and the rest of those boys; and felt my hopes of growing up to be a learned and distinguished man, crushed in my bosom. The deep remembrance of the sense I had, of being utterly without hope now; of the shame I felt in my position; of the misery it was to my young heart to believe that day by day what I had learned, and thought, and delighted in, and raised my fancy and emulation up by, would pass away from me, little by little, never to be brought back any more; cannot be written.

The following paragraphs, from later in the chapter, Dickens also borrowed nearly word for word from the fragment:

> I know I do not exaggerate, unconsciously or unintentionally, the scantiness of my resources or the difficulties of my life. I know that if a shilling were given me by Mr. Quinion at any time, I spent it in a dinner or a tea. I know that I worked, from morning until night, with common men and boys, a shabby child. I know that I lounged about the streets, insufficiently and unsatisfactorily fed. I know that, but for the mercy of God, I might easily have been, for any care that was taken of me, a little robber or a little vagabond.
>
> Yet I held some station at Murdstone and Grinby's too. Besides that Mr. Quinion did what a careless man so occupied, and dealing with a thing so anomalous, could, to treat me as one upon a different footing from the rest, I never said, to man or boy, how it was that I came to be there, or gave the least indication of being sorry that I was there. That I suffered in secret, and that I suffered exquisitely, no one ever knew but I. How much I suffered, it is, as I have said already, utterly beyond my power to tell. But I kept my own counsel, and I did my work. I knew from the first, that, if I could not do my work as well as any of the rest, I could not hold myself above slight and contempt. I soon became at least as expeditious and as skilful as either of the other boys. Though perfectly familiar with them, my conduct and manner were different enough from theirs to place a space between us. They and the men generally spoke of me as "the little gent," or "the young Suffolker." A certain man named Gregory, who was foreman of the packers, and another named Tipp, who was the carman, and wore a red jacket, used to address me sometimes as "David:" but I think it was mostly when we were very confidential, and when I had made some efforts to entertain them, over our work, with some results of the old readings; which were fast perishing out of my rememberance. Mealy Potatoes uprose once, and rebelled against my being so distinguished; but Mick Walker settled him in no time. (11.132–133, 139)

And there are other borrowings as well.

Two questions arise about the truthfulness of this part of the novel, neither of which can be satisfactorily answered. First, is it really more true to life, seemingly validated as it is by the fragment, than the principal fiction of the later part of the novel, in which Copperfield is supposed to be a famous novelist like Dickens? Second, is the special proof of its validity, the presence of the autobiographical fragment within the pages of the novel, to be regarded as altogether trustworthy? To reply to the second of these questions with still another, should we believe that the autobiographical fragment itself is the truth and nothing but the truth? We have some corroborating testimony in Forster's account of how he first came to hear of the episode and little reason to doubt that Dickens, as a boy, experienced something very like what he recalled. But mainly we know that he wrote of the episode in middle life, in words that seemed faithful to his memory at the time; and we have more and more come to feel that whether stories are told and how they are told are more significant questions for interpretation than what the stories are finally "about." Two such thoughtful and different students of Dickens as Albert Hutter and Robert Patten have argued recently that the fragment itself, if we are to appreciate its significance, ought to be regarded as a fiction.[4] Even the "editing" of the fragment that took place as it entered the novel suggests something of the instability of the original. For example, in the last paragraph given above from the novel, Dickens omitted after "beyond my power to tell" this sentence from the fragment: "No man's imagination can overstep the reality."[5] Did he leave out the sentence because its rhetoric was redundant, because it was untrue on the face of it, or because it jarred with his present sense of fiction and reality? Mr. Quinion in the novel supplies the place of "my relative at the counting-house" of Warren's Blacking. In the previous paragraph, did Dickens's substitution of "if a shilling were given me by Mr. Quinion at any time" for "if a shilling or so were given me by anyone" in the fragment[6] perhaps *restore* an element of truthfulness to the memory? By vaguely crediting anyone's occasional generosity, in his first version of the episode, Dickens deprived his relative of credit. Perhaps his family was not so cool to his plight as he pretended. But the reasons for all such differences in the two narratives are matters of speculation.

To the the first question, whether the childhood of the hero is more true to life than his adult years, the answer is equally uncertain. The narrative of childhood is the rarer achievement, but the facts do not correspond any more closely to the life of Dickens. There are just as grave lies, so to speak, in the first fourteen chapters of *David Copperfield* as in the remaining fifty. Dickens's parents were very much alive when he undertook to write both his autobiographical fragment and his autobiographical novel. In the novel, Copperfield is not only a posthumous child, as he states right away, but he loses his mother shortly thereafter, through her marriage to Murdstone and her death in bearing a second child. Dickens provided his hero two stepfathers, the one immediate and sadistic and the other tangential and irresponsible. He gestured perfunctorily at a wicked stepmother in Jane Murdstone and provided lavishly for two surrogate mothers, in the pleasing convention of rough-seeming fairy godmothers. These out-and-out embellishments on his own life enable some remote wish fulfillment to take place immediately. The nurse Peggotty is called Peggotty because her first name, Clara, is the same as that of Copperfield's mother; Peggotty also gets married when the hero is still a child, but only through Davy as an intermediary and for convenience in caring for him. His Aunt Betsey, who will later adopt him as she has already adopted Mr. Dick, disapproves of the hero's actual mother all along and proposes an alternative identity for him as a tough-minded girl like herself, named Betsey Trotwood Copperfield. These powerful allies and surrogate mothers, who are unparalleled in Dickens's life, outlive by many years Copperfield's parents and outweigh his stepfathers and possible fathers-in-law. Three widowed mothers in the novel—Mrs. Steerforth, Mrs. Heep, and Mrs. Markleham—will show how fortunate Copperfield is in Dickens's choice of Peggotty and Aunt Betsey. Instinctively the hero will seek in marriage two women with weak fathers, the first a childish replica of his own childish mother and the second with all the nurturing love of his godmothers but calm and beautiful, with nearly occult powers for writing and encountering death, and abundantly able to resupply what Erikson calls "basic trust." All this emphatic mothering, the sum total of which is remarkable, is a fiction heaped by Dickens upon *his* surrogate Copperfield both early and late in the novel. This fiction alone is large enough to dwarf the "facts" of Dickens's childhood as thinly disguised in chapter 11.

What is more remarkable is that Dickens should feel sure that an account of early days and of trauma would be useful in coming to terms with a lifetime. The narrative that the author led Forster to lead us to believe[7] was inspired by memories of a specific incident in childhood suddenly comprises the entire life, from birth to death, of the very person who is writing it. The writing follows, as Hillis Miller notes in one essay, "exactly the structure of human temporality" and persists, as the same critic observes in his book on Dickens, until "David has that relation to Agnes which a devout Christian has to God."[8] Miraculously, *The Personal History, Adventures, Experience, & Observation of David Copperfield the Younger, of Blunderstone Rookery (Which He never meant to be Published on any Account)*—as the title appeared on the cover of the monthly parts—began with birth and concluded with death. That is quite a stretch in either direction from the days in Murdstone and Grinby's or in Warren's.

> Whether I shall turn out to be the hero of my own life, or whether that station will be held by anybody else, these pages must show. To begin my life with the beginning of my life, I record that I was born (as I have been informed and believe) on a Friday, at twelve o'clock at night. It was remarked that the clock began to strike, and I began to cry, simultaneously.

With the stroke of the clock and no fractional time of day, this secular life begins, and the narrator covers for the unremembered time of infancy with light mockery of the birth of heroes. Even before we read that he is a posthumous child, we find that he was born with a caul, a charm against drowning that initially allows Copperfield and his readers to laugh at the need of others to believe in luck but, at the same time, introduces the possibility of death and hints that the hero will not drown with Ham and Steerforth.[9] Copperfield's is a life dedicated to work and influenced mainly by women. That he should immediately be concerned in the narrative with death and his father's grave nearby—even before his story can arrive at the point of conscious memories of childhood—could not be altogether surprising to readers of Dickens from *Oliver Twist* onward. Erikson, in fact, throws some indirect light on this phenomenon here and elsewhere in Dickens's writings when he attributes similar feelings to Martin Luther: "Premonitions of death occur throughout Luther's career," he contends, "but I think it would be too simple to ascribe them to a mere fear of death. A young genius has an implicit life plan to complete; caught by death before his time, he would be only a pathetic human fragment.[10] Erikson's perhaps too generous defense of genius may help explain the infant half-brother of Copperfield who, buried with his mother at the end of the second number of the novel, "was myself" (9.115), as well as the hero's need throughout his personal history for new beginnings, surrogate mothers, and above all Agnes.

Autobiography in the form of a fairy tale is bound to progress and regress in the same narrative. Fairy tales, as a kind of literature enjoying a vogue in the nineteenth century, insist on telling over and over again the trials of childhood. After the extensive use Dickens made of *Paradise Lost* and *King Lear*—however facetious or partial—in his previous two novels, his use of fairy-tale material in *David Copperfield* might be thought of as regressive even from a literary point of view; for better or worse, it was certainly regressive in personal terms for a man approaching middle age. "But must we call it regression," Erikson asks, "if a man thus seeks again the earliest encounters of his truthful past in his efforts to reach a hoped-for and eternal future?" Like Dickens's autobiographical enterprise in *Copperfield*, Erikson's biography of genius seeks to take in the life from beginning to end, even though its ostensible subject is the young man Luther. In the novel we have the birth of the novelist at the beginning and Agnes pointing upward at the close; in the biography of the religious leader we have a reconstruction of childhood that will explain his rediscovery of eternal life for others as well as himself. "I have implied that the original faith which Luther tried to restore," writes Erikson, "goes back to the basic trust of early infancy."[11]

It may be objected that Dickens was writing a novel by and about a famous novelist, himself, while Erikson has written a study of the formative years of a genius of very different fame, not himself. He is an analyst working at many removes from the memories that comprised the life to construct a biography that still purports to be fact. The way to bring these two very different modes of biography together is to point out that the second is also largely fictional. The admission of fiction does not make either mode dishonest. Dickens alters, suppresses, and above all invents his life, but always within the bounds of trying to make sense of it to himself and his readers. He puts in an excess of mothers, for example, but the resulting life must add up to something, and has added up to something, for readers worldwide. Erikson acknowledges again and again that almost nothing is known of Luther's youth, almost nothing about the man before his strong challenge to an accepted religion. He fills this vacuum in the historical record with extensive analysis, under the aegis of Freud and within the bounds of his own knowledge and readers' acceptance, of a young man's relation to his father and what is possible in that relation. Erikson is frank about this construction and seems to assert the necessity of a fiction not only to biography but to the subject of biography. To the objections of a psychiatrist of a different school, we would reply that most certainly we would ascribe to Luther an Oedipus complex, and not a trivial one at that. We would not wish to see any boy—much less an imaginative and forceful one—face the struggles of his youth and manhood without have experienced as a child the love and the hate which are encompassed in this complex: love for the maternal person who awakens his senses and his sensuality with her ministrations, and deep and angry rivalry with the male possessor of this maternal person. We would also wish him with their help to succeed, in his boyhood, in turning resolutely away from the protection of women to assume the fearless initiative of men.

Thus Erikson provides his subject with an Oedipus complex because he needs one, and because "only a boy with a precocious, sensitive, and intense conscience would *care* about pleasing his father as much as Martin did."[12] Similarly Dickens, recalling his childhood or inventing where necessary, provided himself with conflicts that, he acknowledged, "have worked together to make me what I am" and provided Copperfield with "the endurance of my childish days" that, according to Agnes's letter, "had done its part to make me what I was."

Erikson's notion of what is essential to childish days is steeped in cultural assumptions about the "ministrations" of women and the "initiative" of men. These assumptions are both its strength and its weakness. They establish a coherent idea of Luther's career, but they are more deeply rooted in the nineteenth century than in the sixteenth. Dickens was no less constrained by convictions about hard work and good women, codes he described and inscribed for the use of the culture. Not surprisingly, the two biographers share many beliefs: especially when Erikson writes critically of the culture, he almost seems to take up his pen where Dickens left off. The measure of Luther's sensitivity or of his father's viciousness, now lost in time,

pales before the general problem of man's exploitability in childhood, which makes him a victim not only of overt cruelty, but also of all kinds of covert emotional relief, of devious vengefulness, or sensual self-indulgence, and of sly righteousness—all on the part of those on whom he is physically and morally dependent. Someday, maybe, there will exist a well-informed, well-considered, and yet fervent public conviction that the most deadly of all possible sins is the mutilation of a child's spirit; for such mutilation undercuts the life principle of trust, without which every human act, may it feel ever so good and seem ever so right, is prone to perversion by destructive forms of conscientiousness.

Erikson speculates a good deal about the beatings Luther received as a child, presumably from both parents but especially from the father. Again he generalizes in such a way that the facts hardly matter:

It takes a particular view of man's place on this earth, and of the place of childhood within man's total scheme, to invent devices for terrifying children into submission, either by magic, or by mental and corporeal terror. . . . Special concepts of property (including the idea that a man can ruin his own property if he wishes) underlie the idea that it is entirely up to the discretion of an individual father when he should raise the morality of his children by beating their bodies. . . . The device of beating children down—by superior force, by contrived logic, or by vicious sweetness—makes it unnecessary for the adult to become adult. . . . The child, forced out of fear to pretend that he is better when seen than when unseen, is left to anticipate the day when he will have the brute power to make others more moral than he ever intends to be himself.[13]

Dickens moves in his own fashion toward similar conclusions. Though there is no Dotheboys Hall in *David Copperfield,* readers have come to value the early chapters of the novel for what they imply in general about such an institution. We have no evidence that Dickens as a child was beaten by a father in the least like Murdstone, or experienced in person the systematic torture of a schoolmaster like Creakle—"an incapable brute, who had no more right to be possessed of the great trust he held, than to be Lord High Admiral, or Commander-in-chief: in either of which capacities, it is probable that he would have done infinitely less mischief" (7.77). These are fictions enlisted more for their generalizing value than for their personal significance either to Dickens or to Copperfield, and for quite similar purposes Erikson elaborates the early life of Martin Luther.

Copperfield is about a rise in life and not a fall. The previous two novels, in which Dickens questioned his personal identity much more sharply, invoked the greatest literary models of falling. *Chuzzlewit* hilariously, but also seriously, deployed an epic enactment, from Milton's *Paradise Lost,* of the myth of the fortunate fall. *Dombey* followed heroically in the path of Shakespeare's *King Lear,* to mount an attack on pride and become the novelist's principal study of a tragic fall. *Copperfield* is about a rise, and is a novel more emulated than emulating other literature. Undoubtedly, with its hero so ingeniously and repeatedly positioning himself in relation to mothers, the novel is at least partially what we would call Oedipal in design. But remember that Dickens is beforehand in this regard. Freud read *David Copperfield* well before he invented psychoanalysis or even concentrated on childhood. He named it his favorite, praised the novel for many of the same qualities that Forster saw in it. Like Forster, he thought the later novels less pleasing and less true. He made a gift of *Copperfield* to Martha Bernays and wrote her that it was most nearly free of mannerisms among those he had read: "the characters are individualized; they are sinful without being abominable."[14] At this time Freud was twenty-seven, ten years younger than Dickens had been when writing the novel. He never, so far as we know, linked the early chapters to his own rediscovery of childhood and formulation of the Oedipus complex when he was forty. But of course the novel as a whole tells of ambition, in the guise of a great fairy story about a young man's rise in the world. Now that we are more able to see Freud in historical perspective, it should be evident how intimately psychoanalysis is bound up with the very kinds of narrative for which it has proved useful as a tool of investigation.[15]

The point is not that Dickens and Freud had similar thoughts or personalities, but that the discovery of psychoanalysis is historically much closer to the era of the nineteenth-century novel than to our own era, and that reflection on this fact is overdue.[16] The interest of psychoanalysis in the penetration of secrets, the conditions of repression and scandal, the claim to restore a continuity of self, the coming to terms with ambition opposed by the traditional culture, are some of the ground shared with the institution of the novel. It is tempting to compare the process of self-examination by Dickens that culminated in *David Copperfield* with the origins of psychoanalysis, because Freud attributed his discoveries to his own self-analysis in early middle life. The principal result of this introspective experiment was *The Interpretation of Dreams,* and Freud may be said to have later encouraged his followers to believe that the movement had a personal basis. The counterargument to this myth, which is something like the myth of the blacking warehouse in Dickens studies, is the impressive study of the scientific background of psychoanalysis by Frank J. Sulloway.[17] We have gathered now from many sources how ambition served Freud, just as it has served other scientists and discoverers. The early fame of Dickens obviously did not satisfy *his* ambition as a writer, and he was still carefully trying to control and account for it in *Copperfield*. It is noteworthy that both men first confided their memories of childhood in writing to male friends, John Forster and Wilhelm Fliess, and at about the same age. Here is Freud's famous discovery, as reported privately to Fliess:

> A single idea of general value dawned on me. I have found, in my own case too, [the phenomenon of] being in love with my mother and jealous of my father, and I now consider it a universal event in early childhood, even if not so early as in children who have been made hysterical. (Similar to the invention of parentage [family romance] in paranoia—heroes, founders of religion.) If this is so, we can understand the gripping power of *Oedipus Rex*, in spite of all the objections that reason raises against the presupposition of fate . . . the Greek legend seizes upon a compulsion which everyone recognizes because he senses its existence within himself. Everyone in the audience was once a budding Oedipus in fantasy and each recoils in horror from the dream fulfillment here transplanted into reality, with the full quantity of repression which separates his infantile state from his present one.[18]

As in the case of Dickens, there is a substantial literary component to the self-discovery, here and elsewhere in the writings of Freud: the next paragraph of the letter explores the analogy to Hamlet. And as with most such speculations on personal identity, the writer assumes that "everyone" is either male or an adjunct to the male.

Copperfield is a piece of the culture of the nineteenth century from which the Oedipus complex emerged. It is not hard to see how this is so. Even if a case for infantile sexuality is not quite articulated in the novel, aggression—scarcely concealed beneath a wary passivity and extending as far as death-dealing in the plot—is essential to the rise of the hero. The killing in the novel, in fact, is about equally proportioned among mothers, fathers-in-law to be, and rivals of the hero; the two childlike women, Clara and Dora, are not spared. The psychoanalyst D. W. Winnicott puts the general case well, without recourse to a full Oedipal plot or infantile sexuality, by arguing that "growing up means taking the parent's place. *It really does.* In the unconscious fantasy, growing up is inherently an aggressive act."[19] This perception has more to do with the relative size of parents and children, before the latter are grown up, than it has to do with sexuality. In Dickens's novel it has also to do, by analogy, with the soon-to-be-adult hero's perception of his own death and the need for his angel Agnes. The degree of aggression, like the sexual component of the Oedipus complex, need not be thought of as limited to the nineteenth or twentieth centuries of the modern era, but the reasons that Freud discovers the Oedipus complex, wields it, and uses it to explain human identity or behavior are to be found in texts like *Copperfield* that are predicated on a rise in the world—and not just the rise of a uniquely situated or dangerously ambitious man, nor even the rise of a nefarious hypocrite like Heep, but the rise of tame young men like Copperfield.

Examine again Erikson's mild protest: "We would not wish to see any boy—much less an imaginative and forceful one—face the struggles of his youth and manhood without having experienced the love and hate which are encompassed in this complex." Is not this the story that Dickens has written about himself as Copperfield? It is primarily in the nineteenth and twentieth centuries that *any* boy—never mind the imaginative and forceful novelist—must in theory be prepared "to assume the fearless initiative of men": that is, to pursue a career different from his father's, to enter the market place with his labor, to try his hardest to do well. The necessary ambition is not a matter of personal choice (Copperfield never decides to become a novelist, as we have seen), but the kind of maximizing of personal effort—of selfishness, if you will—that is essential to the body politic and especially to the assumptions of modern economics. When Dickens has Copperfield preach the necessity of work, he deliberately downplays his own extraordinary talent and insists upon the ordinary talent and necessary ambition of any boy. The ambition of all, the energy available to progress for society as a whole, cannot be construed as tragic. And yet—and yet—it is still ambition and demands a more prominent role in life than that enjoyed by our fathers before us. The Oedipus complex assumes and assuages ambition not believed necessary before the nineteenth century for any but exceptional boys. Now all boys are exceptional, and all must identify, as Forster suggests, with the hero who is Copperfield.

The famous complex, as Dickens's novel helps to make clear, is more like a myth of the fortunate fall transposed to childhood than it is like the tragedy of Oedipus; it is a dream of murder and sex from which one turns "resolutely away" after being tempted, in Erikson's terms, and not fate to be endured, as Freud's language sometimes suggests. There is no use experiencing an Oedipus complex unless one can leave it behind, and in *Copperfield* Dickens helps to codify the very assumptions about early life that bring psychoanalysis into being. The tale of childhood that *Copperfield* tells—the weaning of the child from his mother and the biting of the hand that wards him—frees the man for labor and the punctual discharge of duties. It breeds the "stuff to stand wear and tear" and prepares for "thorough-going, ardent, and sincere earnestness" (42.518). Take care of that young man: he bites. The rise of the hero is prepared but also justified by a fall and recovery in childhood.

To show that the Oedipus complex, instead of an etiology, ought to be regarded in the light of an apologetics is well beyond the scope of this book. Yet the main point is clear: both Dickens and Freud made the move to narrate childhood experience when they were entering middle age and were deeply occupied with careers. I have argued that there is enough evidence in the case of Dickens, at least, that the process culminating in a story of childhood began with an adult's awareness of his vulnerability as an adult. The novelist scrambled, as we say of jet fighters, to find and destroy the enemy—who was himself—in *Martin Chuzzlewit*, and once in control of the skies, he concentrated self-criticism in the tragic mode of *Dombey and Son*. Only then was he prepared to present himself in the guise of ambitious novelist and to recall a traumatic childhood in *David Copperfield*. I think it fair to say that Freud's *Interpretation of Dreams* records another scramble, another mastery and justification of the life. From our perspective today these exercises of the will begin to look like cultural appropriations of the self, justifications of essential ambition. No longer can we suppose that fixed patterns of childhood conflict were discovered merely by coincidence at the end of the nineteenth century. Human nature, especially in its social relations, does not remain constant, and almost certainly the Oedipus complex shares in the same assumptions as the "Personal History" of young Copperfield.

NOTES

[1] Charles Dickens, *David Copperfield*, ed. Nina Burgis (Oxford: Clarendon, 1981), ch. 11, p. 233. Further citations are from this edition and will be given by chapter and page in parentheses.

[2] Avrom Fleishman, *Figures of Autobiography* (Berkeley: University of California Press, 1983), p. 207, suggests that the treatment of the mother as a child comes about as "the best excuse . . . for maternal inadequacy."

[3] William C. Spengemann, *Forms of Autobiography: Episodes in the History of a Literary Genre* (New Haven: Yale University Press, 1980), pp. 119–132.

[4] Albert D. Hutter, "Reconstructive Autobiography: The Experience at Warren's Blacking," *Dickens Studies Annual*, 6 (1977), 7; Robert L. Patten, "Autobiography into Autobiography: The Evolution of *David Copperfield*," in *Approaches to Victorian Autobiography*, ed. George P. Landow (Athens: Ohio University Press, 1979), pp. 273–278.

[5] John Forster, *The Life of Charles Dickens*, 2 vols. (London: Everyman, 1927), I, 25.

[6] Ibid., I, 25.

[7] For an essay on the control exerted by Dickens over his autobiography, see Jean Fergusson Carr, "Dickens and Autobiography: A Wild Beast and His Keeper," *ELH*, 52 (1985), 447–469.

[8] J. Hillis Miller, "Three Problems of Fictional Form: First Person Narration in *David Copperfield* and *Huckleberry Finn*," in *Experience and the Novel*, ed. Roy Harvey Pearce (New York: Columbia University Press, 1968), p. 33; and Miller, *Charles Dickens: The World of His Novels* (Cambridge: Harvard University Press, 1958), p. 157.

[9] Robert E. Lougy, "Remembrance of Death Past and Future: A Reading of *David Copperfield*," *Dickens Studies Annual*, 6 (1977), 87, suggests that the drowning of Ham and Steerforth "moves primarily toward a recognition of his own death that David can no longer conceal or evade."

[10] Erik H. Erikson, *Young Man Luther: A Study in Psychoanalysis and History* (1958; rpt. New York: Norton, 1962), p. 83.

[11] Ibid., pp. 264–265.

[12] Ibid., p. 73.

[13] Ibid., pp. 69–70.

[14] Letter of 5 October 1883, quoted by Ernest Jones, *The Life and Work of Sigmund Freud,* 3 vols. (New York: Basic Books, 1953–1957), I, 174; also p. 104.

[15] I have especially in mind the work of social historians, such as William J. McGrath's *Freud's Discovery of Psychoanalysis: The Politics of Hysteria* (Ithaca: Cornell University Press, 1986). The inspiration of this work can be said to be the chapter on Freud in Carl E. Schorske, *Fin-de-Siècle Vienna: Politics and Culture* (New York: Vintage, 1981), pp. 181–207, but in a real sense also Erikson is the one who has taught us to see Freud against the background of his times.

[16] The dependence of psychoanalysis on narrative is now frequently urged. Donald P. Spence, *Narrative Truth and Historical Truth: Meaning and Interpretation in Psychoanalysis* (New York: Norton, 1982), perhaps goes furthest in seeing the analytic narrative as fiction. Though Spence calls on literary theory, he does not see the history of the novel as relevant to his argument.

[17] Frank J. Sulloway, *Freud, Biologist of the Mind: Beyond the Psychoanalytic Legend* (New York: Basic Books, 1979).

[18] Letter of 15 October 1897, *The Complete Letters of Sigmund Freud to Wilhelm Fliess, 1887–1904,* trans. and ed. Jeffrey Moussaieff Masson (Cambridge: Harvard University Press, 1985), p. 272.

[19] D. W. Winnicott, *Playing and Reality* (New York: Basic Books, 1971), p. 144; Hunter, "Reconstructive Autobiography," p. 10, cites Winnicott.

CONTRIBUTORS

HAROLD BLOOM is Sterling Professor of the Humanities at Yale University and Henry W. And Albert A. Berg Professor of English at the New York University Graduate School. He is a 1985 MacArthur Foundation Award recipient, served as the Charles Eliot Norton Professor of Poetry at Harvard University (1987–88), and is the author of nineteen books, the most recent being *The Book of J* (1990). Currently he is editing the Chelsea House series Modern Critical Views and The Critical Cosmos, and other Chelsea House series in literary criticism.

GWENDOLYN B. NEEDHAM was Professor Emeritus of English at the University of California–Davis and co-authored *Pamela's Daughters* (1936; with Robert Palfrey Utter).

JAMES R. KINCAID is Professor of English at the University of Southern California. He is the author of *Tennyson's Major Poems: The Comic and Ironic Patterns* (1975) and *The Novels of Anthony Trollope* (1977), and editor of several other works.

BERT G. HORNBACK is Professor of English at the University of Michigan. He is the author of *The Metaphor of Chance: Vision and Technique in the Works of Thomas Hardy* (1971), *"Noah's Arkitecture": A Study of Dickens's Mythology* (1972), *"The Hero of My Life": Essays on Dickens* (1981), *Great Expectations: A Novel of Friendship* (1987), and *Middlemarch: A Novel of Reform* (1988).

ROBIN GILMOUR is Professor of English at the University of Aberdeen (Scotland). He is the author of *The Idea of the Gentleman in the Victorian Novel* (1981), *Thackeray: Vanity Fair* (1982), and *The Novel in the Victorian Age: A Modern Introduction* (1986).

NORMAN TALBOT is Professor of English at the University of Newcastle (Australia). He is the author of *The Major Poems of John Keats* (1968) and *A Glossary of Poetic Terms* (1982). He has written several works of poetry, of which the most recent are *The Fishing Boy* (1973), *Find the Lady: A Female Universe Rides Again* (1978), and *Where Two Rivers Meet* (1981).

MARK M. HENNELLY, JR., is Professor of English at California State University–Sacramento. He has published essays on Charles Dickens, Nathaniel Hawthorne, Emily Brontë, J. R. R. Tolkien, Ann Radcliffe, Matthew Gregory Lewis, and Wilkie Collins.

JOHN P. McGOWAN is Associate Professor of English at the Eastman School of Music (Rochester, NY). He is the author of *Representation and Revelation: Victorian Realism from Carlyle to Yeats* (1986).

IAIN CRAWFORD is Professor of English at Berry College (Rome, GA). He has published essays on *Great Expectations, Little Dorrit, Oliver Twist,* and *Frankenstein.*

CHRIS R. VANDEN BOSSCHE is Director of Graduate Studies in English at the University of Notre Dame. He has published on Thomas Carlyle and Alfred, Lord Tennyson.

EDWIN M. EIGNER is Professor of English at the University of California–Riverside. He is the author of *Robert Louis Stevenson and Romantic Tradition* (1966), *The Metaphysical Novel in England and America: Dickens, Bulwer, Melville* (1978), and *The Dickens Pantomime* (1989).

237

VIRGINIA CARMICHAEL is Lecturer of Speech and Mass Communications at Mesa State College, Grand Junction, Colorado. She has published essays on Matthew Arnold and *Sir Gawain and the Green Knight*.

ALEXANDER WELSH is Professor of English at the University of California–Los Angeles. He is the author of *The Hero of the Waverley Novels* (1963), *The City of Dickens* (1971), *Reflections on the Hero as Quixote* (1981), and *George Eliot and Blackmail* (1985).

BIBLIOGRAPHY

Adrian, Arthur A. *Dickens and the Parent-Child Relationship*. Athens: Ohio University Press, 1984.

──────. "*David Copperfield*: A Century of Critical and Popular Acclaim." *Modern Language Quarterly* 11 (1950): 325–31.

Andrade, Mary Anne. "Pollution of an Honest Home." *Dickens Quarterly* 5, No. 2 (June 1988): 65–74.

Ashby, Ruth. "David Copperfield's Story—Telling in the Dark." *Dickens Studies Newsletter* 9, No. 3 (September 1978): 80–83.

Bandelin, Carl. "David Copperfield: A Third Interesting Penitent." *Studies in English Literature 1500–1900* 16 (1976): 601–11.

Baumgarten, Murray. "Writing and *David Copperfield*." *Dickens Studies Annual* 14 (1985): 39–59.

Bell, Vereen M. "The Emotional Matrix of *David Copperfield*." *Studies in English Literature 1500–1900* 8 (1968): 633–49.

Berman, Ronald. "The Innocent Observer." *Children's Literature* 9 (1981): 40–50.

Black, Michael. "*David Copperfield*: Self, Childhood, and Growth." In *The Literature of Fidelity*. London: Chatto & Windus, 1975, pp. 82–102.

Bloom, Harold, ed. *Charles Dickens's* David Copperfield. New York: Chelsea House, 1987.

Brook, G. L. *The Language of Dickens*. London: André Deutsch, 1970, pp. 118–22.

Brown, E. K. "David Copperfield." *Yale Review* 37 (1947–48): 651–66.

Buckley, Jerome Hamilton. "Dickens, David and Pip." In *Season of Youth: The* Bildungsroman *from Dickens to Golding*. Cambridge, MA: Harvard University Press, 1974, pp. 28–62.

──────. "The Identity of David Copperfield." In *Victorian Literature and Society*, edited by James R. Kincaid and Albert J. Kuhn. Columbus: Ohio State University Press, 1984, pp. 225–39.

Cain, Tom. "Tolstoy's Use of *David Copperfield*." *Critical Quarterly* 15 (1973): 237–46.

Carabine, Keith. "Reading *David Copperfield*." In *Reading the Victorian Novel: Detail into Form*, edited by Ian Gregor. London: Vision Press, 1980, pp. 150–67.

Carey, John. *The Violent Effigy: A Study of Dickens' Imagination*. London: Faber & Faber, 1973.

Cockshut, A. O. J. "*David Copperfield*." In *The Imagination of Charles Dickens*. London: Collins, 1961, pp. 114–26.

Collins, Philip. "*David Copperfield*: A Very Complicated Interweaving of Truth and Fiction." *Essays and Studies* 23 (1970): 71–86.

Dabney, Ross H. "*David Copperfield and Bleak House*." In *Love and Property in the Novels of Dickens*. Berkeley: University of California Press, 1967, pp. 66–92.

Daldry, Graham. "The Novel as Narrative: *David Copperfield*." In *Charles Dickens and the Form of the Novel: Fiction and Narrative in Dickens's Work*. Totowa, NJ: Barnes & Noble, 1987, pp. 99–130.

Dawson, Carl. " 'The Lamp of Memory': Wordsworth and Dickens." In *Victorian Noon: English Literature in 1850*. Baltimore: Johns Hopkins University Press, 1979, pp. 123–43.

DeGraaff, Robert M. "Self-Articulating Characters in *David Copperfield*." *Journal of Narrative Technique* 14 (1984): 214–22.

Dickensian No. 291 (June 1, 1949). *David Copperfield* Centenary Number.

Dunn, Albert A. "Time and Design in *David Copperfield*." *English Studies* 59 (1978): 225–36.

Dunn, Richard J. *David Copperfield: An Annotated Bibliography*. New York: Garland, 1981.

Dutton, A. R. "Jonson and *David Copperfield*: Dickens and *Bartholomew Fair*." *English Language Notes* 16 (1979): 227–32.

Dyson, A. E. "*David Copperfield*: The Favourite Child." In *The Inimitable Dickens: A Reading of the Novels*. London: Macmillan, 1970, pp. 119–53.

Easson, Angus. "The Mythic Sorrows of Charles Dickens." *Literature and History* 1 (1975): 49–61.

Edwards, Simon. "*David Copperfield*: The Decomposing Self." *Centennial Review* 29 (1985): 328–52.

Eigner, Edwin M. "*David Copperfield* and the Benevolent Spirit." *Dickens Studies Annual* 14 (1985): 1–15.

Engel, Monroe. "The Sense of Self." In *The Maturity of Dickens*. Cambridge, MA: Harvard University Press, 1959, pp. 146–56.

Fielding, K. J. "The Making of *David Copperfield*." *Listener* 46 (July 1951): 93–95.

Flaxman, Rhoda L. "*David Copperfield*: World-Portraits and Verbal Tableaux." In *Victorian Word-Painting and Narrative: Toward the Blending of Genes*. Ann Arbor: UMI Research Press, 1983, pp. 33–49.

Fleishman, Avrom. "The Fictions of Autobiographical Fiction." *Genre* 9 (1976): 73–86.

———. "*David Copperfield*: Experiments in Autobiography." In *Figures of Autobiography: The Language of Self-Writing in Victorian and Modern English*. Berkeley: University of California Press, 1983, pp. 201–18.

Flint, Kate. *Dickens*. Atlantic Highlands, NJ: Humanities Press, 1986.

Frank, Lawrence. "The Autobiographical Imperative." In *Charles Dickens and the Romantic Self*. Lincoln: University of Nebraska Press, 1984, pp. 60–94.

Gard, Roger. "*David Copperfield*." *Essays in Criticism* 15 (1965): 313–25.

Garis, Robert E. *The Dickens Theatre: A Reassessment of the Novels*. Oxford: Clarendon Press, 1965.

Garson, Marjorie. "Inclusion and Exclusion: The Motif of the Copyist in *David Copperfield*." *Etudes Anglaises* 36 (1983): 401–13.

Gaskell, Philip. "Dickens, *David Copperfield*, 1850." In *From Writer to Reader: Studies in Emotional Method*. Oxford: Oxford University Press, 1978, pp. 142–55.

Gold, Joseph. "*David Copperfield*." In *Charles Dickens: Radical Moralist*. Minneapolis: University of Minneapolis Press, 1972, pp. 175–84.

Goldfarb, Russell M. "Charles Dickens: Orphans, Incest, and Repression." In *Sexual Repression and Victorian Literature*. Lewisburg, PA: Bucknell University Press, 1970, pp. 122–27.

Greenstein, Michael. "Between Curtain and Caul: *David Copperfield*'s Shining Transparencies." *Dickens Quarterly* 5, No. 2 (June 1988): 75–81.

Guérard, Albert J. *The Triumph of the Novel: Dickens, Dostoevsky, Faulkner*. New York: Oxford University Press, 1976, pp. 75–76, 139–45.

Hardy, Barbara. "The Change of Heart in Dickens' Novels." *Victorian Studies* 5 (1961): 49–67.

———. "*David Copperfield*." In *Charles Dickens: The Writer and His Work*. Windsor, Eng.: Profile Books, 1983, pp. 63–69.

———. "*David Copperfield*." In *The Moral Art of Dickens*. New York: Oxford University Press, 1970, pp. 122–38.

Harrison, Fraser. *The Dark Angel: Aspects of Victorian Sexuality*. London: Sheldon Press, 1977, pp. 38–44.

Herbert, Christopher. "De Quincey and Dickens." *Victorian Studies* 17 (1973–74): 247–63.

Hirsh, Gordon D. "A Psychoanalytic Rereading of *David Copperfield*." *Victorian Newsletter* No. 58 (Fall 1980): 1–5.

Hornback, Bert G. *"The Hero of My Life": Essays of Dickens*. Athens: Ohio University Press, 1981.

Hughes, Felicity. "Narrative Complexity in *David Copperfield*." *ELH* 41 (1974): 89–105.

Hurley, Edward. "Dickens' Portrait of the Artist." *Victorian Newsletter* No. 38 (Fall 1970): 1–5.

Jackson, Arlene M. "Agnes Wickfield and the Church Leitmotif in *David Copperfield*." *Dickens Studies Annual* 9 (1981): 53–65.

Jackson, T. A. *"David Copperfield*." In *Charles Dickens: The Progress of a Radical*. New York: International Publishers, 1938, pp. 119–28.

Jacobsen, Wendy S. "Brothers and Sisters in *David Copperfield*." *English Studies in Africa* 25 (1982): 11–28.

Johnson Edgar. "His Favorite Child." In *Charles Dickens: His Tragedy and Triumph*. New York: Simon & Schuster, 1952, Volume 2, pp. 677–700.

Jordan, John O. "The Social Sub-text of *David Copperfield*." *Dickens Studies Annual* 14 (1985): 61–92.

Kearney, Anthony. "The Storm Scene in *David Copperfield*." *Ariel* 9, No. 1 (January 1978): 19–30.

Kettle, Arnold. "Thoughts on *David Copperfield*." *A Review of English Literature* 2, No. 3 (July 1961): 65–74.

Kincaid, James R. "The Darkness of *David Copperfield*." *Dickens Studies* 1, No. 2 (May 1965): 65–75.

———. "The Structure of *David Copperfield*." *Dickens Studies* 2, No. 2 (May 1966): 74–95.

———. "Symbol and Subversion in *David Copperfield*." *Studies in the Novel* 1 (1969): 196–206.

Lankford, William T. " 'The Deep of Time': Narrative Order in *David Copperfield*." *ELH* 46 (1979): 452–67.

Leavis, L. R. *"David Copperfield* and *Jane Eyre*." *English Studies* 67 (1986): 167–73.

Leavis, Q. D. "Dickens and Tolstoy: The Case for a Serious View of *David Copperfield*." In *Dickens the Novelist* by F. R. Leavis and Q. D. Leavis. London: Chatto & Windus, 1970, pp. 34–117.

Lougy, Robert E. "Rememberances of Death Past and Future: A Reading of *David Copperfield*." *Dickens Studies Annual* 6 (1977): 72–101.

Lucas, John. "David Copperfield." In *The Melancholy Man: A Study of Dickens's Novels*. London: Methuen, 1970, pp. 166–201.

MacKay, Carol Hanbery. "Surrealization and the Redoubled Self: Fantasy in *David Copperfield* and *Pendennis*." *Dickens Studies Annual* 14 (1985): 241–65.

McGowan, John P. "Dickens: Fancy and the Real." In *Representation and Revelation: Victorian Realism from Carlyle to Yeats*. Columbia: University of Missouri Press, 1986, pp. 103–19.

Manheim, Leonard F. "The Personal History of David Copperfield: A Study in Psychoanalytic Criticism." *American Imago* 9 (1952): 21–43.

Manning, Sylvia. *"David Copperfield* and Scheherazade: The Necessity of Narrative." *Studies in the Novel* 14 (1982): 327–36.

———. "Masking and Self-Revelation: Dickens's Three Autobiographies." *Dickens Studies Newsletter* 7, No. 3 (September 1976): 69–75.

Marshall, William H. "The Image of Steerforth and the Structure of *David Copperfield*." *Tennessee Studies in Literature* 5 (1960): 57–65.

Miller, Michael G. "Murdstone, Heep, and the Structure of *David Copperfield*." *Dickens Studies Newsletter* 11, No. 3 (September 1980): 65–70.

Millhauser, Milton. "*David Copperfield*: Some Shifts of Plan." *Nineteenth-Century Fiction* 27 (1972): 339–45.

Morris, Patricia. "Some Notes on the Women in *David Copperfield*: Eleven Crude Categories and a Case for Miss Mowcher." *English Studies in Africa* 21 (1978): 17–21.

Mundhenk, Rosemary. "*David Copperfield* and 'The Oppression of Remembrance.'" *Texas Studies in Literature and Language* 29 (1987): 322–41.

Myers, Margaret. "The Lost Self: Gender in *David Copperfield*." In *Gender Studies: New Directions in Feminist Criticism*, edited by Judith Spector. Bowling Green, OH: Bowling Green State University Popular Press, 1986, pp. 120–32.

Patten, Robert L. "Autobiography into Autobiography: The Evolution of *David Copperfield*." In *Approaches to Victorian Autobiography*, edited by George P. Landow. Athens: Ohio University Press, 1979, pp. 269–91.

Pattison, Robert. *The Child Figure in English Literature*. Athens: University of Georgia Press, 1978, pp. 122–27.

Pavese, Cesare. "Preface to Dickens: *David Copperfield*." In *American Literature: Essays and Opinions*. Translated by Edwin Fussell. Berkeley: University of California Press, 1970, pp. 206–10.

Pearlman, E. "Two Notes on Religion in *David Copperfield*." *Victorian Newsletter* No. 41 (Spring 1972): 18–20.

Peterson, Carla L. "*Jane Eyre* and *David Copperfield*: Nature and Providence." In *The Determined Reader: Gender and Culture in the Novel from Napoleon to Victoria*. New Brunswick, NJ: Rutgers University Press, 1986, pp. 82–131.

Pettersson, Torsten. "The Maturity of David Copperfield." *English Studies* 70 (1989): 63–73.

Praz, Mario. "Charles Dickens." In *The Hero in Eclipse in Victorian Fiction*. Translated by Angus Davidson. London: Oxford University Press, 1956, pp. 127–88.

Raina, Badri. "*David Copperfield*: The Price of Success." In *Dickens and the Dialectic of Growth*. Madison: University of Wisconsin Press, 1986, pp. 77–101.

Reibetanz, J. M. "Villain, Victim and Hero: Structure and Theme in *David Copperfield*." *Dalhousie Review* 59 (1979): 321–37.

Rodolff, Rebecca. "What David Copperfield Remembers of Dora's Death." *Dickensian* No. 393 (Spring 1981): 32–40.

Sadoff, Dianne F. "The Dead Father: *Barnaby Rudge, David Copperfield*, and *Great Expectations*." *Papers on Language and Literature* 18 (1982): 36–57.

Schwarzbach, F. S. "The Genesis of a Myth." In *Dickens and the City*. London: Athlone Press, 1979, pp. 18–19.

Sell, Roger D. "Projection Characters in *David Copperfield*." *Studia Neophilologica* 55 (1983): 19–29.

Shelston, Alan. "Past and Present in *David Copperfield*." *Critical Quarterly* 27 (1985): 17–33.

Solomon, Pearl Chester. *Dickens and Melville in Their Time*. New York: Columbia University Press, 1975, pp. 38–39, 103, 134–53.

Spengemann, William C. "Poetic Autobiography: *David Copperfield*." In *The Forms of Autobiography: Episodes in the History of a Literary Genre*. New Haven: Yale University Press, 1980, pp. 119–32.

Spilka, Mark. "*David Copperfield* as Psychological Fiction." *Critical Quarterly* 1 (1959): 292–301.

Steig, Michael. "*David Copperfield*'s Plots against the Reader." In *Stories of Reading: Subjectivity and Literary Understanding*. Baltimore: Johns Hopkins University Press, 1989, pp. 127–43.

Stone, Harry. "*David Copperfield:* The Fairy-Tale Method Perfected." In *Dickens and the Invisible World: Fairy Tales, Fantasy, and Novel-Making*. Bloomington: Indiana University Press, 1979, pp. 193–278.

Sucksmith, Harvey Peter. *The Narrative Art of Charles Dickens: The Rhetoric of Sympathy and Irony in His Novels*. Oxford: Clarendon Press, 1970.

Thurley, Geoffrey. "David Copperfield." In *The Dickens Myth: Its Genesis and Structure*. New York: St. Martin's Press, 1976, pp. 132–72.

Tick, Stanley. "On Not Being Charles Dickens." *Bucknell Review* 16 (1968): 85–95.

Vogel, Jane. *Allegory in Dickens*. University: University of Alabama Press, 1977.

Watkins, Gwen. *Dickens in Search of Himself: Recurrent Themes and Characters in the Work of Charles Dickens*. Totowa, NJ: Barnes & Noble, 1987.

Weinstein, Philip M. "A Palimpsest of Motives in *David Copperfield*." In *The Semantics of Desire: Changing Models of Identity from Joyce to Dickens*. Princeton: Princeton University Press, 1984, pp. 22–47.

Welsh, Alexander. *The City of Dickens*. Oxford: Clarendon Press, 1971.

Westburg, Barry. *The Confessional Fictions of Charles Dickens*. DeKalb: Northern Illinois University Press, 1977.

Worth, George J. "*David Copperfield*." *Dickensian Melodrama: A Reading of the Novels*. Lawrence: University Press of Kansas, 1978, pp. 97–110.

ACKNOWLEDGMENTS

"Charles Dickens and *David Copperfield*" by W. Somerset Maugham from *The Art of Fiction: An Introduction to Ten Novels and Their Authors* by W. Somerset Maugham, © 1948, 1954 by W. Somerset Maugham. Reprinted by permission of Octopus Publishing Group Library on behalf of William Heinemann Ltd.

"Dickens' Favourite Child" by Robert Hamilton from *Dickensian* No. 291 (June 1, 1949), © 1949 by *The Dickensian*. Reprinted by permission of *The Dickensian*.

"*David Copperfield*" by J. Hillis Miller from *Charles Dickens: The World of His Novels* by J. Hillis Miller, © 1958 by the President and Fellows of Harvard College. Reprinted by permission of Harvard University Press.

"Art as Experience" by Maurice Beebe from *Ivory Towers and Sacred Founts: The Artist as Hero in Fiction from Goethe to Joyce* by Maurice Beebe, © 1964 by New York University. Reprinted by permission of New York University Press.

"*David Copperfield*" by Angus Wilson from *The World of Charles Dickens* by Angus Wilson, © 1970 by Angus Wilson. Reprinted by permission of Martin Secker & Warburg.

Dickens by A. H. Gomme, © 1971 by A. H. Gomme. Reprinted by permission of Unwin Hyman Publishers Ltd.

"Circumlocution in *David Copperfield*" by Norren Ferris from *Dickens Studies Newsletter* 9, No. 2 (June 1978), © 1978 by The Dickens Society. Reprinted by permission of *Dickens Quarterly*.

"David Copperfield's Names" by Donald Hawes from *Dickensian* No. 385 (May 1978), © 1978 by *The Dickensian*. Reprinted by permission of *The Dickensian*.

"Dickens and the Art of Pastoral" by Rosemarie Bodenheimer from *Centennial Review* 23, No. 4 (Fall 1979), © 1979 by *The Centennial Review*. Reprinted by permission of *The Centennial Review* and the author.

"Home and Homeless in *David Copperfield*" by Neil Grill from *Dickens Studies Newsletter* 11, No. 4 (December 1980), © 1980 by The Dickens Society. Reprinted by permission of *Dickens Quarterly*.

"The Undisciplined Heart of David Copperfield" by Gwendolyn B. Needham from *Nineteenth-Century Fiction* 9, No. 2 (September 1954), © 1954 by The Regents of the University of California. Reprinted by permission of the Editors of *Nineteenth-Century Literature*.

"*David Copperfield*: Laughter and Point of View" by James R. Kincaid from *Dickens and the Rhetoric of Laughter* by James R. Kincaid, © 1971 by Oxford University Press. Reprinted by permission of Oxford University Press.

"Frustration and Resolution in *David Copperfield*" by Bert G. Hornback from *"Noah's Arkitecture": A Study of Dickens's Mythology* by Bert G. Hornback, © 1972 by Bert G. Hornback. Reprinted by permission of the author.

INDEX